Preface

The idea for this project, and so this book, originated in our growing awareness of two things. First, that the courts' decisions about appropriate basis for dividing wealth on divorce or allocating ownership of property on separation were being increasingly influenced by how parties (are perceived to) organise their lives while together and by what that was supposed to indicate, for example, about their intentions regarding ownership or about the economic impact of relationship breakdown, but that the judges were not always apprised of all the research data necessary to make a fully informed decision about those issues. Secondly, that there is a vast social science literature touching on many issues relevant to legal decision-making in this area, but that researchers in those other disciplines generally run along parallel tracks that never meet each other—or lawyers. We thought that we could usefully try to make a contribution on both fronts by bringing together people working in a wide range of disciplines pertinent to the broad theme of money, property, relationships and relationship breakdown, in order to stimulate debate and cross-fertilisation of ideas between them, and to bring their valuable research to the attention of a wider audience.

The project, run under the aegis of the Cambridge Socio-Legal Group, based at the University of Cambridge, adopted a workshop model. Invited contributors circulated draft chapters on their research in advance of a two-day meeting at which each contributor was then able, following a short presentation, to discuss their work with the whole group. This methodology proved highly successful in enhancing inter-disciplinary understanding, not least in identifying and unravelling areas of *mis*understanding, often generated simply by the use of seemingly familiar language in an unfamiliar way. It was also highly productive of ideas for new lines of inquiry in all of the disciplines represented at the workshop, thanks to the fresh perspectives cast on otherwise familiar territory by those whose disciplinary background provided a different vantage point from which to view the material. In light of those discussions, the contributors were then able to revise their chapters before publication, and our introductory chapter benefited considerably from insights offered by members of the group during our discussions over those two days. We hope that the result is a volume that provides a valuable resource, giving access to findings on wide range of issues from a wide range of disciplines, in a way that will both inform legal development in this field and encourage further research.

We are extremely grateful to the Cambridge Socio-Legal Group, the John Hall Fund of the University of Cambridge, and to Trinity College, Cambridge for their financial support for this project, and to the staff of Trinity College who helped the workshop to run so smoothly. In addition to the contributors themselves, whose biographies appear in the following pages, we must also acknowledge a huge debt to the following individuals for their contributions to discussion during the workshop: Belinda Brooks-Gordon, Ceridwen Roberts, Martin Richards, Brian Sloan and Anke Zimmermann. Finally, we must also thank Liam D'Arcy Brown for his assistance with proof-reading and editing.

Sharing Lives, Dividing Assets

An Inter-Disciplinary Study

Edited by
Joanna Miles
and
Rebecca Probert

·HART·
PUBLISHING
OXFORD AND PORTLAND, OREGON
2009

Published in North America (US and Canada) by
Hart Publishing
c/o International Specialized Book Services
920 NE 58th Avenue, Suite 300
Portland, OR 97213-3786
USA
Tel: +1 503 287 3093 or toll-free: (1) 800 944 6190
Fax: +1 503 280 8832
E-mail: orders@isbs.com
Website: http://www.isbs.com

Hart Publishing Ltd, 16C Worcester Place, Oxford, OX1 2JW
Telephone: +44 (0)1865 517530 Fax: +44 (0)1865 510710
E-mail: mail@hartpub.co.uk
Website: http://www.hartpub.co.uk

British Library Cataloguing in Publication Data
Data Available

ISBN: 978-1-84113-259-4

Typeset by Compuscript Ltd, Shannon
Printed and bound in Great Britain by
CPI Antony Rowe Ltd, Chippenham, Wiltshire

Contents

Part IV: A Rational Approach?

Notes on Contributors

Anne Barlow studied Law with French at the University of Sussex and is Professor of Family Law and Policy at the University of Exeter. The main focus of her research has been on family and housing law, and especially cohabitation law, and she has published widely in these fields. In particular, she is author of *Cohabitants and the Law* (Butterworths, 2001) and (with S Duncan, G James, and A Park) of *Cohabitation, Marriage and the Law* (Hart Publishing, 2005). She has, since 2000, directed and co-directed a number of empirical socio-legal projects funded by the Nuffield Foundation, the Ministry of Justice and the Economic and Social Research Council (ESRC) including 'Family Restructuring, the Common Law Marriage Myth and the Need for Legal Realism, Community of Property—A Regime for England and Wales?' and 'The Common Law Marriage Myth and Cohabitation Law Reform Revisited'. She has been consulted by the Law Commission for England and Wales, the Scottish Executive, and the Office of Law Reform, Northern Ireland on reform of cohabitation law and the implications of her empirical research for this process.

Carole Burgoyne is Senior Lecturer in the School of Psychology, University of Exeter. Her main research interests are in economic psychology and include studies of money, marriage, currency change and distributive justice. Her most recent projects are 'The Common Law Marriage Myth Revisited' (led by Anne Barlow); 'Financial Management Practices in Non-traditional Heterosexual Couples' (with Stefanie Sonnenberg and Anne Barlow); 'Beliefs about the Allocation of Money in Marriage' (with Stefanie Sonnenberg); and 'Money management in Lesbian and Gay Couples' (with Victoria Clarke).

Shirley Dex is Professor of Longitudinal Social Research in the Centre for Longitudinal Studies, Institute of Education, University of London. She has held posts at the Judge Business School, University of Cambridge, the Institute for Social and Economic Research at the University of Essex, and the Economics Department at the University of Keele. From 1998 to 2003 she was Research Advisor to the Joseph Rowntree Foundation's Work and Family Life Programme. She has published widely on women's employment and cross-national comparative research, equal opportunities, families and work, ethnic minorities and employment, flexible working arrangements in organisations, work and care, and family policy. Recent books include *Families and Work in the 21st Century* (Joseph Rowntree Foundation, 2003). She has also co-edited (with Heather Joshi) *Children of the 21st Century* (The Policy Press, 2005) and (with Jacqueline Scott and Heather Joshi) *Women and Employment: Changing Lives and New Challenges* (Edward Elgar Publishing Ltd, 2008).

Antony Dnes currently holds a chair in Economics at the University of Hull, and has held previous appointments at the Universities of Birmingham, Edinburgh and St Andrews in the UK, and at the Virginia Tech and the George Mason Law School in the US. He completed his PhD in Economics at the University of Edinburgh, and has an LLB from the University of London. He is a specialist in the economic analysis of law, with a number of published articles dealing with family topics, in both law and economics journals. He co-edited *The Law and Economics of Marriage and Divorce* (CUP, 2002), a collection of articles from leading academics on both sides of the Atlantic.

Gillian Douglas obtained her LLB at the University of Manchester in 1977 and her LLM at the London School of Economics in 1978. She is currently Professor of Law and Head of Cardiff Law School, having previously taught at the University of Bristol and the National University of Singapore. She is the co-editor of the *Child and Family Law Quarterly* and of the Case Reports section of *Family Law*. Her publications include (with Nigel Lowe) *Bromley's Family Law* (9th and 10th editions) and *An Introduction to Family Law* (Clarendon Law Series, 1st and 2nd editions). With colleagues from disciplines including psychology and social work she has conducted a number of empirical studies in law, including *How Parents Cope Financially on Marriage Breakdown* (2000, funded by the Joseph Rowntree Foundation), *Grandparenting in Divorced Families* (2004, funded by the Nuffield Foundation), and *A Failure of Trust: Resolving Property Disputes on Cohabitation Breakdown* (2007, funded by the ESRC).

Sally Dowding is a District Judge based at Birmingham Civil Justice Centre. She obtained an LLB degree from the University of Manchester in 1973 and subsequently qualified as a solicitor. For most of a practising career spanning nearly 30 years she specialised in family law. She was a member of the Law Society's Family Law Committee and Children Law Sub-committee for the 10 years preceding her judicial appointment and chaired the latter committee for nearly four years.

John Eekelaar is Emeritus Fellow of Pembroke College, Oxford, and a Fellow of the British Academy. He has written and conducted research in family law since the 1970s, and is currently Joint Director of the Oxford Centre for Family Law and Policy with Mavis Maclean, with whom he has co-authored several books. His latest book, *Family Law and Personal Life*, was published by Oxford University Press in hardback in 2006, and paperback in 2007. He also co-edits the *International Journal of Law, Policy and the Family*.

Andrea Finney is a Research Fellow in the Personal Finance Research Centre at the University of Bristol. Primarily a quantitative researcher, she previously spent six years at the Home Office and, latterly, the Office for National Statistics, where she was involved in rolling-out the new longitudinal survey of household assets. Andrea's current research interests lie in furthering understanding of saving and borrowing behaviour, financial vulnerability and decision-making. She is co-author of reports on over-indebtedness (for the European Commission), the results from the baseline survey of consumer purchasing (for the Financial Services Authority) and modelling exposure to financial risk (for Genworth Financial).

Hayley Fisher is a PhD student in the Faculty of Economics at the University of Cambridge, supervised by Thomas F Crossley and Hamish Low. Her research interests include family and labour economics, and she is currently considering the economic impact of divorce legislation on the decision to marry or to cohabit.

Emma Hitchings is Senior Lecturer in the School of Law, University of Bristol. She studied law as an undergraduate before taking her PhD in 2003. Her main research interests lie in the field of family law, where she has written and worked on issues concerning domestic violence, adoption, ancillary relief, and the recognition of adult relationships, particularly same-sex couples. She is case commentaries editor for the *Journal of Social Welfare and Family Law* and an academic member on the Family Law Committee of the Law Society of England and Wales. She is currently engaged in research on pre-nuptial agreements for the Law Commission for England and Wales.

Jane Lewis is Director of Research, Evidence and Evaluation at the National Children's Bureau and was formerly Director of the Qualitative Research Unit at the National Centre for Social Research. She practised as a solicitor before moving into social policy research. Her recent research includes *Separating from Cohabitation: Making Arrangements for Finances and Parenting* (2006, funded by the Department for Constitutional Affairs); *Settling Up: Making Financial Arrangements after Divorce or Separation* (2002, funded by the Nuffield Foundation), and *Pensions and Divorce: A Qualitative Study among Solicitors* (2000, funded by the Department for Work and Pensions). She has written widely on research methods and is co-editor of *Qualitative Research Practice,* published by Sage in 2003. She has a long-standing interest in relationship breakdown and more broadly in research on children and young people's lives; social inclusion, inequality and disadvantage; and research methods.

Hamish Low is a Senior Lecturer in the Faculty of Economics at the University of Cambridge and a Fellow of Trinity College, Cambridge. He is also a research fellow at the Institute for Fiscal Studies. His main research interests are in understanding the risks that individuals face over their lifetimes and in analysing the extent to which these risks are insured. A particular interest has been in understanding changing patterns of women's labour supply across different generations. He has published primarily in economic journals, such as the *American Economic Review* and the *Journal of Public Economics.*

Mavis Maclean CBE is Joint Director with John Eekelaar of the Oxford Centre for Family Law and Policy, Department of Social Policy and Social Work, University of Oxford. She also acts as Academic Adviser to the Ministry of Justice. Recent publications include *Parenting after Partnering* (Hart Publishing, 2007), *Cross Currents in Family Law*, edited with Katz and Eekelaar (OUP, 2000), and *Family Lawyers* with Eekelaar and Beinart (Hart, 2000). She is a former President of the Research Committee for the Sociology of Law and a Fellow of the International Institute for Sociology of Law, Onati, Spain.

Joanna Miles is a University Lecturer in the Faculty of Law and Fellow of Trinity College, University of Cambridge. Her research interests lie mainly in the area of family property and financial remedies following relationship breakdown, whether marital or non-marital. Her work has been considered and cited judicially in England and Wales, Ireland, and New Zealand. She was recently seconded to the Law Commission for England and Wales for two years to work as a lawyer on its project 'Cohabitation: The Financial Consequences of Relationship Breakdown'. She is currently embarking on a Nuffield Foundation-funded project examining the first three years' operation of the new remedies between cohabitants in Scotland, introduced by the Family Law (Scotland) Act 2006, with Professor Fran Wasoff at the University of Edinburgh. She is co-author (with Sonia Harris-Short) of *Family Law: Text, Cases, and Materials* (OUP, 2007).

Julia Pearce graduated from the University of Bristol in 1988 with a degree in Law, subsequently practising as a solicitor specialising in family law for seven years. She obtained her LLM in 1996, following which she left private practice to work full-time in socio-legal research. Joining the Law Department of Bristol University she has worked on a number of research studies in family law with colleagues in the Schools of Law and of Social Policy. These include *A Study of Children Act Applications* (1998, funded by the Nuffield Foundation), *An Evaluation of the Family Mediation Pilot Scheme* (1999, for the Legal Services Commission), *A Survey of Ancillary Relief Outcomes* (1999, for the Lord Chancellor's Department), and *A Failure of Trust: Resolving Property Disputes on Cohabitation Breakdown* (2007, funded by the ESRC).

Debora Price is a Lecturer in Social Policy at the Institute of Gerontology at King's College London, where she specialises in the study of pensions and the poverty of older people, issues relating to household money over the life-course, and the legal regulation of the financial consequences of family formation and dissolution. She also has an interest in survey methodology and data analysis, regularly undertaking consultancy work in this area. Formerly a barrister specialising in family law, her ESRC PhD research focused on the impact of family change on pension scheme participation in the UK. She has recently concluded an ESRC/DWP fellowship placement at the Department for Work and Pensions reviewing measures of pensioner poverty. Her current research includes the ESRC-funded project 'Behind Closed Doors: Older Couples and the Management of Household Money'.

Rebecca Probert is a Senior Lecturer at the University of Warwick, teaching family law, child law, and a course on 'law and the intact family'. She has written widely on the topics of cohabitation and marriage, particularly from a historical perspective. Her recent publications include *Marriage Law and Practice in the Long Eighteenth Century: A Reassessment* (CUP, 2009) and 'Looking back on the overlooked: cohabitants and the law 1857–2007' in N Lowe and G Douglas (eds) *The Continuing Evolution of Family Law* (Jordans, 2009). She is also co-author (with J Masson and R Bailey-Harris) of *Cretney: Principles of Family Law* (Sweet & Maxwell, 2008), editor of *Family Life and the Law: Under One Roof* (Ashgate, 2007), and co-editor (with Stephen Gilmore and Jonathan Herring) of *Responsible Parents and Parental Responsibility* (Hart Publishing, 2009).

Jacqueline Scott is Professor in Empirical Sociology at the University of Cambridge and a Fellow of Queens' College. She directs the ESRC's Research Network on Gender Inequalities in Production and Reproduction. Her former positions include Director of Research at the ESRC Centre for Micro Social Change at the University of Essex, where she was involved in the original design and implementation of the British Household Panel Survey. Her research interests include life-course research; gender-role change; attitudinal research; and ageing and well-being. She has recently co-edited (with Judith Treas and Martin Richards) the *Blackwell Companion to the Sociology of Families* (Blackwell, 2004); (with Yu Xie) the *Sage Benchmark Series on Quantitative Sociology* (Sage, 2005); and (with Shirley Dex and Heather Joshi) *Women and Employment: Changing Lives and New Challenges* (Edward Elgar Publishing Ltd, 2008).

Stefanie Sonnenberg is a Lecturer in Psychology at the University of Portsmouth. She graduated from the University of Exeter with an MSc in Economic Psychology (1998) and completed her PhD in Social Psychology at the University of St. Andrews (2004). Her general research interest lies at the intersection between economic psychology and social psychology, and her work primarily focuses on the relationship between identity and economic practices. Her recent projects (with Carole Burgoyne and Anne Barlow) have examined financial management practices in intimate relationships.

Jean Taylor is an Associate Fellow at the Office for Public Management (OPM). Prior to joining OPM, Jean was a Senior Researcher at National Centre for Social Research (NatCen), where she undertook fieldwork for, and co-authored, *Separating from Cohabitation: Making Arrangements for Finances and Parenting* (2006, funded by the Department for Constitutional Affairs). Jean holds an MSc in European Social Policy Analysis from the University of Bath, and a BA in Modern History from the University of Oxford.

Rosalind Tennant is a Research Director at NatCen. She specialises in qualitative research and has worked across a range of social policy areas including families and work, older people's services, and social inclusion. She is co-author of the research report *Separating from Cohabitation: Making Arrangements for Finances and Parenting* (2006, funded by the Department for Constitutional Affairs). Her current work focuses on the areas of learning, skills, and employment, in particular special educational needs. Rosalind graduated in 2000 with a BA in Communication and in 2001 with a MA in Research in Language and Communication, both from the University of Wales, Cardiff. She worked in qualitative and quantitative market research for a number of years before joining NatCen's Qualitative Research Department in 2004.

Carolyn Vogler is Reader in Sociology at City University, London. She has published extensively in the areas of globalisation, social class, unemployment, gender segregation in the labour market, and money and gender relations within intimate relationships. Currently, her main research interests are in the area of money, power, and inequality in new forms of intimate relationships.

Hilary Woodward graduated from the London School of Economics with a degree in Sociology and Social Anthropology in 1967. She worked as a research associate on projects with the Institute of Education, the Institute of Psychiatry and the Medical Research Council, before taking up training in law. She practised as a family lawyer from 1982 to 2003 and was accredited as a Resolution cohabitation specialist in 2001. She has worked as a family mediator with Bristol Family Mediation since 1993, and joined Cardiff Law School as a research associate in 2003. She is co-author of 'Ancillary Relief Outcomes' (2000) 12 *Child and Family Law Quarterly* 43, *Divorce for Dummies* (John Wiley and Sons Ltd, 1st and 2nd editions) and *A Failure of Trust: Resolving Property Disputes on Cohabitation Breakdown* (2007, funded by the ESRC).

Part I

General Issues

whatever is afforded (or demanded) by the law relating to the financial support of children.[14] We outline the details of these laws further below.

It is likely that many people are surprised by these key features of the current law. For example, we know from the British Social Attitudes survey that a majority (albeit shrinking) still positively believe (in general terms[15]) that spouses and cohabitants enjoy similar legal status, leaving many cohabitants disappointed (and seriously disadvantaged) on relationship breakdown.[16] Conversely, a large number of spouses would probably be surprised to discover that they do not automatically—by virtue of marriage—enjoy joint ownership of all or certain assets (particularly the matrimonial home and/or its essential household contents), as is the case in certain European jurisdictions operating systems of 'community of property'.[17]

The Law of 'Ancillary Relief' on Divorce

Upon divorce, the court has a discretion as to how it should exercise its wide-ranging powers to reallocate assets between the former spouses. Until 1984, courts were directed to exercise these powers in such a way as would keep the parties, so far as it was practicable and (having regard to their conduct) just to do so, in the financial position in which they would have been if the marriage had not broken down. Since the removal of that direction by the Matrimonial and Family Proceedings Act 1984 (see further Maclean and Eekelaar, chapter two, this volume), there has been no statutory guidance as to the aims of the process. The legislation simply states that first consideration is to be given to the welfare of any child of the family, that the court is to take all the circumstances of the case into account (referring judges to a list of specific but non-exhaustive factors), and that the court is to consider the desirability of an order that will achieve a clean break between the parties, that is to say, to bring to an end any ongoing financial ties between them. In line with the shift away from a divorce law based on fault to one based on the breakdown of the marriage, the conduct of the parties is rarely a factor that will influence the division of the parties' assets, save where it is 'obvious and gross'[18] or directly affects the assets available for division.[19]

---

[14]   Child Support Act 1991, and Children Act 1989 s 15 and Sch 1.

[15]   Contrast the responses given to more specific questions regarding particular legal entitlements: Barlow et al (2001).

[16]   See Barlow et al (2008).

[17]   See generally the attitudes of those interviewed by Cooke, Barlow and Callus (2006) about what the law *should* be, both for spouses and cohabitants; a majority of British Social Attitudes respondents think that *cohabitants* should pool their resources: Barlow et al (2008) table 2.4; see Harris-Short and Miles (2007) 3.5 for discussion of community of property and joint ownership systems.

[18]   See *Wachtel v Wachtel (No 2)* [1973] Fam 72.

[19]   As in the case of financial or litigation misconduct: see eg *M v M (Financial Misconduct: Subpoena Against Third Party)* [2006] 2 FLR 1253.

The principles underpinning the court's exercise of discretion were discussed by the House of Lords in the cases of *White v White*[20] and *Miller; McFarlane*[21] and subsequently by the Court of Appeal in *Charman v Charman*.[22] Three bases for reallocation were articulated: need, compensation, and sharing. From a theoretical perspective this proliferation poses a problem, in that each of the bases presupposes a slightly different model of marriage; from both a practical and a theoretical perspective, there is the challenge of deciding whether, and if so when, needs should take precedence over sharing, and how compensation fits into the court's assessment. There have also been debates as to what exactly is to be shared: does the principle apply only to assets acquired as a result of the parties' joint efforts during the marriage, or does it extend to other assets acquired before,[23] during, or after[24] this period?[25]

At present the position would appear to be that the court will first consider the needs of the parties, and that any assets owned by either party, whenever acquired, may be used to ensure that such needs are met.[26] In lower-income cases, meeting the needs of the parent with primary care for the children of the marriage may well result in that party receiving more than half of the assets. If there is a surplus after the needs of the parties are met, then the sharing principle comes into play. This principle does not, however, simply dictate that all assets, or even all assets acquired during the marriage, are to be divided equally between the parties: the duration of the marriage and the contributions of the parties may suggest that a different distribution would be fairer.[27] As the Court of Appeal put it in *Charman v Charman*, 'property should be shared in equal proportions unless there is good reason to depart from such proportions'.[28]

This flexible approach reflects the way in which the modern courts have consistently eschewed a formulaic approach.[29] They have also been reluctant to develop the idea of compensation introduced in *Miller; McFarlane*. While there is now a greater awareness of the impact of sacrificing a career,[30] such sacrifices tend to be addressed by means other than including a specifically compensatory element

---

[20]   [2001] 1 AC 596.
[21]   [2006] UKHL 24.
[22]   [2007] EWCA Civ 503.
[23]   A clear answer in the negative was given in *B v B (Ancillary Relief)* [2008] EWCA Civ 543; see also *McCartney v Mills McCartney* [2008] EWHC 401 (Fam).
[24]   See eg the debates regarding post-separation property in *Rossi v Rossi* [2006] EWHC 1482 (Fam); *S v S* [2006] EWHC 2339 (Fam); *H v H* [2007] EWHC 459 (Fam).
[25]   See also *Vaughan v Vaughan* [2007] EWCA Civ 1085, in which Wilson LJ drew a distinction between equality of *assets* and equality of *outcome*.
[26]   See eg *S v S (Non-Matrimonial Property: Conduct)* [2006] EWHC 2793; *S v S (Ancillary Relief: Importance of FDR)* [2007] EWHC 1975.
[27]   See eg *S v S (Non-Matrimonial Property: Conduct)* [2006] EWHC 2793; *NA v MA* [2006] EWHC 2900; *McCartney v Mills McCartney* [2008] EWHC 401 (Fam).
[28]   [2007] EWCA Civ 503 [65].
[29]   See eg *H v H* [2007] EWHC 459 (Fam).
[30]   See eg *Lauder v Lauder* [2007] EWHC 1227 (Fam); *VB v JP* [2008] EWHC 112 (Fam).

in that party's share of the assets.[31] In lower-income cases the ongoing effect of sacrifices made during the marriage (for example giving up paid employment to care for the children of the marriage) will be dealt with as an aspect of that party's needs;[32] in higher-income cases the sharing principle may produce more than the spouse would have earned as a result of paid employment,[33] and, or alternatively, the loss of earning capacity will be recognised through a 'generous assessment' of that party's needs.[34] In other cases the principle is not seen as relevant, either because the spouse had not developed a career before the marriage,[35] or because giving up work was a 'lifestyle choice' rather than a necessity.[36] And even if the principle is seen as appropriate, courts may struggle with its application to the case before them: one judge suggested that it was neither possible nor desirable to attempt to ascertain the career that the spouse would have had.[37] As yet, therefore, there have been few cases in which the concept of compensation has played an independent role in the court's deliberations.

The Law of Property and Trusts: Dividing the Assets when Cohabitants Separate

Decisions made during the lifetime of the relationship have a profound, if not necessarily anticipated, effect on the parties' property rights on separation. Most couples who have purchased a home together in the past decade will be jointly registered as legal owners of that property and will have made an express declaration as to their beneficial interests in the property[38] (even if some of them may not have realised the effect of so doing[39]). Such a declaration is determinative of their rights—in the absence of fraud or common mistake—regardless of their respective contributions.[40] The recent House of Lords decision in *Stack v Dowden*[41] made clear that if a couple purchase a home in joint names without making any such declaration, the starting point will be that they too intended that the beneficial title should be held jointly,[42] and strong evidence will be required

---

[31] See eg *H v H* [2007] EWHC 459 (Fam).

[32] See eg *Lauder v Lauder* [2007] EWHC 1227 (Fam).

[33] *CR v CR* [2007] EWHC 3334 (Fam).

[34] See eg *Lauder v Lauder* [2007] EWHC 1227; *VB v JP* [2008] EWHC 112.

[35] *NA v MA* [2006] EWHC 2900.

[36] *S v S (Non-Matrimonial Property: Conduct)* [2006] EWHC 2793.

[37] *P v P* [2007] EWHC 779 (Fam). See also *VB v JP* [2008] EWHC 112 (Fam) and *CR v CR* [2007] EWHC 3334 (Fam).

[38] Since 1998 the relevant Land Registry forms have invited those purchasing a home in joint names to indicate whether they hold the beneficial title as joint tenants, or as tenants in common in equal shares, or on some other trusts. However, the Land Registry will not reject a form that fails to complete this declaration.

[39] See Douglas, Pearce and Woodward, ch 7, this volume.

[40] *Goodman v Gallant* [1986] 1 FLR 513.

[41] [2007] UKHL 17.

[42] See also *Abbott v Abbott* [2007] UKPC 53.

to show that, 'unusually', a different arrangement was intended. By contrast, if the home was purchased in the name of one party (or was owned by him or her before the relationship began), then the onus is on the other party to establish a beneficial interest under the law of trusts. This may be done by showing either that the claimant made a financial contribution to the initial purchase price or that there was an agreement, arrangement or understanding between the parties on which the claimant has relied to his or her detriment.[43] The former may give rise to a resulting trust (which will yield an interest in the property proportionate to the original contribution), or, more probably in the domestic context,[44] will lead the court to infer a constructive trust on the basis that there was a common intention that the beneficial interest should be shared, the financial contribution establishing the necessary element of detrimental reliance. The extent of the parties' interests under a constructive trust will be determined by reference to the whole course of dealing between the parties.

Such distinctions lead to some stark differences in outcome. In *Fowler v Barron*,[45] for example, the property had been conveyed into joint names, but during the 17 years of the parties' relationship it was Mr Barron who made all the payments under the mortgage and who met other household expenses. Miss Fowler's salary was used for more transient items, such as holidays, meals out, and clothes in particular for the children and herself. The court's interpretation of this was that, despite the lack of a joint bank account, the parties had effectively pooled their assets and did not care who paid for what, or how much; the inference was that they had not intended that their different contributions should lead to them having different interests in the property. Each party was thus entitled to 50 per cent of the equity in the property. By contrast, in *James v Thomas*,[46] Miss James moved into a home already owned by Mr Thomas, and he was reluctant to convey it into their joint names. Although she worked unpaid in his business for the better part of their 15-year relationship and the mortgage was paid from the profits of that business, the court held that there was no common intention that she should have an interest in the property, and that her contributions were simply attributable to the fact that she and Mr Thomas 'were making their life together as man and wife'.[47] She was therefore not entitled to any interest in the home.[48]

Whether these outcomes truly reflected the intentions of the parties is open to question: Mr Thomas acknowledged that it would be fair for Miss James to receive some interest in the property, while Mr Barron argued that, while he had intended that Miss Fowler should inherit the property if he pre-deceased her, he had not intended that she should be entitled to half if they separated. This is not an

---

[43] *Lloyds Bank v Rosset* [1991] AC 107.

[44] At least where the parties are sharing a home: see eg *Adekunle and Others v Ritchie* [2007] EW Misc 5 (EWCC); cf *Laskar v Laskar* [2008] EWCA Civ 347.

[45] [2008] EWCA Civ 377.

[46] [2007] EWCA Civ 1212.

[47] ibid [36] (Chadwick LJ).

[48] See also *Morris v Morris* [2008] EWCA Civ 257.

unusual view: it has been suggested that many in this situation would be perfectly happy for their partner to inherit all their property in the case of their death, but are far less willing to split their assets equally in case of separation.[49] The sharing that is part of a loving relationship is often fiercely resisted by the parties when that relationship has come to an end, whether they were married or cohabiting (as is evident from the research of Lewis et al in this volume). The law, however, takes the view that while the parties' intentions regarding the shares each has in the property may change over time, those intentions—and so those shares—must at any given point in time be the same for all purposes.[50]

Financial Provision for Children whose Parents Live Apart

In order to complete the picture of the current law relating to the distribution of wealth on relationship breakdown, it is necessary briefly to outline the law governing provision for children. This law applies almost identically to children of married and unmarried parents.[51] However, given the very different background of provision/division of property between the adults, described above, the overall outcomes for formerly marital and cohabiting households and the children within them are very different.

The Child Support Act 1991, as amended, declares the responsibility of each parent to maintain his children,[52] regardless of the nature of the parents' relationship. In the case of a 'non-resident parent' (a parent with whom the child does not principally live), this responsibility is met by the payment of child maintenance calculated by reference to a formula which (subject to possible variation on limited grounds set out in the Act) requires payment of a given percentage of that parent's income, depending on the number of children to be supported. Recent changes effected by the Child Maintenance and Other Payments Act 2008 mean that child maintenance is now viewed principally as a matter to be resolved by (non-binding) private agreement between the parties.[53] The statutory agency, its formula and enforcement powers are intended to provide a fallback where such agreement is unattainable or breaks down.

Basic child maintenance (generally made by way of regular payments) is not a matter for the courts, except where agreed by the parties and enshrined in a

---

[49]   See Douglas, Pearce and Woodward, ch 7, this volume.

[50]   Contrast the findings of Douglas, Pearce and Woodward, ch 7, this volume, who find that parties may have precisely the sort of multiple intention that the law does not accommodate.

[51]   The only key distinction pertains to the responsibility of step-parents: only an individual who is married to (or a civil partner of) a child's legal parent may be required to maintain the child; someone who has merely lived with that parent may not: see the concepts of 'parent' in Children Act 1989 Sch 1 para 16(2); and 'child of the family' in Matrimonial Causes Act 1973 s 52(1).

[52]   Child Support Act 1991 s 1. Only 'qualifying children', as defined by ss 3 and 55 of the Act, are owed this duty.

[53]   Prior to these reforms, if the parent with care was claiming a means-tested benefit, the Child Support Agency's involvement was effectively mandatory.

'consent order'.[54] However, the courts have exclusive jurisdiction to order various forms of capital provision 'for the benefit of the child'.[55] Crucially, that qualification has been interpreted in such a way as effectively prevents the outright transfer of property to the parent with care. Generally, any capital transferred must either be spent for the child's benefit during the child's minority (for example on depreciating assets such as a car for taking the child to and from school and other activities, or 'white goods' for the child's home), or, in the case of the transfer of a house, the property must revert to the other parent once the child attains independence.[56] Provision for dependent children of a formerly married or cohabiting couple can therefore offer no long-term or direct security for the parent with care. But, as we have seen, that limitation of these remedies is of far greater significance for former cohabitants (who have no personal financial remedy and may have no claim in property law) than for former spouses (who have the benefit of financial relief under the matrimonial legislation, whatever their property rights may be).

Future Reform?

As increasing numbers of couples cohabit outside marriage and as more children are born outside marriage, reform providing statutory financial remedies between cohabitants—already available in a number of other jurisdictions[57]—has been actively considered. The Law Commission for England and Wales recently published its recommendations for a scheme of remedies between separating cohabitants who had either had a child together or lived together beyond a minimum duration (fixed somewhere between two and five years), unless they had executed a valid 'opt-out agreement' excluding the operation of the scheme and (perhaps) made their own arrangements.[58] Under this scheme, the courts would have largely the same powers to reallocate assets as they enjoy on divorce, but those powers would be exercisable on a different basis. The Law Commission concluded that, given broadly observable differences between many cohabiting and marital relationships (including the substantial heterogeneity of the cohabiting population; the lack of express, public commitment to the relationship; and various patterns

---

[54] The courts also have exclusive jurisdiction (see Child Support Act 1991 s 8) to order periodical payments for meeting educational expenses, costs associated with extra needs created by a child's disability, and 'top-up' payments where the non-resident parent's income exceeds the jurisdictional limit of the statutory agency responsible for child maintenance: Children Act 1989 Sch 1; Matrimonial Causes Act 1973 s 23(1)(d) and (e). In the last case, in particular, payment may include a 'carer's allowance' to cover the parent with care's needs as carer: *Re P (A Child: Financial Provision)* [2003] EWCA Civ 837.

[55] These powers are exercisable by the courts under various statutes. In the case of married parents who are divorcing, jurisdiction would usually be exercised under the Matrimonial Causes Act 1973; in the case of unmarried parents, under the Children Act 1989 Sch 1.

[56] *A v A* [1995] 1 FCR 309.

[57] Most recently, Scotland: Family Law (Scotland) Act 2006.

[58] Law Commission (2007). See also Law Commission (2006) for its earlier consultation paper.

of money management and property ownership), provision between cohabitants should not be based on the needs of the parties or a norm of equal sharing. Instead, the court would exercise a principled discretion with restitutionary and compensatory purposes designed to respond to the enduring economic impact of the parties' contributions to their life together. The court would therefore aim broadly to reverse gains ('retained benefits') made by one party as a result of the other's contributions, such as the latter's direct or indirect financial contribution to the acquisition of property held in the former's sole name; and to share the burden of losses ('economic disadvantage') suffered by one party for the benefit of the family, for example, the loss of future earnings arising from having given up paid employment to care for children.

The Role of Empirical Data in Developing the Law

The consequence that, following *Stack v Dowden*, the proceeds of sale of the family home will be divided 50:50 in most joint ownership cases between cohabitants on separation may seem to resemble the approach in the context of ancillary relief in the wake of cases such as *White v White* and *Miller; McFarlane*. There is, however, a difference: the 'sharing principle' established in the latter context rests upon the view that the assets accrued during the 'partnership' of marriage should as a matter of principle be shared, while the presumption that equity follows the law in the context of the family home rests on the assumption that this is what such couples would usually have intended. The role that individual intentions play in the context of ancillary relief remains a moot point,[59] whereas evidence as to the parties' intentions may play a crucial role under the law of trusts.[60]

This brings us on to the crucial distinction between empirically based presumptions and normative judgments. The principles developed and asserted in the recent House of Lords decisions may be put into these two inter-related categories:

(i) empirically based presumptions about what parties to particular relationships may be taken to intend in particular circumstances: for example, that couples who purchase a home in joint names intend to hold it in equal shares; that couples who manage their money separately may not have that intention.

(ii) normative judgements about what consequences ought to be taken to flow from particular situations: for example, that marriage is a partnership

---

[59] For example, pre-nuptial agreements retain a rather limited role, just one factor for the court to take into account in the exercise of its discretion, although in some cases an agreement may be a factor of 'magnetic importance': *Crossley v Crossley* [2007] EWCA Civ 1491.

[60] See eg *Williamson v Sheikh* [2008] EWCA Civ 990 (house in sole name of male partner, intentions gauged from an unexecuted declaration that female partner would be entitled to £10,000 plus 60% of proceeds).

which should entitle the partners to equal shares of certain property, regardless of need or financial contribution; that 'special contributions' should nevertheless receive recognition; that needs arising during a marriage (and perhaps to some extent afterwards) should generally be met by the other spouse; that some measure of 'compensation' ought to be afforded to recompense one spouse for economic disadvantage incurred, typically as a result of sacrificing paid employment to care for home and family.

To some extent, these empirically based presumptions and normative judgements articulated by the House of Lords were consciously based not just on the courts' assessment of the position of individual litigants who have appeared before them or on 'common sense' views adopted by the courts over time, but also on observations yielded from social science data, including socio-legal research. The speeches of Baroness Hale, in particular, are distinctive for and often enriched by her use of such material.[61]

Whether legal development is to be driven by reference to how people actually think or behave in their relationships, or by reference to what society considers the law ought to be seeking to achieve, or (perhaps most likely) a combination of both, social science data and analysis have central roles to play in informing the deliberations of appellate courts, law reformers and policy-makers. Such information is always essential to obtaining a proper understanding of the context in which the current law is operating and how that law is impacting on those to whom it applies. For example, data regarding participation in paid employment during relationships and about the economic disadvantage experienced following relationship breakdown by those who have been absent from the labour market may readily prompt the preliminary conclusion that remedies should be provided in response to this hardship.[62] Determining precisely *how* that should be achieved, on what basis and in which cases may, of course, be more difficult to resolve, but research data may have a valuable contribution to make here too. In a rather different vein, data about how couples deal with the financial implications of separation, and about the obstacles that they encounter in the process, may prompt us to re-examine both procedural and other contextual aspects of dispute resolution and the extent to which complexity in the substantive law may itself impede settlement. Moreover, without a clear understanding of the social context in which the law is to operate, the law of unintended consequences is likely to rule the day.

---

[61] In *Miller, McFarlane* and *Stack v Dowden* she refers to Pahl (1989), Ermisch (2000), Barlow et al (2001), Lewis (2001), Arthur et al (2002) and Douglas, Pearce and Woodward (2007) (*cf* the contribution by the latter authors to this volume (ch 7)). See also her extra-judicial writing: eg Hale (2004) draws on Rake (2000).

[62] Although see remarks in the conclusion to this chapter regarding the relative responsibility of private family law and other areas of law and policy to deal with the issues explored in this volume.

The importance of empirical data can only grow as those considering legal reform in this field explore schemes based not on the exercise of a wholly individualised, strong discretion, with which many are becoming disenchanted,[63] but on a more 'standardised' basis, such as community of property regimes, guidelines for wealth distribution,[64] or 'structured discretion' of the sort recently recommended for cohabitants by the Law Commission.[65] If a (more or less) standardised scheme is to 'fit' the population to which it is to apply—to supply a satisfactory measure of 'average rather than individualised justice'[66]— its development must be fully informed by data on a wider range of issues such as: patterns of property ownership, money management, employment and so on, and what (if anything) these patterns imply about parties' intentions, commitment and so on; the degree of disparity in earning capacity or standard of living between partners following separation; and public attitudes towards the provision of remedies in particular cases and about the appropriate basis for remedies.[67]

It is also important that the judges in our appellate courts should refer to social science data when developing the current law, as they have done in recent cases such as *Stack v Dowden*.[68] All too often their Lordships are not referred to key findings bearing on the empirical questions which they inevitably have to address in the course of their decision-making.[69] One major obstacle is, of course, the accessibility of such data: those presenting the case to the court will not usually be *au fait* with literature in non-legal disciplines, and even research assistants employed by the court may find it difficult to discover and interpret papers written by economists, sociologists and psychologists. It is equally unlikely, of course, that empirical researchers will be aware of ongoing legal proceedings to which their findings may be highly relevant, and terminological differences sometimes pose a barrier to mutual understanding. There is thus a role for intermediaries to make empirical research from one discipline more accessible—both physically and intellectually—to another.

It must, however, be conceded that no distillation of the existing research evidence will ever be value-free. Indeed, it is clear from academic criticisms of *Stack v*

---

[63] See eg the disadvantages of the current Matrimonial Causes Act scheme identified by the Law Society (2003) [71]; concerns reported in the wake of *Miller, McFarlane* by the Court of Appeal in *Charman v Charman (No 4)* [2007] EWCA Civ 503 [120]; and proposals for presumptive formulae for the calculation of periodical payments awards: eg Eekelaar (2006).

[64] See for example the Canadian spousal support guidelines: Department of Justice Canada (2008).

[65] Law Commission (2006, 2007).

[66] Rogerson and Thompson (2005) 10.

[67] Cf the view of Maclean and Eekelaar, in ch 2, this volume at p 34 regarding the difficulty today of identifying shared expectations and values on which reform might be based.

[68] See for example Harris-Short and Miles (2008), Probert (2008a, 2008b), and Douglas, Pearce and Woodward, ch 7, this volume.

[69] For example, there is no reference in *Stack v Dowden* to research into couples' money management practices, data which have been central to many commentators' criticisms of the case—see previous note.

Dowden that the research data cited in that case is open to interpretations different from those adopted by the House of Lords. Since such different interpretations can generate different conclusions about the appropriate response from the law, there is a need for constant evaluation of the interplay between such research evidence and judicial decision-making—an example of which appears in this volume, in chapter seven, by Douglas, Pearce and Woodward.

THE ISSUES AND THE DATA

As Maclean and Eekelaar indicate in chapter two of this volume, much research to date has focused on divorced or separating couples. But every separating couple was once an intact family, and the choices made while the relationship was subsisting will obviously be a significant constraint on the options available on relationship breakdown. Part II of the book, 'Work, Money and Property within Intimate Relationships: Expectations and Actions', examines data relevant to these questions.

Problems originating during the relationship are particularly acute where one or both of the parties are in debt. There has to date been relatively little discussion of this aspect of relationships or its legal implications: for example, we now recognise a loose concept of 'matrimonial property'—should we also recognise more explicitly the reality of 'matrimonial debt', and if so how should we distinguish it from personal debt?[70] Finney's discussion of debt within relationships and the links between debt and relationship breakdown in chapter six highlights key background data about both indebtedness and saving habits, and their association with particular types of relationship and life events such as relationship formation, the arrival of children, and relationship breakdown.

In addition, the House of Lords in both *Miller; McFarlane* and *Stack v Dowden* placed some importance on the way in which the couple dealt with their assets during the relationship, both when dividing assets on divorce and when discerning the parties' intentions regarding their property. But without empirical data it is difficult to know what forms of behaviour are unusual, or what light such behaviour can throw on the parties' intentions. The assumption that Mr Stack and Ms Dowden were unusual in keeping their finances separate is clearly contradicted by several studies. The chapters by Vogler (chapter four), Burgoyne and Sonnenberg (chapter five), and Douglas, Pearce and Woodward (chapter seven) cast valuable light on this area, showing in particular that what we might instinctively assume certain money management practices indicate about parties' intentions regarding ownership and use of their money might be incorrect.

Of course, an individual's behaviour may reflect constraints as well as their preferences, as is evident from the analysis by Scott and Dex in chapter three

---

[70] *cf* the findings of Cooke et al (2006), where respondents to their qualitative survey were largely not supportive of debts, as well as assets, being treated as joint as between spouses.

of the division of labour in the context of the UK labour market.[71] Given the difficulties of changing the underlying conditions that produce such inequality, it is likely that it will persist for the foreseeable future, and it is therefore necessary to consider its effect both during relationships and upon separation. Unequal earnings may, for example, affect the way in which couples manage their money and generate differing concepts of 'equality' in this sphere, as chapter four by Vogler, and chapter five by Burgoyne and Sonnenberg show. For some, inequality in income is seen as mandating inequality in contributions, with each contributing according to their ability;[72] for others, equal contributions are made despite differences in earnings. But as the next section shows, contributions, in whatever proportions, do not always translate into a share of the assets, equal or otherwise, upon relationship breakdown.

In the third part of the book, 'Dividing the Assets on Relationship Breakdown', the discussion of married and cohabiting couples of necessity diverges, owing to the very different legal regimes that apply to each on divorce and separation. Douglas, Pearce and Woodward in chapter seven draw on empirical research to highlight how difficult it is to ascertain the 'common intention' required by the law of trusts, particularly by reference to the factors identified by the House of Lords in *Stack v Dowden*. They show that the law has set itself a daunting task in seeking to give effect to parties' intentions, given the difficulties encountered in practice in attempting to ascertain from the parties' conduct of their relationship any shared intention specifically regarding property ownership.

Lewis, Tennant and Taylor in chapter eight identify those disadvantaged by the current law relating to cohabitants and consider whether the Law Commission's recommendations for reform in this area would do any better at addressing those individuals' problems. Their study shows, in particular, how *legal* ownership (specifically) rather than the needs of the parties (or beneficial entitlements under the law of trusts) currently dominates the way in which assets are divided when a cohabiting relationship breaks down. By contrast, upon divorce needs assume far greater importance: indeed, as Hitchings shows in chapter nine, the needs of the parties, and the range of practical options available to meet those needs, are of crucial importance in determining the nature of any settlement in most everyday cases. The emphasis on needs may help to achieve a degree of consistency in the disposal of these cases, despite the lack of guidance in the legislation. Further research is necessary in this area, not least given the concerns expressed by the Law Society in 2003 about uncertainty of outcome, which may vary between different county courts.[73] 'Local knowledge' may be extremely important in practice, which poses a particular problem for the growing number of litigants in person appearing

---

[71] And see further La Valle, Clery and Huerta (2008).

[72] See also *Stack v Dowden* [2007] UKHL 17 [91], where Baroness Hale refers to the idea of 'each doing what they could', as a form of organisation that could then reflect an intention that the property be equally shared.

[73] Law Society (2003) [60]–[70]. See also Hitchings, ch 9, this volume.

before the family courts, who will almost certainly lack the insider knowledge garnered by repeat players.

Moreover, public misconceptions about the role of the law in this context may hinder a speedy settlement, and Dowding's chapter ten sets the issue of settlement in its practical context, identifying the many opportunities which parties have— and are strongly encouraged by their legal advisors to use—to reach agreement without recourse to litigation, and the cost implications of their choices in this respect. As the chapters in this volume by Vogler (chapter four), Burgoyne and Sonnenberg (chapter five), and Douglas, Pearce and Woodward (chapter seven) indicate, couples often find it difficult to discuss money and property during their relationships—or easy to avoid having to do so. Inevitably if their relationship breaks down, such discussions become unavoidable and the earlier the couple can be helped to resolve their disagreements, the lower will be the costs of their dispute, both financial and emotional. But in the case of cohabitants (where there are no judicial powers of the sort enjoyed on divorce to adjust property rights and where the special matrimonial procedures described by Dowding in chapter ten do not apply), by the time the couple do belatedly address the issue of who owns what (and so who leaves the relationship with what), it may be too late for one party to guard against disadvantage of the sort discussed by Lewis, Tennant and Taylor in chapter eight.

One feature, however, is common to both cohabiting and married relationships, especially where there are dependent children, and that is inequality on relationship breakdown arising in particular from decisions made during the relationship about each party's participation in paid employment. The impact of these decisions on the income of men and women after divorce and the end of cohabitation is made manifest by Fisher and Low in chapter eleven, based on an analysis of several sweeps of the British Household Panel Survey. Their conclusion that income recovers over time gives some cause for optimism, although it is clear from their analysis that in many cases income recovery following divorce is achieved by repartnering rather than by improvements in personal income from employment. While this may guard against poverty following divorce, repartnering may be said simply to substitute a new dependency for the old one, and as such fails to address what for many is the underlying problem. Moreover, as Fisher and Low demonstrate, repartnering is less likely for older women and for women with children, leaving them economically disadvantaged unless able substantially to increase their labour market participation, which few appear to do.

Price's chapter on pensions (chapter twelve) builds on this theme of post-divorce inequality, providing powerful evidence that under current conditions divorced women do not and cannot catch up in pension building, and that, contrary to government's expectations, pension sharing on divorce is rare rather than routine, leaving divorced women facing poverty in old age. The reasons for the rarity of pension-sharing orders are hard to diagnose, although some anecdotal evidence suggests that pensions are not routinely included in parties' schedule of assets ('Form E') on divorce, so potentially rendering that valuable asset 'invisible' and not a 'matrimonial asset' to be shared. The assumption may be that women will create their own pension fund by 'downsizing' once the children reach independence, or that they will protect themselves via repartnering; and we know from research that some women are principally motivated to ensure their short-term security (for example in securing accommodation for themselves and the children) to the neglect of their long-term interests.[74] But as Fisher and Low's data show, the latter assumption may be misplaced, and the inherent uncertainty about prospects of repartnering and about the security of any new relationship makes it difficult to factor that possibility into any individual settlement. Moreover, the principles developed by the House of Lords in *Miller; McFarlane* have clear application to pension savings: savings accumulated during the marriage should be treated as matrimonial property and in principle be brought into account in dividing those assets pursuant to the 'sharing' principle; and women's disadvantage in relation to pensions offers a clear example of the sort of economic disadvantage to which the 'compensation' strand is intended to alert us. However, we also lack information about the characteristics of the tiny minority of cases in which such orders *are* made. This is clearly an area ripe for further investigation and, given the uncertainty that surrounds future state provision beyond retirement age, is a matter of considerable importance as the proportion of older women who are divorced, and living longer, increases.

Fisher and Low's data also provide material against which they evaluate alternative principles on which financial remedies following relationship breakdown might be based—comparing income-based measures (reflecting the impact of the relationship on each party's human capital) with consumption-based measures (based on needs or expected living standard)—and so for analysing the outcomes in and the incentive effects created by *Miller; McFarlane*. This theme—how to choose the most appropriate basis for financial relief—is developed further in the contrasting contributions of Dnes and Barlow in the final part of the book, 'A Rational Approach?'. Barlow in chapter fourteen draws on recent social attitude surveys and demographic changes to support her argument in favour of a 'bottom-up' approach to law reform: a reconfiguration of remedies on relationship breakdown according to whether the parties (married or not) had children, with a focus on needs-based remedies between couples with children and on greater autonomy for childless couples. Meanwhile, Dnes' chapter thirteen offers an economist's view of the law governing financial and property disputes on divorce and the end of cohabitation, demonstrating the potential for economic analysis to provide greater clarity to discussions in this area, for example by articulating welfare goals more explicitly and highlighting the different incentive effects of various settlement rules, including the introduction of financial remedies at the end of cohabitation.[75]

---

[74] Douglas and Perry (2001).
[75] See generally Dnes and Rowthorn (2002).

These chapters also provide competing views on the ability of the law to influence behaviour within the family context, and how different research methodologies can be used to detect such influences at work. This discussion has been described by Barlow and others as being concerned with 'legal rationality', that is the idea that people respond to the framework of family regulation created by the law and order their intimate relationships in line with the law's expectations.[76] Barlow argues, in light of data yielded from various research projects conducted by herself and other socio-legal scholars, that legislators in the family-law sphere are in danger of making a 'rationality mistake', overestimating law's ability to influence behaviour in the family field. She considers the evidence of people's changing attitudes to relationships and property and how well or otherwise this fits with the law's expectations, arguing that the legal and financial consequences of marriage rarely figure in the decision whether to marry (at least for first marriages). Even assuming that the parties have an accurate understanding of the law, to marry for such pragmatic reasons is seen by many as distasteful, despite the potentially far-reaching economic consequences of this decision when the relationship ends, whether by separation or by death. Dnes, by contrast, explains the insights that can be provided by positivistic, quantitative analysis of longitudinal samples (such as that undertaken by Fisher and Low), arguing that how people explain their own behaviour to qualitative researchers may not necessarily correspond with independent indicators about what people are in fact doing, and highlighting a number of studies identifying significant changes in certain types of behaviour, including partnering behaviour, in response to legal change. This debate about the influence of law on family behaviour is undoubtedly one that will continue and requires further examination. It may be that some laws, such as those relating to welfare benefits and tax credits[77] have greater influence over family practices than those relating to financial settlements following relationship breakdown,[78] not least given what to the individuals concerned is the relative complexity and perceived remoteness of those laws from decisions about marriage and conduct within ongoing relationships.

WHERE SHOULD WE GO FROM HERE?

One clear finding that emerges from the empirical research is the great diversity of practices within families. Whether such diversity militates against devising proposals for reform on the basis of shared values, as Maclean and Eekelaar

---

[76] In the language of economists, 'rationality' is simply concerned with observations about the consistency or otherwise of a subject's decisions, and is entirely unrelated to the desirability of those decisions, the information on which they are based, or their compatibility with or conformity with a particular policy goal or objective perception of the subject's best interests, given the current legal framework.

[77] See eg Anderberg (2008).

[78] Although see Mechoulan (2006), who found that the rules governing allocation of property on divorce had a stronger effect on the divorce rate than the grounds for divorce.

suggest in chapter two, is a moot point. The surveys discussed by Barlow in chapter fourteen suggest that there is still a considerable degree of common ground in the wider population, and a solution that does not resonate with individuals' values may be difficult to implement in practice.

As noted above, there are difficulties in ascertaining the parties' intentions regarding their property from their money management practices during their relationship. There is also a more fundamental question to be posed, which is how far the law *should* be guided by the parties' intentions when dividing assets at the end of a relationship. To date, as we have seen, the answer to that question has differed according to the nature of the relationship, rather than the extent of the disadvantage experienced by the individual in question. This has resulted in a situation in which very similar contributions may result in very different outcomes (as demonstrated by Lewis, Tennant and Taylor, in chapter eight, who compare the results that their cohabitants might have expected had they been married with the actual arrangements that were made).

Yet although individual experiences differ, some common trends can be observed. While we have, as a society, departed from the pure version of Lloyd Cohen's profile of marriage,[79] it remains the case that women tend to earn less than men and spend more time on unpaid household tasks. Whether the first causes the second, or vice versa, is difficult to determine; still more difficult is the task of devising a solution to encourage greater equality in both spheres.[80] The positive story of women's enhanced earning capacity and labour market participation has a negative consequence: the extent of downward mobility for those who move out of the labour market even for a short period is greater for today's women than it was for previous generations. And although remaining out of the labour market to care for children and other dependants should be respected as a choice, this does not mean that the financial detriment of doing so should fall on the carer alone. A division of responsibilities that works within the intact family may well leave the partner who has not pursued a career vulnerable on relationship breakdown (as demonstrated by Fisher and Low and by Price in chapters eleven and twelve).

To the extent that the other party—whether married or cohabiting—has benefited from the contribution of the one who provided care or other non-tangible contributions, then there is a justification for the court to intervene as between the parties themselves. But on what basis? Underlying much of the discussion in this volume is the concept of 'equality'. But this is a multi-faceted concept which could support a variety of solutions to the problems experienced on relationship breakdown. Should equal sharing of assets arise only following equality of contribution? Is contribution to be regarded as equal only where it is of equal value,

---

[79] Cohen (1987).

[80] See eg recent comments of Nicola Brewer, chief executive of the Equalities and Human Rights Commission, regarding the negative impact that improved maternity rights have had on women's progression in the labour market: Bennett and Ahmed (2008).

or made as equal proportions of individual wealth? Are domestic contributions assumed to carry equal value? Or ought we instead to focus on substantive equality of outcome, and if so how is that to be achieved? This brings us back to the ideas of equality of consumption level (needs) or 'compensation'.[81] Studies suggest that the division of responsibilities during the relationship has a direct impact upon both the reduced earnings of married women[82] and the enhanced earnings of married men.[83] The courts' lack of enthusiasm for the concept of 'compensation' is to a large extent attributable to their perceived inability to put a value on the loss that needs to be compensated. Human capital projections of the sort necessary to put a precise figure on future earnings losses and reduced pensions are unfamiliar territory for family lawyers, and potentially costly tools for parties in dispute to have to provide.[84] However, that there will have been *some* disadvantage to the primary carer of children will in many cases be self-evident, and the research by Fisher and Low reveals what the average effects of divorce on the parties' income are, at least for the general population. One possible way forward might be to use that data as a starting point for deciding compensation awards on divorce, rather than, as at present, starting from an assumption that there is no loss to be compensated, and requiring individualised proof by the applicant. Although a 'one-size-fits-all' approach is likely to be inappropriate in this complex area, there is scope for a more standardised approach to ancillary relief than currently exists.[85]

While the focus of this volume is on informing the development of private law entitlements and obligations in light of the research data, it is important to retain a wider perspective and an awareness of the limited horizons and capacities of private family law. Many of the issues arising from the work discussed here go to fundamental issues of *social* rather than merely inter-personal justice, in particular relating to *equality of opportunity*. Where individuals' or families' choices about their behaviour—in particular regarding participation in paid employment, pensions and other saving, and indebtedness—are constrained by social and labour market conditions, created, fostered or maintained by a particular web (or absence) of legal regulation and other policy levers, we must critically examine those areas of law and other tools of governance. Moreover, to the extent that disadvantage and hardship experienced on separation can be characterised as a product of

---

[81] See Miles (2008) for a recent discussion of how a principle of compensation should be used as a tool for achieving equality of outcome on divorce.

[82] See eg Bryan and Sevilla Sanz (2008), who suggest that the timing and nature of housework has an impact on women's wages, since they tend to be responsible for daily tasks that have to be fitted around the working day.

[83] Korenman and Neumark (1991), based on US evidence; although compare Bardasi and Taylor (2005) in the UK context, who use a different methodology and find a rather smaller premium: see further Fisher and Low, ch 11, this volume.

[84] But note, for example, the evidence provided in a recent Scottish cohabitation case, *CM v STS* [2008] CSOH 125 from [284].

[85] Compare, for example, the work of Rogerson and Thompson (2005) and Department of Justice Canada (2008).

social constraints rather than private preferences—and of socially *beneficial* work in caring for dependants—we need to ask whether responsibility for supporting the carer should fall on the other partner at all. It could instead be argued that it is a matter (to that extent) of public rather than private responsibility.[86] Reform beyond the traditionally-understood ambit of 'family law' (in particular, in the fields of labour law and social security law) may well—in the long term—provide a more satisfactory remedy to many of the problems to which family law is currently endeavouring, not without difficulty in some instances, to provide an adequate response.[87]

This is not to say, however, that family lawyers and law-makers can or should simply rely on other areas of the law to produce greater equality between men and women and so mitigate the impact of relationship breakdown. There will always be many who choose to prioritise caring for the family above paid employment, and family law must respond to the economic consequences of relationship breakdown in a way which reflects as closely as possible the real-life experiences of those involved. For this ongoing project to succeed, we need to ensure a constant cycle of empirical research to feed into the 'life-cycle' of legal development. First, research has a vital role to play in informing the creation or development of the applicable legal regime. This should include research on the experience of jurisdictions whose legal regimes we are contemplating borrowing: without such research, there is a real danger of 'faulty transplant' or of assuming on the basis of the face of the legislation and case law that all is well in practice. Then, once reform is enacted, research is needed to monitor how the new law is operating in practice, in part to identify any unintended consequences, not least where people behave in ways that do not conform with the law-makers' expectations. Meanwhile, it remains necessary to maintain a programme of research into contemporary attitudes, norms, and behaviours in the fields of money management, labour market and household work participation, and so on; and, as discussed in the previous paragraph, to revisit the appropriate division of responsibilities and functions between family law and other areas of law and policy with the power to affect behaviour in these spheres. And so, as norms and behaviour change, such research will have a role to play in shaping the next reform of family law.

BIBLIOGRAPHY

Anderberg, D (2008) 'Tax credits, income support and partnership decisions' 15 *International Tax and Public Finance* 499.
Arthur, S, Lewis, J, Maclean, M, Finch, S and Fitzgerald, R (2002) *Settling Up: Making financial arrangements after divorce or separation* (London, NatCen).

---

[86] See eg Fineman (2004).
[87] See Price, ch 12, and Scott and Dex, ch 3, this volume.

divorce, by holding financial responsibilities to continue in the event of the ending of the marriage, and by penalising conduct (although the courts swiftly eroded this element limiting the definition to obvious and gross and misconduct).[3] While this kind of normative purpose lay behind the divorce reforms the policy-maker's task was clear: to ensure that the law would support the generally agreed aim of protecting marriage. But as divorce law became altogether more pragmatic, and the goal on separation became making the best of the resources available to the parties bearing in mind the needs of the children, then it became more important to develop a better understanding of how family finances were operating.

Two social changes in particular affected the way in which the law operated, and became a matter to be studied and understood. First, the increasing rate of home ownership made the power to transfer the home more significant. If the husband's interest in the matrimonial home could be transferred to the wife either outright or for the period while the children were dependent, the wife's bargaining position was strengthened immeasurably. Secondly, women's increasing participation in the workforce, although their work was often part time with low pay, provided a different perspective on the need to remain in an unhappy marriage from that of the woman with no independent resources at all.

During the 1970s, public debate on the financial consequences of divorce developed, as calls for reform were prompted by the 'no-fault' approach, combined with the possibility that 'innocent' men might be losing the homes that were in their names and on which they were paying the mortgage. The Campaign for Justice in Divorce (CJD) was established in 1978, and ran a skilful media campaign on behalf of divorcing men and their second wives. The Law Commission again addressed the issue, and in 1980 published its discussion paper (Law Commission, 1980) agreeing that the current objective of the courts of trying to avoid loss for all parties was simply not working. But to avoid any extension of the judicial discretion which could lead to variation in decision-making and uncertainty (see Barrington Baker and Eekelaar, 1977) the factors to be taken into account in making financial arrangements on divorce, while giving priority to the interests of the children, also included the suggestion that the desirability of the parties becoming self-sufficient should be formulated as a positive principle: that is women should work, and a clean financial break between spouses should be the aim.

The situation was a striking example of the failure of the government to respond to deep-rooted changes to family patterns, particularly the growth in the number of separated and reconstituted families and the increasing complexity of cross-household parental responsibilities, leading to the emergence of an angry interest group. The CJD made effective use of anecdotal evidence, but there was little scientifically based information to go on. Were men being hard done by? Were wives rejecting their husbands, stealing their houses and children, and going

---

[3] See *Wachtel v Wachtel* [1973] Fam 72.

on to live what was referred to as 'the life of Riley' at the expense of the happiness of their former husbands and their new families?

As social science developed, and a better understanding of the state of society began to be part of general knowledge, it is not surprising that the matter of rising divorce rates and post-divorce finance began to attract the attention of researchers. In 1980, John Eekelaar and I began our study of the financial consequences of divorce. When we began to speak with other 'divorce' researchers in the UK we were isolated, as the main thrust of such research was focused on the psychological and social consequences of divorce. But we were encouraged to find researchers in other jurisdictions tackling the same issues, (see Weitzman and Maclean, 1992). In 1981, with the support of the Economic and Social Research Council, we carried out a survey of a nationally representative sample of divorced men and women and found clear evidence, as Lenore Weitzman had found in the United States (Weitzman, 1985), of the economic detriment which women experienced after divorce. As soon as our findings began to emerge (Eekelaar and Maclean, 1986) we were targeted by the CJD, who circulated a pamphlet to all Members of Parliament entitled 'Mud on her Gown ... a critique of Mavis Maclean'. But our findings were, we hoped, the basis for a better-informed approach to the matter, as it was clear that the major factor in the economic difficulties experienced by the women was their responsibility for children (see also Funder, 1992). The typical household situation pre-divorce was two adults with one-and-a-half jobs and dependent children. After divorce, there were two households: one household with one earner and possibly a second partner earning something also; and one household, possibly in the former matrimonial home, with one half-time earner and dependent children. Women's wages were low, child care expensive and hard to find, and women therefore needed either to earn enough to cover the costs of child care and other work-related expenses such as travel, or to stay at home and live on state benefits plus whatever periodical payments were made by the former husband. These might be minimal if he had left the wife and children in the former matrimonial home (Eekelaar and Maclean, 1986). With hindsight these findings seem totally predictable. But at the time they were highly original, based on sound empirical research, and offered a counter-balance to the anecdotal claims of the pressure group of the day, CJD.

We were asked to give evidence to a special standing committee of the House of Commons during the passage of the 1984 legislation. And the Act which followed (the Matrimonial and Family Proceedings Act 1984) was more restrained in approach than early drafts had indicated, as the minimal loss principle was removed, but the courts were to give first consideration to the needs of the children. The so-called 'clean break' was not to be a positive principle. Instead, the court should merely consider whether self-sufficiency was appropriate.

Despite the isolation of the researchers in the UK, we felt supported by the comparable findings emerging from other jurisdictions. And when the government undertook a larger study to replicate our work, our findings were consistently confirmed (see Weitzman and Maclean, 1992, following a conference in

1989). The 1984 Act—which amended the Matrimonial Causes Act 1973, still in force today—gained public acceptance, and remains the basis for our regulation of financial arrangements after divorce. We suggest that the firm research base made a major contribution to the good fit between the aims of the legislation and the contemporary situation of divorcing and repartnering families. The more pragmatic the intentions of the drafters become, the more important it becomes to have a good understanding of the social context into which the legislation is inserted.

THE CHANGING POLICY FOCUS: FROM ADULTS TO CHILDREN

Although the divorce arrangements described above concerning spousal support and property division remain in place, they were rapidly overtaken in public debate by the issue of child support. In this matter, legislation in the form of the Child Support Act 1991 was made rapidly and without research support, at the insistence of the then Prime Minister, Margaret Thatcher. The results may be considered as unsuccessful in that the law was universally unpopular, both with men who were asked for larger sums of money and with women on welfare whose households, without any disregard for maintenance they received, failed to secure any benefit. Child support assessments were subject to long delays and puni-tive emergency assessment, and compliance was low. The legislation was swiftly amended and is currently being replaced by the Child Maintenance and Other Payments Act 2008, setting up a system which should benefit from a better evi-dence base following a large research programme carried out by the Department for Work and Pensions (Wikeley et al, 2008). The government now has a much clearer picture of the characteristics of the families involved in cross-household parenting, and in particular the rapidly changing job, housing, and household circumstances experienced. The problems associated with the Child Support Act 1991 are not, of course, caused by of lack of research, but rather by the intransi-gent nature of the problem of persuading non-resident parents to part with much larger sums of money than they had been used to. But had there been a better background knowledge base there would at least have been warning of some of the issues which were going arise, and at least some aspects of the 1991 legislation might have been handled differently. For example, requiring detailed informa-tion as to non-resident parents' actual housing costs might have been modified if it had been appreciated how often these were likely to alter in the period after separation, and how informal they tended to be and difficult to evidence. But, in this case, the empirical work which preceded the reform concentrated on poverty among lone parents. There was little attempt to examine the way the judicial part of the process was working, nor enough attention paid to investigating the cir-cumstances of the non-resident parents , a notoriously difficult group to reach for research purposes. And the work on understanding the underlying social norms about parental obligations came too late to inform this first attempt at solving the problem through statute (see Maclean and Eekelaar, 1997, an empirical study of the attitudes towards and support in place between parents who had divorced, separated, or never lived together), although it has been used in the policy work in preparation for the 2008 Act. This study clarified the difference between men's and women's attitudes to social and biological parenting. For the parents with care, mainly women, support for the first family was a clear priority, and any second family was expected to take second place in the call on the limited resources of the non-resident parent. But the non-resident parents, mainly men, were torn between meeting the needs of their first and second families and prioritised their current household, which might include step-children, that is children of their new partner, as well as new children, that is children of the new relationship.

The difficulties which followed the Child Support Act 1991 made it clear that, although quantitative research into the circumstances of lone parents had been rigorous and helpful, there was also a need for qualitative work to provide information about the attitudes and expectations of all the parents concerned. Serial partnering with children is an expensive exercise, and there is a continuing division of opinion as to whether the cost should be born by the individuals concerned (in which case licence to repartner might be made contingent on earning capacity) or whether the state should step in. The only broad consensus is around the need to protect the children from the poverty associated with living in a single-parent household.

MOVING FROM DIFFERENTIATION TOWARDS INCLUSIVENESS IN ALLOCATING RESOURCES ON SEPARATION

We noted earlier how the early divorce legislation differentiated between men and women, and how the Matrimonial Proceedings and Property Act 1970 (now Part II of the Matrimonial Causes Act 1973) for the first time removed this distinction in allocating resources after the marriage ended. Before the child support legislation, there had always been a differentiation between the approach to children whose parents had married and children whose parents had lived together, or never formed a common household. This distinction in providing financial support was swept away by the Child Support Act 1991, which dealt with the financial obligations of all non-resident parents to all of their children. But the distinction remains between the approach to the division of property and other assets to be made at the end of a marriage compared with those made at the end of cohabitation, and this necessarily impacts indirectly on the children of such relationships.

This differentiation between the protection offered by the law to the children of separating cohabitants and the children of divorcing parents, which flows from the lack of remedies for the benefit of parents with care outside the marital context, and the lack of public awareness of the distinction between the legal position of wives and that of cohabiting women, were key stimuli to calls for legislation to extend the protection offered to divorcing mothers and children to separating mothers and children. Brenda Hale's article in *Family Law* puts the case forcefully (Hale, 2004). When the Law Commission received the reference to examine the issue, they approached the issue with rigour and energy and began by collating the available research evidence on the characteristics of these families (age, housing status, children, work status, earning capacity and so on). The importance of this background information to any proposed change in the law is now no longer in question. But the thrust of the story of the increasingly close relationship between research and policy-making is consistent. The development of the research knowledge base available to policy-makers, despite concerns about lack of funding and lack of research capacity (see Genn et al, 2006) is at last bringing together not only the necessary large-scale survey work but also the detailed and nuanced qualitative research which will enable us to see how individuals manage family change, particularly when uncertainty or dispute arises.

To summarise, increasingly diverse and flexible family forms mean that there are no longer clear, universally held assumptions to be made about family circumstances; the increasing pragmatism of family law reform, aiming to offer management of family matters rather than abstract justice based on moral or religious principles, means that it becomes ever more important for the policy-maker to understand what individuals expect and value.

THE WAY AHEAD

We have now reached the position where active discussion and the development of proposals to regulate the financial outcomes of separation, as opposed to divorce, have added to the growing interest in looking again at the checklist of factors in section 25 of the Matrimonial Causes Act 1973, as amended in 1984, which guide the court's discretion in granting financial remedies. It might be argued that as the differences between marrying and cohabiting couples seem to be diminishing (the cohabitants are becoming older, economically better off, experiencing longer partnerships, and approaching the level of stability of the married population (see Law Commission, 2006: Part 2)) there is little point in attempting to deal with one group without the other. The other stimulus for looking again at the situation of the married group lies in the decisions made recently in some rather unusual 'big money' cases where the abundance of assets to be disposed of seems to have encouraged an abundance of ideas about how this might be done.

In the past, by far the largest group of divorces were those affecting couples with limited means, where the courts used their discretion to attend first to the need to house the children and the parent with care (nine times out of ten the mother). The Child Support Act 1991 then required the non-resident parent to make an administratively calculated regular payment to the parent with care for the children. In most cases, these two aspects of the arrangements exhausted the available resources. There is still some spousal support of limited duration to support the mother of young children or to enable the former wife to find work and adjust to the new situation. But long-term spousal support is becoming more and more rare. There may be adjustments to be made with respect to pensions, but often the amounts available do not justify the cost of the actuarial work required to make the allocation. A roof and child maintenance is the general expectation. But recent cases have highlighted the confusion around what kind of outcomes the courts are seeking. The legal arguments range around the importance of the duration of the marriage which has ended, the extent of the responsibility to provide for a former spouse's needs, how to share the combined benefits accruing from the marriage and, conversely, how far one party should be compensated by the other for any detriment incurred during the marriage. In the unusual case of *White v White*,[4] where there were no dependent children and the considerable assets were agricultural, Lord Nicholls said:

> [W]here the assets exceed the financial needs of both parties why should the surplus belong solely to the husband? … If, in their different spheres each contributed equally to the family, then in principle it matters not which of them earned the money and built up the assets … Before reaching a firm conclusion and making an order along these lines, a judge would be well advised to check his tentative views against the yardstick of equality of division. As a general guide, equality should only be departed from if, and to the extent that, there is good reason for doing so.[5]

This case and the following cases of *Miller; McFarlane*[6] are discussed elsewhere in this volume. But the issue for those seeking to respond to current concerns about the lack of certainty facing those who divorce, and the extent of judicial discretion, is how to respond to the disproportionate impact which these cases have had on the average high-street case.[7] Given that any case reaching the House of Lords is unlikely to be a typical run-of-the-mill case, but instead one with unusual circumstances and sufficient assets to be worth the argument, the decision is unlikely to help the average case. Such a decision may even cause additional problems by appearing to set out a clear principle, for example, equality of division, where there is an excess above what is required to meet needs. Fisher's (2002) small study of high-street solicitors in the year following *White v White*[8] did indeed find that clients of modest means were expecting all assets to be sold and shared. In low- to average-income households this would mean that the family home must be sold and that, while the male earner would be able to start again in the mortgage market, a woman with child-care responsibilities and no qualifications would find it all but impossible to get started as an owner-occupier. With the decline in public housing provision and the lack of low-cost privately rented accommodation, this is a serious issue. Under the existing rules,

---

[4] [2001] AC 596.
[5] ibid at 605–8.
[6] [2006] UKHL 24.
[7] Although compare Hitchings, ch 9, this volume.
[8] [2001] AC 596.

the court has a duty to give first consideration to the needs of the children, which in practice requires attention to be paid to keeping a roof over the heads of the children and the parent with care and ensuring that there are sufficient funds to maintain the position.

The judiciary struggle for clarity and consistency in these wealthy cases. The high-street solicitor tries to create a survival package for his client, stretching one-and-a-half incomes to support two households. Is it possible to set out meaningful rules to help people struggling to reorder their lives in such a wide variety of circumstances? Or has the judicial discretion which we have accepted for so long given us the flexibility to keep a roof over the children's heads and enable the mother to gather herself together and adjust to life after marriage, without killing the goose who lays the golden egg, that is the major earner? Members of the Bar have recently called for more certainty, arguing that they cannot advise their clients in negotiation when the parameters are so broad. But whenever a scheme is suggested as a basis for decision-making, there is little sign of agreement. At a seminar held in Oxford in March 2007, John Eekelaar put forward a scheme based on duration of marriage to a group similar to the contributors to this volume and including members of the senior judiciary and legal practitioners. While many supported the idea of a framework, none would accept any of the proposals put forward.

What is the policy-maker to do, given professional concerns but relatively little information other than anecdote as to what kinds of values and expectations men and women have about the financial arrangements to be made on divorce, or about what happens in practice? Nor should we ignore the continuing debate about the values and expectations at the end of cohabitation, and the relatively limited information about what happens to both opposite-sex couples and same-sex couples, who may or may not have entered into a civil partnership.

We suggest that the first step would usefully be a substantial quantitative research project to examine the socio-economic characteristics of the adult separating population, both those who had married or entered into a civil partnership and those who had been cohabiting (and those referred to by demographers as 'Living Apart Together': Haskey, 2005). We need to understand the history of such relationships, the patterns of money and asset management and ownership, what the the parties' financial expectations would have been if the relationship had not broken down, and the obligations of the parties to others including children and other dependants of this and previous relationships. We need to understand what they thought should be the financial outcome of their separation, what this expectation was based on, and how close it is to what the current family justice system would accept. Finally, we would need to discover what arrangements were made, how they were made, what professional intervention there was, and whether the arrangements have been upheld and whether they are thought to be satisfactory. Such a survey would have to begin from a general population sample, and could not be completed in less than two years, but it would provide the baseline data for future policy-making and evaluation. In the absence of shared values and expectations it is not possible to develop new law that will be widely acceptable or enforceable. In the absence of the information set out above we do not even know how the current system is working and whether it is already working as well as can be hoped, given that the divorcing/separating population is unhappy and unlikely to be enthusiastic about any legal framework. The child support legislation is an example of an attempt to legislate for the benefit of children, an uncontentious goal. The support obligation is almost universally accepted. But very few non-resident parents find their own assessment satisfactory. For the policy-maker, family disputes are dangerous territory.

But while we wait for this research to be funded and completed, we suggest that it may also be helpful to look in depth at the way in which separating couples approach the making of financial arrangements. Some manage to make their own arrangements informally, others seek the advice of family solicitors to reach agreement, and a minority fail to resolve matters without the help of the courts and the family Bar. These conflicted cases may tell us a great deal about the kinds of expectations men and women bring to this situation, what kinds of issues lead to dispute, and how the justice system tries to contain and manage these conflicts and help the parties to reach a practicable arrangement which takes into account their needs, their resources, and above all their children.

RESOLVING FINANCIAL DISPUTES WITH THE HELP OF THE FAMILY BAR

At the Oxford Centre, we have carried out research (Eekelaar, Maclean and Beinart, 2000) into the divorce work of family courts and lawyers that reveals something of how individuals in dispute approach the issues and how they are guided towards settlement by legal advisers, only rarely requiring adjudication by the court. We studied family solicitors, and observed the careful supportive process by which these lawyers lead their clients towards settlement. The lawyer negotiates with his client to reach a position which falls within the parameters which he knows from experience to be acceptable to a court. If the other party's solicitor follows a similar process, then both parties should be within reach of agreement by the time their representatives begin to negotiate with each other. Difficulties arise when a client will not accept the lawyer's advice and presses for a position which is beyond the scope of what a judge could accept.

Our current qualitative research (Maclean and Eekelaar, 2009) looks at the work of the family Bar and includes observational data on financial disputes at the end of a marriage. These detailed accounts are based on our observation of the day-to-day work of counsel in ancillary relief cases, and provide a starting point for considering potential reform of section 25 of the 1973 Act. Would rules help?

We observed big-money cases, middle-income cases, and cases where there were no resources to argue about but rather the apportionment of debt and access to welfare benefits. In the big-money category, one case we observed turned on the belief of the wife that her husband had additional substantial assets which he had not disclosed. A great deal of time and money was spent in trying to pursue this issue, until she eventually accepted that more efforts could be made but that they would be unlikely to add to the existing information, and her legal advisers finally convinced her that it was probable that all substantial assets had now been discovered. How the assets were to be divided was not the cause of the conflict, but what the assets comprised. The skills required from the barrister were meticulous attention to the detail in the multiplicity of financial papers, perhaps more akin to the forensic work of an accountant rather than a lawyer. In a second big-money case, the issue again was not the proportion of the assets to go to each party, which was not at issue. The dispute centred rather on the way the assets were to be valued, as they included hedge funds which could not be given a precise valuation at the time of the divorce hearing. One side wanted to agree the date at which a valuation should be made for the assets to be divided in a certain ratio. The other side wanted a fixed amount regardless of the precise date of valuation.

Of the cases where the assets were modest and the debts considerable, the matters in dispute again included questions about disclosure of information. One wife could simply not believe that all the money raised by a second mortgage had been spent, but according to the evidence provided it clearly had. In addition, there were questions about how to make best use of the assets available to the parties. The dispute centred around whether the husband would be able to keep his job and hold on to the former matrimonial home, which would then increase in value to the benefit of both parties in the longer term, or whether it should be sold and the proceeds shared now even though this would be of little benefit to either side as the wife was in receipt of benefits and her entitlement would be threatened. In a second low-money case, the problem was lack of financial knowledge and experience. Both parties had modest incomes (he earned £20,000 per annum and she earned £3,000 per annum) but each had run up debts totalling £50,000 on a number of different credit cards. He had moved in with a new partner. She hoped to hold on to the former matrimonial home, while he wished to sell and settle his debts. The judge asked how she might finance her plan, and she said that friends would help but she had no definite figures or firm commitments. The court required the sale and equal sharing of the equity in the house. It is hard to see how any more precise rules about property division could have helped in any of these cases, all of which were based in the facts of the matter and not in the application of legal doctrine.

In the big-money cases, resources were more than adequate to meet needs, and this is where questions about the role of compensation or equality may emerge, although we did not see this. In the 'no-money' cases, resources cannot even meet needs, never mind do any more than this, and so we saw questions about disclosure and how to best manage debt and welfare benefit entitlements.

Perhaps the middle-money cases, where both parties are trying to continue to support their present standard of living but with divided resources, is where the division of assets might benefit from further regulation or guidance on principle? But even here the major task is to meet the needs of both parties for housing and the income necessary to maintain it. Here, the arguments are about house prices in various areas, about the distance from the children's schools, and, increasingly often, about the need for two homes large enough for the children to spend time comfortably in as part of shared parenting arrangements. When contact visits did not involve staying more than the odd night in school holidays, makeshift arrangements were more acceptable. But in a middle-class, middle-income family with shared care, there is now a need to fund a bedroom in each home for each child, an additional burden on the financial arrangements.

These brief accounts may serve to illustrate the problems that would arise on trying to devise principles for property division on divorce or separation. It would be possible to abandon the aim of meeting need and move towards a formulaic division of the assets. But, as can be seen from these examples, the conflicts which reach the courts arise from lack of trust in the other party, and involve refusal to accept the other side's account of the financial position without full forensic enquiry, supported by the authority of the court, to obtain disclosure of bank and credit card details and the questioning of statements from accountants and employers about actual and potential earnings and expenses. The task of the legal advisers we observed was not to argue points of law but to obtain the trust of their client and then to painstakingly comb through the figures and reach an agreed statement of the assets on the table, that is, the size of the 'pot'. The division of the pot was usually a less contentious matter.

Any attempt to establish clearer guidance about the factors to be taken into account in assessing need would have to consider for example whether this should include provision for shared parenting. Any attempt to regulate how to share resources available after needs have been met would have to consider whether the ratio should be 50:50, or a sliding scale depending on contributions or length of relationship or numbers of children or a shared understanding of the wife's contribution to family finances. Any codification of how to look at the situation where needs have been met and compensation made for any financial loss result-ing from the relationship becomes the issue, must consider, for example, whether the loss was due to any other cause such as illness, although this might be included if caused by the spouse (for instance as a result of passive smoking), but excluded if genetic and unknown at marriage. Taking into account the length of the rela-tionship would not help with establishing the facts or increasing trust between the parties. As Ira Ellman has said, 'in view of the inherently uncertain nature of the outcomes of legal interventions in family law, it matters less what rules are chosen than that whatever is done is clear and applied with consistency, for that at least will be fair' (Ellman, 2003).

To conclude, pointing out that any attempt to legislate for the regulation of the financial arrangements to be made at the end of a relationship is difficult is hardly necessary. What we have tried to show in this chapter is how the task has changed over the last 25 years, and how these changes have made a firm knowledge base for the policy-maker increasingly necessary. In a homogeneous, stable society with agreed norms and values, law can be made according to agreed principle. For many years judges followed the practice of the ecclesiastical courts in awarding the petitioning wife roughly one-third of her husband's income (Barton, 1957). Now that family forms are complex, changing, flexible, and not encompassed within a single value system, law-making has become more pragmatic and concerned to manage disputes so that people can get on with their lives rather than the more abstract pursuit of truth and justice. If we are to be pragmatic and flexible, we need to know who we are dealing with, what they want, and how to best meet their often conflicting needs.

BIBLIOGRAPHY

Barrington Baker, B, Eekalaar, J, Clarke, K and Raikes, S (1977) *The Matrimonial Jurisdiction of Registrars* (Oxford, Centre for Socio-Legal Studies).

Barton, JL (1957) 'The Enforcement of Financial Provisions' in RH Graveson and FR Crane (eds), *A Century of Family Law* (London, Sweet & Maxwell).

Department of Education and Skills (2003) *Every Child Matters*, Cm 5860 (London, HMSO).

Eekelaar J (2000) 'The End of an Era?' in S Katz, J Eekelaar and M Maclean (eds), *Cross Currents: Family Law and Policy in the US and England* (Oxford, OUP).

Eekelaar, J and Maclean, M (1986) *Maintenance after Divorce* (Oxford, OUP).

Eekelaar, J, Maclean, M and Beinart, S (2000) *Family Lawyers, The Divorce Work of Solicitors* (Oxford, Hart Publishing).

Ellman, I (2003) 'Why making family law is hard' 35 *Arizona State Law Journal* 699.

Fisher, L (2002) 'The unexpected impact of *White*—taking equality too far?' 32 *Family Law* 208.

Funder, K (1992) 'A Proposal for Reform' in L Weitzman and M Maclean (eds), *Economic Consequences of Divorce* (Oxford, OUP).

Genn, H, Partington, M and Wheeler, S (2006) *Nuffield Foundation Report: Law in the Real World: Improving our Understanding of How Law Works* (London, Nuffield Foundation).

Hale, B (2004) 'Unmarried couples in family law' 34 *Family Law* 419.

Haskey, J (2005) 'Living Arrangements in Contemporary Britain: Having a partner who lives elsewhere and Living Apart Together' 122 *Population Trends* 35.

Law Commission (1980) *The Financial Consequences of Divorce*, Cmnd 8041 (London, TSO).

—— (2006) *Cohabitation: The Financial Consequences of Relationship Breakdown*, Law Com CP 179 (London, TSO).

—— (2007) *Cohabitation: The Financial Consequences of Relationship Breakdown*, Law Com No 307 (London, TSO).

Maclean M and Eekelaar J (1997) *The Parental Obligation* (Oxford, Hart Publishing).

—— (2009) *Family Law Advocacy: How Barristers help the Victims of Family Failure* (Oxford, Hart Publishing).

Weitzman, L (1985) *The Divorce Revolution* (New York, Free Press/Macmillan).

Weitzman, L and Maclean, M (eds) (1992) *Economic Consequences of Divorce* (Oxford, OUP).

Wikeley, N, Ireland, E, Bryson, C and Smith, R (2008) *Relationship Separation and Child Support Study*, DWP Research Report 503 (London, Department for Work and Pensions).

Part II

Work, Money and Property within Intimate Relationships: Expectations and Actions

3

Paid and Unpaid Work

Can Policy Improve Gender Inequalities?

JACQUELINE SCOTT AND SHIRLEY DEX

INTRODUCTION

WOMEN'S POSITION IN the labour market has improved enormously in recent decades, both in terms of employment and in relative earnings. It was predicted that increasing gender equality within the labour market would lead to greater egalitarianism in unpaid work within the household. However, this has proved to be only partially true. Although employment reduces women's unpaid work, changes in men's contribution to domestic labour have been slight and uneven.

The last decade or so has seen a Europe-wide explosion of interest in the way social policies, labour markets, and motherhood are inter-related (Del Boca and Wetzels, 2007). In Europe, population decline is an issue and forecasts suggest that below-population replacement levels of total fertility will continue, with an average European total fertility rate of about 1.5 through to 2020 (Kohler, Billari and Ortega, 2006). With people living longer, there is concern that the proportion of people who are of working age compared with those who are too young or too old to work (the dependency ratio) will steadily decline. Thus there is an interest in improving the dependency ratio by alleviating family–work conflicts, so that women employees will continue to have children (the labour market of the future), and so that mothers will continue to participate in the labour force.

In this chapter we review some of the ways policies under different welfare regimes seek to influence work–family balance. Policy rhetoric in the UK tends to emphasise the importance of individual choice in making decisions about work–family balance, but this masks the degree to which people's choices are differentially constrained by gender. In particular, unless the unequal division between men and women of unpaid work can be addressed, policies that seek to reconcile paid work and family life are likely to be extremely limited in their capacity to improve gender inequalities both in the labour force and in the realm of unpaid domestic work and care.

In order to understand what policies might facilitate or mitigate against change in men's and women's division of labour, we review the changes that have occurred in division of labour within couples in Britain over the past decade and explore why gender inequalities in unpaid work are so slow to change. While much attention has been paid to child-care provision and parental leave policies, far less attention has been given to whether policies can be devised that will equalise men's and women's contributions to unpaid work (Dex, forthcoming). Our review leads to the rather pessimistic conclusion that, on the basis of the existing evidence, it is unlikely that state policies will have more than a minimal influence in reducing gender inequalities in a couple's share of unpaid domestic work. However, before examining in more detail the division of labour within couples, and associated policy initiatives, we first consider how far gender equality has been achieved in the UK labour market.

GENDER EQUALITY AND THE UK LABOUR MARKET

There are two very different stories that can be told about labour market changes over the past half-century or so, in terms of gender equality. One story emphasises the positive, while the other offers a somewhat less rosy picture. The positive perspective has plenty of evidence on which to draw: the proportion of women in the labour market has grown markedly; the pay gap has narrowed; notions that a woman's place is in the home have eroded markedly; and women have overtaken men in numbers pursuing higher education.

Half a century ago, the situation was very different. The 1949 Royal Commission on Population report was concerned that the then existing employment bars against married women working were harmful all round—to women, the family, and the community. True, the Commission was hardly giving a ringing endorsement to employed mothers. For example it observes that 'there is often a real conflict between motherhood and a whole-time career' (Royal Commission on Population, 1949: 160). Nevertheless it went on to acknowledge that, at least in part, the conflict is due to artificial barriers that restrict the contribution that women can make to the cultural and economic life of the nation. The report urged that a 'deliberate effort should be made to devise adjustments that would render it easier for women to combine motherhood and the care of a home with outside activities' (at 160).

In 1951, less than a quarter of married women in Britain were in the workforce; by 1991 this was the case for half of all married women, and the proportion continued to rise. By 2001, 65 per cent of married women were in the labour force and there is no longer any difference between the participation rates of married and single women (Gallie, 2000; Scott, 2008). In 1951, 30 per cent of women aged 20–59 were in full-time employment (Joshi, 1989). Forty years later in 1991 this figure had risen only slightly to 34 per cent. In the same period, the extent of women being employed part-time has quadrupled from 11 per cent of all female employees in 1951 to 45 per cent in 1991 (Gallie, 2000). In 2002, 70 per cent of working-age women were economically active, with 42 per cent of those in employment working part time (WEU, 2004).

On the positive side, the UK has already surpassed the Lisbon target for a female labour force participation rate of 60 per cent by 2010. But there is little to be complacent about. Women and mothers in particular are often caught in part-time jobs that frequently bring disadvantages in pay and promotion trajectories. Mothers, according to national surveys, overwhelmingly prefer to work part time. However, whether their preferences reflect the fact that shorter hours help women to juggle family and work roles, or whether part-time work is the only realistic option because of lack of child-care alternatives and a traditional gender-role division of labour in the home, is less clear. What is clear from analysis of British Cohort Survey data is that although overall there has been a decrease in the downward mobility of women following childbirth, if women have longer breaks out of the workforce or return after childbirth to a part-time job, the occupational penalties in terms of downward mobility have *increased* over time.

Even professional women experience increasing occupational costs for taking longer periods away from work following the birth of their first child. As Figure 3.1 shows, a teacher born between 1922 and 1936 and between 1943 and 1953 (data from WES—the Women and Employment Survey) had a one in five chance of moving down the occupational scale after taking one year off work; for a woman taking five years off work, this increased to just over a one in four chance. For a teacher born in 1958 (data from the NCDS—National Child Development Survey), there was a one in four chance of moving down the occupational scale following a one-year break, which increased to a one in three chance if the gap was five years.

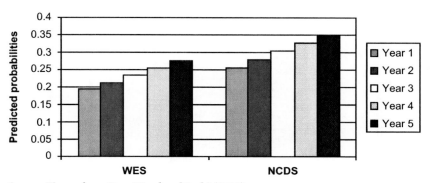

Source: Figure from Dex, Ward and Joshi (2008).

Figure 3.1: Predicted Probabilities of Downward Occupational Mobility after Childbirth (WES and NCDS teachers by years before first return to work)

There has been an overall trend of ever-faster rates of mothers' return to work after childbirth, as Figure 3.2 shows. For example, 50 per cent of mothers born in 1946 had returned to work by the time their first child was six years old. For mothers born in 1958, 50 per cent had returned within two years after the birth, and of those born in 1970 half had returned after just one year. However, these figures vary greatly for recent cohorts depending on the level of educational qualifications the mothers held, and it is those with higher education who were born in 1958 and 1970 who have returned to work fastest (less than a year after the birth of their first child), whereas those with lower levels of education or no qualifications return at a much slower rate.

The analysis of women's changing patterns of employment over time makes it clear that there has been some improvement in women's employment prospects. Moreover, these improvements go hand in hand with improvements in women's tertiary educational qualifications and the lessening of the pay gap. The percentage of women who had tertiary qualifications increased from 11 per cent of those born in 1946, to 25 per cent of those born in 1958, and 32 per cent of those born in 1970; whereas the equivalent percentages for men were 22 per cent, 28 per cent,

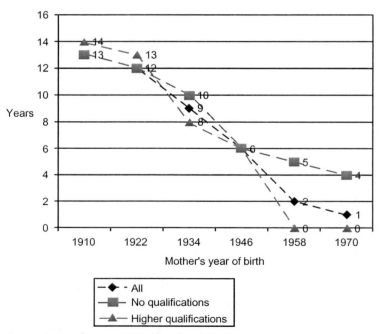

Source: **Figure from Dex, Ward and Joshi (2008).**

Figure 3.2: Median Number of Years between First Birth and Return to Next Job by Mothers' Date of Birth and Qualifications

and 31 per cent. If we look at the ratio of women's to men's hourly wage at age 26 for those working full time, then for those born in 1946 it was 0.63, for those born in 1958 it had increased to 0.84, and for those born in 1970 it was 0.91 (Joshi and Paci, 1998). This is a genuine lessening of the gender pay gap.

But there is also a story that is far less rosy. If we look at the average annual gross earnings of graduates, where one might expect to find younger generations of women with the opportunities and inclinations to achieve financial rewards comparable to their male peers, we find this is not the case. Using data from a longitudinal study of over 3,000 graduates who gained their first degrees in 1995, Purcell and Elias (2008) found that young women, even at this early stage in their careers, do not appear to have achieved equal earnings with their male peers and, moreover, that the gender pay gap continues to increase as their careers develop. As we can see in Figure 3.3, women graduates reported full-time gross earnings in their first job after graduation that were on average, 11 per cent less than those of male graduates. Three and half years later the gap had risen to 15 per cent, and by 2002/03 to 19 per cent.

So how can this 19 per cent pay gap be accounted for? The top bar on the chart shown in Figure 3.4 gives the unadjusted difference in the annual earnings of male and female graduates in full-time employment seven years after graduation. Each bar beneath this shows the effect on the gender difference in pay of introducing statistical controls for the different relevant factors. Thus controlling for weekly hours alone reduces the differential to about 16 per cent. Next, controls are added for sectors of employment. Women are much more likely than men to work in the public sector, which pays less than the private sector but may have more 'family-friendly' working conditions. The sector controls reduce the wage

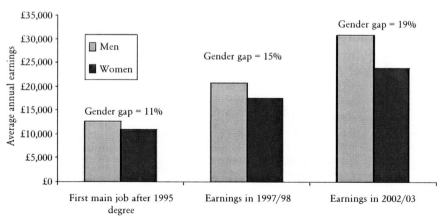

Source: **Figure from Purcell and Elias (2008).**

Figure 3.3: Average Annual Gross Earnings of 1995 Graduates by Gender

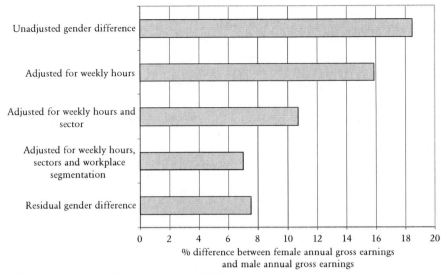

Source: **Figure from Purcell and Elias (2008).**

Figure 3.4: The Combined Effects of Various Factors on the Gender Difference in Annual Earnings of 1995 Graduates Seven Years after Graduation

gap to nearly 11 per cent. Finally the additional impact of gender segregation at the workplace brings the gender gap down to only 7 per cent.

There may be some unmeasured workplace discrimination that helps explain a small fraction of the remaining gender inequality in pay. But, beyond the operation of any outstanding workplace inequalities in pay and promotion prospects, a more important explanation lies in the day-to-day practices of unequal division of paid work and caring activities in the household (Gershuny, 2004). The persistence of the pay gap between men and women is likely to be attributable in part to a gender division of labour among couples in paid and unpaid work.

HOW FAR HAS THE DIVISION OF LABOUR WITHIN COUPLES IN BRITAIN CHANGED?

The main question addressed in this section is to what extent the divide of paid and unpaid work in couple households in Britain has changed over the last decade. The data used are from the British Household Panel Survey, which is a longitudinal survey of over 5,000 households in Britain. Here we report analysis by Harkness (2008) which concentrates on couples where the women are in their prime working age between 25 and 49. Couples need not be legally married but they must be cohabiting. Thus '*lat*' couples (those living apart together) are excluded, not only because they are problematic to identify but also because, given the sampling rules of the survey, data for both partners would be available only if they had children. The analysis looks at aggregate patterns of change over time—and does not follow individuals longitudinally.

In Figure 3.5 we can see the employment rate for women in couples by whether or not they have children. While employment rates for childless women have always been high, there has been a marked rise in the employment of mothers from 1992 onwards, with the greatest rise among mothers of young children. There is no evidence of any decline in the employment of the male partners in these couple households. The division of paid work in households is very dependent on the presence of young children.

While there has been a rise of 6 per cent overall in the proportion of female workers, as Table 3.1 shows, this increase rises to 10 per cent for households with small children (under the age of five). These figures combine dual-earner households (both parties working full time) and the one-and-a-half earner model (where the female partner works part time). This increase in labour may in part reflect the impact of a series of government initiatives supporting maternal employment, including increased support for child care and improved maternity leave.

In terms of hours spent on paid work and housework (including cooking, cleaning and doing the laundry, but excluding child care) we can see in Table 3.2 that the paid work hours of women rose on average by two hours per week from 1993/94 to 2003/04; whereas, for women with pre-school children, the increase over the same period was three hours per week to 18 hours in 2003/04. As paid

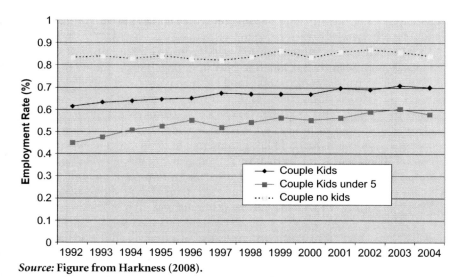

Source: **Figure from Harkness (2008).**

Figure 3.5: Employment Rates for Women in Couples (aged 25–49) (British Household Panel Survey)

Table 3.1: Household Work Patterns: Women aged 20–49 in Couples

	Dual career (both full time)	Modified (male full time and female part time)	Male bread-winner	Female bread-winner	No earner	Sample size
All						
1993/94	0.38	0.27	0.21	0.05	0.07	3,182
2003/04	0.42	0.29	0.2	0.04	0.04	2,760
Change	0.04	0.02	−0.01	0.01	−0.03	
With children under 5						
1993/4	0.17	0.29	0.41	0.03	0.1	871
2003/4	0.2	0.36	0.38	0.02	0.03	772
Change	0.03	0.07	−0.03	−0.01	−0.07	

Source: Table from Harkness (2008).

Table 3.2: Hours of Paid and Unpaid Work within Households

	Paid Work Hours			Unpaid Work Hours		
	female	male	total	female	male	total
All couple households						
1993/94	23.4	41.4	64.8	20.8	5.7	26.5
2003/04	25.2	41.7	66.9	16.2	5.5	21.7
Change	1.8	0.3	2.1	−4.6	−0.2	−4.8
Children under 5						
1993/94	14.9	41.8	56.7	24.7	5.9	30.6
2003/04	17.8	42.9	60.7	18.7	5.2	23.9
Change	2.9	1.1	4	−6	−0.7	−6.7

Source: Table from Harkness (2008).

employment rose there was a corresponding decrease in housework—a six-hour drop for women with pre-school children. By contrast, men's paid and unpaid work hours changed very little over this period.

Of course, households with different employment patterns do differ in the amount of time men and women spend on both paid and unpaid work; while full-time working mothers are employed for shorter hours than their partners (39 hours compared with 46 hours in 2003/04) they continue to do the bulk of the housework (14 hours compared with 7 hours for their male partner).

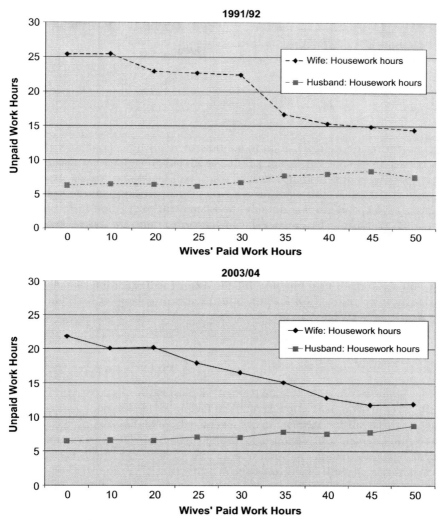

Source: Figures from Harkness (2008).

Figure 3.6: Husbands and Wives: Unpaid Work Hours by Wives' Paid Work Hours (British Household Panel Study)

Figure 3.6 shows the way the women's and men's unpaid housework hours are associated with the woman's employment hours. The figures for 1991/92 and 2003/04 show that the pattern has not changed over time: women's unpaid work diminishes rapidly, while men's participation in unpaid work increases only very slightly.

Other analysis, using the longitudinal panel data that follow changes in individual patterns of paid and unpaid work over time (Gershuny, Bittman and Brice, 2005), points to a pattern of 'lagged adaptation'. Thus although women decrease their unpaid work immediately and dramatically on returning to full-time work, their male partner's corresponding increase in unpaid work is both delayed and somewhat unreliable. Gershuny et al find a similar pattern for men in the UK, the US and West Germany. Their findings raise the interesting question as to who is doing the work—whether unpaid chores are being left undone, or whether there has been an increase in the use of paid domestic services. There has been a clear growth in the demand for and supply of domestic services in recent years, but such services are often arranged and paid for by women and do little to ameliorate the gender imbalance in unpaid work. These findings also suggest that different national policies towards work–family balance have little effect on the gender division of labour in paid and unpaid work.

POLICY INITIATIVES CONCERNING WORK–FAMILY BALANCE

It is usually considered desirable to have greater equality between men and women in the labour market—and a lot of policy initiatives and anti-discrimination legislation have been orientated towards that goal. A related issue that is less visible in policy debate is whether steps should be taken to try to equalise women's and men's unpaid work loads in the home. In this section we consider the types of policy interventions used by governments which might, in principle, change unpaid work behaviour within households.

As Lewis (2008) and others have pointed out, the policy regimes of many industrialised countries were designed and devised around the model of a male breadwinner family where the man worked full time and the women cared for the family and was not expected to be employed. This male breadwinner behaviour, in its pure sense, is hardly visible in industrialised countries of the twenty-first century because of the huge increases in women's employment that have taken place. Although, as we showed earlier, many women do take time out of the labour force to have and to care for children, these periods have been getting successively shorter over recent generations (Macran, Joshi and Dex, 1996). For policy purposes the male breadwinner model still exists, albeit in a modified form. A common modification is for the male partner to be in paid work and working full-time hours, and the female partner to be in paid work but working part-time hours.

A range of models that address work–family balance, together with the associated policies and example countries, is set out in Table 3.3. Policies have grown up in very different ways in different countries, and the logic underlying the policies can vary considerably from country to country. Moreover, some countries have adapted more quickly to the new models of family behaviour that have emerged, whereas other countries are slow to change (Lewis, 2006).

Table 3.3: Range of Models of Work–Family Balance

Model/author	Description	Associated policies	Example countries
Adult worker model family (Lewis, 2001). Comes in two forms:	Men and women are responsible for participating in the labour market.	Stimulate provision of formal child-care services, possibly subsidised.	Model encouraged in EU.
a) supported	Focus on getting lone parents and low earners into work.	In work-benefits, tax credits acting as subsidy to low paying employers. Tax relief or subsidy for child care if women in paid work.	UK since 1999, more so since 2003.
b) unsupported	Gender neutral, equality defined as sameness.	Earned income tax credits to make sure it is economic to work. No support for workers, except what is provided in the market. Market may provide cheap affordable domestic services and child care (eg, via high levels of immigration to offer low-wage work if the state colludes). Little support in leave or pay for childbearing, or income replacement while childbearing and child-rearing.	USA
Gender participation model, sometimes called the Nordic model, or 'gender-differentiated supported adult worker model' (Hobson, 2004; Lewis, 2008)	Gender equality promoted, but makes allowances for difference.	Generous cash support for parental leave, services for child care and elderly dependents, but also for women to have extensive periods of leave (three years if two children born in quick succession) and rights to work part time until child is eight.	Sweden To a lesser extent in other Scandinavian countries. To a lesser extent in Germany.
Gender equality based on a women's model of equality (Knijn, 2004)	All workers encouraged to reduce their weekly paid working hours to be part time.		The Netherlands

In principle there are two extremes that policy regimes can adopt: they can either support adults as paid workers, undifferentiated by gender, or they can acknowledge that men and women are likely to offer different levels of contributions to the labour market. No policy regime takes the extreme adult worker position, but the US comes pretty close to this, having only offered women rights to unpaid maternity leave since 1996. Scandinavian countries are often heralded as being more focused on providing equal opportunities to women and men, but their policies also allow women's employment contribution to be different from men's in having longer parental leave, and long periods of part-time work following childbirth. When policies allow or encourage women to behave differently in terms of their employment participation or their hours of work, gender differences in the home and in domestic contributions are tacitly endorsed.

In order to link specific country policies with different time use patterns, Table 3.4 shows the mean time in minutes per day that men and women spend on different types of work and unpaid work, in the UK, the US, Sweden, the Netherlands and West Germany. These data are taken from time diaries of a longitudinal cross-national sample (Gershuny, 2000). 'Paid work' is contrasted with 'core domestic work' (referring to housework and cooking) and 'other unpaid work' (child care, shopping and odd jobs).

Table 3.4 makes it clear that women in all these countries do a greater share of unpaid work than men. However, two other facts about the gender division of work are also worth noting. First, adding up women's and men's paid and unpaid work leads to near equality in the amounts of total work done by men and women (as in the Harkness figures cited earlier), or men doing slightly more total work

Table 3.4: Mean Time Spent per Day on Different Types of Work, in Minutes

	The Netherlands	UK	US	Sweden	West Germany
Core domestic work					
Men	29	28	33	56	11
Women	188	177	182	143	238
Other unpaid work					
Men	84	83	97	117	84
Women	124	111	142	146	132
Paid work					
Men	325	367	406	379	418
Women	94	178	187	262	168
Total work					
Men	438	478	536	552	513
Women	406	466	511	551	538

Source: Gershuny (2000: ch 7).

than women (the only exception being West Germany). Such figures suggest that claims of the 'double burden' (Hochschild, 1989) carried by women who are employed and still do the larger share of unpaid work may be exaggerated. Secondly, the average amounts of domestic work and paid work vary by country as by well as by gender, with relatively high total work hours in the US, Sweden and West Germany, and the lowest total work hours in the Netherlands.

We suggested above that policies that make allowance for gender differences in employment practice are likely to reinforce gender differences in domestic work.

In Sweden it is clear that women are spending more time on core domestic work than men, despite an explicit policy commitment to gender equality (Table 3.4). Nevertheless there is some evidence that policies supporting equality have some effect. The figures reported in Table 3.4 show Swedish men spending more time than their male counterparts elsewhere on core domestic work (56 minutes) and Swedish women spending the least time (143 minutes). However, even in Sweden, equality of unpaid domestic work seems an elusive goal.

Policies restricting working time affect the potential time available to share in unpaid work. The EU has taken the initiative to direct members to limit weekly hours of paid work to a maximum of 48 hours per week. However, the UK allows opt-outs from this 1993 Directive[1]: it is not mandatory in the UK for all of its workers to comply with the 48-hour rule, and, not surprisingly, the UK now has the highest mean weekly paid working hours among men in Europe. Some countries have allowed parents the right to reduce their hours of work (for example Sweden and the Netherlands). But it is very largely women that use this ability to work part time. In 2003, the UK offered the right to request flexible working arrangements of their choice to parents of a child under the age of six. Employers were required to consider their request. This marked a new idea in UK industrial relations, moving away from voluntarism, but not as far as making this a statutory requirement. While such requests may be made by either parent, surveys show it is mainly women who make requests for and are offered flexible working arrangements (Palmer, 2004; Holt and Grainger, 2005).

Is it possible for policies to influence gender shares of unpaid work? There is no compelling evidence that policies addressing work–family balance have had a significant or sizeable effect on the male and female share of unpaid work within households where they have been used. Policies however, can affect whether and

---

[1] The European Union Working Time Directive was introduced in 1993 by the EU member states, with the aim of improving employment conditions. It was a legislative breakthrough, which changed employment law and set a maximum 48-hour working week. The 1993 Working Time Directive included Article 18, which allowed member states to opt out of the directive, and not apply the 48-hour working week if a number of conditions were met. These included: workers must sign individual opt-out agreements, and must not suffer any penalty if they refuse to do so; employers must keep records of staff who work more than 48 hours a week, and make them available to the appropriate authorities. The opt-out from the Working Time Directive was not specific to the UK, but the UK was the only country within Europe to make widespread use of its provisions. In 2009 the EU Parliament voted to end the opt-out, but the UK government says it will appeal.

when women and men are in paid work during periods of childbirth and family formation. For example, 'Daddy leave' in Sweden (which is lost to the household if not taken by the male partner) has increased slowly from its initiation in 1995 rising to a 17 per cent take-up by 2003. Of course, even small increases in father involvement in child care might be highly beneficial in terms of child outcomes. Research in Britain (Dex and Ward, 2007) has suggested that fathers who took some parental leave around the birth of a child were more likely to read to a child aged three on a daily basis than fathers who did not take such leave (53 per cent as compared to 43 per cent). Also they found a correlation between fathers taking parental leave and three-year-old children having fewer behavioural and emotional problems.

Studies have found women's returns to work after childbirth have been sensitive to the conditions of their maternity or parental leave period (Ruhm, 1998; Brewer and Paull, 2006). In some cases, and with the most recent policies, it is perhaps too early to say that they have not achieved the goal of changing shares of unpaid work. But in the case of the policies based on gender difference, one could argue that they give to women with one hand, but take away with the other, as they reinforce the traditional gender role divide.

This begs the question of whether the traditional gender role divide is what most women want. The case for preferences driving decisions about paid work has been argued by Hakim (2000), mainly in the context of the UK, although 'preference theory' is not without critics (Crompton, 2006). Hakim argues that it is possible to divide the female population into three groups according to their preferences: there are the career women who are focused on paid work; there are the homemakers who are focused on unpaid work and care; and, between these two, there is the adaptive group who will do paid work, but will give it up when it gets in the way of family commitments, since these have priority. The adaptive group is argued to be the majority of women among whom part-time work is very popular.

It is certainly the case that part-time work is popular among some women, despite it being low paid and low skilled in some countries. There is also evidence in many countries that many women who are in full-time paid work would prefer to work fewer hours per week although this is also true of many men (OECD, 2001). The desire for flexibility in working hours and the extension of maternity leave rights has also been evident in Britain, especially among women (DTI, 2000). In expressing support for such options, women could be seen as embracing the difference approach to being paid workers, with lower hours, less attachment, less work experience, and, consequently, less pay and fewer career promotion prospects than men. Such policies facilitate an accommodation of gender inequality and a continuation of the unequal domestic division of unpaid work since they do not require the household boat to be rocked. Contemporary theorists emphasise that both men and women are 'doing gender', and both partners are living out traditional expectations of who does what. O'Brien's review on 'shared caring' (2005) suggests that fathers do see the 'good father' role as including the role of primary breadwinner, but are happy for partners to contribute to the household income.

Counter to this claim that a redistribution of unpaid work is not what women want, others would point out that the so-called 'choices' that parents make are still being made on a playing field that is not level or equal between genders. There are a range of other policies that support the (higher-paid) male partner working longer paid hours than the female, and there is still the unequal wage rate issue. Nonetheless, we cannot discount people's expressed preferences. Fathers are largely content with the hours they work, even when their work hours are as much as 60 hours per week (O'Brien, 2005). Mothers like part-time paid work; they like flexibility in their working hours; they are generally happy with the care policies that acknowledge that women are different and treat them differently. It seems unlikely that equality in either paid or unpaid work will come from such preferences.

DOES GENDER IMBALANCE IN PAID AND UNPAID WORK MATTER?

If women do less paid work outside the home than men, then it seems only equitable that they should do more unpaid work in the home than men. In principle, the female partner could do more paid work than the man, but the relative wage rates are against this choice and in favour of women's specialisation in home work (Becker, 1991). Men will be able to earn more per hour, on average, than women. So it is more efficient for the man to work, and thus, he accumulates more human capital which will bring him higher wages in future. But this reinforces the unequal wage rates for men and women and locks women into unpaid home work. Does this matter? If the couple have committed themselves to living together as a unit, then they both stand to gain financially by this gender specialisation. In the past, couples were happy to do this, but times are changing. It is now seen as riskier for the woman to compromise her earning potential. She needs to maintain human capital (in terms of work experience and training) to cope with future uncertainties, such as unemployment or divorce (see Fisher and Low, chapter eleven, this volume). Moreover, the traditional female career pattern has exerted a heavily penalty on older women who are reliant on state pensions (see Price, chapter twelve, this volume). It is also a problem in countries like the US where health insurance is tied to employment.

So, what can be done and what should be done to address the gender imbalance? Is it possible to change the wage ratio in order to make a more level playing field for men's and women's intra-household decision-making? Is it desirable to coerce men to do more of the unpaid work and family care, even if that were possible?

It is sometimes suggested that compulsion to care goes against the inherent meaning of the caring activity. It is claimed that one cannot force someone to be responsible and attentive in a competent manner. Caring usually requires some feeling of empathy to shape appropriate actions. The most that is possible is to give people the choice to care and to provide favourable conditions in which they can exercise such choice. One could argue, however, that many women are constrained to care because of lack of alternatives, whether nursery places or a partner who is willing and able to share in the caring. There are positive signs, however, that in practice men have increased their contribution to child care more than to other core domestic duties. Policies such as 'daddy leave' are surely to be welcomed, in so far as they help support men's wish to take a more active fathering role.

A more problematic and contentious issue is how to address the unequal wage rates of men and women. State policy attempts to change the female-to-male wage ratio in order to achieve changes in the shares of unpaid work are not in evidence. The idea of giving wages for housework has been suggested and discussed, but never implemented (for example Young and Halsey, 1995). In the US in the 1970s, the possibility of crediting homemakers with social security contributions was discussed but not adopted. Women's behaviour in entering the labour market in large numbers has made redundant any policy interest in such ideas. Cash for parental care is a policy that has many examples, including parental leave. More recent examples used in Finland and Norway offer parents the choice between cash to care for their own children at home or a subsidised place in formal child care. Such policies have been popular among lower-paid women, who are the ones who have taken the cash and stayed at home rather than choosing the child-care places. These policies are criticised by feminists, who think that women will only be emancipated through employment. But none of these policies have tried to manipulate women's wages in the labour market.

It is not likely to be possible suddenly to change the amounts of human capital that are embedded in individuals' wage rates, such as the differing amounts of paid work experience that men and women have. But legislating for equal pay for equivalent work is a policy that starts to tackle the issue, so long as it is actually implemented in workplaces. Similarly, gender pay audits and pay reviews, as well as enforced monitoring of pay and equal opportunities, can assist in making sure women do not fall behind when they are in paid jobs. Unfortunately, the current move in the UK to 'reflexive regulation' adopted by the Discrimination Law Review consultation document is unlikely to be effective in achieving greater pay equality, especially outside the public sector, at a time when collective bargaining has diminished and when there are no appropriate institutional mechanisms for carrying through equality change (Deakin and McLaughlin, 2008). Deakin and McLaughlin's pessimistic appraisal of the likely success of the current 'encouragement' of redressing gender pay inequalities is born out by cross-national data. The result of several decades or more of trying to achieve gender wage equality is that both raw and adjusted-for-work-experience female-to-male wage ratios remain resistant to equality in nearly all countries.

One approach to raising the wages of partnered women relative to men would be to tax partnered men's wages sufficiently to give women in paid work a sizeable tax credit to boost their hourly wage rate to the same level as their partner's after-tax hourly rate. This policy could, in principle, equalise wage rates and eliminate the incentive for the female partner to be the person who did more of the unpaid work. Whether equality in wage rates would be sufficient to get the women to do more paid work is not clear, since there is still considerable evidence that women like caring (Houston and Marks, 2005) and some evidence that men cannot do ironing (for example, Moir and Moir, 2000).

Such a policy initiative, however, is not going to happen. No government would see such an aggressive approach for reducing gender inequalities in division of labour within couples as either feasible or desirable. So we are back to token or symbolic steps to try to encourage men to do a more equitable share of domestic and care work. Tokens and symbolic gestures, however, do matter, and signals from the state encouraging greater male participation in unpaid work could help advance the slow pace of gender convergence. There might also be useful steps that parents and schools could take to help the next generation reduce gender inequalities. According to data from the youth survey of the British Household Panel, the contribution that boys and girls aged 11–15 are making to housework show clear gender differences—with more than a third of boys doing little or no housework compared with one fifth of girls (Harkness, 2008). But whether such a difference is increasing or diminishing only time will tell. It may, however, be more feasible to tackle gender inequalities in youth through educational and parental encouragement than to change ingrained gender inequalities in paid and unpaid work among the adult population.

BIBLIOGRAPHY

Becker, G (1991) *A Treatise on the Family* (Cambridge, MA, Harvard University Press).

Brewer, M and Paull, G (2006) *Newborns and New Schools: Critical Times in Women's Employment* (London, Department for Work and Pensions).

Crompton, R (2006) *Employment and the Family* (Cambridge, Cambridge University Press).

Deakin, S and McLaughlin, C (2008) 'The Regulation of Women's Pay: From Individual Rights to Reflexive Law?' in J Scott, S Dex, and H Joshi (eds), *Changing Patterns of Women's Employment over 25 Years* (Cheltenham, Edward Elgar).

Del Boca, D and Wetzels, C (2007) *Social Policies, Labour Markets and Motherhood: A Comparative Analysis of European Countries* (Cambridge, Cambridge University Press).

Dex, S (forthcoming) 'Policy Interventions to Equalize Men's and Women's Time Spent in Unpaid Work: Are they Possible and Realistic?' in J Treas and S Drobnic (eds), *Dividing the Domestic: Men, Women and Household Work in Cross-National Perspective* (Stanford, CA, Stanford University Press).

Dex, S and Ward, K (2007) *Parental Care and Employment in Early Childhood: Analysis of the Millennium Cohort Study (MCS) Sweeps 1 and 2* (Manchester, Equal Opportunities Commission Report).

Dex, S, Ward, K and Joshi, H (2008) 'Changes in Women's Occupations and Occupational Mobility over 25 years' in J Scott, S Dex and H Joshi (eds), *Changing Patterns of Women's Employment Over 25 Years* (Cheltenham, Edward Elgar).

DTI (Department of Trade and Industry) (2000) *Work and Parents: Competitiveness and Choice, a Research Review* (London, DTI).

Gallie, D (2000) 'Labour Force Change', in A Halsey with J Webb (eds), *British Social Trends*, 3rd edn (Houndsmill, Macmillan Press Ltd).

Gershuny, J (2000) *Changing Times: Work and Leisure in Post Industrial Society* (Oxford, Oxford University Press).

—— (2004) 'Time through the Life-course in the Family' in J Scott, J Treas and M Richards (eds), *The Blackwell Companion to Sociology of Families* (Oxford, Blackwell).

Gershuny, J, Bittman, M and Brice, J (2005) 'Exit, Voice and Suffering: Do Couples Adapt to Changing Employment Patterns?' 67 *Journal of Marriage and Family* 656.

Hakim, C (2000) *Work–Lifestyle Choices in the 21st Century: Preference Theory* (Oxford, Oxford University Press).

Harkness, S (2008) 'The Household Division of Labour: Changes in Families Allocation of Paid and Unpaid Work' in J Scott, S Dex and H Joshi (eds), *Changing Patterns of Women's Employment Over 25 Years* (Cheltenham, Edward Elgar).

Hobson, B (2004) 'The Individualised Worker, the Gender Participatory and the Gender Equity Models in Sweden' 3 *Social Policy and Society* 75.

Hochschild, A (1989) *The Second Shift, Working Parents and the Revolution at Home* (London, Piatkus).

Holt, H and Grainger, H (2005) *Results of the Second Flexible Working Employee Survey*, DTI Employment Relations Research Series No 39 (London, Department of Trade and Industry).

Houston, DM and Marks, G (2005) 'Working, Caring and Sharing: Work–Life Dilemmas in Early Motherhood' in D Houston (ed), *Work–Life Balance in the Twenty-first Century* (London, Palgrave Macmillan).

Joshi, H and Paci, P (1998) *Unequal Pay for Women and Men: Evidence from the British Birth Cohort Studies* (Cambridge, MA: MIT Press).

Joshi, H (1989) 'The Changing Form of Women's Economic Dependency' in H Joshi (ed), *The Changing Population of Britain* (Oxford, Basil Blackwell).

Knijn, T (2004) 'Challenges and Risks of Individualisation in the Netherlands' 2 *Social Policy and Society* 57.

Kohler, H-P, Billari, F and Ortega, JA (2006) 'Low Fertility in Europe: Causes, Implications and Policy Options' in F Harris (ed), *The Baby Bust: Who will do the Work? Who will Pay the Taxes?* (Lanham, MD, Rowman & Littlefield Publishers).

Lewis, J (2001) 'The Decline of the Male Breadwinner Model: The Implications of Work and Care' 8 *Social Politics* 152.

—— (2006) 'Men, Women, Work, Care and Policies' 16 *Journal of European Social Policy* 387.

—— (2008) 'Work–Family Balance Policies: Issues and Development in the UK 1997–2005 in Comparative Perspective' in J Scott, S Dex and H Joshi (eds), *Changing Patterns of Women's Employment Over 25 Years* (Cheltenham, Edward Elgar).

Macran, S, Joshi, H and Dex, S (1996) 'Employment after childbearing: A survival analysis' 10 *Work Employment and Society* 273.

Moir, A and Moir, B (2002) *Why Men Don't Iron: The Science of Gender Studies* (London, Citadel, Kensington Publishing Corps).

O'Brien, M (2005) *Shared Caring: Bringing Fathers into the Frame* (London, Equal Opportunities Commission).

OECD (Organization for Economic Cooperation and Development) (2001) *Employment Outlook 2001* (Paris, OECD).

Palmer, T (2004) *Results of the First Flexible Working Employee Survey*, DTI Employment Relations Occasional Papers URN 04/703, www.dti.gov.uk/er/emar.

Purcell, K and Elias, P (2008) 'Achieving Equality in the Knowledge Economy' in J Scott, S Dex and H Joshi (eds), *Changing Patterns of Women's Employment Over 25 Years* (Cheltenham, Edward Elgar).

Royal Commission on Population (1949) *Report* (London, HMSO).

Ruhm, C (1998) 'The Economic Consequences of Parental Leave Mandates' 113 *Quarterly Journal of Economics* 285.

Scott, J (2008) 'Changing Gender Role Attitudes' in J Scott, S Dex and H Joshi (eds), *Changing Patterns of Women's Employment Over 25 Years* (Cheltenham, Edward Elgar).

WEU (Women and Equality Unit) (2004) *Women and Men in the Workplace*, www.womenandequalityunit.gov.uk/research/gender_briefing_nov04.doc.

Young, M and Halsey, AH (1995) *Family and Community Socialism* (London, Institute for Public Policy Research).

4

Managing Money in Intimate Relationships

Similarities and Differences between Cohabiting and Married Couples

CAROLYN VOGLER

INTRODUCTION

THIS CHAPTER AIMS to explore what we can learn from two recent, large-scale, nationally representative surveys, about the similarities and differences between different subcategories of cohabiting and married couples, in terms of the financial context of their relationships and how they handle money within them.[1] The latter is important, not only because it has serious implications for the distribution of property and possessions when relationships end (Tennant, Taylor and Lewis, 2006), but also because it has important implications for the well-being and satisfaction of each individual during the life of a relationship (Vogler, Lyonette and Wiggins, 2008). There is now a rich sociological literature showing how the different ways in which couples manage money can be seen as a tangible expression of how they resolve the tensions at the heart of all intimate relationships between, on the one hand, individual autonomy versus commitment to the welfare of the couple as a collective unit, and, on the other, equality versus inequalities in power and living standards between individuals within the same relationship (Blumstein and Schwartz, 1983; Pahl, 1989; Burgoyne, 1990; Treas, 1993; Vogler and Pahl, 1993; Fleming, 1997; Singh, 1997; Nyman, 1999; Treas and Widmer, 2000; Elizabeth, 2001; Rake and Jayatilaka, 2002; Heimdal and Houseknecht, 2003). Traditionally, of course, these polarities have been institutionally rooted in the marriage contract and the labour market. While

[1] I am grateful to the Economic and Social Research Council (ESRC) for providing funding to undertake this research (ESRC grant no R000239727). I am also grateful to Rosemary Crompton for acting as the principal applicant, and to the ESRC's anonymous referees for insightful comments and very helpful suggestions.

the marriage contract requires spouses to support each other financially, both during marriage and after it ends (Barlow et al, 2005), we enter the labour market as individuals who are in some sense deemed to 'own' the money we have earned: it is 'ours' and we are seen as having a legitimate right to do what we like with it (Burgoyne 1990; Burgoyne and Lewis 1994; Singh, 1997; Nyman and Reinikainen 2002; Rake and Jayatilaka, 2002).

In the past, these tensions were resolved in a highly gendered way. Men were expected to act as breadwinners for the whole family and were therefore seen as having a legitimate right to more control over, and access to, money for their own personal use. Wives, on the other hand, were constructed as economically dependent on husbands and primarily responsible for unpaid caring and household tasks, regardless of how much they actually earned (Zelizer, 1989, 1994). Today, of course, this has changed dramatically. Both men and women now participate in the labour market as 'individuals' with their 'own' incomes, and intimate relationships are almost invariably regarded as partnerships between equals, in which all resources are ideally shared equally, regardless of who contributes what to the household. At the same time, however, men still earn more than women, while women are still seen as responsible for unpaid caring and household tasks (see Scott and Dex, chapter three, this volume). In these circumstances, the problem couples face is that individual autonomy and equality are inevitably in tension with each other, because equality requires higher earners to give up a degree of individual autonomy and control over their 'own' income in order to redistribute equally within the couple. The intra-household economy can therefore be seen as a crucially important dimension of intimate relationships, sitting at the interface between the couple and the wider society, mediating the extent to which gender inequalities in the labour market are transposed into inequalities in access to and control over money within the relationship (Vogler and Pahl, 1994).

One fundamental question that arises in this context is whether different forms of money management are adopted in different types of relationships. In recent years, the dramatic increase in cohabitation outside marriage has led to an important debate about the similarities and differences between cohabiting and married couples. But, despite its obvious relevance, given the different legal and financial ties between married and cohabiting couples, one issue that has seldom been addressed in the context of this debate is the financial dimension of intimate relationships. While qualitative studies indicate that in many ways cohabiting couples tend to be very similar to their married counterparts, especially in relation to commitment, attitudes, values and the rhythm of their everyday lives together (McRae, 1993; Lewis, 2001; Jamieson et al, 2002; Eekelaar and Maclean, 2003), two large-scale international studies indicate that there may nevertheless be some very big differences in both the financial context of their relationships and how they handle money within them (Treas and Widmer, 2000; Heimdal and Houseknecht, 2003). In the UK, these have important implications for policy when couples split up.

Drawing on quantitative, nationally representative British data from two annual sweeps of the International Social Survey Programme (ISSP),[2] in 1994 and 2002, for modules focusing on 'Family and Changing Gender Roles', this chapter seeks to explore the similarities and differences between cohabiting couples and their married counterparts in the same age range and family situations, by addressing four key questions. First, are there any differences between different subcategories of married and cohabiting couples in terms of their background characteristics and socio-economic circumstances? Secondly, how far do different subcategories of cohabiting and married couples manage money differently from each other, after controlling for a range of demographic, socio-economic, and ideological/discursive factors which have been found to be important predictors of how couples manage money in previous studies, such as age, the presence of children, both partners' relative economic contributions to the household, ideologies/discourses of breadwinning, and social class? Or how far, on the other hand, are cohabiting couples just like married couples without an official licence? Thirdly, how far are cohabiting couples now coming to be more egalitarian than their married counterparts in terms of (1) access to money for personal spending and saving and (2) who has the final say over important expenditure decisions? And, finally, although there is little previous research in this area, how far is power over expenditure decisions related to satisfaction with the relationship and happiness with life in general?

In order to put the analysis in context, I begin with a brief discussion of existing research on patterns of money management and how they have changed over time, before focusing on this specific data and the four questions raised above. Finally, I conclude by highlighting the main findings and drawing out their implications for policy.

SYSTEMS OF MONEY MANAGEMENT

When couples first set up home together they inevitably have to establish some way of managing the money coming into the household from earnings, state benefits and so on, in order to meet bills for basic living expenses such as mortgage/rent, council tax, fuel, food and so on, as well as personal spending money (Pahl, 1989). However, given that couples usually earn different amounts and that one or both partners may have no income, except possibly state benefits, this is not necessarily straightforward. If couples have different ideas about money or different assumptions about who should pay for what and how much it is legitimate to spend on oneself, without consulting the other partner first, it can all too easily lead to disagreement, underlying resentment and sometimes open conflict.

---

[2] The ISSP is a voluntary grouping of study teams in 38 nations each of which agrees to run a short annual self-completion survey containing an agreed set of questions asked of a probability-based nationwide sample of adults aged 18 and over (see Davis and Jowell, 1989; also www.issp.org.uk/info.htm).

Organising money can also be difficult because in Western societies the financial aspects of intimate relationships tend to be a 'taboo subject', which couples dislike talking about, even in private, particularly during the course of an ongoing relationship (Blumstein and Schwartz, 1983; Hertz, 1986, 1992; Rake and Jayatilaka, 2002). Qualitative studies indicate that there is very little explicit discussion or negotiation about how to manage money: couples frequently say they never sat down and tried to work out rationally the best system for them, instead they often claim they just did 'what came naturally' (Pahl, 1989; Tennant, Taylor and Lewis, 2006). This supports the finding by Douglas, Pearce and Woodward (chapter seven, this volume) that patterns of money management tend to emerge more by default or force of personality, than, as economists have traditionally assumed (Becker, 1993), by rational consideration and open negotiation. Not surprisingly, this tends to result in partners' having different assumptions and expectations from each other when relationships end (Tennant, Taylor and Lewis, 2006).

In the early 1980s, Pahl (1989) devised a typology of the main ways in which couples organise money, based on how couples *manage* money on a day-to-day basis, rather than how they exercise *strategic control* (or power) over it. This is because, as in a company or a work environment, the person who manages money on a daily basis may be different from the person with ultimate control over strategic financial decision-making. Traditionally, wives have been more likely to manage money as part of their domestic responsibilities for shopping, while control has more often been a male prerogative, associated with the breadwinner or primary earner status (Edwards, 1981; Blumstein and Schwartz, 1983; Pahl, 1989; Vogler and Pahl, 1993). The typology is divided into two subsections depending on the extent to which money is either constructed as jointly owned by both partners, so that individual autonomy is to some degree subordinated to the needs of the couple as a collective unit; or whether couples prioritise individual freedom and operate largely as two separate, autonomous individuals, each with their own individually owned money, so that neither is completely financially dependent on the other (Treas, 1993; Treas and Widmer, 2000; Elizabeth, 2001; Nyman and Reinikainen, 2002).

Systems in which couples operate more or less as single economic units include:

— the *female whole wage* system in which women manage all the money except the man's personal spending money;
— the *male whole wage/housekeeping allowance* system in which men either manage all the money (which may leave non-earning wives with no personal spending money) or men manage most of the money, except for the woman's housekeeping allowance;
— the *joint pooling* system in which couples pool all the money, usually in a joint bank account and in theory manage it jointly, each taking money out as needed.

Individualised systems in which couples operate largely as two separate autonomous economic units include:

— the *partial pool* in which couples pool some of their income to pay for collective expenditure and keep the rest separate to spend as they choose, without having to discuss it with the other partner;
— finally, the *independent management* system in which both partners have their own independent incomes from earnings or state benefits which they keep completely separate, and each partner has responsibility for different items of household expenditure.

While the female whole wage and housekeeping allowance systems involve separate spheres of expenditure for men and women based on a discourse of breadwinning in which men are constructed as the main breadwinners, with a legitimate right to more control over money and more money for their own use, the joint pool is less internally structured and in theory offers greater scope for discussion and negotiation over the use of pooled money (Shove, 1993). While pooling is in theory based on a discourse of equality in which all money is defined as jointly owned and both partners have equal access to and control over money, this tends to be achieved in practice only when both partners are in full-time employment and *also* see themselves as co-providers, equally responsible for providing the income. When the male partner is constructed as the main breadwinner, equal outcomes tend to be undermined by a more implicit and pervasive discourse of earner control, legitimating inequalities in personal spending money, favouring men (Pahl, 1989; Burgoyne, 1990; Shove, 1993; Vogler and Pahl, 1993, 1994; Fleming, 1997; Singh, 1997; Elizabeth, 2001).

So far there has been little research on the two privatised systems, although the little that does exist indicates that couples using the independent management system attempt to establish both equality and individual autonomy by constructing all money as individually owned and by defining equality not as equal access to and control over money, as in the joint pool, but as making equal contributions towards collective expenditure (going 50:50) regardless of income (Brines and Joyner, 1995; Singh and Lindsay, 1996; Elizabeth, 2001; Nyman, 2003). While keeping money separate thus avoids problems of financial dependency, it does not necessarily produce equal outcomes, because, if one partner earns more than the other, the higher earner ends up with more financial power in the relationship and more money for his or her own use (Pahl, 2005; Burgoyne et al, 2006). In a series of qualitative interviews with couples in New Zealand, Fleming (1997) found that partial pooling couples often seemed to have a foot in each camp. While they saw the household unit as important and liked the idea of pooling, they were often not fully committed to it in practice and sometimes disagreed over the extent to which money was jointly or separately owned. He concluded that the partial pool could therefore be thought of as a hybrid between systems in which households operate as single economic units and those in which money is kept completely separate, acting as a way of accommodating the two conflicting principles of jointness and autonomy.

Changing Patterns of Money Management among all British Heterosexual Couples

In order to provide a rough indication of the use of Pahl's (1989) systems among British (heterosexual) couples as a whole (married and cohabiting), as well as how this has changed over time, Table 4.1 compares the use of different allocative systems at three different points in time: 1987 (Vogler and Pahl, 1993, 1994), 1994 and 2002 (Vogler, Brockmann and Wiggins, 2006).[3] As can be seen in the table, the most commonly used system at all three points in time was clearly the joint pool, chosen by approximately half of respondents. The table also shows a slight decline in the use of the two traditional systems based on the male breadwinner model of gender (the female whole wage and housekeeping allowance systems) and a slight increase in the use of the partial pool, so that by 2002 it had overtaken the female whole wage system as the second most frequently used system. In the samples as a whole, there were no significant differences between male and female respondents' answers.

Table 4.1 also shows that the female whole wage system was associated with the lowest average standardised household income, while the partial pool and the independent management systems were associated with the highest incomes, with the housekeeping allowance and joint pooling systems falling between the two extremes. This supports previous studies showing that female partners are most likely to manage money in low-income households where there is insufficient money to meet the bills and the task is likely to be a chore or a burden rather than a source of power, while male partners, on the other hand, are more likely to manage money when income is high enough to allow for discretionary spending and it is possible for real decisions to be made about how to spend money (Pahl, 1989; Vogler and Pahl, 1993, 1994; Singh, 1997; Goode, Callender and Lister, 1998; Rake and Jayatilaka, 2002). Given that they presuppose two separate sources of income, the partial pool and the independent management system were, not surprisingly, most likely to be used by the highest-income couples who, as we shall see later, were more likely than other couples to both be in full-time employment.

Previous research indicates that allocative systems are largely the result of two inter-related factors: first, the relative economic resources each partner

---

[3] The 1987 data consist of a sub-sample of 1,211 individuals living in couple relationships, who were initially included as part of the Social Change and Economic Life Initiative. This was based on interviews with a random sample of 6,000 adults aged 20–60, living in six towns in Britain in 1986 (Gallie, 1988). In terms of their economic and demographic characteristics the 1,211 individuals broadly corresponded to an national sample (Vogler and Pahl, 1994).

Table 4.1: Proportion of Opposite-sex Couples in Britain using Different Household Allocative Systems in 1987, 1994 and 2002, together with Mean Standardised Household Income in 2002 (male and female respondents in couple relationships)

	1987	1994	2002	2002
	Allocative Systems (All)	Allocative Systems (All)	Allocative Systems (All)	Mean Standardised Household Income
	%	%	%	£ per year
Female whole wage	26	14	10	16,861
Housekeeping allowance	22	10	8	19,879
Joint pool	50	54	55	24,398
Partial pool	(not included)	13	17	30,799
Independent management	2	9	10	29,807
Total (%)	100	100	100	
Respondents (N)	(1,211)	(686)	(1,308)	
Significance level				$p < 0.001$

Note: Income was standardised using the McClelland Equivalence Scale, according to the number of adults and children in the household, obtained from the *British Household Panel Survey User Manual Volume A* (Taylor, 2005: table 29). No significant differences between men's and women's answers in 1987, 1994, or 2002.

Source: 1987 figures from the Social Change and Economic Life Initiative (Vogler and Pahl, 1994), and 1994 and 2002 figures from the ISSP (Vogler, Brockmann and Wiggins, 2006).

contributes to the household (as measured by household employment status rather than income, because not all couples are economically active) and, secondly, cultural ideologies/discourses of gender, particularly those of male breadwinning versus newly emerging discourses of co-provisioning (Vogler and Pahl, 1993, 1994; Ellingsaeter, 1998). One factor which has seldom been included in British research on this topic is the type of relationship couples establish. To see how far different subcategories of cohabiting and married couples organise money differently after controlling for selection effects, we therefore need to turn to our own data.

DATA USED IN THE ANALYSIS

Our own comparison of different subcategories of cohabiting and married couples is based on British data from two cross-sectional, national surveys of 'Family and Changing Gender Roles,' undertaken by the UK's National Centre For Social Research, as part of the 1994 and 2002 ISSP. Both surveys were based on nationally representative samples of the adult population (aged 18 and over) living in Great

Britain (that is, England, Wales and Scotland, south of the Caledonian Canal). Each respondent participated in a face-to-face interview and was left with a self-completion questionnaire to fill in after the interview, which was returned by post. The 1994 survey yielded 688 male and female respondents aged 18 and over, living in married and opposite-sex cohabiting relationships, of whom 9 per cent were cohabiting and 91 per cent were married. The 2002 survey yielded 1,308 similar respondents, of whom 13 per cent were cohabiting and 87 per cent were married. Comparison with the 2002 General Household Survey (GHS) indicated that the level of cohabitation in the ISSP was broadly representative of the population as a whole (for more details, see General Household Survey, 2004; Vogler, Brockmann and Wiggins, 2006, 2008; Vogler, Lyonette and Wiggins, 2008).

Identifying Subcategories of Cohabiting and Married Respondents

Our first objective was to identify the three main subcategories of cohabiting respondents identified by Kiernan and Estaugh (1993) in their analysis of the 1989 GHS, namely, 'never-married childless cohabitants', 'never-married cohabiting parents', and 'post-marital cohabitants', together with their married counterparts in the same age range and family situations. Unfortunately, we were unable to use the 2002 ISSP for the entire analysis because, unlike the earlier 1994 survey, it did not include questions on marital or partnership histories and thus did not enable us to identify post-marital cohabiting and remarried respondents separately. For this, we had to return to the earlier 1994 data.

Our sub-samples of 'never-married childless cohabitants' and 'never-married cohabitants with children' were drawn from the 2002 data. Since national statistics (Summerfield and Babb, 2003; Walker, 2003), indicate that never-married cohabitants are overwhelmingly young (under 35 years old), both samples consisted of all respondents under 35 years old, who were cohabiting with a partner at the time of the 2002 survey. They were then matched with a sample of married couples in the same age range. This yielded 306 male and female respondents under 35 years old, over a third (36 per cent) of whom were cohabiting while just under two thirds (64 per cent) were married. Both groups were then divided into those with and without children aged 16 or under living with them. This generated four subcategories which we refer to as 'childless cohabiting respondents', 'cohabiting parents', 'childless married respondents' and 'married parents,' respectively. It is important to note that the category of cohabiting parents needs to be treated with extreme caution, partly because of the small number of respondents in this category (38), but also because the 1994 data indicate that in 1994, approximately one quarter of cohabiting parents under 35 were post-marital cohabitants, who as we see later, tend to be very different from never-married cohabiting parents. Our findings about cohabiting parents therefore need to be seen as indicative rather than conclusive, although it was reassuring to find that they were broadly consistent with the findings of previous research (Kiernan and Estaugh, 1993;

McRae, 1993, 1999; Pickford, 1999; Smart and Stevens, 2000; Lewis, 2001; Lewis, Papacosta and Warin, 2002; Ermisch, 2005).

Our sub-sample of 'post-marital cohabitants' consisted of 27 post-marital cohabitants aged between 26 and 56 in the 1994 survey, who were matched with 92 remarried respondents in the same age range. We refer to them as 'post-marital cohabitants' and 'remarried respondents', respectively. Both groups include those with and without children under 16 living with them. Given the small number of post-marital cohabitants, it was not possible to subdivide them further, but age and the presence of children are controlled for in all our later multivariate analysis. It needs to be stressed that since the three subcategories of cohabiting and married respondents were drawn from different data sets and constructed on the basis of different criteria, they are not directly comparable with each other. However, since the aim is to compare cohabiting and married respondents *within* sub-samples rather than between them, we can still make meaningful inferences, although the results clearly need to be treated as tentative.

Tables 4.2 and 4.3 show the proportion of respondents living in each type of relationship at the time of the respective surveys, together with their average age in years. As can be seen in the tables, the data are consistent with previous studies showing that cohabiting respondents tend to be younger than their

Table 4.2: Relationship Status and Mean Age of Partnered Respondents (aged under 35) in Britain, in 2002

Relationship Status	%	Mean Age in Years	
		Men[a]	Women[b]
Childless married respondents	20	29.2	29.6
Childless cohabiting respondents	24	27.6*	26.1***
Married parents	44	30.3	30.6
Cohabiting parents	12	29.3	27.9***
Total (%)	100		
Respondents (N)	(306)		

Notes: $*p < 0.1$; $**p < 0.05$; $***p < 0.01$.

a. Overall differences between men ANOVA $F = 3.5$; d.f. $= 3$; $p < 0.05$. T tests showed childless cohabiting men were marginally younger than childless married men ($t = -1.7$; $d.f = 126$; $p < 0.1$) but the difference between married and cohabiting fathers was not significant.

b. Overall differences between women ANOVA $F = 14.2$; d.f. $= 3$; $p < 0.001$. T tests showed childless cohabiting women were significantly younger than childless married women ($t = -4.073$; d.f. $= 171$; $p < 0.001$), and cohabiting mothers were significantly younger than married mothers ($t = -3.087$; d.f. $= 171$; $p < 0.01$). No significant differences between men and women within relationship categories.

Source: ISSP 2002, Vogler, Brockmann and Wiggins (2008).

Table 4.3: Relationship Status and Mean Age of Repartnered Post-marital Respondents (aged between 26 and 56), in Britain in 1994

Relationship status	%	Mean age in years	
		Men[a]	Women[b]
Post-marital married respondents	77	39.1	41.8
Post-marital cohabiting respondents	23	39.2	37.2
Total (%)	100		
Respondents (*N*)	(119)		

Notes: $^*p < 0.1$; $^{**}p < 0.05$; $^{***}p < 0.01$.

[a] Age differences between men not significant.
[b] Age differences between women not significant.
No significant differences between men and women within relationship categories.

Source: ISSP 1994, Vogler, Brockmann and Wiggins (2008).

married counterparts, although in the case of cohabiting fathers and post-marital cohabitants, the differences did not reach statistical significance (Kiernan and Estaugh, 1993; Ermisch, 2005). The main findings will be presented in four sections corresponding to the research questions specified above. The first two sections draw on both the 1994 and 2002 data to compare the three different subcategories of cohabiting couples with their married counterparts in the same age range and family situations. In contrast, the third and fourth sections attempt to boost the number of cohabiting couples available for analysis in the same data set by using *all* cohabiting and married couples in the 2002 data, without separating out couples over 35 years old who may have been married before. What sort of people, then, cohabit rather than marry, and how do they compare with married people in terms of their background characteristics and socio-economic circumstances?

Background Characteristics and Socio-economic Circumstances

Tables 4.4 and 4.5 show the main differences between different subcategories of cohabiting and married couples in terms of education, employment status, mean standardised household income, housing tenure and social class. Our findings broadly support Kiernan and Estaugh's (1993) analysis of the 1989 GHS, showing that, in terms of education, income and social class, childless and post-marital cohabitants were quite similar to their married counterparts, although they were less likely to be living in owner-occupied accommodation and more likely to be living in households in which both partners were in full-time

Table 4.4: Socio-economic Characteristics of Cohabiting and Married Respondents (aged under 35) in Britain, in 2002

	Childless Married Respondents	Childless Cohabiting Respondents	Married Parents	Cohabiting Parents
A. Educational qualifications				
Men				
% with A-levels and above	93	81	53	36
% with O-levels	3	16	43	43
% with no formal qualifications	4	3	4	21
	n.s.		$\chi^2 = 4.794$; d.f. = 2; $p < 0.1$	
Women				
% with A-levels and above	81	71	52	32
% with O-levels	16	29	44	54
% with no formal qualifications	3	–	4	14
	n.s.		$\chi^2 = 4.769$; d.f. = 2; $p < 0.1$	
B. Household Employment Status				
% both employed full-time	74	85	18	18
% man FT woman PT	12	4	34	26
% man FT woman not employed	2	4	34	1
% no earners in the household	2	1	6	18
	n.s.		$\chi^2 = 19.331$; d.f. = 4; $p < 0.05$	
C. Mean Standardised Household Income (£/year)	39,249	36,999	22,626	19,522
	n.s.		n.s.	
D. Housing tenure				
% owner occupiers	87	65	77	46
% renting form local authority	3	4	15	43
% renting privately	10	31	7	11
	$\chi^2 = 8.84$; d.f. = 2; $p < 0.05$		$\chi^2 = 15.1$; d.f.= 2; $p < 0.001$	
E. Social Class				
Women				
% managerial/professional	50	56	40	24
% intermediate class	29	21	27	9
% working class	21	23	33	67
	n.s.		$\chi^2 = 7.771$; d.f. = 2; $p < 0.05$	

Notes: Total household income was standardised by the number of adults and children in the household using the McClement's Equivalence Scale (Taylor, 2005). Class was measured on the Goldthorpe three-class model (Goldthorpe, 1987).
Source: ISSP 2002, Vogler, Brockmann and Wiggins (2008).

Table 4.5: Differences in Socio-economic Characteristics between Post-marital Cohabiting and Remarried Respondents (aged between 26 and 56) in Britain, in 1994

	Remarried Respondents	Post-marital Cohabiting Respondents
A. Household Employment Status		
% both employed full-time	29	61
% man FT; woman PT	24	11
% man FT; woman not employed	18	11
% other	30	18
	$\chi^2 = 9.73$; d.f. $= 3$; $p < 0.05$	
B. Housing Tenure		
% owner occupiers	75	54
% renting from local authority	17	39
% renting privately	9	7
	$\chi^2 = 6.538$; d.f. $= 2$; $p < 0.05$	

Source: ISSP 1994, Vogler, Brockmann and Wiggins (2008).

employment. As Kiernan and Estaugh (1993) point out, in the case of young childless cohabitants, these differences may be at least partly because they are younger than their married counterparts and thus likely to be at an earlier stage in their partnership and housing histories.

Turning to those with children, however, the picture was very different: cohabiting parents stood out in being socio-economically disadvantaged compared with their married counterparts. They were more likely than married parents to have no formal qualifications, to be living in social housing (43 per cent and 15 per cent, respectively) and to have no earners in the household (18 per cent and 6 per cent, respectively). This was mainly because cohabiting fathers were only half as likely as married fathers to be in full-time employment (53 per cent and 87 per cent, respectively; $\chi^2 = 12.114$; d.f. $= 3$; $p < 0.01$).[4] While there were no differences in employment status between cohabiting and married mothers, cohabiting mothers were twice as likely as married mothers to be in the working class (67 per cent and 33 per cent, respectively). These findings are consistent with previous studies (McRae 1993, 1999; Smart and Stevens, 2000; Lewis, Papacosta and Warin, 2002; Ermisch, 2005), showing that cohabiting parents may therefore replace or mirror some of the unstable shotgun marriages of former times, as well as with Holtermann et al's (1999) analysis of the 1997 Labour Force Survey,

---

[4] The 1994 data indicate that our 2002 findings are likely to underestimate the differences in employment status and income between cohabiting and married parents, because a few post-marital cohabitants may have been included in the category of cohabiting parents. Post-marital cohabitants, however, are far more likely than cohabiting parents to both be in full-time employment. In 1994, for example, differences in income between married and cohabiting parents were much bigger (£15,406 and £7,348 per annum, respectively; $p = <0.05$).

showing that in all these respects, cohabiting mothers were much more similar to lone mothers than to married mothers. In McRae's (1993) study, for example, cohabiting mothers with the most resources married soonest after the birth, while those with no resources saw marriage as irrelevant. McRae also makes the point that given the high rate of dissolution of cohabiting unions with children, there is likely to be considerable movement between the categories of cohabiting and lone motherhood (McRae, 1997).

In short, then, our findings strongly support the argument put forward by a number of authors that, despite women's increased participation in the labour market in recent years, marriage still has an important economic dimension: economic well-being is much more strongly associated with marriage than with cohabitation, especially in the case of couples with children (McRae, 1993, 1997, 1999; Smock and Manning, 1997; Ermisch and Francesconi, 2000; Rake, 2000; Taylor, 2000; Kiernan, 2003; Ermisch, 2005).[5] As White and Rogers (2000) suggest, in a climate of more liberal attitudes towards births outside marriage, it is possible that economic decisions may have become even more important in the decision to marry.[6] How far then, did different subcategories of cohabiting and married couples differ from each other in terms of how they organised household money?

Managing Money in Intimate Relationships

In order to get an idea of how couples organised household money, respondents were shown a card describing Pahl's (1989) allocative systems, and asked to say which came closest to the way in which they managed money within their own households. We begin by focusing on young never-married cohabiting and first-time married respondents, and then go on to those in post-marital relationships.

Were there any differences between young cohabiting and married couples in terms of how they managed money in their relationships, or were they similar to each other, as Lewis (2001) found in her qualitative study? As can be seen in Table 4.6, the most striking feature of the data was that cohabiting parents were very similar to married respondents (with and without children) in being most

[5] There are a number of reasons for this. First, the most important factor predicting whether cohabiting unions are converted into marriages is higher earnings by the male partner (Smock and Manning, 1997; Ermisch and Francesconi, 2000); secondly, the increase in women's labour market participation during the 1990s was mainly confined to married women with young children and employed partners, while the proportion of cohabiting women with young children in employment hardly changed at all (Taylor, 2000); and thirdly, cohabiting men and women, especially men, also earn less than their married counterparts (Rake, 2000).

[6] This finding was partly based on ethnographic work with young unmarried mothers, showing that neither the young women themselves nor their parents saw any point in marrying an unemployed man (White and Rogers, 2000). For an interesting argument along the same lines see Ermisch (2005).

Table 4.6: Household Allocative Systems used by Cohabiting and Married Respondents (aged under 35) in Britain, in 2002

Allocative Systems	Childless Married Respondents %	Childless Cohabiting Respondents %	Married Parents %	Cohabiting Parents %	All %
Female whole wage	8	–	9	11	7
Housekeeping allowance	4	–	12	4	7
Joint pool	58	39	59	52	54
Partial pool	20	40	9	15	19
Independent management	10	21	9	19	13
Total (%)	100	100	100	100	100
Respondents (N)	(50)	(52)	(106)	(27)	(235)

Notes: Difference between childless married and cohabiting couples: $\chi^2 = 13.772$; d.f. = 4; $p < 0.01$.
Difference between married and cohabiting parents not significant.
Difference between childless married respondents and married parents not significant.
Source: ISSP 2002, Vogler, Brockmann and Wiggins (2008).

likely to use one of the three systems in which households operated more or less as single economic units, especially the joint pool, whereas respondents in childless cohabiting unions stood out in being far more likely to keep money partly or completely separate.[7] Although the numbers were very small and the differences did not reach statistical significance, there were also indications in the data that male and female respondents in childless cohabiting relationships were more likely than men and women in other types of relationships to perceive the way in which they managed money differently from each other. Female cohabitants, for example, were more likely than male cohabitants to see themselves as using the partial pool (48 per cent and 27 per cent, respectively) while male cohabitants, on the other hand, were more likely than female cohabitants to perceive themselves as using the joint pool (55 per cent and 29 per cent, respectively). In other words, men in these unions appeared to see themselves as pooling to a greater extent than their female counterparts. This may relate to the blurring that Burgoyne and Sonnenberg refer to in chapter five of this volume. As mentioned earlier, however, since our male and female respondents are not partnering each other, we cannot be sure that these differences of perception exist in any given relationship; this is something which requires more attention in future research.

---

[7] This supports previous findings on cohabiting parents (McRae, 1993, 1999; Winkler, 1997; Lewis, 2001).

How far were these differences between childless cohabiting and married respondents due to pre-existing differences between the two groups (selection effects) such as age, the relative income each partner contributes to the household, ideologies/discourses of breadwinning and so on; or to state effects, namely the actual experience of living in a cohabiting relationship? In order to find out, we carried out a series of multinomial logistic regression analyses with allocative systems as the dependent nomial variable and the large heterogeneous joint pooling system as the reference category. Our independent variables consisted of sex (where relevant), age (entered as a covariate at the individual level ranging from 18 to 34) and social class (professional/managerial, intermediate, working class), together with relationship status (childless cohabitants, childless married respondents, cohabiting parents, married parents) both partners' relative economic contributions to the household, as indicated by household employment status (both full-time; man full-time, woman part-time; man full-time, woman non-employed; other combinations of employment statuses), as well as a score for ideologies/discourses of breadwinning, in which high scores indicated more traditional ideologies. The entries for age and ideologies of breadwinning represent the difference in odds between the oldest (or highest) compared with the youngest (or lowest) points on the scales (Vogler and Pahl, 1994). In the case of the categorical variables, the last-named category was the reference group.

Table 4.7 shows the odds of using the female whole wage, the housekeeping allowance, the partial pool and the independent management systems as compared with the joint pool, for respondents under 35 years old in 2002. While the parameter estimates are sometimes unreliable due to data sparsity and the results are therefore indicative rather than conclusive, they nevertheless provide some indication of the extent to which relationship status was independently linked to each of the individual allocative systems, as compared with the joint pool, after controlling for other factors. The results indicate that the experience of living in a childless cohabiting relationship plays a hugely significant role in keeping money partly separate: childless cohabitants were over five times as likely as married parents to use the partial pool rather than the joint pool, after controlling for other factors. Female respondents were also 60 per cent more likely than male respondents to perceive themselves as using the partial pool rather than the joint pool, and respondents in the managerial/professional and intermediate classes were also more likely to do so, as compared with those in the working class, after controlling for other factors.

Separate equations for men and women (not shown) indicated that for men, relationship status was the *only* significant factor predicting keeping money partly separate: men in childless cohabiting relationships were nearly 20 times more likely than married fathers to keep money partly separate rather than pooling money. For women, however, relationship status was interrelated with social class. Women in cohabiting unions (with and without children) were more likely than married mothers to perceive themselves as using *both the partial pool and*

Table 4.7: Multinomial Logistic Regression Showing the Independent Predictors of Financial Allocative Systems (as compared with the Joint Pool) among Cohabiting and Married Respondents (aged under 35) in Britain, in 2002

	Female Whole Wage	Housekeeping Allowance	Partial Pool	Independent Management
	(Odds)	(Odds)	(Odds)	(Odds)
(constant)	0.6	0.01	0.03	1.1
Sex				
Male	0.5	0.5	0.4**	1.1
Female (ref.)	–	–	–	–
Age	0.4	2.0	2.5	0.4
Relationship status				
Childless cohabitants	UE	UE	5.1**	2.6
Childless married	0.7	0.5	1.3	1.0
Cohabiting parents	1.3	0.7	3.2	3.4
Married parents (ref.)	–	–	–	–
Employment status				
Both full time	0.7	0.6	1.1	1.2
Man full time, woman part-time	0.2*	1.4	1.0	1.5
Man full time, woman non employed	0.2*	2.0	0.2	0.6
Other (ref.)	–	–	–	–
Ideologies of breadwinning	17.7	8.3	0.6	0.1
Social class				
Managerial/professional	0.8	0.7	4.5***	2.5
Intermediate	0.8	1.2	3.2*	3.5**
Working class (ref.)	–	–	–	–

Notes: ***$p < 0.01$, **$p < 0.05$, *$p < 00.1$; $N = 220$, Pseudo $R^2 = 0.34$, Likelihood 457.5 d/f 44; Reference category is the joint pool; age and ideologies of breadwinning were not statistically significant; UE = unreliable estimate due to empty cells.
Source: ISSP 2002, Vogler, Brockmann and Wiggins (2008).

the independent management systems rather than the joint pool, as did women in the managerial and intermediate classes, with incomes high enough to facilitate partially or completely separate finances, as compared with women in the working class.

Turning to post-marital and remarried couples, the analysis shows that, once again, cohabitants were more likely to keep money partly or, indeed, completely separate, while those in remarried unions were most likely to use one of the three systems in which couples operate more or less as single economic units, especially the joint pool (Table 4.8).[8] Table 4.9 confirms that this is still the case after controlling for age, sex, social class, the presence of children, both partners' relative economic contributions to the household and ideologies/discourses of breadwinning: cohabitants were dramatically more likely than those who had remarried to use either the partial pool or the independent management system rather than the joint pool, after controlling for other factors. In addition, older respondents were also more likely than younger respondents to keep money partly separate rather than pooling money, as were those living in households in which both partners were either in full-time employment or in which the man was in full-time while the woman was in part-time employment, as compared with those in other employment situations. Finally, women were also 80 per cent more likely than men to perceive themselves as keeping money completely separate rather than pooling money, after controlling for other factors.

In summary then, both marriage and remarriage appear to be strongly associated with pooling money, whereas childless and post-marital cohabiting relationships are far more likely to be associated with keeping money partly or completely separate.

Table 4.8: Household Allocative Systems used by Post-marital Cohabiting and Remarried Respondents (aged between 26 and 56) in Britain, in 1994

Allocative Systems	Remarried Respondents	Post-marital Cohabiting Respondents	All
	%	%	%
Female whole wage system	18	7	15
Housekeeping allowance system	9	4	8
Joint pool	54	25	47
Partial pool	12	46	20
Independent management system	8	18	10
Total (%)	100	100	100
Respondents (N)	(91)	(28)	(119)
Significance: $\chi^2 = 20.814$; d.f = 4; $p = <0.001$.			

Source: ISSP 1994, Vogler, Brockmann and Wiggins (2008).

[8] The 1994 data show that remarried couples were not significantly different from first-time married couples.

Table 4.9: Multinomial Logistic Regression showing the Independent Predictors of Financial Allocative Systems (as compared with the Joint Pool) among Post-marital Cohabiting and Remarried Respondents (aged between 26 and 56) in Britain, in 1994

	Female Whole Wage	Housekeeping Allowance	Partial Pool	Independent Management
	(Odds)	(Odds)	(Odds)	(Odds)
(constant)	0.67	75.5	0.39	5.23
Sex				
Male	1.1	0.1**	2.3	0.2*
Female (ref.)	–	–	–	–
Age	11.0*	0.07	42.5***	18.4
Children under 16 years old present in the household				
Yes	0.3*	0.6	2.2	2.3
No (ref.)	–	–	–	–
Relationship status				
Cohabiting	1.8	0.4	16.7***	14.8***
Remarried (ref.)	–	–	–	–
Employment status				
Both full time	1.0	UE	7.9***	0.3
Man full time, woman part time	1.8	0.06**	20.0***	0.3
Man full time, woman non-employed	0.9	0.2	0.9	0.3
Other (ref.)	–	–	–	–

Notes: ***$p < 0.01$, **$p < 0.05$, *$p < 0.1$; $N = 117$, Pseudo $R^2 = 0.50$; Likelihood 326.104; d/f 28. Reference category is the joint pool. Ideologies of breadwinning and social class were not statistically significant. UE = unreliable estimate due to empty cells.
Source: ISSP 1994, Vogler, Brockmann and Wiggins (2008).

EQUALITY AND INEQUALITIES ASSOCIATED WITH INDIVIDUALISED PATTERNS OF MONEY MANAGEMENT

Given that qualitative studies (Elizabeth, 2001; Pahl, 2005) indicate that cohabiting couples often keep money partly or completely separate in order to try to overcome gender inequalities and financial dependencies associated with traditional heterosexual marriage, an important question is how far the newly emerging individualised systems of money management are more egalitarian than other systems in terms of each partner's access to personal spending money and power over important expenditure decisions, as Giddens' (1992) thesis would lead us to expect? Or how far, on the other hand, are increasingly individu-alised and unstable intimate relationships still associated with marked gender inequalities, albeit perhaps, in new and impersonal marketised forms, which as Beck and Beck-Gernsheim (1995) suggest, may make intimate relationships a relatively good deal for men but even riskier for women. This section draws on all cohabiting and married couples surveyed in the 2002 ISSP. We begin with personal spending money and then go on to power over important expenditure decisions.

Although the ISSP did not ask respondents directly about each partner's rela-tive access to personal spending money, it was notable that, contrary to Giddens' (1992) thesis that cohabiting couples are now in the vanguard of shifts to highly egalitarian and radically democratic 'pure relationships', the partial pool and independent management systems were most likely to be used by cohabiting respondents when one partner (usually the man) earned more than the other, whereas when both earned similar amounts they were most likely to use the joint pool (80 per cent and 20 per cent respectively) (Vogler, Brockmann and Wiggins, 2008). To the extent that cohabiting couples contribute equally to collective expenditure (or indeed even in proportion to earnings), as previous research suggests, they may therefore be even less egalitarian than some of their married counterparts who pool money, because inequalities in the labour market, as well as in assets acquired before the current relationship, are likely to be directly transposed into inequalities in earning power within relationships, so that the higher earner ends up with greater access to money for discretionary spending (Brines and Joyner, 1999; Singh and Lindsay, 1996; Burgoyne and Morison, 1999; Roman and Vogler, 1999).

Previous research indicates that one of the most important sources of con-flict and disagreement between couples is who has the final say over large one-off expenditure decisions for the home, particularly when one partner feels they have less influence over spending than the other (Kirchler et al, 2001; Sutton, Cebulla and Middleton, 2003). As Blumstein and Schwartz (1983) point out, this is because while money tends to be a taboo subject which couples prefer not to talk about, decisions about large one-off expenditures usually involve so much deliberation between partners that they tend to bring to the surface differences in underlying values or attitudes which are usually kept hidden. Not surprisingly then, the nature of decision-making has also been found to be associated with relationship satisfaction (Blumstein and Schwartz, 1983; Kirchler et al, 2001), which is in turn likely to impact on each individual's well-being and happiness with life in general (Layard, 2006). Pahl (1989), for example, found that when male partners controlled finances, both male and female partners were less happy with their relationships than when responsi-bilities were shared.

In the 2002 ISSP, our main indicator of power over important expenditure decisions was the respondents' answers as to who had the final say when they and their partner made decisions about buying major things for the home: mostly the male partner, mostly the female partner, both decided together, or sometimes one partner and sometimes the other partner decided. This generated four different types of decision-making: male-dominated, female-dominated, joint and varying. It is important to note that although neither joint or varying decision-making necessarily indicates *equal* decision-making in a 50:50 sense, they may be at least *potentially* more egalitarian than either male- or female-dominated decisions (Blumstein and Schwartz, 1983; Kirchler et al, 2001). However, Kirchler et al (2001) also found that while men tended to have more influence over and more benefit from financial decisions than women, they were far more likely than women to claim that control 'varied'. Given that male control is no longer in keeping with the egalitarian spirit of the times, the authors suggest this is likely to be one of the ways in which men try to gloss over or suppress their own greater influence (for discussion, see Vogler et al, 2008a). In the sample as a whole, 63 per cent of respondents reported that decisions were joint, 17 per cent that they varied, 14 per cent that they were female dominated, and 6 per cent that they were male dominated. Our main finding (Table 4.10) was that, contrary to Giddens' (1992) thesis that cohabiting couples are markedly more democratic and egalitarian than married couples, the partial pool—and to some extent the independent management system—were just as likely to be associated with inequalities in who had the final say over important expenditure decisions, as were more traditional ways of managing money based on the male breadwinner model of gender, even after controlling for age, sex, social class, who earned more, ideologies/discourses of gender and whether respondents were cohabiting or married (Vogler, Lyonette and Wiggins, 2008).

In short then, our findings support qualitative studies showing that while individualised systems of money management are often used to try to overcome traditional gender inequalities and create non-financially dependent relationships (Elizabeth, 2001; Pahl, 2005), in the context of a gendered labour market (Nyman, 2003), individualised systems of money management tend to have highly unequal outcomes, and inequality also tends to be more visible to female respondents than in systems in which money is merged and treated more as a joint resource. The partial pool, and to a lesser extent the independent management system, tend in practice to end up benefiting the higher earner, in a very similar way to the traditional housekeeping allowance system. Indeed, the reason why cohabiting couples earning different amounts are more likely than those earning similar amounts to use one of these systems may be precisely because they enable the higher earner to retain control over higher levels of discretionary spending, despite the decline of traditional discourses of male breadwinning and the increasing importance of egalitarian ideologies of co-provisioning.

Table 4.10: Multinomial Logistic Regression showing the Independent Predictors of Female-dominated, Male-dominated and Varying Decisions (as compared with Joint Decisions) for All Respondents in Couple Relationships in Britain, in 2002

	Female-dominated Decisions	Male-dominated Decisions	Varying Decisions
	Odds	Odds	Odds
(constant)	0.1	0.6	0.4
Age	0.6	0.1**	0.1***
Ideologies of women's responsibilities	1.8	1.9	1.8
Sex			
Male	1.3	1.4	1.9***
Female (ref.)	–	–	–
Relationship status			
Childless married	1.1	1.8	0.8
Childless cohabiting	2.5***	0.7	1.0
Cohabiting parents	1.8	0.5	1.1
Married parents (ref.)	–	–	–
Social class			
Managerial/professional	1.0	1.2	1.1
Intermediate	0.7	0.7	1.0
Working class (ref.)	–	–	–
Relative income			
Woman more	1.6*	1.2	0.4**
Both the same	1.6*	0.7	1.2
Man more (ref.)			
Household allocative systems			
Female whole wage	5.0***	2.6*	2.2**
Housekeeping allowance system	0.4	6.5***	0.8
Partial pooling system	1.6*	4.5***	1.2
Independent management system	0.8	2.0	1.6*
Joint pool (ref.)	–	–	–

Notes: ***$p < 0.01$, **$p < 0.05$, *$p < 0.1$; $N = 1016$; Pseudo $R^2 = 0.14$, Likelihood 1842.659, 42d/f. The last-named category is always used as the reference, labelled (ref.) above.
Source: ISSP 2002; Vogler, Lyonette and Wiggins (2008).

SATISFACTION WITH FAMILY LIFE AND HAPPINESS WITH LIFE IN GENERAL

Finally, how far was having the final say associated with individuals' satisfaction with family life and happiness with life in general?

Our main findings indicate that, while causation is likely to operate in both directions, both men and women were least satisfied with family life when the man had the final say and most satisfied when they made decisions jointly. As can be seen in the regression analysis in Table 4.11, after controlling for a wide range of other factors, both male and female respondents were less satisfied with family life when either partner controlled spending autonomously and female respondents were also less satisfied when decisions varied. Finally, as can be seen in Table 4.12, after controlling for a wide range of other factors, satisfaction with family life was also a crucial predictor of both men's and women's overall happiness with life in general: the more satisfied respondents were with family life, the happier they were with life in general (Vogler, Lyonette and Wiggins, 2008).

Table 4.11: Selected Multiple Linear Regression Estimates for Satisfaction with Family Life for Male and Female Respondents in Couple Relationships in Britain, in 2002

	Beta	*t*
Male respondents		
Adjusted R² = 0.04; Std. Error .768		
(Constant)		17.775***
35–54 years old (vs 55+)	−0.144	−2.1**
Female-dominated decisions (vs joint decisions)	−0.103	−2.1**
Male-dominated decisions (vs joint decisions)	−0.095	−2.0**
Female respondents		
Adjusted R2 = .08; Std. .9488		
(Constant)		15.413***
Female-dominated decisions (vs joint decisions)	−0.203	−4.4***
Varying decisions (vs joint decisions)	−0.121	−2.7***
Living in a childless married relationship (vs married with children)	−0.149	−2.5**
Male dominated decisions (vs joint decisions)	−0.108	−2.4**
Living in a childless cohabiting relationship (vs married with children)	−0.105	−2.0**

Notes: This table shows, for example, that on average a male respondent living in a household in which the female partner makes important decisions about buying things for the home is approximately 10% less satisfied with family life than a male respondent living in a household in which decisions are made jointly.

***p < 0.01; **p < 0.05. Parameter estimates are only shown for estimates with *t* ratios <2.0 for a full model, which includes a set of dummy variables for decision-making, age, relationship status, social class, and who earns more, as well as covariates for total household income and ideologies/discourses of women's traditional responsibilities for family life. The reference categories for the remaining predictors are entered in parentheses.

Source: ISSP 2002; Vogler, Lyonette and Wiggins (2008).

Table 4.12: Selected Multiple Linear Regression Estimates for Happiness with Life in General, for Male and Female Respondents in Couple Relationships in Britain, in 2002

	Beta	*t*
Male respondents		
Adjusted R2 = .43 Std. Error .6453		
(Constant)		
Satisfaction with family life	0.505	11.1***
Satisfaction with job	0.300	6.3***
Living in a childless cohabiting relationship		
(vs married with children)	0.107	2.1**
Female respondents		
Adjusted R^2 = .592 Std. Error . 5743		
(Constant)		.908
Satisfaction with family life	0.694	18.8***
Satisfaction with job	0.207	5.8**

Notes: This table shows, for example, that on average a male respondent who is very satisfied with family life is approximately 50% happier with life in general than one who is very dissatisfied with family life.

***$p < 0.01$, **$p < 0.05$. Parameter estimates are only shown for estimates with t ratios <2.0 for a full model, which includes a set of dummy variables for decision-making, age, relationship status, social class, and who earns more, as well as covariates for total household income, ideologies/discourses of women's traditional responsibilities for family life, satisfaction with family life, and satisfaction with job. The reference category for relationship status is entered in parentheses.

Source: ISSP 2002; Vogler, Lyonette and Wiggins (2008).

CONCLUSION

This chapter has attempted to compare the similarities and differences between different subcategories of cohabiting and married couples, in terms of the financial aspects of their relationships. I would like conclude by highlighting our main findings and drawing out their implications for policy debates about whether cohabitation should be treated more like marriage for legal purposes.

Despite the limitations of the data, our analysis indicates that whether couples were cohabiting or married was strongly related to the financial aspects of their relationships, but in different ways among different subcategories of cohabiting couples. Cohabiting parents tended to be poorer than married parents, less likely to be living on income from paid work and more likely to be living in social housing, although they were similar to low-income married parents in that they were more likely to pool money, simply to make ends meet (Goode, Callender and Lister, 1998). As Burgoyne (2008) points out, these findings support calls for future legal regulation of cohabiting partnerships to take a functional approach (see Smart and Stevens, 2000; Barlow, 2008).

In contrast, however, respondents in childless and post-marital cohabiting unions were more likely than their married counterparts to both be in full-time employment, but less likely to own their own homes, and less likely than married couples with two full-time incomes to pool money; however, contrary to Giddens (1992), they were just as likely to be characterised by gender inequalities in power over expenditure decisions and access to personal spending money, favouring the higher earner, usually the man. Moreover, when either men or women made autonomous decisions about spending, both male and female partners were less satisfied with family life, as well as with life in general, than those who made joint decisions. Rather than being in the vanguard of shifts towards more egalitarian and radically democratic 'pure relationships' (Giddens, 1992), couples in these unions may therefore operate at least partly on the basis of free market forces (that is, equity rather than equality), resulting in considerable inequalities between individuals in the same relationship, as well as bigger differences perceived between his and her relationship than among comparable married couples, despite the decline of traditional discourses of male breadwinning and the increasing importance of co-provisioning (Burgoyne and Lewis, 1994; Vogler, Brockmann and Wiggins, 2008). These findings can therefore be seen as strengthening Smart and Stevens' (2000) argument that after a period of living together, when cohabiting unions continue for a period of time and start to slide into marriage by another name, the law should also treat childless cohabitants more like married couples, in order to protect the more economically vulnerable partner, providing there was some sort of opt-out for those couples where both partners wished to dissent and make their own arrangements.

Finally then, our analysis indicates that, apart from the different legal ties, one of the biggest differences between different subcategories of cohabiting and married couples, at least in the UK, is probably money. Moreover, the financial and legal aspects of intimate relationships are likely to be closely bound up with each other. In a society characterised by gender inequalities in both earnings and responsibilities for caring, the risks of cohabitation for women may not just be those of property rights, but also that cohabitation may now be providing an increasingly important context for the persistence of old inequalities.

BIBLIOGRAPHY

Barlow, A (2008) 'Cohabiting relationships, money and property: the legal backdrop' 37 *Journal of Socio-economics* 502.

Barlow, A, Duncan, S, Jones, G and Park, A (2005) *Cohabitation, Marriage and the Law* (Oxford, Hart Publishing).

Beck, U and Beck-Gernsheim, E (1995) *The Normal Chaos of Love* (Cambridge, Polity).

Becker, G (1993) *A Treatise on the Family* (London, Harvard University Press).

Blumstein, P and Schwartz, P (1983) *American Couples: Money Work and Sex* (New York, William Morrow).

Brines, J and Joyner, K (1999) 'The ties that bind: principles of cohesion in marriage and cohabitation' 64 *American Sociological Review* 333.

Burgoyne, CB (1990) 'Money in marriage: how patterns of allocation both reflect and conceal power' 38 *The Sociological Review* 634.

—— (2008) 'Introduction: Special issue of the household economy' 37 *Journal of Socio-economics* 455.

Burgoyne, CB and Lewis, A (1994) 'Distributive justice in marriage: equality or equity?' 4 *Journal of Community and Applied Social Psychology* 101.

Burgoyne, CB and Morison, V (1997) 'Money in remarriage: keeping things simple—and separate' 45 *Sociological Review* 363.

Burgoyne, CB, Clarke, V, Reibstein, JR and Edmunds, AE (2006) '"All my worldly goods I share with you"? Managing money at the transition to heterosexual marriage' 54 *The Sociological Review* 619.

Davis, JA and Jowell, R (1989) 'Measuring national differences: an introduction to the International Social Survey Programme' in R Jowell, S Witherspoon and L Brook (eds), *British Social Attitudes: Special International Report* (Aldershot, Gower).

Eekelaar, J and Maclean, M (2003) 'Marriage and the moral bases of personal relationships' in M Maclean (ed), *Family Law and Family Values* (Oxford, Hart Publishing).

Elizabeth, V (2001) 'Managing money, managing coupledom' 49 *The Sociological Review* 389.

Ellingsaeter, AL (1998) 'Dual Breadwinner Societies: Provider Models in the Scandinavian Welfare States' 41 *Acta Sociologica* 59.

Ermisch, J (2005) 'The puzzling rise of childbearing outside marriage' in AF Heath, J Ermisch and D Gallie (eds), *Understanding Social Change* (Oxford, Oxford University Press).

Ermisch, J and Francesconi, M (2000) 'Patterns of household and family formation' in R Berthoud and J Gershuny (eds), *Seven Years in the Lives of British Families* (Bristol, The Policy Press).

Fleming, R (1997) *The Common Purse* (Auckland, NZ, Auckland University Press).

Gallie, D (1988) *The Social Change and Economic Life Initiative: An Overview* (Oxford, Nuffield College).

General Household Survey (2004) *Living in Britain: Results from the 2002 GHS* (London, HMSO).

Giddens, A (1992) *The Transformation of Intimacy* (Cambridge, Polity Press).

Goldthorpe, J (1987) *Social Mobility and Class Structure in Modern Britain* (Oxford, Clarendon Press).

Goode, J, Callender, C and Lister, R (1998) *Purse or Wallet?* (London, Policy Studies Institute).

Heimdal, KR and Houseknecht, S (2003) 'Cohabiting and married couples' income organisation: approaches in Sweden and the United States' 65 *Journal of Marriage and the Family* 525.

Hertz, R (1986) *More Equal Than Others* (California, CA, The University of California Press).

—— (1992) 'Financial affairs: money and authority in dual earner marriage' in S Lewis, D Izraeli, and H Hootsmans (eds), *Dual Earner Families* (London, Sage).

Holtermann, S, Brannen, J, Moss, P and Owen, C (1999) *Employment, Lone Parents and the Labour Market. Results from the 1997 Labour Force Survey and Review of Research* (Sheffield, Employment Service, ESR23).

Jamieson, L, Anderson, M, McCrone, D, Bechhofer, F, Stewart, R, and Li, Y (2002) 'Cohabitation and commitment: partnership plans of young men and women' 50 *The Sociological Review* 356.

Kiernan, KE (2003) 'Unmarried parenthood: new insights from the Millennium Cohort Study' 113 *Population Trends* 26.

Kiernan, KE and Estaugh, V (1993) *Cohabitation* (London, Family Policy Studies Centre).

Kirchler, E, Rodler, C, Holzl, E and Meier, K (2001) *Conflict and Decision Making in Close Relationships* (Hove, The Psychology Press).

Layard, R (2006) *Happiness* (London, Penguin).

Lewis, C, Papacosta, A and Warin, J (2002) *Cohabitation, Separation and Fatherhood* (York, The Joseph Rowntree Foundation).

Lewis, J (2001) *The End of Marriage* (Cheltenham, Edward Elgar).

McRae, S (1993) *Cohabiting Mothers* (London, Policy Studies Institute).

McRae, S (1997) 'Household and labour market change: implications for the growth of inequality in Britain' 48 *British Journal of Sociology* 384.

—— (1999) 'Introduction: family and household change in Britain' in S McRae (ed), *Changing Britain* (Oxford, Oxford University Press).

Nyman, C (1999) 'Gender equality in "the most equal country in the world"? Money and marriage in Sweden' 47 *The Sociological Review* 767.

—— (2003) 'The social nature of money: meanings in Swedish families' 26 *Women's Studies International Forum* 79.

Nyman, C and Reinikainen, L (2002) 'Equality, Dependency, and Independence in Swedish Couples', Paper presented at the American Sociological Association meeting, Chicago, IL.

Pahl, J (1989) *Money and Marriage* (Basingstoke, Macmillan).

—— (2005) 'Individualisation in couple finances: who pays for the children' 4 *Social Policy and Society* 381.

Pickford, R (1999) *Fathers, Marriage and the Law* (London, Family Policy Studies Centre).

Rake, K (2000) *Women's Incomes Over the Lifetime* (London, HMSO).

Rake, K and Jayatilaka, G (2002) *Home Truths* (London, Fawcett Society).

Roman, C and Vogler, C (1999) 'Managing money in British and Swedish households' 1 *European Societies* 419.

Shove, E (1993) 'Accounting for power: formal financial systems and domestic power' in G Dunne, R Blackburn, and J Jarman (eds), *Inequalities in Employment, Inequalities in Home Life*, Conference Proceedings for the 20th Cambridge Stratification Seminar, University of Cambridge 9–10 September, Sociological Research Group, Faculty of Social and Political Sciences.

Singh, S (1997) *Marriage Money* (St Leonards, Australia, Allen and Unwin).

Singh, S and Lindsay, J (1996) 'Money in heterosexual relationships' 32 *The Australian and New Zealand Journal of Sociology* 57.

Smart, C and Stevens, P (2000) *Cohabitation Breakdown* (London, Family Policy Studies Centre).

Smock, P and Manning, W (1997) 'Economic circumstances and marriage' 34 *Demography* 331.

Summerfield, C and Babb, P (2003) 'Households and Families' in *Social Trends 33* (London, HMSO).

Sutton, L, Cebulla, A and Middleton, A (2003) *Marriage in the Twenty-first Century*, CRSP 482 (Cardiff, Care for the Family).

Taylor, M (2000) 'Work, non-work, jobs and job mobility' in R Berthoud and J Gershuny (eds), *Seven Years in the Lives of British Families* (Bristol, The Policy Press).

Taylor, MF (ed), with Bryce J, Buck, N and Prentice-Lane, E (2005) *British Household Panel Survey User Manual Volume A* (Colchester, University of Essex).

Tennant, R, Taylor, J and Lewis, J (2006) *Separating from Cohabitation: Making Arrangements for Finances and Parenting* (London, Department of Constitutional Affairs), www.dca. gov.uk/research/resrep.htm.

Treas, J (1993) 'Money in the bank: transaction costs and the economic organisation of marriage' 58 *American Sociological Review* 723.

Treas, J and Widmer, E (2000) 'A multi-level analysis of financial management in marriage for 23 countries' in J Weesie and W Raub (eds), *The Management of Durable Relations* (Amsterdam, Thela Thesis).

Vogler, C and Pahl, J (1993) 'Social and economic change and the organisation of money within marriage' 7 *Work, Employment and Society* 71.

—— (1994) 'Money, power and inequality within marriage' 42 *The Sociological Review* 263.

Vogler, C, Brockmann, M and Wiggins, RD (2006) 'Intimate relationships and changing patterns of money management at the beginning of the twenty-first century' 57 *The British Journal of Sociology* 454.

Vogler, C, Lyonette, C and Wiggins, RD (2008) 'Money, power and spending decisions in intimate relationships' 56 *The Sociological Review* 117.

Vogler, C, Brockmann, M and Wiggins, RD (2008) 'Managing money in new heterosexual forms of intimate relationships' 37 *Journal of Socio-economics* 552.

White, L and Rogers, S (2000) 'Economic circumstances and family outcomes: a review of the 1990s' 62 *Journal of Marriage and the Family* 1035.

Winkler, A (1997) 'Economic decision making by cohabitors: findings regarding income pooling' 29 *Applied Economics* 1979.

Zelizer, V (1989) 'The social meaning of money: special monies' 92 *American Journal of Sociology* 342.

—— (1994) *The Social Meaning of Money* (New York, Basic Books).

5

Financial Practices in Cohabiting Heterosexual Couples

A Perspective from Economic Psychology

CAROLE BURGOYNE AND STEFANIE SONNENBERG*

INTRODUCTION

THE INCREASING PREVALENCE of couples living together outside legal marriage has given rise to a growing body of research on cohabitation. As the present volume demonstrates, it has also raised a variety of policy concerns and opinions on whether and how the law should be changed to deal with a cohabiting couple's finances and property when their relationship ends. It seems essential to gain a better understanding of cohabitants' relational (ie interpersonal) as well as financial practices. The need for more accurate, in-depth information regarding the latter is especially pertinent in the light of *Stack v Dowden*.[1] This case set a legal precedent for establishing the property rights of a cohabiting couple on separation by taking into account whether the couple had arranged their finances jointly or separately during their relationship. In the particular case of *Stack v Dowden*, the absence of a joint bank account seems to have been taken as evidence that the couple had never operated as a single financial unit, and had never intended an equal split of the equity in their property. As a result, the existence of joint versus separate bank accounts may now be seen as one important marker of a couple's *intentions* regarding the division of their assets when their relationship ends.

The specific findings we discuss later suggest that psychological—or perceived—ownership of money and property may be a better indication of intentions than whose name is actually on a bank account. Although there has been a steady

* Our grateful thanks go to the Nuffield Foundation and the Economic and Social Research Council (ESRC) for their contributions to the funding of our research. Thanks also to Dr KJ Ashby for her valuable assistance with the ESRC-funded study, and to David Routh for drawing our attention to some recent literature on the psychology of ownership.
[1] [2007] UKHL 17.

growth of interest in the intra-household economy, it is only recently that studies have begun to compare the relational and financial practices of cohabiting and married couples (for example Singh and Lindsay, 1996; Vogler, 2005; Ashby and Burgoyne, 2008; also, Vogler, chapter four, this volume). Other forms of partnership are also being explored, such as same-sex relationships (Clarke, Burgoyne and Burns, 2006; Burns, Burgoyne and Clarke, 2008) and 'living apart together' couples, or 'LATS' (Duncan and Phillips, 2008). This chapter explores the issues from the perspective of economic psychology. The first section offers a brief review of earlier findings on money management in married and cohabiting relationships. We then discuss more recent evidence from two in-depth studies of money management in cohabiting couples. We conclude this chapter by reflecting on whether there is any compelling information about financial practices that might serve as potential markers of a couple's intentions.

RESEARCH ON HOUSEHOLD MONEY MANAGEMENT

There has been a growing interest among social scientists in the issue of how household members organise, manage and control their financial resources. Researchers interested in this issue tend to describe and distinguish between households (or couples) by attempting to classify their systems of money management. The prototypical classification of systems originated in the work of Jan Pahl (1980, 1989). She was one of the first researchers in the UK to investigate the financial practices of married couples in detail. Her findings demonstrated that—contrary to earlier assumptions of a common standard of living within households—women and children could be living in relative poverty even when household income was more than adequate. Her typology of common practices of household money management have been described elsewhere (see Vogler, chapter four, this volume); in this chapter we will be adopting the same typology, but investigating how a given case may be assigned to one category on the basis of certain information but to quite another if different information is provided.

The specific ways in which money is allocated and managed within the household can have far-reaching consequences for individual well-being, since these different systems of money management have implications for access to and control of resources—and, of course, for individual spending. For example, if a couple decide to keep their incomes completely separate and split the cost of bills and other expenditure 50/50, this can lead to a situation in which the lower-paid partner has significantly less disposable income once their share of essential expenses has been covered.

In the UK, the normative definition of marriage is that of an equal partnership in which resources are shared (Burgoyne and Routh, 2001; Sonnenberg, Burgoyne and Routh, submitted). Since large-scale surveys show that around half the UK married population report use of a pooling system (Vogler and Pahl, 1994; Pahl, 1995), the norm of sharing in marriage appears to be well founded. However, in-depth, qualitative studies reveal that even when money is said to be pooled in a joint account, it is often the case that the main (or sole) earner retains overall control and has the final say on how the money will be used (Burgoyne, 1990). There is an important distinction between money *management* (which may give the household manager circumscribed power over finances) and overall (executive) *control* (Pahl, 1989). For example, it is possible for an ostensibly joint management system to be operated as either a whole wage or housekeeping allowance system if the main earner retains a high level of overall control of the 'pooled' money, thus obliging the other partner to seek permission before making any non-routine expenditure. The right to control one's earnings can therefore militate against equal sharing, even when partners are aiming for equality (Burgoyne and Lewis, 1994). Given that men are still (typically) the main earners when a couple have dependent children (see Scott and Dex, chapter three, this volume), one consequence is that non-earning mothers are especially prone to inequality in access to and control over money. Moreover, those women who do earn tend to spend a greater proportion of their incomes (compared with their partners) on the family (Vogler and Pahl, 1994; Pahl, 1995). Such gender-related asymmetries in responsibilities and access to resources in heterosexual marriage also mean that women and children are often found to be at greater risk of poverty following relationship breakdown (Maclean, 1987).

Two key issues arise from previous research on household money management that are important in the current context. First, as already indicated, the use of a joint bank account—and the inferred intention of equal sharing underlying its use—does not always, in practice, translate into equal access to and control over the household's financial resources. There are many other factors that potentially undermine equal access to common resources—including those of a psychological nature—that might remain concealed. Also, as we have argued elsewhere, whilst the above classification of money management provides a very useful tool to differentiate between households, the day-to-day interactions or practices on which these systems are based tend to disappear from view (Sonnenberg, 2008). This adds another layer of complexity which is often manifested in the difficulties qualitative researchers encounter when trying to map these systems onto people's in-depth accounts of their monetary practices (for example Nyman, 1999; Sonnenberg, 2008).

Secondly, the manner in which the household's financial resources are managed and controlled is often intimately linked with the traditional division of labour (especially in the case of the whole wage and housekeeping allowance systems). The key findings in this area of research indicate that financial control and access to monetary resources within marriage can be highly gendered, thus contributing to the persistence of financial inequalities in the domestic sphere. Since past research has tended to focus on married couples, there is a certain degree of difficulty (both theoretical and empirical) in trying to disentangle financial management issues from notions of marital power (Vogler, 1998). In other words, our current understanding of household money management is not independent of our conceptions of marriage. This echoes the finding that, for some, the institution of marriage is seen as linked inextricably with the traditional division of labour and the demarcation of different gender roles. In fact, there is some evidence to suggest that, for an increasing minority of people, marriage has indeed become almost synonymous with the perpetuation of gender inequalities (Elizabeth, 2000, 2001), and that contributes, at least in part, to the current rise in cohabitation rates. So what do we know so far about cohabitants and their financial practices?

RESEARCH ON COHABITATION

Although there is a growing literature on heterosexual cohabitation, thus far our knowledge of unmarried couples' finances remains limited. Researchers have instead focused on the duration and stability of cohabiting relationships, studying the relationship between cohabitation and marital breakdown (Teachman and Polonko, 1990; Axinn and Thornton, 1992; Lillard, Brien and Waite, 1995) and examining notions of 'commitment' and 'equality' in cohabitation relative to marriage (Brines and Joyner, 1999). Cohabiting relationships have tended to be described as inherently less stable than marriage and, if they turn into marriage, as more likely to end in divorce (Morgan, 1999). For these reasons, cohabitation is often seen as lying in the 'contingent' position on Smart and Stevens' (2000) commitment dimension. The latter runs from 'no commitment' at one end to 'mutual commitment' (often considered more typical of marriage) at the other. Commitment is more likely to be 'contingent' in shorter-term cohabitations, and where there has been little explicit planning (or else uncertainty) about the future of the relationship. Such couples may stay together only as long as they feel that the relationship is working. In contrast, mutual commitment describes partners who are committed not only to each other, but also to the maintenance of the relationship. However, recent studies have suggested that, contrary to earlier findings, cohabitation prior to marriage (or remarriage) does not necessarily lead to less stable marriages (Lichter, 2008; Teachman, 2008; Sassler, Cunningham and Lichter, 2009).

Whilst comparisons between marriage and cohabitation have been made along various dimensions, thus far 'money' has not figured much as a topic for comparative interest. To date, two key findings have emerged. In comparison with their married counterparts, cohabitants seem more likely to view each other as individual economic entities (Blumstein and Schwartz, 1983) and, as a consequence, partners are more likely to keep their incomes separate (Blumstein and Schwartz, 1983; Heimdal and Houseknecht, 2003; Singh and Lindsay, 1996). Some researchers claim that, in the transition from cohabitation to marriage, the symbolic meaning(s) of money are transformed. According to this view, 'cohabitation money' is characterised by its calculability and separateness whilst 'marriage money' is assumed to be joint and consequently eludes calculation or quantification (Singh and Lindsay, 1996). Thus, Singh and Lindsay define marriage money as 'domestic, personal, private, nebulous and joint' (at 58) and cohabitation money as 'separate, individual, calculable and accountable' (at 61).

However, recent studies of newly married couples suggest that individualised ways of dealing with money are not necessarily confined to cohabitation. Many married couples also start off with an independent management or partial pooling system, although some of these move towards a more collective view of their finances during the first year of marriage (Burgoyne et al, 2006, 2007). The interesting analytic issue that arises in relation to this finding is whether it is possible to establish the degree to which this move towards pooling is determined by marriage per se (that is, by normative or ideological factors) as opposed to broader economic factors (such as obtaining a joint mortgage or the birth of a child).

In sum, while previous findings on the treatment of money in cohabitation provide a useful starting point, several important issues require further examination. First, much of our knowledge on cohabitation has come from research with non-British samples. Secondly, the methodological robustness of some studies is questionable, either because of their broad-brush approach to qualitative analysis (see for example Singh and Lindsay, 1996) or because of their use of very rough quantitative measures to examine household financial organisation (see for example Heimdal and Houseknecht, 2003). Thirdly, the *reasons* for the apparent tendency amongst cohabitants to keep their incomes separate have so far remained under-explored. For instance, whilst the laws applying to cohabitants differ from country to country (Barlow, 2004; Barlow and James, 2004; Kiernan, 2004) and the subjective or normative meanings attached to cohabitation can vary across (Heimdal and Houseknecht, 2003), as well as within, national contexts (Le Bourdais and Lapierre-Adamcyk, 2004), we know little about how these broader factors might impinge on cohabitants' actual money management practices. For instance, cohabitants' greater tendency, on average, to keep their incomes separate is often interpreted as indicating their lack of commitment to the relationship—in other words, financial practices are seen as a reflection of relationship factors. However, it is equally plausible that keeping their finances separate is simply a pragmatic or rational response to an uncertain legal context and is thus independent of relationship factors such as commitment. Also, there is some evidence to suggest that some cohabitants keep their individual accounts in an attempt to avoid the inequalities they associate with marriage (for example Elizabeth, 2001)—although this does not render cohabitants immune to financial inequalities which can still creep into the relationship, especially when there is a disparity in earnings. One of the most important questions then that arises from these issues is: *who* cohabits? In other words, how should we conceptualise cohabitation?

Until recently, the literature was dominated by two main approaches to cohabitation. Some researchers conflated cohabitation and marriage and treated them as essentially the same (for example Stocks, Diaz and Hallerőd, 2007). Others regarded married and cohabiting couples as inherently different—but homogeneous—groups (for example Singh and Lindsay, 1996; Amato, 2006). However, as critics have pointed out (for example Barlow et al, 2005; Vogler, Brockmann, and Wiggins, 2008), cohabitation is frequently used as an umbrella term for very different kinds of couple relationship. For instance, cohabitation can be: (a) transitory, evading long-term commitment; (b) part of the courtship process or a 'prelude' to marriage; (c) a 'trial marriage'; and (d) an ideological alternative to marriage in an attempt to circumvent traditional gender stereotypes (Sassler, 2004). Thus, more recent research has begun to examine some of the important differences between sub-groups of cohabitants (for example Lichter and Qian, 2008; Teachman, 2008; Vogler, Brockmann and Wiggins, 2008; Sassler, Cunningham and Lichter, 2009).

FINANCIAL PRACTICES IN COHABITATION: RECENT EVIDENCE

In the two studies to be described here, we aimed to sample a range of different kinds of cohabitants. The remainder of this chapter draws on data from the qualitative phases of these studies and delineates some of the key factors that shape a couple's financial arrangements. We also consider the extent to which different financial arrangements allow for inferences regarding a couple's underlying intentions. First, however, we provide some background details for the studies on which the present findings are based.

Research Background

Study 1 was funded by the Nuffield Foundation and primarily aimed to gauge how far attitudes and behaviours had changed since 2000, when the 'common law marriage myth' was first identified (Barlow et al, 2001, 2005). The study took place following attempts by the (now) Ministry of Justice to raise legal awareness amongst cohabitants through its *Living Together* Campaign.[2] The findings contributed to the Law Commission's consultation on possible reform of the law governing cohabiting couples (Law Commission, 2007). The study comprised a quantitative survey as well as a qualitative interview component. Interviewees were selected from a nationally representative survey in England and Wales which, in turn, formed part of the British Social Attitudes Survey 2006 (see Barlow et al, 2008). Forty-eight cohabitants (including ex-cohabitants who had recently separated from their partners) were interviewed, 27 women and 21 men (some of these were interviewed together as a couple). Participants' ages ranged from 25 to 60 years, with a mean cohabitation period of six years. Thirty-one participants had children, 24 with their current or most recent partner. Twenty-six participants owned their homes (16 of these in joint names) and eight were living in rented accommodation. The interview questions were open-ended and aimed to elicit a detailed account of respondents' financial arrangements. The interviews also explored participants' attitudes and behaviours in relation to the broader legal and financial implications of being in a cohabiting relationship.

Study 2 was funded by the ESRC and also comprised a quantitative survey as well as a qualitative interview component. The overall objective of this study was to examine cohabitants' financial practices in the context of their broader views

---

[2] See www.advicenow.org.uk/livingtogether.

on money, relationships (for example on cohabitation versus marriage; commitment; the perceived quality of their relationship and so on), gender (for example traditional gender roles) and the law (in terms of both their awareness of and views on various legal aspects relating to cohabitation). This study specifically aimed to sample the views of a wide range of cohabitants—not just those who had 'drifted' into cohabitation. The interview participants, in particular, were selected on the basis of their self-definition as 'non-traditional' (that is, they were ambivalent about or rejected marriage for ideological reasons). In-depth interviews were designed to explore how these couples organised their finances, and to elicit cohabitants' views on marriage, as well as their understandings of their financial rights and responsibilities in the light of possible law reform. Both partners were interviewed in 16 couples, the majority giving a joint interview. Participants' ages ranged between 24 and 60 years, with a mean cohabitation period of six years. Nine couples had children from either the current or a past relationship. Eight couples owned their house in joint names, two had homes owned by one of the partners, and six couples were living in rented accommodation or had some other accommodation arrangement.

Money Management

We begin with the way that the couples from both studies organised and managed their financial resources. As a first analytic step, we drew on cohabitants' references to external markers (for example, type and number of bank accounts, name(s) on bank accounts) and attempted to map these onto an adjusted version of Pahl's typology of household money management. The results are summarised in Table 5.1, column 1. Across the two interview samples, only 7 out of 52 couples had a joint account and no separate accounts for managing all of their finances. These couples were categorised as operating a joint pool. The majority of couples were either classified as using a partial pooling or independent management system. Those initially categorised as independent management had separate, individual accounts only, whereas those classed as partial pooling had at least one joint account in addition to using individual accounts. One couple appeared to be operating an allowance system where one partner had virtually no income and was being given a sum for 'housekeeping' by her partner. Two couples had such

Table 5.1: Classification of Household Money Management

	Based on Bank Accounts	Based on Day-to-day Practices
Independent management	20	16
Partial pool	22	22
Allowance	1	0
Joint pool	7	11
Whole wage	0	3
Other	2	0

complex financial arrangements that it was not possible to classify them on the basis of their bank accounts, so they were initially labelled 'other'. At first glance, given the relatively high incidence of independent management and partial pooling, this sample seems to echo previous findings on the prevalence of individualised finances in cohabiting couples (for example, Elizabeth, 2001; Vogler, Brockmann and Wiggins, 2006).

However, the picture changed to some degree when we examined couples' day-to-day financial practices more closely. As a second analytic step, we paid close attention to interviewees' detailed descriptions of how their financial resources were controlled, managed, accessed and used in the context of their everyday lives. For instance, we focused on who actually had access to the various bank accounts, the extent to which negotiation seemed to take place before using money from these accounts, which accounts partners drew on for their personal spending and which accounts were used to pay for the mortgage or rent, the household bills, leisure spending, or holidays, and savings or debts. We also paid attention to more subtle indicators, such as the extent to which money was *perceived* as a common resource (see the discussion below on 'perceived ownership'). This resulted in the re-classification of the financial arrangements of a number of cohabitants and is summarised by the figures provided in column 2 of Table 5.1.

As mentioned earlier, qualitative researchers are often faced with some difficulty when trying to classify a couple's financial arrangements (for example, should one focus on bank accounts, or try to arrive at a synthesis that takes into account the details of everyday practices and an individual's sense of entitlement to certain financial resources?). In re-categorising cohabitants' financial arrangements on the basis of their everyday practices, we employed the criteria outlined below.

Joint Pool

Where a couple only had accounts in joint names, identification of a joint pooling system was generally straightforward. However, we also classified a couple as operating a joint pool (in practice) if their individual incomes were initially paid into a joint account and only small transfers were made into individually named accounts for personal spending (or conversely, if individual incomes were paid into individual accounts but were then for the most part transferred into a joint account). For example, Julie and Adam[3] used a variety of separate and joint accounts but essentially treated all income as a collective resource. Julie had experienced problems in the past when bank cards had been lost or cancelled and she explained that they kept their separate accounts as a safeguard so that each partner would always have access to some funds:

> **Well then Adam lost his credit card and they cancelled all my cards and so I couldn't get any money out of the joint account. And I was a bit freaked**

---

[3] Pseudonyms are used for all interview respondents.

'cause [...] I hadn't quite closed down my private account at that point [...]. It just made me realise that if I'd shut it down, neither of us would have been able to get any money out at all. And that could be really quite disastrous if you're on holiday or something [...]. So it was purely that. So it's not because we didn't want to share our money. (Julie, Joint Pool)

However, having an account in joint names was not a necessary condition for allocating a couple to the joint pool category. Some couples had no joint account, but were defined as pooling in practice because their day-to-day treatment of money made it clear that it was regarded by both partners as a common 'pot' or resource (see the section on 'perceived ownership' for more details). For example, some couples relied on internet banking and only used individual accounts. However, in some of these cases, the individual accounts were functionally equivalent to joint accounts in so far as partners knew each other's passwords and could therefore not only access but also control and manage the funds in these accounts. In other words, these couples operated a virtual pool in practice.

In general, the number of cohabiting couples who operated a joint pool in practice was greater than suggested by the existence (or absence) of joint bank accounts alone. Interestingly, the majority of couples who pooled all their financial resources also had dependent children.

Partial Pooling

Partial pooling was differentiated from the joint pool by the lesser extent to which resources were pooled in the context of a couple's everyday monetary practices. Cohabitants in this category typically paid their individual incomes into their own personal accounts. Each partner then transferred a certain amount (usually agreed upon and fixed) into a joint account; partners either contributed equal or different amounts. The money transferred to the joint account tended to be used mainly for covering household expenses, whereas any money left in partners' individual accounts was treated as separate, that is, as their own affair.

However, when exactly does a joint pool become a partial pool (and vice versa)? There was a considerable degree of overlap between these two systems of money management, and their boundaries often remained blurred, depending on how much money each partner had left in their personal account once they had contributed to joint expenses. In some cases, this actually amounted to only a small sum for personal spending. In practice, therefore, such couples were very similar to those operating a joint pool where a little money for personal spending (for example, for individual leisure activities or buying gifts) is 'siphoned off' into separate accounts (or where there is an agreed sum of money that each partner can spend from the joint account). Partial pooling also came close to the joint pool in many cases where partners tried to compensate for the existence of large income disparities between them by contributing to the joint pool in proportion to their individual earnings. In such cases, the higher earner also tended to pay more towards joint leisure activities, holidays, and so on. The way in which these couples approached money was qualitatively different from cohabitants who contributed equal amounts to the joint account regardless of the income differences existing between them. The latter were less concerned with equality in terms of achieving equal *outcomes* (that is, having equal amounts of money to spend or save after paying for joint expenses) and tended to emphasise equality in terms of making strictly equal *contributions*, often referred to as 'paying one's own way'. These couples were also more inclined to emphasise autonomy over their own income (which rendered their financial arrangements functionally similar to independent managers, who operate a 50:50 split of all expenses).

On the whole, the classification of couples' financial arrangements is by no means a straightforward matter—especially if we take their day-to-day monetary practices into account. Determining the degree to which finances are pooled often involves a qualitative judgement and the boundaries between different types of arrangements can be rather blurred. The money management categories presented in Table 5.1 also omit important details, such as how the individual partners in the non-pooling couples contributed to joint expenses and leisure. As already indicated, the independent management and partial pooling categories can be subdivided further to take account of *equal*, *proportional*, or simply *different* contributions. It could be argued that those who contributed on a proportional basis (that is, according to income when there was a large disparity in earnings) operated far less like separate financial entities than those who contributed on a strict 50/50 basis. Thus, the findings summarised in Table 5.1 suggest that when couples' everyday monetary practices are taken into account, some cohabitants' finances are merged to a greater extent than might be inferred from their banking arrangements. As will be described in more detail below, a couple could have a variety of individual and joint accounts, but might treat all of the money as a pooled resource, moving funds around in a flexible way to deal with different expenses as they arise. If we combine the joint pooling couples with those who had some degree of pooling, this amounts to nearly two-thirds of our interviewees. Why then did so many cohabitants keep at least one bank account in their individual name?

Reasons for Using Separate Accounts

The main reasons provided by interviewees for using separate accounts included practical or pragmatic factors and concerns about keeping some financial control and independence. We provide some examples of these reasons below. However, for some couples it was immaterial whether the money was in a separate or joint account, as all of their money was regarded as a common resource. This reason relates to perceived ownership of money and will be discussed below.

Pragmatic Reasons
When partners move in together, they often start off with just their individual accounts. This also tends to be the case for couples who cohabit for a short period

before getting married, or who only start living together after the wedding (Burgoyne et al, 2006). Opening a joint account takes a certain amount of planning and negotiation, and for many couples in our sample, it had simply been inertia and the perceived effort of getting both names on the account that had prevented them from doing so. There were other logistic factors as well: for example, one respondent's partner was often away for long periods at a time (for work-related reasons) and it was therefore more practical for them to keep their individual accounts. Some couples also wanted to take advantage of having access to two overdrafts, and in some cases (as already mentioned) the shared use of online management facilities made it unnecessary to have a physical joint account. For example, some couples like Jeff and Tina kept their separate accounts, rather than pooling *all* of their incomes in the joint account, in order to use the money in these accounts 'as reserve, really, in case we lose our cards [...] emergency money' (Jeff and Tina, Partial Pooling).

Jeff explained that one of the individual accounts would shortly be used as his business account, even though both partners agreed that this was still joint money:

If I have to keep a certain amount of money in my business account, what I'll have to do is get some money that we've got and put it into the business account. (Jeff, Partial Pooling, his emphasis)

In some cases, one of the partners was responsible for child support payments to a previous partner, and kept a separate account to avoid implicating their current partner in these payments. When one partner had significant debts which they regarded as their own responsibility to repay, it was often easier to manage this by having a separate account. Finally, some respondents indicated that their partners were 'feckless' or 'hopeless' with money, which would have made a total pooling system more difficult to manage. Related to the last point, although not necessarily because one partner lacked management skills, some participants decided against having just one joint account because they felt they would have to be constantly checking and monitoring each other's spending to make sure that there was still enough left in the account each month to cover the bills. Using their individual accounts for any additional or personal expenditure meant that it was easier to control and manage their resources. For example, Kim and her partner had separate accounts for savings and control of spending:

Everything goes through the joint account for the bills, so we want to always make sure there's money there [...] that's the only reason the sole accounts are used. It's not any other reason. (Kim, Partial Pooling)

Control and Independence

The right to decide about the disposal of one's own income is usually taken for granted unless a couple has agreed to set that entitlement aside (Burgoyne and Lewis, 1994). However, as we have seen, even when all money is pooled physically, it is not always easy to ignore where it has come from. This often means that the earner has more 'say' in how 'household' money will be used, a phenomenon that applies to marriage as much as to any other form of partnership (Burgoyne,

1990). Some of our participants valued the control and independence afforded by keeping their money separately. There were some cases where one partner would have preferred to have a joint account, but the other would not contemplate it as they would lose control of their own earnings. For others, it was less about control and more about financial 'identity' and, sometimes, privacy. Having a fund of money that was separate from the general pool meant that one partner was able to surprise or 'treat' the other from time to time. For example:

> One of the things that's nice is also to treat the other without having a bill come in and everyone knowing exactly how much it cost. Sometimes it's nice to buy Kyla a bunch of flowers without having her being able to look at the account and know exactly how much they cost. I can take it directly out of my account and go 'there you are, darling' whether it cost £10 or £30 and no one is none the wiser. (Matt, Partial Pooling)

On the whole, the reasons respondents provided for keeping some accounts in individual names seemed to have very little to do with their commitment, future intentions or expectations regarding their relationship. We discussed earlier the way that pooling all income can give a misleading impression of equal sharing. Here, we have seen the converse—namely that having separate accounts does not necessarily imply that partners are operating as separate financial entities. Of course, some respondents did value the independence and autonomy afforded by individually-named accounts. But that was not the whole story. As indicated above, some couples *saw* all their money as being 'in one pot', making it irrelevant whose name was on the account. Thus, a key factor in the way that money is treated is not necessarily whose *name* is *on* the account, but whose *money* is *in* the account. In other words, as we discuss in the following section, one of the main determinants of a couple's financial arrangements is psychological—or *perceived*—ownership of money.

PERCEIVED OWNERSHIP: WHOSE MONEY IS IT?

In our interviews with couples in all kinds of intimate relationships, it has proved impossible to establish how household money is controlled and managed without reference to a range of subjective factors, including notions of entitlement and responsibility as well as ownership. A full discussion of these is beyond the scope of the present chapter. Instead, we focus on the notion of ownership, as this seems to underpin the individual or collective treatment of financial resources.

Perceived ownership is far from being an all-or-nothing concept—it seems to have many shades of meaning, and these are not fixed, but subject to negotiation, change, and redefinition over time. Moreover, the notion of perceived ownership would appear to be distinct from the concept of legal ownership in a number of important ways. For example, one partner may have no independent earnings or other assets to contribute to the relationship, but the couple might nevertheless decide that the income of the other partner 'belongs' psychologically to them both, with both partners having an equal right to decide how it will be used. A similar point can be made about other sources of money, such as an inheritance: some couples would regard this as an individual asset—solely the affair of the inheritor—whereas others would see such a windfall as 'family money' for the couple to own and use collectively. Perceived ownership thus captures the degree to which partners are seen as, and feel themselves to be, psychologically entitled to access and control money, regardless of its source.

Perceived ownership matters in so far as it tends to interact in rather subtle ways with the meanings and expectations couples attach to their relationships. At one extreme, there are couples who have a strong ideological commitment to collective ownership of all resources, seeing this as an expression of their identity as a couple. At the other extreme, there are couples for whom the maintenance of a sense of individual identity and ownership take priority within the relationship— and this may be reflected in their financial arrangements. Between these two extremes are many positions, depending on the specific assets in question and the couple's circumstances. For example, even when money is clearly perceived as separately owned, most cohabitants emphasised that the money would be used for collective purposes if the need arose.

In addition, couples' views of ownership are likely to evolve in response to changes in the nature of their relationship, or to economic changes such as movements into and out of employment, the birth of a child, or the purchase of a house. Of course, partners may not always agree about these matters and may have to reach a compromise in order to avoid conflict—keeping at least some money separately can be a conflict-avoidance strategy (Burgoyne et al, 2007).

Earlier studies of money in newly-weds and cohabiting couples have traced some of the ways that perceived ownership translates into practice (Burgoyne et al, 2006; see also Ashby and Burgoyne, 2008). Burgoyne et al (2006) identified a broad dimension of ownership of household income with three main categories: distinct (or separate), blurred (or transitional), and shared (although of course, in practice, the demarcation of each category shades into the next). The same degrees of perceived ownership became apparent in the ways in which cohabitants interviewed for the current studies talked about money in their relationships.

Distinct Ownership

Those with 'distinct' ownership perceptions were more likely to be using partial pooling or independent management, although not all couples using these forms of management regarded money in this way (see also Ashby and Burgoyne, 2008). Most of the couples in this category drew a clear distinction between money that had been earmarked for collective expenses (especially when this was held in a joint account) and money that was considered to be individually owned. For example:

I'd earned my money and that were my savings and he earned his money and if he wished to save or spend it that was his, up to him. But as long as our bills were paid, what we did with our own money was up to us. (Alexa, Independent Management)

Blurred Ownership

When a couple seemed to be in the process of moving from distinct towards collective ownership, or when partners differed in their perceptions (on which see further Vogler, chapter four, this volume), they were categorised as having 'blurred' ownership. For example, Mark, who was the main earner in his relationship, would have preferred to pool all their money in a single joint account. He felt that he and Sally should have equal amounts of personal spending money after the bills had been met. However, Sally would not have been comfortable with that arrangement, feeling that Mark should retain a higher degree of individual ownership and control of hiss income than he seemed to want for himself:

> No. The way I look at it is that Mark goes to work and earns a salary, and that is really nothing to do with me [...] once our bills and our mortgage and everything is paid at the end of the month, whatever's left over is his and I shouldn't have an entitlement to that. (Sally, Partial Pooling)

Shared Ownership

As the label implies, those with shared ownership tended to treat all resources collectively, and generally did not distinguish between money from different sources in terms of their individual access to and control over finances. Whereas those with a 'distinct' view of ownership exercised a great deal of autonomy over spending from their personal accounts, this group were more likely to discuss most of their spending decisions. Not surprisingly, shared ownership was typical of those who managed all their household finances by means of a joint account, but it was not limited to such couples. For example, Natalie and her partner had separate accounts but her view of money came very close to the idea of pooled resources that is normatively associated with marriage:

> We don't feel a need to have a joint bank account [...] because even if we've got two separate accounts, we consider it as his money is my money and my money is his money. (Natalie, Partial Pooling)

Similarly, Sarah and her partner had income from a variety of sources (employment, joint business ventures, and property). They had many accounts, some in individual names and some in joint names (so we had initially categorised their system as 'Other'). Yet the degree to which *none* of this money was perceived as individually owned was striking. Sarah expressed almost a sense of nostalgia for the time when she did have some money that she could call her own:

> I miss perhaps having my own income that is very clearly mine [...] that I used to spend without even thinking about [...] it's nice not to think about it

Table 5.2: Clues to Shared versus Distinct Ownership

	Shared	Distinct
Money	Seen as 'all in one pot' (even if in separate accounts)	Differentiation of 'mine', 'yours' and 'ours'
Assets/Inheritance	Defined as 'ours' to decide about—to save or use	Emphasis on separate ownership and individual decision-making
Debts	Joint responsibility—repaid from collective funds	Individual responsibility for repayment
Who pays?	Irrelevant who pays (for leisure, house deposit, etc)— 'it's all the same money'	Careful tally kept of who spends on what
Borrowing from partner	Money 'given' to partner and not repaid	Small amounts of money lent and assiduous repayment
The meaning of trust	Openness and transparency (no secrets)	Trusting one's partner to pay their share

in that—any income is both of ours […] but equally it's perhaps—you've lost something as well in that you don't have your own personal money. (Sarah, Joint Pool)

However, Sarah seemed ambivalent about changing the way they organised their finances just so that she would have some identifiable spending money:

I mean probably my only thing is it would be quite nice to have a certain— We've talked about it but we've just never bothered really—[…] having your own money, a little bit of your own money to, to spend and—Not because I'd want to not tell about it but just to feel it's mine to spend. You know sort of takes out some of the fun of buying presents for each other and things if it's all your joint money and that sort of thing. So—but we've never really found a way to do that so, so that's the only thing that we could try and do something about. But it just seems a bit false, just to make me sort of psychologically feel a bit better about it [laughs].

Additional clues about perceived ownership emerged from specific financial practices as well as in response to direct questions in the interviews. Table 5.2 provides a summary of some of the key indicators.

CONCLUSIONS

In this chapter, we have indicated that trying to understand how couples deal with money is a potential minefield. We have seen that a joint account may not always mean equal sharing in practice, and that individual accounts may not necessarily signify separate financial entities or a lack of commitment. It appears that many couples keep individual accounts for a whole host of reasons that may have little to do with their commitment to each other or to the relationship. Thus, our findings suggest that there may be problems associated with relying solely on 'external' markers, such as named bank accounts, as a proxy for couples' legal intentions. However, we have also touched on the thorny issue of how we, as researchers or policy-makers, can obtain an accurate picture of couples' financial practices. The findings presented here were from qualitative research that typically draws on a wide range of in-depth, detailed information. Such an approach is valuable in exposing some of the hidden complexities of a potentially sensitive topic such as money. We found that financial practices involve issues of, for example, ownership and control, fairness, responsibility and entitlement, and that the ways in which couples navigate this terrain can be complex, idiosyncratic and fluid.

At the same time, qualitative research is often costly and time-consuming, and does not allow us to make broader claims about the general population of cohabitants. Survey research also raises difficulties—albeit of a different kind. If, as is sometimes the case, survey data are derived from no more than a few simple questions, then some caution is needed in taking people's responses at face value. In some of our earlier studies, for example, we found that when people are asked about money issues, they do not simply treat these questions as factual probes into financial matters but also as probes into the quality of, or commitment to, their relationships; in other words, people interpret and respond to such questions in specific ways (Sonnenberg, 2008). Given that marriage, and harmonious relationships more generally, tend to be discursively defined by notions of sharing and collectivity, there may be a tendency to over-report 'pooling', or at least to under-report arrangements perceived as counter-normative, such as independent management (Sonnenberg, 2008). In addition, some participants may say they operate a pooling system because of the way they *think* about money in the relationship, rather than because they actually have a joint account.

Perceived *ownership*, on the other hand, may provide a more nuanced picture of the ways that couples deal with money in practice—and perhaps a better indication of their financial intentions. Another possible indication is the extent to which partners try to compensate for any large disparities in income by, for example, contributing to collective expenses on a proportional basis. This may be more important from the point of view of 'intentions' than whether or not they actually have a joint account. However, as we have indicated, unless a couple have decided that all resources really are collective, it is not easy to get a handle on day-to-day practices or perceptions. Couples have to negotiate and decide on many details of money management, such as what counts as a collective or individual expense (for example, buying and running a car that might be used by one of the partners); whether savings and debts are to be a collective or individual responsibility; how they should pay for shared and individual leisure activities; whether or not small sums 'borrowed' from one's partner should always be repaid, and so on. Couples also vary widely in the extent to which partners consult each other about spending from their various accounts; whether they keep precise records of each partner's spending or contributions; and whether they try to balance up the latter over time.

Most researchers now accept that the notion of 'marriage money' versus 'cohabitation money' is too simplistic. We would also argue that having separate accounts does not necessarily indicate a lower degree of commitment: Pahl (2005) observes that the more individualised ways of managing money seem to be gaining in popularity, and many of the married couples in Burgoyne et al's (2007) study still exhibited degrees of separation in their finances a year after the wedding. Thus, we may be witnessing more of a cohort effect than a marital status effect. As mentioned earlier, it is also important to consider different types of cohabitants: for example, perceptions of ownership among long-term cohabitants are likely to differ in significant ways from those among cohabitants in shorter-term relationships, and factors such as having children or buying a house may have a greater impact than getting married (see Vogler et al, 2008).

So, finally, is there a compelling answer to the conundrum of how to gauge intentions? The problem—as we have demonstrated—is that perceptions of ownership and entitlement (and hence intentions) concerning the treatment of money and property are not only difficult to ascertain at any particular point in time, they are also likely to change in the course of a relationship. Partners who start off with separate accounts may come to see their resources in a more collective way but may not get around to opening a joint account. The converse may also apply: Ashby (2007) found that many of her cohabiting participants took a more or less collective view of money and property during the lifetime of the relationship, and would wish the law to treat their property accordingly if one partner died. However, if the relationship were to end in separation, then many felt that individual ownership should prevail. It is arguable that if the law permitted it, many divorcing partners might also like to make such a distinction (cf *Stack v Dowden*, and see further Douglas, Pearce and Woodward, chapter seven, this volume). Thus, there are questions about the extent to which 'intentions' can be reliably assessed or given legal weight in the absence of a specific contract. The business of gauging people's intentions on the basis of certain financial arrangements is fraught with difficulty and thus may not always result in a fair judgement.

BIBLIOGRAPHY

Amato, P (2006) 'Strengthening marriage as a context for child development: Lessons learned from intervention approaches', Keynote presentation at International Academy of Family Psychology Meeting, Cardiff, Wales, *Family Psychology in Context: Linking Research, Policy, and Practice*, 10–13 June.

Ashby, KJ (2007) 'Money, cohabitation and the law: A story of diversity', Unpublished PhD thesis, University of Exeter.

Ashby, KJ and Burgoyne, CB (2008) 'Separate financial entities? Beyond categories of money management' 37 *Journal of Socio-economics* 458.

Axinn, WG and Thornton, A (1992) 'The Relationship Between Cohabitation and Divorce: Selectivity or Causal Influence?' 29 *Demography* 357.

Barlow, A (2004) 'Regulation of cohabitation, changing family policies and social attitudes: a discussion of Britain within Europe' 26 *Law and Policy* 57.

Barlow, A and James, G (2004) 'Regulating marriage and cohabitation in 21st century Britain' 67 *Modern Law Review* 143.

Barlow, A, Duncan, S, James, G and Park, A (2001) 'Just a piece of paper? Marriage and cohabitation in Britain' in A Park, J Curtice, K Thomson, L Jarvis and C Bromley (eds), *British Social Attitudes: The 18th Report—Public policy, social ties* (London, Sage).

—— (2005) *Cohabitation, Marriage and the Law: Social Changes and Legal Reform in the 21st Century* (Oxford, Hart Publishing).

Barlow, A, Burgoyne, C, Clery, E and Smithson, J (2008) 'Cohabitation and the law: Myths, money and the media' in A Park, J Curtice, K Thomson, M Phillips, M Johnson, and E Clery (eds), *British Social Attitudes: The 24th Report* (London, Sage).

Blumstein, P and Schwartz, P (1983) *American Couples: Money, Work, and Sex* (New York, William Morrow).

Brines, J and Joyner, K (1999) 'The Ties that Bind: The Principles of Cohesion in Cohabitation and Marriage' 64 *American Sociological Review* 333.

Burgoyne, CB (1990) 'Money in marriage: how patterns of allocation both reflect and conceal power' 38 *The Sociological Review* 634.

Burgoyne, CB and Lewis, A (1994) 'Distributive Justice in Marriage: Equality or Equity?' 4 *Journal of Community and Applied Social Psychology* 101.

Burgoyne, CB and Routh, DA (2001) 'Beliefs about financial organisation in marriage: The "Equality Rules OK" norm?' 32 *Zeitschrift fuer Sozialpsychologie* 162.

Burgoyne, C, Clarke, V, Reibstein, J and Edmunds, AM (2006) '"All my worldly goods I share with you"? Managing money at the transition to heterosexual marriage' 54 *The Sociological Review* 619.

Burgoyne, CB, Reibstein, J, Edmunds, A, and Dolman, V (2007) 'Money management systems in early marriage: factors influencing change and stability' 28 *Journal of Economic Psychology* 214.

Burns, ML, Burgoyne, CB and Clarke, V (2008) 'Financial affairs? Money management in same-sex relationships' 37 *Journal of Socio-economics* 481.

Clarke, V, Burgoyne, CB and Burns, ML (2006) 'Just a piece of paper? A qualitative exploration of same-sex couples' multiple conceptions of civil partnership and marriage' 7 *Lesbian and Gay Psychology Review* 141.

Duncan, S and Phillips, M (2008) 'New families? Tradition and change in modern relationships' in A Park, J Curtice, K Thomson, M Phillips, M Johnson and E Clery (eds), *British Social Attitudes: The 24th Report* (London, Sage).

Elizabeth, V (2000) 'Cohabitation, Marriage, and the Unruly Consequences of Difference' 14 *Gender and Society* 87.

—— (2001) 'Managing money, managing coupledom: A critical examination of cohabitants' money management practices' 49 *The Sociological Review* 368.

Heimdal, KR and Houseknecht, SK (2003) 'Cohabiting and Married Couples' Income Organization: Approaches in Sweden and the United States' 65 *Journal of Marriage and Family* 525.

Kiernan, K (2004) 'Redrawing the boundaries of marriage' 66 *Journal of Marriage and Family* 980.

Law Commission (2007) *Cohabitation: The Financial Consequences of Relationship Breakdown*, Law Com No 307 (London, TSO).

Le Bourdais, C and Lapierre-Adamcyk, É (2004) 'Changes in Conjugal Life in Canada: Is Cohabitation Progressively Replacing Marriage?' 66 *Journal of Marriage and Family* 929.

Lichter, DT and Qian, Z (2008) 'Serial cohabitation and the marital life course' 70 *Journal of Marriage and the Family* 861.

Lillard, LA, Brien, MJ and Waite, LJ (1995) 'Premarital Cohabitation and Subsequent Marital Dissolution: A Matter of Self-Selection?' 32 *Demography* 437.

Maclean, M (1987) 'Households after divorce' in J Brannen and G Wilson (eds), *Give and Take in Families* (London, Allen & Unwin).

Morgan, P (1999) *Marriage-Lite: The Rise of Cohabitation and its Consequences* (London: Institute for the Study of Civil Society).

Nyman, C (1999) 'Gender equality in "the most equal country in the world"? Money and marriage in Sweden' 47 *The Sociological Review* 766.

Pahl, J (1980) 'Patterns of money management within marriage' 9 *Journal of Social Policy* 313.

—— (1989) *Money and Marriage* (London, Macmillan).

—— (1995) 'His money, her money: Recent research on financial organisation in marriage' 16 *Journal of Economic Psychology* 361.

—— (2005) 'Individualisation in couple finances: who pays for the children?' 4 *Social Policy and Society* 381.

Sassler, S (2004) 'The process of entering into cohabiting unions' 66 *Journal of Marriage and Family* 491.

Sassler, S, Cunningham, A and Lichter, DT (2009) 'Intergenerational patterns of union formation and marital quality' (available online) *Journal of Family Issues*, doi:10.1177/0192513X09331580.

Singh, S and Lindsay, J (1996) 'Money in heterosexual relationships' 32 *Australian and New Zealand Journal of Sociology* 55.

Smart, C and Stevens, P (2000) *Cohabitation Breakdown*, Joseph Rowntree Foundation Report (London, Family Policy Studies Centre).

Sonnenberg, SJ (2008) 'Household financial organization and discursive practice: managing money and identity' 37 *Journal of Socio-economics* 533.

Sonnenberg, SJ, Burgoyne, CB and Routh, DA (submitted) 'Income Disparity and Norms Relating to Intra-household Financial Organisation: Some Experimental Evidence from the UK'.

Stocks, J, Diaz, C and Hallerőd, B (eds) (2007) *Modern Couples Sharing Money, Sharing Life* (Basingstoke, Palgrave MacMillan).

Teachman, J (2008) 'Complex life course patterns and the risk of divorce in second marriages' 70 *Journal of Marriage and Family* 294.

Teachman, JD and Polonko, KA (1990) 'Cohabitation and Marital Stability in the United States' 69 *Social Forces* 207.

Vogler, C (1998) 'Money in the household: some underlying issues of power' 46 *The Sociological Review* 687.

—— (2005) 'Cohabiting couples: rethinking money in the household at the beginning of the twenty first century' 53 *The Sociological Review* 1.

Vogler, C and Pahl, J (1994) 'Money, power and inequality within marriage' 42 *The Sociological Review* 263.

Vogler, C, Brockmann, M and Wiggins, RD (2006) 'Intimate relationships and changing patterns of money management at the beginning of the twenty-first century' 57 *British Journal of Sociology* 455.

—— (2008) 'Managing money in new heterosexual forms of intimate relationships' 37 *Journal of Socio-economics* 552.

6

The Role of Personal Relationships in Borrowing, Saving and Over-indebtedness

A Life-course Perspective

ANDREA FINNEY[*]

INTRODUCTION

I N THE PUBLIC perception, financial difficulties are commonly linked with relationship breakdown. Empirical research supports this notion, with relationship breakdown implicated as both contributing to and resulting from over-indebtedness. However, it is an over-simplification to view this connection in isolation from other factors. Instead, it should be seen in the wider context of relationship formation and duration, taking into account associated life events such as setting up home, becoming a parent and raising a family. Moreover, over-indebtedness is related to the accumulation and reduction of savings and consumer borrowing over the life-cycle, both of which also vary with relationship status and progression.

This chapter examines patterns of consumer borrowing,[1] saving and over-indebtedness (used interchangeably with 'financial difficulties') over the life-course, with a special focus on the formation and dissolution of intimate relationships and child-rearing. Unlike other chapters in this volume, which consider the treatment of money at the intra-household level, the focus here is on how these aspects of personal finance vary in the general population and the extent to which they are influenced by family status and transitions in relationships. It presents a synthesis

---

[*] I am very grateful to Professor Elaine Kempson for her assistance with mapping the existing body of research literature and for commenting on earlier drafts of the chapter.

[1] Only unsecured credit use is considered here, since there is insufficient scope additionally to consider mortgage borrowing in any great detail. It is worth noting, however, that among home owners there is considerable overlap between mortgage and unsecured borrowing (Finney, Collard and Kempson, 2007).

of findings from the existing body of qualitative and quantitative empirical research from the UK (and some new analysis of national survey data),[2] drawing together what are often separate studies of borrowing, saving, and financial difficulties. It is clear that sums of money that are saved or borrowed are susceptible to changes in household structure brought about by relationship formation and dissolution if they are measured at the household level. To avoid this problem, studies that examine the role of life events on saving and borrowing tend to do so at the individual level: a share (usually a half) of any savings or outstanding borrowing held jointly with a partner is assigned to each partner and combined with any they own in their sole name.

The first parts of this chapter present an overview of levels of borrowing, saving, and over-indebtedness in the general population; the extent to which they can be explained by personal and socio-economic characteristics; and the reasons for borrowing and saving and routes into over-indebtedness. Factors associated with family or relationship status are not necessarily the *main* determinants of financial difficulties, but are important nonetheless. The final substantive section therefore focuses on the role of three aspects of personal relationships: partnering, raising a family, and relationship breakdown. Whilst relationship breakdown is itself implicated in over-indebtedness, there are also complex links between borrowing, saving, and over-indebtedness and the formation of relationships and raising a family. The findings underline the importance of recognising the complex influences on the financial well-being of people facing relationship breakdown, some of which relate to the life-course of relationships.

CONSUMER BORROWING

Credit use is widespread. Three quarters of all households in Great Britain have unsecured credit facilities and about a half of households owe money on these—excluding credit and store cards that are paid off in full each month—at any point in time (Kempson, 2002). This is equivalent to a third of all individuals (Kempson, McKay and Willetts, 2004).

Given the large increases in the aggregate sums owed in consumer credit that have been recorded in Bank of England statistics, it is perhaps surprising that the proportion of the adult population using unsecured credit has remained quite stable over the last decade or so (Kempson, McKay and Willetts, 2004).[3] Instead, it is the average amounts owed by the credit users that have increased: from £890 in 1995 to £2,000 in 2000, and to £3,100 in 2005.[4] Consequently, credit use is

---

[2] The new analysis uses data from the British Household Panel Survey (BHPS)—University of Essex, Institute for Social and Economic Research, British Household Panel Survey: Waves 1–15, 1991–2006 [computer file], 3rd edn, Colchester, Essex: UK Data Archive [distributor], June 2007. SN: 5151.

[3] The figure for 2005 is based on new analysis of the 2005 BHPS.

[4] Source: BHPS: median values. These figures have not been adjusted to take account of inflation.

becoming increasingly concentrated among a small number of heavy credit users (Tudela and Young, 2003), a conclusion evidenced by the finding that the highest-owing 10 per cent of credit users owed £5,000 or more in 1995 and £9,000 or more in 2000 (Kempson, McKay and Willetts, 2004), rising to £15,000 or more in 2005.[5] Still, heavy borrowing remains rare. According to recent surveys, only about one in 20 people were heavy credit users on a range of measures, these being five or more active credit commitments, owing £10,000 or more, and spending more than a quarter of income on repaying consumer credit (Kempson, 2002; Finney, Collard and Kempson, 2007).

Although the proportion of people who are active credit users has remained stable over time, it is not necessarily the same individuals who are borrowing from one snapshot in time to the next. There is, in reality, a fair degree of movement in and out of the credit market. Whilst a third of people had outstanding credit commitments in 1995 and 2000, only a quarter had commitments in both years. Between the two years similar proportions of the population switched from being non-borrowers to borrowers (14 per cent) as switched from being credit users to credit-free (16 per cent) (Kempson, McKay and Willetts, 2004).

With this in mind, it is helpful to examine the key correlates and drivers of borrowing found in previous research.

Correlates of Consumer Borrowing

The existing body of evidence indicates that age, family structure, and housing tenure are important determinants of consumer borrowing, whilst attitudes are especially powerful predictors of heavy borrowing. However, and perhaps surprisingly, income-related characteristics are not directly important for explaining patterns of credit use.

Age has been found to be the single most important predisposing factor in credit use (Berthoud and Kempson, 1992; Finney, Collard and Kempson, 2007). Research has shown consistently that borrowing climbs sharply from a relatively low rate among those in their late teens to early 20s to a peak during the late 20s to mid 40s, declining fairly steeply thereafter (Berthoud and Kempson, 1992; Cox, Whitley and Brierley, 2002; Kempson, 2002; Del-Rio and Young, 2005a; Finney, Collard and Kempson, 2007). Heavy credit use charted a similar course with age, and these patterns held true when other characteristics that were also related to borrowing were controlled in regression analysis (Finney, Collard and Kempson, 2007).

However, the role of attitudes towards spending, borrowing, and saving are also important for understanding variations in credit use (Berthoud and Kempson, 1992; Livingstone and Lunt, 1992). A person's attitude was, in fact, the strongest

---

[5] The figure for 2005 is based on new analysis.

independent predictor of heavy credit use in the recent study (Finney, Collard and Kempson, 2007).

The relationship between economic factors and borrowing are not so straight-forward. Full-time workers were among those most likely to be active credit users, and this relationship remained strong when other factors were controlled (Finney, Collard and Kempson, 2007). However, although people living in higher-income households were disproportionately more likely to use credit, this relationship disappeared when other factors such as age, employment status, and family structure were taken into account. An earlier study similarly found that disposable income did not predict having any borrowing, although it did predict the amount owed among active credit users (Livingstone and Lunt, 1992). It seems, therefore, that while measures linked to income appear to relate to the propensity to use credit, the relationship is in fact spurious.

In contrast, credit use is strongly correlated with housing tenure: mort-gagors were the most likely of all housing tenure groups to use credit, fol-lowed by people who rented privately, while outright owners had the lowest propensity of all (Kempson, 2002; Waldron and Young, 2006; Finney, Collard and Kempson, 2007). Housing tenure largely reflects socio-economic status, not least because only the poorest of families are normally eligible for social housing in the UK. However, home ownership also reflects life-stage: aspiring young adults who have yet to raise sufficient capital for a deposit are largely excluded from the market (most rent privately and therefore have a higher average level of credit use), whilst home owners who are nearing retirement age are typically moving towards outright ownership; mortgagors therefore are concentrated in the middle, family years. Despite this, the relationship of housing tenure with credit use remained strong when these other charac-teristics were controlled (Berthoud and Kempson, 1992; Finney, Collard and Kempson, 2007).

Mortgage borrowing itself has been described as a 'gateway' to unsecured bor-rowing (Pannell, 2002; Bridges and Disney, 2004). This appears to operate at two levels; the first being that lenders are often more willing to lend to people who own their homes; and the second the fact that the financial commitment involved in buying (and furnishing) a home can place greater demands on the budget, resulting in the increased need for unsecured borrowing.

Finally, turning to the influence of marital status and family structure, existing research evidences a potent but complex relationship. Overall, people who were married or cohabiting were more likely to use credit than those who were not (Whyley and Kempson, 2000b). Credit use—and heavy credit use—was also com-mon among families with dependent children, reflecting the increased demands on the household budget at this stage of the life-course, and this was true of lone parents and couples alike (Kempson, McKay and Willitts, 2004; Finney, Collard and Kempson, 2007). In another study, the effect of children was less on the pro-pensity to borrow per se and more on the ability to keep up with the repayments (Berthoud and Kempson, 1992).

In a recent study (Finney, Collard and Kempson, 2007), there were slightly lower rates of credit use among lone parents compared with two-parent families, but these were compensated for by higher rates of borrowing from friends and family among lone parents. In addition, the pattern was reversed, with lone parents being at the higher end of the range when other socio-demographic characteristics were controlled in multivariate analysis. This suggested that, once the lower incomes of lone-parent families are taken into account, their rates of borrowing are high relative to other groups. In another study, lone mothers were the household type most likely to owe money on consumer credit commitments, although they owed smaller amounts on average (Westaway and McKay, 2007), which is likely to indicate lower affordability of credit or credit-worthiness for this group. Lone parents spent a relatively large amount of their income on servicing borrowing (19 per cent), compared with couples with children (14 per cent) and all low-income groups (11 per cent). In short, the propensity to use credit by lone-parent families reflects the multiplicative effect of being single and having dependent children, but is often suppressed by the relative low socio-economic status of these groups (Kempson, McKay and Willitts, 2004).

Reasons for Borrowing

Traditional economic theories describe consumer borrowing as one of the tools used to help smooth consumption over the life-course in the face of changing levels of income. In reality, the explanations for borrowing are more complex. At its broadest, people use consumer credit either to help to relieve financial difficulties or to help service spending on a consumer lifestyle (Berthoud and Kempson, 1992). As already seen, attitudes play an important role, with some people seemingly predisposed to borrow whilst others prefer instead to save or to cut back on spending. Finally, credit use also depends on supply factors as well as demand (Berthoud and Kempson, 1992).

A more recent quantitative study found little evidence of borrowing for reasons of hardship (Finney, Collard and Kempson, 2007). This is not surprising, given strong economic growth in the UK over the course of the previous decade or so. Instead, for the majority of borrowers, credit was helping to augment a consumer lifestyle, although for some heavy credit users this was contributing to a need to borrow to get by. Moreover, the qualitative element of the same study found that the distinction between 'needs' and 'wants' was blurred for many consumers. For some young people, they were virtually indistinguishable, whilst some parents appeared to have restructured wants to justify them as needs, especially where spending on their children was concerned. Finally, 'pre-requisite' borrowing, for example to buy a home or to fund further or higher education, predominantly affecting young adults and people in their family years, emerged as an important feature, appearing in some cases to result in people borrowing far more than they needed for these purposes (Finney, Collard and Kempson, 2007).

Underpinning these findings was evidence of a marked shift in attitudes towards borrowing in recent years. Quantitative research previously observed only a gradual softening of attitudes since the 1970s (Berthoud and Kempson, 1992; Kempson, 2002). However, the recent qualitative study found that, among some young people in particular, borrowing was considered a way of life; credit was even perceived by a core minority as 'money' to which they had a right (Finney, Collard and Kempson, 2007).

Finally, putting aside the extraordinary conditions that took hold in the lending markets during the second half of 2008,[6] there has been little evidence of widespread constraint in the supply of consumer credit in recent years (Finney, Collard and Kempson, 2007). Where constraint occurs it is most common among the most marginalised sectors of society, especially those on the lowest incomes (HM Treasury, 2007). The aforementioned qualitative study identified strong pressures to consume and a preparedness to borrow to do so, especially among young adults and those in the middle, child-rearing years. Moreover, people were aware of, and often responding to, the relative cheapness and availability of credit (Finney, Collard and Kempson, 2007).

SAVING

Whilst levels of borrowing have reached a record high, the savings ratio is low and has been falling in recent years. A substantial minority of households do not have any liquid savings, and few who do have large sums saved. Routine, active saving is also the preserve of the minority and is seemingly more sporadic than consumer borrowing.

National survey data show that about one in three families had no savings whatsoever in 2007 (32 per cent), and a further one in five (19 per cent) had less than £1,500 in savings (DWP, 2007).[7] At the other end of the spectrum, one in five families (22 per cent) had more than £10,000 saved in liquid assets (DWP, 2007). In terms of depositing money, fewer than a half of individuals said they had put money into savings or investments in the previous 12 months in 2000, and the average amount deposited was £100 per month (McKay and Kempson, 2003). Forty-three per cent of individuals said they currently saved from their regular income, three in ten reported saving regularly, and just under two in ten reported saving for no specific purpose.

Rates of saving account-holding by families remained relatively steady between 1998 and 2006 on aggregate (DWP, 2007). People from most age groups had

---

[6] The February 2009 Bank of England statistical release shows that the monthly amounts lent in unsecured consumer credit declined during the second half of 2008 and into 2009 although the total amount outstanding at January 2009 (over £230 million) was about £7.5 million higher than at January 2008 (Bank of England, 2009).

[7] Here, a 'family' refers to a single adult or couple living as married and any dependent children.

similar levels of account-holding compared with their peers 10 years previously. The one exception was people born between 1975 and 1985. This group—most of whom were in their 20s in 2006—had lower rates of saving than the cohort born in the previous 10-year period (DWP, 2007).

At the level of the individual, however, saving was more variable. Among adults interviewed every year between 1991 and 2000, only eight per cent reported saving every year and 16 per cent did not save in any year (McKay and Kempson, 2003). Analysis across each consecutive pair of years found that about a fifth of non-savers in any given year were saving the next year and about three in ten savers were not saving the following year.

Savings provide a cushion during times of financial strain. However, the ability to save assumes surplus income to expenditure. The remainder of this section explores the characteristics of savers and the drivers of saving and considers the overlap between saving and borrowing.

Correlates of Saving

Compared with consumer borrowing, economic characteristics are much more important for explaining saving. However, family and relationship factors also play a role, especially in regular saving, and many kinds of life events coincide with starting and ceasing saving.

Economic factors explain much of the variation in saving behaviour. Even after taking into account the effect of other characteristics, the likelihood of saving at all in the 2000 BHPS (British Household Panel Survey) was much higher among people reporting to be 'living comfortably' than those who were 'getting by' (McKay and Kempson, 2003). The difference was even more marked compared with those who were finding things quite or very difficult financially. People in full-time employment had the highest odds of saving and, conversely, being in the bottom income quintile independently predicted the lowest rates of saving. There were similar patterns for regular saving. Moreover, when interviews from 10 years of the BHPS were pooled together, enabling the effects of changes in circumstances to be examined whilst controlling for non-changing characteristics, these economic factors were again important (McKay and Kempson, 2003).[8]

The effects of family circumstances—family structure and marital status—on saving at all were largely mediated by economic factors (McKay and Kempson, 2003). There was a clear, independent association of family characteristics with saving regularly, however. Family structure and marital status were independently related to regular saving, although the number of children was not. So, couples without children were most likely to be saving regularly, whilst lone parents, at the other end of the extreme, were least likely to do so, all other things being

[8] Using the 1992 to 2000 BHPS.

equal. Another study confirmed that families with children were less likely than those without children to be able to save £10 a month. Lone parents were especially unlikely to be able to do so, and this was more marked for lone mothers than lone fathers (Westaway and McKay, 2007). Surprisingly, when other factors including the presence of children were controlled, people who were divorced, and, especially, those who were separated, were the most likely of all marital status groups to be saving regularly, while cohabitants were the least likely (McKay and Kempson, 2003).

It would appear contradictory that family and marital status does not predict *any* saving but does predict *regular* saving. One explanation might be that people who are separated or divorced for example, if able or inclined to save at all, place great importance on doing so regularly, whilst childless cohabitants, in contrast, may be saving more sporadically if they are saving at all.

Using data from working-age adults interviewed in consecutive years of the 1991 to 2000 BHPS, researchers explored the links between saving and certain life events (McKay and Kempson, 2003). There were step-increases in the propensity to save between the ages of 21 and 22 and, to a lesser extent, between 29 and 30. Changes in economic indicators such as unemployment, an increase or decrease in earnings, and receipt of a windfall had a strong effect in the expected directions.

Notably, a change in legal marital status and starting and expanding a family were also linked with reductions in saving on various measures (a finding that is explored further below). Across all these life events, wealthier groups were more likely to start saving than lower income groups, and women were more likely to stop saving than men (McKay and Kempson, 2003). The differential effect by gender is likely to reflect, at least in part, the greater tendency for women to cease or reduce paid employment at these times. However, the additional finding that women were less likely to stop saving than men following a drop in earnings, but more likely to stop following a drop in income indicates complexities here that have yet to be fully explored.

Overall, the life events that independently predicted saving cessation among people of working age included—in order of magnitude—unemployment, bereavement, divorce or separation, starting a new family, increasing the family size, and taking out a mortgage. Correspondingly, among other events, divorce and separation, increasing the family size, and becoming unemployed were also associated with a lower likelihood of starting saving, all other things being equal (McKay and Kempson, 2003). The next section explores some of the reasons for this.

Reasons for Saving

Economic factors are clearly important for explaining the propensity to save. Again, however, the picture is more complex: there are important interactions between factors, attitudes play an important role, and when people do save they do it for different reasons.

Previous research found that the interplay between disposable income and life-stage was a key factor in saving behaviour, affecting even the most committed savers. For example, in addition to retirement, settling down and child-rearing were two of the life-stages during which levels of disposable income clearly impacted on saving behaviour (Whyley and Kempson, 2000a).

Attitudes have been found to play an important role in saving behaviour, as they did in consumer borrowing. Previous qualitative research explored the links between saving and spending and found that when people do save they can have different motivations for doing so, falling into two broad camps (Whyley and Kempson, 2000a). Most people find it more satisfying to spend rather than to save; indeed, if they save money up, it is in order to spend it (instrumental savers). Only a minority prefer saving to spending, and save in the long term for reasons of financial security, whether for old age or for no specific reason (rainy day savers).

Four in ten regular savers in the 2000 BHPS were 'rainy day' savers, who were saving reportedly for no specific reason. Among the remaining 'instrumental savers', the most common reason given was for a holiday (22 per cent). Perhaps surprisingly, only a tiny minority of savers (three per cent) reported saving for their children (McKay and Kempson, 2003).

However, previous authors have noted the distinction between the ability to save and the inclination or aspiration to do so, and that these can have conflicting effects on saving behaviour (McKay and Kempson, 2003; NS&I, 2008). Some events make saving more desirable, whilst others may make it more—or less—possible. In some instances, such as was noted by NS&I during the period of rising retail prices and the then threatening economic slowdown in early 2008, saving may be both more desirable and less likely (NS&I, 2008). Parents face a particular dilemma when it comes to saving: having children may increase the inclination to save but reduce the ability to do so. This is borne out by research relating to the Child Trust Fund: a study at its inception found that seven in ten parents anticipated that they would make additional deposits into the accounts (Kempson, Atkinson and Collard, 2006); in fact, only about a quarter of accounts have so far received additional contributions.[9]

Overlaps between Borrowing and Saving

For an individual both to save and to use credit may appear incompatible; and previous authors have described the ways in which they appear to be 'opposites' (Berthoud and Kempson, 1992). Nonetheless, research demonstrates a fair degree of overlap between saving and borrowing by individuals, and that it can be a deliberate strategy.

---

[9] Figures correct as at October 2007. Source: Her Majesty's Revenue and Customs.

New analysis of the 2005 Baseline Survey of Financial Capability (BSFC) showed that the population could be divided into four fairly equal-sized groups based on whether or not they had saved in the previous 12 months and whether or not they had outstanding borrowing: 25 per cent of people had saved in the previous 12 months *and* currently had some level of outstanding borrowing (Kempson, 2008).

Qualitative research among people on low-to-moderate incomes provides explanations for different groups in terms of their saving and borrowing behaviour patterns (Whyley and Kempson, 2000a). People who were savers only were mostly rainy day savers who were resistant to borrowing. Some owned credit cards but settled the balance in full each month, using them as a convenient payment method or to access short-term interest-free credit. This approach enabled these savers to safeguard or delay dipping into their savings. People who were borrowing and not saving were mostly complete non-savers or instrumental saver types. They had positive attitudes towards credit and were not prepared to wait and save up for things they wanted. Often, having committed a large part of income to repaying their borrowing, people in this group could not afford to save.

Concurrent saving and borrowing was often part of a well thought-out strategy and was especially common among single people in their thirties (Whyley and Kempson, 2000b). Savings were often earmarked, whether for a 'rainy day' or for something specific. Consumer credit enabled other needs to be met whilst safeguarding these savings. As such, savings and credit served two different needs. Naturally, the overlap between borrowing and saving diminishes where there are larger sums involved: people with the highest levels of savings were least likely to be using credit, and, conversely, the more credit a person used the less likely they were to have savings or to save regularly (Whyley and Kempson, 2000b).

Net liquid assets—which describe the balance between an individual's liquid assets and their outstanding unsecured credit—fell consistently between 1995, 2000, and 2005 for every age group up to and including people aged 60 to 65 in 2005 (Boreham and Lloyd, 2007). The fall is explained primarily by increases in liquid borrowing, compounded by a small decrease in liquid assets for the younger groups (those aged 16 to 24, 20 to 29, and 25 to 34 in 2005). This was largely a cohort rather than an ageing effect: as each cohort aged, net assets stayed relatively flat, except for older cohorts for whom net assets increased. These findings suggest that it is the younger generations who are increasingly at risk of over-indebtedness.

OVER-INDEBTEDNESS

Over-indebtedness, also referred to as financial difficulties, describes the situation in which a household has insufficient income or other resources to service all their financial commitments on an ongoing basis without jeopardising their basic standard of living (Davydoff et al, 2008). It manifests itself in an inability to keep up with household bills and credit commitments without either having to resort to using credit cards and overdrafts to make those payments or compromising on basic needs such as food or heating. Regardless of the precise measure used, over-indebtedness is a minority experience.

According to the 2005 European Survey of Income and Living Standards, six per cent of UK households had been in arrears on credit, housing or utility payments in the previous 12 months. Eleven per cent of adults in Britain reported difficulties in paying bills to the 2006 Eurobarometer survey (Davydoff et al, 2008).

Despite the dramatic changes in the economy in the intervening years, levels of over-indebtedness were remarkably similar in 2002 as they were in 1989, reflecting the relatively buoyant economies at both points in time. In a survey in 2002, 18 per cent of households in Britain had been in arrears on at least one payment in the previous 12 months (Kempson, 2002) compared with 19 per cent in a similar survey undertaken in 1989 (Berthoud and Kempson, 1992). Additionally, six per cent were in arrears on two or more commitments when interviewed in 2002, whilst in the 1989 survey eight per cent had (any) current arrears that they were worried about.

The 2002 study additionally found that only six per cent of households reported a movement into difficulties and six per cent out of difficulties over the previous 12 months (Kempson, 2002). Despite this, and as the next section explores—along with age, economic status and family structure—changes in circumstances appear especially relevant for explaining variations in over-indebtedness.

Correlates of Over-indebtedness

A recent review of research found consistently that financial difficulties were most common among householders aged under 30 and remained higher than the average for people in their thirties and forties, after which the rate declined steeply with age (Davydoff et al, 2008). Another study found that 25- to 34-year-olds were especially susceptible to debt problems that lasted longer than a year (Balmer et al, 2005).

Previous research suggests that economic factors alone are reasonable indicators of debt problems (Webley and Nyhus, 2001). In the 2002 survey, unemployed householders were especially likely to report financial difficulties, as were lone mothers who were not in work. Compared with the population as a whole, financial difficulties were also twice as common among households headed by a part-time worker and those unable to work through long-term sickness or disability (Kempson, 2002). Among non-pensioners, low household incomes relative to the number of people living in the household ('equivalised income') rather than low income per se predicted over-indebtedness (Berthoud and Kempson, 1992; Kempson, 2002). Finally, home ownership was associated with decreased risk of financial difficulties, independently of other characteristics including income (Kempson, 2002; Kempson, McKay and Willitts, 2004).

Research has shown with some consistency that the likelihood of experiencing over-indebtedness varies by household structure (Davydoff et al, 2008). Married couples were at least risk of over-indebtedness, and this was especially true for a first marriage. In the 2002 study, single adult households under pension age had relatively high risks of financial difficulties, as did two-parent families (Kempson, 2002).

However, the prevalence of arrears was especially high among lone-parent households: nearly a half had been in arrears in the past 12 months, compared with 18 per cent of the population as a whole (Kempson, 2002). These findings are reflected in another national survey, which showed that, of all the family types, lone parents had clearly the highest rates of debt problems, followed by couples with children (Balmer et al, 2005). Previous research indicated that the relationship between lone parenthood and a heightened risk of over-indebtedness requires careful interpretation. The relationship was explained not by lone parenthood per se, but income, age, the presence of children, and a fall in income or relationship breakdown (Berthoud and Kempson, 1992; Kempson, McKay and Willitts, 2004).

The risk of over-indebtedness was especially high among families with younger, or higher numbers of, children (Davydoff et al, 2008). The influence of children has been found to be independently predictive of problem debt in multivariate analysis (see, for example, Berthoud and Kempson, 1992; Webley and Nyhus, 2001; Bridges and Disney, 2004).

Notably, households that had experienced a drop in income in the previous 12 months were at heightened risk of financial difficulties, independently of actual income (Herbert and Kempson, 1995; Kempson, McKay and Willitts, 2004). Households that had experienced a change in family circumstances such as having a baby or relationship breakdown were also at increased risk (Davydoff et al, 2008). Some changes in household structure are likely to be accompanied by a reduction in earnings and/or an increase in household expenditure relative to equivalised income. The birth of a child, in particular, is often accompanied by reduced working hours within a household. Family changes were more strongly related to problems with consumer credit than household bills (Kempson, McKay and Willitts, 2004). Financial shocks are, accordingly, identified as one of the two main causes of over-indebtedness.

Reasons for Over-indebtedness

There are two main routes into over-indebtedness: financial shocks and a persistent low income. Poor money management, over-commitment, and over-spending potentially compound the effects of both of these (Davydoff et al, 2008).

Financial shocks are the most commonly cited reason. For example, in the 2002 survey almost a half of struggling households (45 per cent) reported loss of income as the reason for their situation, while 15 per cent reported a persistent low income (Kempson, 2002). Specifically, almost one in five households reported a drop in income through job loss or redundancy as the reason for their financial difficulties (Kempson, 2002). Another study found that hardly anyone was immune to an income shock—occurring across a broad cross-section of society—and that a third of those who did experience a financial shock experienced financial difficulties as a result (Kempson and Atkinson, 2006).

Notably, however, factors relating to personal relationships also featured highly in the 2002 study. Relationship breakdown was cited as the cause by about one in ten households, either because it resulted in a loss of income (five per cent) or because of debts left by a former partner (four per cent). A further 12 per cent reported that an increase in expenditure was the reason for their difficulties, although the causes of these increases were not specified (Kempson, 2002). Similarly, in a survey of Citizens Advice Bureaux 'debt clients', 20 per cent reported relationship breakdown as a reason for their debt problems, three per cent reported bereavement, including the death of a partner, and the related expenses as a cause, whilst six per cent reported the actions of others, including having borrowed money on behalf of a former partner (Edwards, 2003).

While poverty typically related to difficulties meeting essential utility services payments, financial shocks were more often linked with difficulties repaying consumer credit commitments (Davydoff et al, 2008). Previous authors have noted that manageable credit commitments can become problematic when unexpected events present a shock to income or expenditure (Mitchell, Mouratidis, and Weale, 2005). Studies by the Bank of England have asked people with consumer credit commitments how much of a burden they found making their contracted repayments. Following a financial shock, people with the highest levels of borrowing relative to income were most likely to report finding their repayments a burden, and this effect was stronger the more recent the shock (Del-Rio and Young, 2005a, 2005b). A qualitative study of credit card debt found that a shock to income typically resulted in one of two polarised reactions: either to cut up the credit card to prevent further use, or to begin to depend on it more heavily (Kempson, Bryson and Rowlingson, 1994).

Underlining the link with savings, earlier research found that younger people and those on low incomes faced increased risks of finding credit commitments a burden following a financial shock because they were less likely to have savings to support them (Del-Rio and Young, 2005a, 2005b). A qualitative study concluded that people do not take into account the possibility of a change in circumstances that might lead to a drop in income when taking on credit commitments (National Consumer Council, 2002), although in an exception to this rule, concern about a partner dying did partly explain lower credit use among low-income pensioners (Kempson, Collard and Taylor, 2002).

Finally, researchers have observed that there is rarely a single cause of over-indebtedness (Kempson, Bryson and Rowlingson, 1994; Ford, Kempson and Wilson, 1995; Elliott, 2005). Instead, problems often occur in combination. A national survey in England and Wales noted the co-occurrence of a number of civil justice and social problems with debt problems (Balmer et al, 2005). Among the CAB debt client study mentioned above, multiple—and frequently inter-related—reasons were common (60 per cent), and these often impacted on clients' income and expenditure. In a study of mortgage arrears in Scotland, researchers found that a range of interacting factors such as job loss, relationship breakdown, and health problems were common in repossession cases, whilst those who had only a single problem that was resolved over time were able to recover from arrears and retain their homes (McCallum and McCaig, 2002).

THE ROLE OF RELATIONSHIPS OVER THE LIFE-COURSE

To recap, the preceding discussion indicates that personal relationships and family characteristics play a role in explaining consumer borrowing, saving, and financial difficulties. On the whole, people who were married or living as married were more likely to use credit than those who were not; they were also more likely to be saving (Whyley and Kempson, 2000b). Credit use was common among families with dependent children, and heavy credit use was especially common where two children were present (Kempson, McKay and Willitts, 2004; Finney, Collard and Kempson, 2007).

Although marital status did not relate to *any* saving independently of other factors, it did predict *regular* saving: cohabitants were the least likely to be saving regularly, while divorcees and people who were separated were relatively more likely to be doing so, all other things being equal (McKay and Kempson, 2003). Families with dependent children were less likely to save regularly, all other things being equal (McKay and Kempson, 2003) and were less likely to report being able to save £10 a month (Westaway and McKay, 2007). Increasing numbers of children in the household were independently associated with a decreasing propensity to save (McKay and Kempson, 2003).

Finally, experience of over-indebtedness also varied by marital status, with married couples being least at risk; this was especially true for a first marriage (Davydoff et al, 2008). The presence of children was independently predictive of financial difficulties (see, for example, Berthoud and Kempson, 1992; Bridges and Disney, 2004; Webley and Nyhus, 2001); the risk was especially high among families with a larger number of children and younger children (Davydoff et al, 2008).

However, over and above the effects of current marital and family status, *changes* in these play a role in borrowing, saving, and over-indebtedness. This section considers the relevance of personal relationships, and in particular relationship transitions, to financial circumstances in more detail. The focus turns first to relationship formation (partnering), then to raising a family, and finally to relationship breakdown.

Partnering

The finding that people who are married or living as married are more likely to use credit than those who are not masks important differences within these groups. In the short term, at least, new partnerships appear to have largely negative effects on people's financial circumstances. In the longer term, marriage is associated with lower rates of borrowing and higher rates of saving.

Previous research has shown that single young people still living in the parental home had lower levels of credit use than those who had set up home independently (Ford, 1990; Berthoud and Kempson, 1992; Kempson, 2002). Meanwhile, couples (married and cohabiting couples combined) had higher levels of credit use than these young, single householders (Berthoud and Kempson, 1992). In turn, within couples, people who were cohabiting in 2005 and who had never been married had much higher rates of credit use (55 per cent) than people who were married (31 per cent).[10] Cohabitants were also less likely than people who were married or who were single and had never been married to be saving regularly, taking into account other factors such as age and income (McKay and Kempson, 2003). The natural assumption might be that cohabitants were at increased risk of financial difficulties. Unfortunately, studies of over-indebtedness have not tended to distinguish cohabitants from people who are married.

A few studies have, however, examined the effects of transitions into relationships on financial circumstances. Household changes such as setting up home with a new partner were associated with an increased likelihood of using credit (Kempson, 2002). Two-thirds (65 per cent) of people who had married within the previous year reported using credit to the 2005 survey, compared with 31 per cent of all married couples.[11] The transition into marriage from cohabiting in the previous year was associated with a small decrease in the likelihood of saving (from 51 per cent to 48 per cent), and among savers a decrease in the median amount saved (from £135 to £123; McKay and Kempson, 2003). It was slightly more common for people who had been saving at the time of the interview prior to marriage to have ceased saving in the survey year directly after (29 per cent) than it was for previous non-savers to have begun saving (26 per cent). The earlier study also found that major changes including setting up home with a new partner were linked with financial difficulties (Kempson, 2002).

When viewed in simple economic terms, these findings are surprising: partnering should result in increased disposable income (by pooling resources and sharing living expenses), thereby facilitating saving and making borrowing less necessary. In practice, however, cohabitation and marriage typically occur at a time in life when demand on financial resources is heavily concentrated (and when the available resources, especially savings, are relatively limited). Along with the concomitant costs of setting up home, they often reflect the earlier, more

[10] New analysis of the BHPS.
[11] Ibid.

carefree stages of relationships in which personal, discretionary spending remains high. In the longer term, however, marriage is associated with increased financial stability, all other things being equal, and this is reflected in the generally lower levels of borrowing and higher rates of saving reported above.

Despite this overarching pattern, qualitative research highlights nuances in the effect of partnering on financial behaviour and complexities between the inclination and propensity to save at this time. A study of people on low-to-middle incomes found that partnering was marked by a period of intense saving followed by periods of much reduced saving, withdrawing savings, or increases in borrowing. These related predominantly to the large expenses associated with partnering and settling down: getting married, setting up a home, and buying a house. Settling down appeared to trigger a switch from non-saving to saving, and from instrumental saving to rainy day saving. Existing rainy day savers may even start to save more (Whyley and Kempson, 2000a).

Getting married and buying a home were events that many long-term savers had previously been putting money aside for. However, planning for these events had the effect of increasing the amounts long-term savers were saving. They also encouraged regular saving among people who were previously instrumental savers. For many, the additional, incidental, costs of moving into home ownership resulted in a shift towards more general rainy day saving. One instrumental saver in the study, who had recently got engaged to her partner and bought a house with him, said she felt this had enabled her to start planning for the longer term (Whyley and Kempson, 2000a). Additionally, although most people learn their saving habit as children, some started saving as adults because they had a partner who took saving seriously and 'converted' them (Whyley and Kempson, 2000a). Consequently, there is a fairly high coincidence of saving behaviour among couples: in two-thirds of couples, either both partners saved from their regular income or neither did (McKay and Kempson, 2003).

Notwithstanding the increased inclination to save at this time, the additional expense of a wedding or home ownership meant that people found it more difficult to save, or that they found themselves using up their savings. Many who were still able to save found that they had to scale down their level of saving (Whyley and Kempson, 2000a).

The longer-term effects of getting married on consumer borrowing and saving are also more mixed than they first appear when differences by gender are considered. In a recent study, researchers examined the average relative increase in savings and borrowing from 1995 to 2005 among adults cohabiting with a partner in 1995 whom they went on to marry by 2005. They compared these with those who remained in a cohabiting relationship (Westaway and McKay, 2007). Women who married saw larger relative increases (on average 3.0 times the amount held in 1995) in their savings than those who did not marry (2.0 times). Among men, the relative increase in the median amounts saved was similar (3.0 times) regardless of whether they married or not. Women who went on to marry also saw smaller relative increases in their outstanding borrowing (2.4 times) than those who remained in the cohabiting relationship (4.0 times); whilst for men the pattern was reversed (4.2 times for those who married compared with 3.6 times for those who did not).

In other words, the impact of marriage on the longer-term finances of women who were previously cohabiting was positive (reflected in a larger increase in savings and a smaller increase in borrowing), whilst for men it was neutral in terms of saving, but impacted somewhat negatively on borrowing. It is difficult to explain these patterns (especially in relation to savings) in the absence of any qualitative research—particularly at the intra-household level—to elucidate them. These are of course averages, which will disguise wide variations in behaviour, and the base is limited to those who were cohabiting in 1995, which reflects only a subset of pre-marital relationships. It is also important to note that these findings do not take other factors into account, such as age, work status and household income, length of relationship prior to 1995, or the presence (and age) of children, all of which influence financial well-being (as previously outlined), as well as how finances are organised within households (see for example Singh and Lindsay, 1996, and Burgoyne et al, 2007). The negative impact of marriage on borrowing may partly be because with marriage comes a greater expectation (whether by the couple themselves or the lenders) that the man will take on credit on behalf of the household in the traditional role of main earner, reminiscent of the findings of Pahl (1994).

Having Children and Raising a Family

Whilst the relationship between financial circumstances and partnering appears quite complex, the influence of children on household finances is much clearer. Often occurring after a period of relative financial stability, starting a family presents a time of considerable disruption to the financial situation of a household, with increases in resultant expenditure compounded by a drop in income if one parent gives up work or reduces their working hours. Having children is associated with increased levels of borrowing, a decline in saving, and a greater propensity to fall into arrears.

Lone and coupled parents of dependent children were over-represented among credit users (see for example Kempson, McKay and Willitts, 2004; Finney, Collard and Kempson, 2007). Heavy credit use was especially common where two children were present (Finney, Collard and Kempson, 2007), and the presence of children has been found consistently to be independently predictive of financial difficulties (see, for example, Berthoud and Kempson, 1992; Webley and Nyhus, 2001; Bridges and Disney, 2004). Higher numbers of children in the household were associated with a decreasing propensity to save, independently of other factors, and families with any dependent children were also less likely to save regularly than those without children (Kempson and McKay, 2003).

The apparent financial strain that families are under is likely to be due at least in part to a particularly high proportion of expenses that cannot be reduced when there are dependent children present (Davydoff et al, 2008). This is likely to be compounded by lowered incomes due to reduced paid working hours within the family unit—especially when children are young—to meet child-care responsibilities (see Scott and Dex, chapter three, this volume).

Research supports the notion that raising a family makes saving more difficult and borrowing more likely. Although children were rarely cited in a general population survey as the main reason for saving (McKay and Kempson, 2003), qualitative research shows children are both the focus for saving and also very often the reason why parents cannot afford to do so (Whyley and Kempson, 2000a). This again touches on the tension between the inclination and the ability to save. Saving was given a lower priority than meeting children's immediate needs. In another qualitative study, there was a general consensus across different life-stage and income groups that the costs of raising a family make borrowing at that stage of life more or less inevitable. Among lower-income people who were in their family years, there was a strongly held view that it was not possible to reduce levels of borrowing once you had a family, although young adults who had not yet had children discussed it as something they would aim to do (Finney, Collard and Kempson, 2007).

Christmas has been identified as a particularly hard time for low-income families, providing for children at this time being of paramount importance, putting additional strain on resources. People reported trying to save up and cutting back on other spending (Kempson, Bryson and Rowlingson, 1994; Finney, Collard and Kempson, 2007). But Christmas was also a big trigger for borrowing, and it was often the trigger for falling into arrears (Kempson, Bryson and Rowlingson, 1994). A study of borrowers at high risk of default noted the pressure on parents to provide for their children and families with the various trappings of modern life and that this was especially acute at Christmas time (Ellison, 2008).

Apart from the *presence* of children, the *birth* of a child seems especially likely to trigger financial strain, since this is often the point at which financial shocks occur. Indeed, studies have found clear links between the arrival of a new baby within the previous 12 months and higher than average rates of credit use (Kempson, 2002), as well as higher numbers of credit commitments (Berthoud and Kempson, 1992). In an early, retrospective study of mortgage arrears, three per cent of people in arrears and five per cent of people whose homes were possessed reported giving up work to have a baby as the main reason for their difficulties (Ford et al, 1995). And in a more recent, longitudinal study, 41 per cent of savers ceased saving in the year following the birth of their first child, whereas only 23 per cent of new parents who were previously non-savers began to save (McKay and Kempson, 2003). In other words, new parents were more likely to stop saving than to start. In addition, the proportion of people saving fell by six percentage points from 45 per cent in the year after birth. The average amounts saved among savers also fell, quite substantially from £135 to £116. The authors suggested that this might reflect two complementing factors: previous saving in anticipation of a child's birth, and the effect of increased strain on family resources following the arrival of the child.

The arrival of a subsequent child or children was associated with a further decline in the likelihood of saving (from 36 per cent to 31 per cent), although among those saving the median amounts saved increased slightly (from £98 to £105; McKay and Kempson, 2003). In this case, previous savers were almost three times as likely to stop saving (38 per cent) as non-savers were to start saving (14 per cent). An increase in family size made starting to save less likely independently of other factors (relative odds of 0.7).

The 2003 study found the negative effect of an increase in family size on saving was more pronounced for women than men. A more recent study also identified gendered effects of starting and expanding a family on saving (Westaway and McKay, 2007). The decrease in the propensity to save in the year following the birth of a first child was much more marked for women, falling from 46 per cent to 34 per cent, compared with men (45 per cent to 42 per cent). Ten years on from the first child's birth, saving rates also recovered better for men on average (to 46 per cent) than they did for women (to 40 per cent). The differential effect of subsequent children on men's and women's saving was even more pronounced, and the differences were also reflected in the median amounts saved.

Examined in a different way, the relative increase in sums held in saving between 1995 and 2005 was lower among people who had become a parent during that time compared with those who had not, and this was true for both men and women (Westaway and McKay, 2007). On the other hand, the relative increase in median outstanding borrowing was lower for men if they had a child, whereas for women it was higher. Overall, therefore, the impact of raising a family on women's finances was largely negative, whereas for men it was mixed. The authors concluded that the differences existed largely due to gender inequalities in income and income stability caused by gendered patterns of paid and unpaid work, although spending and saving preferences also played a part (Westaway and McKay, 2007).

Relationship Breakdown

Whilst the financial strain of starting and raising a family is evident, relationship breakdown is a time of considerable financial turmoil. The shocks brought about by decreased incomes and increased expenditure that are typically experienced when households split can plunge people into financial difficulties (see Fisher and Low, chapter eleven, this volume). These can alleviate as the financial situation stabilises with time, albeit often on a lower income than when married. Consequently, we would expect to see higher levels of financial difficulties among people who are recently separated than those who are divorced, and this is supported by the existing research literature. Equally, however, whilst relationship breakdown is implicated in financial difficulties, financial problems can themselves create strain within relationships that result in breakdown.

Studies that have examined the role of marital status indicate that, on the whole, people who were separated or divorced were likely to have outstanding borrowing and to be experiencing financial difficulties, although they were also likely to be saving regularly. Borrowing was more likely among divorcees (42 per cent) and people who were separated (53 per cent) than among people who were married (31 per cent).[12] Correspondingly, people who were divorced, and especially those who were separated, were very likely to be saving regularly compared with other groups after controlling for other factors (McKay and Kempson, 2003). People who had previously been married or had cohabited had the highest risk of self-reported bill payment difficulties: this was especially true if they were separated rather than divorced, most likely reflecting the impact of a relationship breakdown itself (since separation precedes divorce; Davydoff et al, 2008).[13]

Some studies have examined the link between recent relationship breakdown and financial behaviour and well-being. One study found no apparent effect on the propensity to borrow among households that had split in the previous three years (Berthoud and Kempson, 1992). Another found that average outstanding unsecured borrowing among newly created households (those created between the 1995 and 2000 BHPS interviews) headed by a divorcee were slightly higher compared with those headed by someone who was married or cohabiting, and slightly higher again among those headed by someone who was separated (Mitchell, Mouratidis and Weale, 2005).[14] The lack of any clear link may be explained in part by the fact that responses to financial shocks differ, as noted above.

Saving behaviour was negatively affected in quantitative studies—on a number of measures—around the time married people divorced or separated (McKay and Kempson, 2003).[15] Separation or divorce in the previous year was associated with a decrease in the likelihood of saving (from 34 per cent to 29 per cent) and the average amounts saved among savers also fell (from £117 to £108). After controlling for the influence of other factors, people who were saving previously were much more likely to stop saving after divorce or separation. Qualitative research found that breaking up with a partner put a strain on the budget such that people found they were no longer able to save. Rainy day savers might stop saving but often resisted borrowing, whilst instrumental savers more readily switched to borrowing (Whyley and Kempson, 2000a).

Considering borrowing and saving (and other measures of assets) together, Mitchell, Mouratidis and Weale (2005) found that newly created households headed by a divorcee were more likely than the average household to have outstanding borrowing in excess of 10 per cent of their income, a pattern which

---

[12] New analysis of the 2005 BHPS.
[13] Based on 2006 Eurobarometer data for 25 countries across Europe, including the UK.
[14] Based on small samples; treat with caution.
[15] Due to small samples divorce and separation were combined in this analysis.

held true after taking the age of the household head into account. Unsecured borrowing was also relatively high compared with their financial wealth (liquid assets) as was total borrowing (including mortgage borrowing) compared with total wealth (including housing wealth). The total borrowing among new households headed by people who were separated (rather than divorced) was also high on average relative to their income or wealth, but only for householders aged under 35; as a whole, those who were separated had both high borrowing *and* high wealth. Nevertheless, the high borrowing to wealth hints at the increased risk of over-indebtedness following relationship breakdown found clearly in a number of studies.

A national survey in 2001 found that people who had suffered a relationship breakdown in the previous three years were more likely to have experienced debt problems in that same period, and this was independent of other influences (Balmer et al, 2005).[16] In another study, people with mortgage arrears were four times more likely to have experienced separation or divorce in the past three years (18 per cent) than those who were not in arrears (five per cent; Ford, Kempson and Wilson, 1995).

As noted earlier, relationship breakdown is one of the commonly cited reasons for financial difficulties in self-report studies (Davydoff et al, 2008). Moreover, it is seemingly cited more often for more serious financial difficulties. In the 2002 survey of over-indebtedness in Britain, three per cent of people self-reporting financial difficulties specifically cited relationship breakdown as a reason, and this rose to six per cent among those reporting household bill or credit payment arrears (Kempson, 2002). In a national survey of mortgage arrears in 1993, 10 per cent of people gave relationship breakdown as the *main* reason for arrears; while 14 per cent cited it as the main reason for their home being repossessed (Ford, Kempson and Wilson, 1995).

In summary, relationship breakdown was not clearly implicated in consumer borrowing, but it has been linked with an increased inability to save, self-reported debt problems, falling into arrears, and repossession of the home. However, whilst studies have found a clear link between relationship breakdown and financial difficulties, the association is more complicated than the discussion so far implies.

In particular, the economic effects of relationship breakdown are not experienced equally by men and women. Women have been identified as being especially vulnerable to the economic shocks of relationship breakdown; for men it often leads to an improvement in economic well-being (Holden and Smock, 1991; Sayer, 2006; Westaway and McKay, 2007). Economic modelling of the BHPS has illustrated the stark difference in real incomes that men and women are exposed to on marital breakdown, with women's equivalised income

---

[16] However, relationship breakdown was not an independent predictor of longer-term debt problems (those persisting for more than a year).

falling considerably in the short-term compared with modest to high increases among men, although the gap has closed to a degree in recent years (Fisher and Low, chapter 11, this volume, Jarvis and Jenkins, 1999, Jenkins, 2008). Again, these differences are likely to reflect gendered patterns in previous paid and unpaid work and the likelihood that any dependent children remain in the care of the mother (and so limit employment options). Notably, a 1984/85 study of divorcees found that those with children were the most likely to be in arrears (Gregory and Foster, 1990).

It is perhaps not surprising, therefore, that women who divorced between 1995 and 2005 experienced a greater increase in their average borrowing than women who remained married: divorced women's borrowing had increased at twice the rate of women who remained married (Westaway and McKay, 2007). Women who divorced also saw smaller relative increases in their savings holdings compared with women who stayed married. In contrast, the relative increases in the amounts borrowed and saved were similar for men regardless of whether they remained married or got divorced. In a separate study, women were more likely than men to report having stopped saving in the interview following divorce or separation (McKay and Kempson, 2003). Finally, the study by Mitchell, Mouratidis and Weale (2005) found that the financial circumstances of divorced women, whether or not they had children, and lone mothers were distinct from all other categories considered. Unlike all other groups, these women had negative net financial worth, and this was not due to high rates of unsecured borrowing, but to a lack of savings. On the other hand, although the earlier study of mortgage arrears found that it was generally the women who were left with financial difficulties after marital breakdown, this was not invariably the case (Ford, Kempson and Wilson, 1995).

Secondly, whilst relationship breakdown has been identified as a cause of financial difficulties, financial strain is also implicated in relationship outcomes. Many of the CAB 'debt clients' said their financial problems had impacted on relationships with partners (and children), resulting in arguments or relationship breakdown (Edwards, 2003). Sequencing based on dates of the onset of problems as reported to the 2001 survey confirmed that relationship breakdown preceded debt problems (and may therefore have been a contributory factor) in only 60 per cent of instances; in the remaining cases, it followed the onset of debt problems (and were possibly caused by it; Balmer et al, 2005).[17] Similarly, relationship breakdown preceded mortgage arrears in about a half of cases but mortgage arrears followed separation in the other half (Ford, Kempson and Wilson, 1995). People have also reported being taken advantage of financially by their partners, including borrowing money against their better judgement, and suffering as a result on relationship breakdown (for example Edwards, 2003; Atkinson, Kempson and Collard, 2008). The complexities are underlined

---

[17] Notably, domestic violence and relationship breakdown were the only social justice problems that correlated with debt problems for which a predominant direction of effect was identified.

further by recent qualitative work which found that separation sometimes brought about a relief from financial pressures if one partner spent more than the other, whilst in other cases it led to more serious financial difficulties for individuals who did not have the means to support themselves (Atkinson, Kempson and Collard, forthcoming).

Due to small samples, it is difficult to study the mechanisms through which financial problems may influence relationship breakdown directly. However, some US studies have examined the effects of assets and credit on other marital outcomes such as conflict and satisfaction, and these throw some light on the likely processes, sometimes direct and sometimes indirect, involving the mediating effects of feelings of economic pressure, psychological depression, emotional stress, or loss of (quality) time together (Dew, 2007, 2008; Gudmunson et al, 2007).

A third consideration is that the association is complicated by the co-occurrence of other problems. The 2001 survey (Balmer et al, 2005) found a high level of coincidence of debt problems with other social justice problems. Looking retrospectively at the previous three years, people who had debt problems self-reported an average of 3.8 problems altogether. People in financial difficulties who also reported relationship breakdown had a higher mean number of problems overall. The independent relevance of relationship breakdown is therefore difficult to disentangle.

Related to this is a lack of understanding regarding the extent to which debt problems during a relationship or following its breakdown are a manifestation of domestic violence. Financial abuse is recognised by the Home Office as a form of domestic violence (Home Office, 2005: 10) and 'being prevented from having a fair share of household money' by a partner is not especially uncommon, being reported as having happened at least once since age 16 by seven per cent of women and three per cent of men to the 2004/05 British Crime Survey (Finney, 2006). Qualitative research has observed that this situation can lead to the abused partner having to borrow unmanageable amounts of money and falling into arrears on fuel and rent payments that they were held accountable for after leaving the relationship (Wilcox, 2000). Furthermore, some abusive partners have borrowed in their spouse's name (either without their knowledge or without their consent), forced their partner to borrow on their own behalf, or put all liabilities in the partner's name, thereby passing all debts on to them (Westaway and McKay, 2007). The extent to which these latter forms of financial abuse occur or have implications for financial difficulties on relationship dissolution is not known, although they may account for some of the four per cent of over-indebted householders who said this was due to debts left by a former partner (Kempson, 2002).

Finally, few studies have investigated the effects of divorce, marital separation and cohabitation breakdown separately, or considered the compounding effects of dependent children. The importance of understanding the effects of these subtly, but substantively, different relationship transitions is underlined by the recent study by Westaway and McKay (2007) in which the average effect on financial well-being of cohabitation breakdown was markedly different to that of marital breakdown (Westaway and McKay, 2007). Women whose cohabiting relationship broke down saw *smaller* relative increases in borrowing and *higher* increases in savings than those who remained with their partner; as reported above, the reverse was true for married women. Among cohabiting men, average borrowing and savings had both increased at a much higher rate if they had split up, whereas the effect of divorce on men's finances was largely similar to that of men who remained married. The reasons for these patterns have not yet been the subject of enquiry.

CONCLUSIONS

Relationships are strongly implicated in an individual's overall financial well-being throughout the life-course of their formation and their dissolution as well as raising a family.

The associations between marital status and family structure with borrowing, saving, and over-indebtedness are mediated, at least in part, by socio-economic characteristics, age, and attitudinal dimensions. Relationships, therefore, are not the most important determinants of overall financial circumstances but they are important nevertheless for explaining variations in these financial outcomes, and this is particularly true for over-indebtedness. Studies that have examined changes in family and marital status are especially insightful and highlight the largely negative impact these can have, whilst the maintenance of a marital relationship appears to have beneficial effects over longer periods. The drops in income and increases in expenditure that accompany these structural changes are the mechanisms through which financial strain seems to arise. So, whilst divorce and marital separation have been associated clearly with an increased propensity to experience over-indebtedness, so have partnering and starting or expanding the family. The findings underline the importance of recognising the complex influences on the financial well-being of people facing relationship breakdown, many of which relate to the life-course of relationships.

However, even accounting for the life-course perspective, the association between relationship breakdown and financial difficulties is not always straightforward. Differences appear to exist in the extent to which relationships impact on financial well-being by gender, financial strain can itself impact adversely on relationships, and relationship breakdown and over-indebtedness rarely occur in isolation from other social problems. Finally, gaps in the existing research—notably in the (typical) lack of distinction between cohabiting and marital relationships, opposite- and same-sex relationships, and first and subsequent relationships—suggest other complexities may exist. There is clearly a need for further research on the correlation between relationship status and an individual's propensity to borrow or save.

BIBLIOGRAPHY

Atkinson, A, Kempson, E and Collard, S (forthcoming) *Snakes and Ladders: A Longitudinal Study of Financial Difficulty* (London, Financial Services Authority).

Balmer, N, Pleasance, P, Buck, A and Walker, HC (2005) 'Worried sick: the experience of debt problems and their relationship with health, illness and disability' 5 *Social Policy and Society* 39.

Bank of England (2009) *Lending to Individuals: February 2009* (London, Bank of England Statistical Release).

Berthoud, R and Kempson, E (1992) *Credit and Debt: The PSI Report* (London, PSI).

Boreham, R and Lloyd, J (2007) *Asset Accumulation across the Life Course* (London, International Longevity Centre).

Bridges, S and Disney, R (2004) 'Use of credit and arrears on debt among low-income families in the United Kingdom' 25 *Fiscal Studies* 1.

Burgoyne, CB, Reibstein, J, Edmunds, A, and Dolman, V (2007) 'Money management systems in early marriage: factors influencing change and stability' 28 *Journal of Economic Psychology* 214.

Cox, P, Whitley, J and Brierley, P (2002) 'Financial pressures in the UK household sector: evidence from the British Household Panel Survey' *Bank of England Quarterly Bulletin* (Winter).

Davydoff, D, Dessart, E, Naacke, G, Jentzsch, N, Figueira, F, Rothemund, M, Mueller, W, Kempson, E, Atkinson, A, Finney, A and Anderloni, L (2008) *Towards a Common Operational European Definition of Over-indebtedness* (Brussels, European Commission).

Del-Rio, A and Young, G (2005a) 'The impact of unsecured debt on financial distress among British households', Bank of England Working Paper 262 (London, Bank of England).

—— (2005b) 'Unsecured debt in BHPS: determinants and impact on financial distress', Bank of England Working Paper 263 (London, Bank of England).

Dew, J (2007) 'Two sides of the same coin? The differing roles of assets and consumer debt in marriage' 28 *Journal of Family and Economic Issues* 89.

—— (2008) 'Debt change and marital satisfaction change in recently married couples' 57 *Family Relations* 60.

DWP (Department for Work and Pensions) (2007) *Family Resources Survey, United Kingdom 2005–06* (London, DWP).

Edwards, S (2003) *In Too Deep: CAB Clients' Experience of Debt* (London, Citizens Advice and Citizens Advice Scotland).

Elliott, A (2005) *Not Waving but Drowning: Over-indebtedness by Misjudgement* (London, CSFI).

Ellison, A (2008) *Transitioning High Risk Low-income Borrowers to Affordable Credit* (London, Department for Business, Enterprise and Regulatory Reform).

Finney, A (2004) *Domestic violence, sexual assault and stalking: findings from the 2004/05 British Crime Survey*, Home Office Online Report 12/06 (London, Home Office).

Finney, A, Collard, S and Kempson, E (2007) *Easy Come, Easy Go: Borrowing over the Life-cycle* (Edinburgh, Standard Life Assurance Limited).

Ford, J (1990) 'Credit and default amongst younger adults: an agenda of issues' 13 *Journal of Consumer Policy* 133.

Ford, J, Kempson, E and Wilson, M (1995) *Mortgage Arrears and Possessions; Perspectives from Borrowers, Lenders and the Courts* (London, HMSO).

Gregory, J and Foster, K (1990) *The Consequences of Divorce* (London, HMSO).

Gudmumson, C, Beutler, I, Israelsen, C, Mccoy, J and Hill, E (2007) 'Linking financial strain to marital instability: examining the roles of emotional distress and marital interaction' 28 *Journal of Family and Economic Issues* 357.

Herbert, A and Kempson, E (1995) *Water Debt and Disconnection* (London, PSI).

HM Treasury (2007) *Financial Inclusion: The Way Forward* (London, The Stationery Office).

Holden, K and Smock, P (1991) 'The economic costs of marital dissolution: why do women bear a disproportionate cost?' 17 *Annual Review of Sociology* 51.

Home Office (2005) *Domestic Violence: A National Report* (London, Home Office).

Jarvis, S and Jenkins, SP (1999) 'Marital splits and income changes: evidence from the British Household Panel Survey' 53 *Population Studies* 237.

Jenkins, SP (2008) 'Marital splits and income changes over the longer term', ISER Working Paper No 2008-07 (Colchester, Institute for Social and Economic Research).

Kempson, E (2002) *Over-indebtedness in Britain: A Report to the Department of Trade and Industry* (London, Department of Trade and Industry).

—— (2008) 'Saving and borrowing in the UK: a household perspective', Presentation to the Association of British Insurers 2008 Research Conference, London, 21 February.

Kempson, E. and Atkinson, A. (2006) *Over-stretched: People at Risk of Financial Difficulties* (Bristol, University of Bristol).

Kempson, E, Atkinson, A and Collard, S (2006) *Saving for Children: A Baseline Survey at the Inception of the Child Trust Fund* (London, HMRC).

Kempson, E, Bryson, A and Rowlingson, K (1994) *Hard Times? How Poor Families Make Ends Meet* (London, PSI).

Kempson, E, Collard, S and Taylor, S (2002) *Social Fund Use amongst Older People*, Department for Work and Pensions Research Report No 172 (Leeds, Corporate Document Services).

Kempson, E, McKay, S and Willitts, M (2004) *Characteristics of Families in Debt and the Nature of Indebtedness*, Department for Work and Pensions Research Report No 211 (Leeds, Corporate Document Services).

Livingstone, S and Lunt, P (1992) 'Predicting personal debt and debt repayment: psychological, social and economic determinants' 13 *Journal of Economic Psychology* 111.

McCallum, E and McCaig, E (2002) *Mortgage Arrears and Repossessions in Scotland* (Edinburgh, Scottish Executive).

McKay, S and Kempson, E (2003) *Savings and Life Events*, Department for Work and Pensions Research Report No 194 (Leeds, Corporate Document Services).

Mitchell, J, Mouratidis, K and Weale, M (2005) *Poverty and Debt*, NIESR Discussion Paper No 263 (London, National Institute of Economic and Social Research).

National Consumer Council (2002) *Credit: Choice or Chance* (London, National Consumer Council).

NS&I (National Savings and Investments) (2008) *NS&I Savings Tracker: Examining Saving across Britain*, Quarter Savings Survey (London, NS&I).

Pahl, J (1994) 'Couples and their money: patterns of accounting and accountability in the domestic economy' 13 *Accounting, Auditing and Accountability Journal* 502.

Pannell, B (2002) *Coping with Mortgage Debt*, CML Housing Finance 48 (London, Council of Mortgage Lenders).

Sayer, L (2006) 'Economic aspects of divorce and relationship dissolution' in MA Fine and JH Harvey (eds), *Handbook of Divorce and Relationship Breakdown* (Philadelphia, Lawrence Erlbaum Associates).

Singh, S and Lindsay, J (1996) 'Money in heterosexual relationships' 32 *Journal of Sociology* 57.

Tudela, M and Young, G (2003) 'The distribution of unsecured debt in the United Kingdom' *Bank of England Quarterly Bulletin* (Winter).

Waldron, M and Young, G (2006) 'The state of British household finances: results from the 2006 NMG research survey' *Bank of England Quarterly Bulletin* (Q4).

Webley, P and Nyhus, EK (2001) 'Life-cycle and dispositional routes into problem debt' 92 *British Journal of Psychology* 423.

Westaway, J and McKay, S (2007) *Women's Financial Assets and Debts* (London, The Fawcett Society).

Whyley, C and Kempson, E (2000a) *Understanding Small Savers II: Saving Behaviour amongst Low-to-middle Income Groups* (Peterborough, Pearl Assurance).

—— (2000b) *Understanding Small Savers: Patterns of Saving amongst Low-to-middle Income Groups* (Peterborough, Pearl Assurance).

Wilcox, P (2000) 'Lone motherhood: the impact on living standards of leaving a violent relationship' 34 *Social Policy and Administration* 176.

Part III

Dividing the Assets on Relationship Breakdown

7

Money, Property, Cohabitation and Separation

Patterns and Intentions

GILLIAN DOUGLAS, JULIA PEARCE
AND HILARY WOODWARD

INTRODUCTION

THE RULES GOVERNING the resolution of property disputes between separating cohabitants have been notorious for their complexity and uncertainty (Law Commission, 2006: Part 3). In *Stack v Dowden*,[1] the House of Lords had the opportunity to offer a definitive ruling on how the law should be applied. The majority of the House agreed with Baroness Hale of Richmond that the concept of the 'constructive trust' is the most appropriate mechanism to apply to determining this matter in the domestic context of intimate relationships.[2] However, establishing such a trust, and determining the implications of so doing, remains difficult. Basically, a claimant must show that there was a 'common intention' to share the equity in the property. Such common intention may be established by evidence either of some agreement between the parties to this effect, or of some conduct pointing towards their intention. Once such evidence is provided, it must also be established that one of the parties acted to their detriment in reliance on it.[3] It can be seen that much will turn on what evidence the parties are able to furnish to demonstrate their intentions. Baroness Hale provided detailed guidance on the kinds of factors that would be relevant to this exercise, which we set out below. In this chapter, we consider each of these factors in the light of the findings of our recent empirical study on separating cohabitants and property issues (Douglas, Pearce and Woodward, 2007).

---

[1] *Stack v Dowden* [2007] UKHL 17, [2007] 2 AC 432.
[2] Lord Neuberger of Abbotsbury preferred to take a different approach to determining the parties' interests, based on a 'resulting' rather than 'constructive' trust basis: see [110]–[122].
[3] *Lloyds Bank plc v Rosset and Another* [1991] 1 AC 107.

BARONESS HALE'S LIST OF FACTORS

In *Stack v Dowden*, the couple had cohabited for at least 19 years and had four children together. Their first home was purchased in the woman's sole name, at a favourable price under the terms of a relative's will. Some years later they purchased a property in joint names, using the proceeds of sale from the former home, the woman's savings, and a joint mortgage. The mortgage loan was repaid by lump sums provided by both parties, although the woman paid more than half of these. Throughout their cohabitation, they held separate bank accounts, savings and investments. When they separated, the man sought an order for sale of the property and an equal division of the proceeds. The woman claimed that she was entitled to 65 per cent of these, having contributed more than the man. The House of Lords upheld the woman's claim. In her speech, with which the majority of the House agreed, Baroness Hale stated:

> In law, 'context is everything' and the domestic context is very different from the commercial world. Each case will turn on its own facts. Many more factors than financial contributions may be relevant to divining the parties' true intentions.[4]

She then provided a list of factors,[5] which we set out here:

— any advice or discussions at the time of the transfer which cast light upon their intentions then;
— the reasons why the home was acquired in their joint names;
— the reasons why (if it be the case) the survivor was authorised to give a receipt for the capital monies;
— the purpose for which the home was acquired;
— the nature of the parties' relationship;
— whether they had children for whom they both had responsibility to provide a home;
— how the purchase was financed, both initially and subsequently;
— how the parties arranged their finances, whether separately or together or a bit of both;
— how they discharged the outgoings on the property and their other household expenses.

The parties' individual characters and personalities may also be a factor in deciding where their true intentions lay.

Baroness Hale added that:

> In the cohabitation context, mercenary considerations may be more to the fore than they would be in marriage, but it should not be assumed that they always take pride

---

[4] *Stack v Dowden* [2007] UKHL 17, [2007] 2 AC 432 at [69].
[5] Compare the factors pertaining to divorce set out in s 25 of the Matrimonial Causes Act 1973 and the increasing pragmatism of divorce law described by Maclean and Eekelaar, ch 2, this volume.

of place over natural love and affection. At the end of the day, having taken all this into account, cases in which the joint legal owners are to be taken to have intended that their beneficial interests should be different from their legal interests will be very unusual.[6]

This extract highlights the factors (albeit not intended to be exhaustive) which Baroness Hale considered relevant to the search for the parties' true intentions in relation to their property, in the context of the established principle that: 'The onus is on the person seeking to show that the beneficial ownership is different from the legal ownership'.[7] Although the case involved a jointly owned property, this basic principle was held to be the starting point in relation to any property dispute regardless of whether the property is solely or jointly owned.[8] Whether this judgment will have the effect desired by the House of Lords of discouraging claims to a beneficial interest will depend on whether cases are regarded as 'unusual' enough to warrant departure from the legal title. This begs the question of what might be regarded as 'usual', and whether this question is to be answered by reference to empirical research or on some other basis. As Probert (2007) has observed, it is not easy to determine whether any given case is exceptional or not, a point which appears to have been confirmed by subsequent decisions.[9] The particular features in *Stack v Dowden* which were identified as unusual enough to justify the finding that the beneficial interests differed from the legal title included the parties' unequal financial contributions and the 'rigid' separation of their financial arrangements despite a cohabitation of about 19 years and a relationship of 27 years. Drawing on findings from our study, we seek to show that the factors highlighted are not necessarily reliable indicators of the parties' intentions, and especially not the 'common intention' to be established under the law of constructive trusts.

THE STUDY

Our study investigated the experience and views of separating opposite-sex cohabitants by means of a set of 24 contemporaneous case studies (the 'core sample'), interviews with 61 practitioners, and focus groups with four barristers and four district judges. The 29 cohabitants in the core sample (which included five couples) were mostly recruited through their professional practitioners and were interviewed shortly after their first consultation and again following the

---

[6] *Stack v Dowden* [2007] UKHL 17, [2007] 2 AC 432 at [69].

[7] ibid at [56].

[8] *Stack v Dowden* being essentially a case relating to joint ownership, this chapter focuses on the cases from our study which involved joint ownership.

[9] *James v Thomas* [2007] EWCA Civ 1212, [2008] 1 FLR 1598, *Adekunle and Others v Ritchie* [2007] EW Misc 5 (EWCC), *Morris v Morris* [2008] EWCA Civ 257, *Laskar v Laskar* [2008] EWCA Civ 347, [2008] 2 FLR 589.

conclusion of their cases, with email and telephone contact in between. The practitioners comprised 41 family and civil solicitors, 10 family mediators, and 10 conveyancers, and included those who had introduced the cohabitants to the project. The case studies were supplemented by a secondary sample of 24 cases, described to us in detail, on an anonymous basis, by the solicitors during their interviews. The cases covered a wide range in terms of the cohabitants' ages, length of cohabitation, attitudes towards marriage, whether there were dependent children, the value of their property, and how hard fought they were. Thus, although not statistically representative, our sample was sufficiently diverse to illustrate a number of commonplace situations and key themes (Douglas, Pearce and Woodward, 2007: 155–61).

It should be noted at the outset, in order to contextualise our discussion below, that the majority of cohabitants in our study showed little interest in, or understanding of, their legal position and a significant proportion *mis*understood their position, believing that they had property (and possibly other) rights by virtue of their cohabitation (see also Smart and Stevens, 2000; Barlow et al, 2001; Barlow et al, 2008). The following comments were typical:

> I thought there would be something there. I don't think I knew quite what it was. I thought that, given the situation and that this was not something I fell into—a joint decision to move in—I thought there would be something.

> [I appreciated that my] rights were not as good as if I had been married, but I thought I might come out with some sort of money … I was surprised by exactly how the law does differentiate.

THE FACTORS RELEVANT TO DIVINING THE PARTIES' TRUE INTENTIONS

Any Advice or Discussions at the Time of the Transfer which Cast Light upon their Intentions then

Discussions at the Time of the Transfer

All but one of the cases involved an owned property. The cases were approximately equally divided between those in joint and those in sole names, amongst both the core and the secondary samples. Within the core sample, 11 of the 12 properties owned in joint names were held under a joint tenancy. We asked the cohabitants what their understandings and assumptions were at the time of the purchase or transfer and how the decisions had been made about the ownership arrangements. The question of intentions did not feature very prominently in their responses to these questions and, regardless of whether the properties were held in joint or sole names, relatively few of the cohabitants could recall any real discussion at all.

In four of the core sample cases there had clearly been some form of more serious discussion between the couple about the beneficial shares, and written agreements had been drafted. However, none of these agreements had been formally executed (or even signed in two cases), and they appeared to have been inconclusive in so far as any common intention was concerned. Of the five other cases in which there was any recollection of a discussion, only one appeared to have clarified the intentions with respect to ownership to any meaningful extent.[10]

Cohabitants' Recollection of Advice

Almost all the cohabitants were very hazy in their recollections of the advice they had received about the ownership arrangements at the time of the purchase or transfer. Whilst all knew whether they owned the property in joint or sole names, very few appeared to have understood the full implications of their ownership choices.

Of those whose properties were in joint names, most could not initially recall the nature of their joint ownership, and it was typically the case that only when we probed further and mentioned the survivorship rule that they remembered that they held the property under a joint tenancy. It became clear that the only feature of a joint tenancy which had really impinged on them had been the survivorship rule. A fairly typical response was, after some deliberation and memory searching:

> ... Sorry, we're joint tenants. That's the one where if someone dies the other gets the house.

Very few had taken fully on board the fact that the shares would be presumed equal on separation, regardless of the circumstances or of their initial or subsequent contributions:

> We went for a joint tenancy at that stage, but not with our eyes completely open. At that stage, things seemed okay. We had more important things to think about.

Confidence in the relationship was one reason why the cohabitants did not always inform and/or protect themselves legally. The cohabitants naturally preferred not to think about the possibility of their relationship breaking down even if they had experienced a previous separation or divorce. This was especially so when they were at the point of buying a home together. Some simply did not consider the possibility of separation at all; others assumed that it would not happen to them; some perhaps consciously or subconsciously kept the whole

---

[10] See *Laskar v Laskar* [2008] EWCA Civ 347, [2008] 2 FLR 589 for an example of how difficult it can be to prove discussions at the time of purchase.

thing a bit woolly or did not ask the questions for fear that they would not like the answers:

> It runs counter to your natural instincts ... planning to fail.

> It didn't even cross my mind ... when I look back, I think what a silly woman you were. Now I think I didn't ask the questions because I didn't want to know the answers.

Ashby and Burgoyne (2008) found a similar bias towards optimism in their study of household financial organisation of unmarried cohabitants.

The Advice Received at the Time

Our interviews with conveyancers suggested that purchasers were generally more interested in getting the keys to their new home than in the legal implications. Ownership options were just one aspect of a whole raft of advice to purchasers, including surveys, searches, mortgages, insurances, wills, and the procedure and implications of exchange of contracts and completion. Whilst we do not underestimate the tasks facing conveyancers, the standard written conveyancing material for joint purchasers shown to us was not as helpful as it could have been. It varied in quality, and, in explaining the differences between a joint tenancy and a tenancy in common (as the first quotation in the previous section illustrates), emphasised the position on death rather than separation. One conveyancer described the oral advice that he gave to his cohabiting purchasers:

> I just tend to do this on a practical basis. I explain that with one, if one passes away, their share goes to the other, and with the other the share goes to whoever. So it could be the survivor might end up owning a property with someone they've never met or who they don't like. That's the main practical difference. Also, if it's a large amount, I would advise on the tax benefit of owning as joint tenants as opposed to tenants in common. Anything more and I just see the eyes glaze over.

The potentially daunting volume and complexity of advice which conveyancers have to impart, and purchasers to absorb, may go some way towards explaining why jointly purchasing cohabitants do not always appear to take fully on board the implications of the ownership options. This potential gap in purchasers' understanding is exacerbated by the language of the joint ownership options and declaration of trust and the evident difficulties of explaining the concepts in lay terms. However, both family solicitors and barristers criticised conveyancers and suggested that their advice was frequently inadequate and/or given in circumstances which made it difficult for individuals to consider or act on it:

> You do find—quite often there are unequal contributions and you ask what advice they got at the time. You get a blank stare. That's where there are a lot of missed opportunities. Conveyancing solicitors need to advise much more fully.

Family lawyers referred to conveyancing files which showed no evidence of advice on ownership options at all. Our sample certainly included cohabitants who had purchased jointly with their partners in ways which, on their separation, they regretted. Frank,[11] for example, who put £90,000 of his own money into a property with his fiancée whilst she contributed nothing, described the advice he was given on the TR1:[12]

> I think he just said, 'this one means this, this one means that, that means that'. He didn't say, 'well, it's your money', or 'have you thought about your children?'

Although most conveyancers assured us that they warned their cohabitant clients of their lack of legal protection should their relationship break down, and were aware of the risks of a negligence action if they did not advise on the implications of this in relation to joint ownership, such advice was not always evident from the standard written material on the joint ownership options. We also had the impression that the conveyancers may have preferred not to probe too deeply for fear not only of offending their clients but also in case enquiries revealed a potential conflict of interest which would make it impossible for them to continue to act:

> We try and lead it in a nice way, but quite frankly, what we're saying is a little unpalatable.

A similar difficulty was described in relation to sole purchasers and the requirement for independent advice to be given to the non-owning cohabitant:

> It's almost a situation where we don't want to know, because if you think about it, we could very easily find ourselves in a conflict of interest as a conveyancer—and that's three quarters of the way through buying a property, and that's really not helpful to anybody to be honest.

The Reasons why the Home was Acquired in Joint Names

Baroness Hale expressed the view that:

> [I]t will almost always have been a conscious decision to put the house into joint names ... Committing oneself to spend large sums of money on a place to live is not normally done by accident or without giving it a moment's thought.[13]

Half the couples within our core sample owned property in their joint names, and three quarters of all the couples had purchased their property together during

---

[11] Pseudonyms are used throughout this chapter.
[12] The TR1 is the Land Registry document which is required, now under the Land Registration Rules 2003, on the sale or purchase of registered land.
[13] *Stack v Dowden* [2007] UKHL 17, [2007] 2 AC 432 at [66].

the course of their relationship. However, in all except one case, one partner had already previously owned their own home. Thus, it appeared that there was a preference to set up in a new home together and that putting ownership of their home into joint names was indeed a deliberate and significant act. However, given the underlying lack of legal understanding found among the cohabitants in the study, it seems probable that this was perceived more as a gesture of commitment to the relationship, made in the hope or expectation that they would stay together as a couple, than as a fully considered expression of their respective property rights. If that is the case, questions then arise as to how far such motivation should equate to intention and whether it is sufficient to bind for ever. Ewan, for example, who appeared to have thought more about the issue than most, chose not to protect his initial contribution of £41,000 to the joint purchase (to which his partner had contributed nothing) because:

> I just thought it was not very romantic … she was pregnant, sitting there next to me … you just don't do that.

As Lord Neuberger pointed out in *Stack v Dowden*:

> The property may be bought in joint names for reasons which cast no light on the parties' intentions with regard to beneficial ownership. It may be the solicitor's decision or assumption, the lender's preference for the security of two borrowers, or the happenstance of how the initial contact with the solicitor was made.[14]

Amongst our core sample, there was a group of three cases where a property owned by one of the partners when the relationship started was not sold, but refinanced to include the new partner's income. In these cases there appeared to be an expectation from the lenders that both names would go on the title. All three involved women who owned the property before the relationship commenced. In each of these cases the new partner made no initial financial contribution towards the property but the property was nevertheless transferred into joint names and made subject to a joint tenancy. In Emma's case, for example, even though she was the property owner, the transaction was set up by her partner's financial advisor, and was dealt with remotely by a conveyancer, instructed by the lender, whom Emma never met. She certainly had no idea at the time that she was, in effect, making a gift to her partner of half the equity in her property. Refinancing arrangements (as compared to sales and purchases) have, in recent years, formed by far the bulk of conveyancing transactions in a highly competitive market, and this must represent a risk for would-be transferors. In such circumstances we would question whether Emma's case would be regarded as sufficiently unusual to justify a departure from the legal title.

Although *Stack v Dowden* was a joint ownership case, one might ask an equivalent question as to why, in sole ownership cases, the home was acquired in one party's sole name. Amongst our core sample, two of the 11 solely owned

---

[14] ibid at [113]. Indeed, Baroness Hale made the same point at [67].

properties were already in the name of one of the couple at the start of the relationship, and in another, one was an existing council tenant with the right to buy. In six cases the initial funds to purchase the property came from only one of the couple and in at least some of those cases this was seen as an obvious reason as to why the property should be purchased in their sole name:

> I'm sure there were conversations about it, but I don't think there was any view one way or the other. It was a question, I'd found the house and arranged the conveyancing, it was all my money. We were pretty much happy at the time.

Some simply did not appreciate how significant the legal ownership could be. In Linda's case, her partner had provided the deposit for their home, which was registered in his sole name. Later in the relationship they discussed putting her name on the deeds, but did not pursue the idea:

> [H]e was more than willing to make things formal and make me part owner of the home ... I really wish I'd done it.

The Reasons why (if it be the case) the Survivor was Authorised to give a Receipt for the Capital Moneys

In approximately half the joint ownership cases the transfer preceded the introduction of the TR1 in April 1998. Before its introduction, all that was required where property was purchased jointly was to declare whether the survivor of the purchasers was entitled to give a valid receipt for capital money arising on the disposition of the property (a point at issue in *Stack v Dowden* itself). Since 1998, the purchasers are now required to indicate on the TR1 whether they hold as 'joint tenants' or 'tenants in common', and if the latter, whether in equal or other shares. This change was intended to reduce the scope for disagreement between the owners subsequent to the purchase.[15] However, it was not apparent from the study that joint owners had understood their legal position any more clearly following this change compared with those in which the transfer pre-dated the TR1, and none of the solicitors raised this as a significant factor in their handling of separation disputes. To the cohabitants, as already mentioned, the survivorship aspect of the joint tenancy was very important. Whether this was for considered personal or 'property-based' reasons, or to save themselves the bother and expense of making a will and/or a declaration of trust is debatable. As one conveyancer put it:

> We try to make sure they understand it. You sometimes get the impression that they are plumping for the easier option. One of the aspects of joint ownership is the position on death. If they're unmarried and it's explained

---

[15] The Land Registry announced in July 2008 that, following a public consultation on a review of the Land Registration Rules 2003, it would conduct a further separate review on the particular issues arising from the form and procedure for the declaration of trust on the TR1: see Land Registry (2008) at 59–62.

that they wouldn't inherit from each other and therefore they should make a will … their reaction may well be that that's an extra expense—'all we're doing is buying a house now. We want each other to benefit'. So there may be a certain amount of inertia and they will go for the simpler option of joint tenancy rather than thinking about a will and joint ownership agreement.

Baroness Hale rejected the suggestion that the declaration in the pre-TR1 form of transfer should be treated as a declaration of trust. She went on to say:[16]

> Nor could it be relied upon for the purpose of drawing an inference as to their intentions, unless the parties had understood its significance,

and in *Stack v Dowden* there was no evidence that they had. Lord Neuberger agreed with this conclusion and added:[17]

> [I]t seems to me that, in the absence of any evidence of contemporaneous advice to the parties as to the effect of the declaration, the alleged inference would simply be too technical, sophisticated, and subtle to be sustainable, at least in the context of the purchase of a home by two lay people.

We suggest that similar reasoning might also apply to the declaration on the TR1, given its general opacity to the lay-person and the apparent lack of discussion, advice, recollection, and understanding of the consequences of joint ownership amongst the cohabitants in the study.

The Purpose for which the Home was Acquired

Most commonly in our study, the purpose of the purchase was to provide a joint home for the parties (and their children). However, in around one quarter of cases in both the core and secondary samples, more than one property was owned concurrently. In most of these cases the second property appeared to have been bought for investment or development purposes. Our study reflected the trend in recent years towards investment in buy-to-let properties and the fact that there are now large numbers of people who own more than one property. Although this situation did not arise in *Stack v Dowden* and was therefore not considered, it is likely to arise in an increasing number of cases, raising the question: how are the parties' intentions to be understood in relation to these properties?

In all the core sample cases from our study, and in all but two of the secondary sample cases, the second property was owned in one partner's sole name. In most cases, the second property was the subject of dispute, along with the first. Although the context of the purchase of the second property remained a domestic one, the purpose of its acquisition was more commonly a commercial one. It

---

[16] At [84].
[17] At [130].

seems likely, in the light of Lord Neuberger's judgment in *Laskar v Laskar*,[18] that a resulting trust approach towards the beneficial ownership of such properties may be more appropriate, but this remains uncertain for cases involving cohabitation. There were additional factors in several cases in the study; for example, the money for the second property was raised with the benefit of finance secured on the first property, usually the family home, or the purchase formed part of a complicated history of inter-related property transactions. In a few cases, one party had contributed more of the finance while the other had building skills which were used to create or renovate the properties. More often than not, the second property appears to have been viewed as a joint venture for the benefit of the family by at least one of the couple, although this had evidently not been clarified between the couple sufficiently to establish a *common* intention.

The Nature of the Parties' Relationship

Researchers have categorised types of cohabiting relationships in a variety of ways. Haskey (2001: 27), for example, used age and relationship history as the basis of his categorisation: 'youthful first time'; 'pre-marital' (those that end in marriage); 'post-marital' (where one or both of the cohabitants has previously been married); and 'subsequent' (where one or both of the cohabitants have previously cohabited). Kiernan and Estaugh (1993) used a similar classification, but added in the dimension of parenthood: 'nubile cohabitors', namely young, never married, childless cohabiting couples; 'cohabiting parents', namely young, never married, cohabiting couples with a biological child together; and 'post-marital cohabitants', namely those who cohabit after one or both have experienced a previous divorce.

Our sample, however, did not fit easily into these categories. For 17 of the 29 individuals in our core sample, the relationship from which they were disengaging had evidently been their first major relationship, but few of them could be described as 'youthful', or at least by the time of their separation—only two were below the age of 30. The average age of our core sample (41) was, in fact, similar to that for divorcing couples (ONS, 2008: Table 4.1). In seven cases, one or both of the partners had been married before, and in three, there had been a previous cohabitation. We could find no obvious correlation between any of these factors and either the legal title or the couple's intentions with regard to the property.

---

[18] *Laskar v Laskar* [2008] EWCA Civ 347, [2008] 2 FLR 589 [15]–[21]. This was a mother and daughter case in which it was found that the primary purpose of the purchase was as an investment, not as a home, and where a resulting trust analysis was applied. See, however, [33] where his Lordship acknowledged the principle established in *Stack v Dowden* that what seems fair to the court is not the basis on which one reaches a decision in such a case, but he nevertheless suggested that: 'It is sensible to stand back and see whether that looks a fair result'.

Baroness Hale may have had in mind the four rather more subjective categories of unmarried couples identified by the Law Society (2002), which she had discussed extra-judicially in 2004 (Hale, 2004):

— 'informed'—'both parties are fully aware of the limited rights that they may have and have come to a conscious decision that they wish to live together without marriage and without entering into financial responsibility for each other';
— 'uninformed'—'[t]he parties do not think they need to get married ... neither have given the matter much thought and probably have common misconceptions about what their legal position may or may not be';
— 'reluctant'—'[o]ne party wishes to marry but the other does not ...', and
— 'no choice'—'[t]he parties are unable to marry'.

Most of our cohabitants fell into either the 'uninformed' or the 'reluctant' category; there were none who could be described as 'fully aware' (although in some cases it appeared that one was more informed than the other) and none who were unable to marry had they chosen to do so. Although not obvious from our sample, it seems quite possible that if the parties had different intentions with regard to marriage, they may have had different intentions with regard to the property too, so that the search for a *common* intention could prove fruitless.

Barlow, Burgoyne and Smithson (2007) adopted a similarly subjective categorisation, focusing on the couple's attitude towards marriage and commitment (which we consider further below) which they found *was* linked to their financial arrangements. They took the view that the different categories of cohabitants have very different needs and issues requiring different solutions (see also Barlow, chapter fourteen, this volume). In *Stack v Dowden*, Baroness Hale criticised the trial judge for placing so much emphasis on the couple's relationship, 'rather than the matters which were particularly relevant to their intentions about [the] property', although she acknowledged the problems of making precise findings on many factors after a long relationship.[19] Our study reflected such problems, with our sample indicating generally that the longer the relationship, the more enmeshed and complex the financial and property arrangements became. Nevertheless, it was the length of the relationship, *combined* with the way in which the parties arranged their finances, which her Ladyship identified as making the case of *Stack v Dowden* very unusual:

> There cannot be many unmarried couples who have lived together for as long as this, who have four children together, and whose affairs have been kept as rigidly separate as this couple's affairs were kept. This is all strongly indicative that they did not intend their shares, even in the property which was put into both their names, to be equal.[20]

---

[19] *Stack v Dowden* [2007] UKHL 17 at [86].
[20] ibid at [92].

We look at how the couples in our sample arranged their finances and how that factor related to others in more detail below.

Whether they had Children for whom they both had Responsibility to Provide a Home

We assume that Baroness Hale had in mind those couples who have children together, and possibly also those where there are dependent children of only one or possibly neither of the couple but who have been treated as children of the family.[21] Our core sample included 15 cases where there were dependent children of the relationship but, once again, we found little correlation between whether the couple had children or not and either the nature of the ownership or the respective capital contributions towards the property. Clearly, having children affected the division of roles and responsibilities between the partners in terms of breadwinning and child care, and our sample reflected the population at large in having a majority of women taking the child-caring role. But these arrangements tended to evolve over time in response to the family's changing circumstances and could not be said obviously to have reflected the couple's specific intentions with regard to their beneficial ownership of the property.

Having children also appeared an unreliable indicator of commitment between the partners. The Law Commission (2006: [5.74]–[5.86]; 2007: [2.78]) recommended that having a child together should be enough to trigger eligibility under their scheme without any duration requirement, in part because it implied or ought to have implied a measure of commitment. Our study found that, where couples came or stayed together because of an unplanned pregnancy, each partner could hold quite inconsistent views about their commitment to each other, and for at least one of them, commitment to the relationship might have been described, in the words of Smart and Stevens (2000) in their study on cohabitation breakdown, as 'contingent'. In those circumstances and in others where the level of commitment differed between the couple despite the existence of children, the relationship between having children and the couple's intentions with regard to the property became somewhat obscure.

How the Purchase was Financed, both Initially and Subsequently

Initial Financial Contributions

The majority of the 23 core cases concerning owned property involved unequal initial financial contributions. In just over half of the total, the parties' initial financial contributions were not reflected in the legal title. However, there was

---

[21] For an interesting discussion of who might be regarded as 'responsible', eg in step-parent cases, see the Law Commission (2007: [3.46]–[3.56]).

a marked difference between jointly and solely owned properties. Ten out of the 12 jointly owned properties involved substantially unequal initial financial contributions. Conversely, eight or possibly nine (depending whom you believed) of the 11 solely owned properties were bought solely with funds from one of the parties. Thus the legal title was an accurate reflection of the initial financial contributions in most of the sole ownership cases but a poor reflection in most of the joint ownership cases. The secondary sample showed a similar picture, with the legal title being an unreliable indicator of financial contributions overall, but particularly so in joint ownership cases.

Where the legal title was not a reliable reflection of the initial financial contributions, the question then arises as to whether *either* the legal title *or* the initial financial contributions in fact accurately reflected the couple's intentions. Financial contributions were clearly determined in part by how much each partner actually had available to contribute. In sole ownership cases, where there was a closer correlation between financial contributions and legal ownership, a more financially astute or dominant partner tended to have taken the property into their name, in some cases on the basis that they were the one with the mortgage capacity, or occasionally for more dubious reasons:

> I talked to him about me going on the mortgage, and he said yes … then he turned round and said that [his mother] had found something that wouldn't allow me to be on the mortgage at that point in time. I can't remember what the reason was. In the end, once we'd moved in, he then produced a document and said, '[r]ight, you're allowed to sign this now because, in the future, because you live here and you're my partner—practically my wife—you can sign this document and then in the future, whenever we get a remortgage, I need you to sign this document'. That was it. Me being me, I didn't even question what I was signing.

The ways in which the couples in our study subsequently managed the issue of their beneficial interests on the breakdown of their relationship also suggested that the legal title and initial contributions were not reliable indicators of intention. Despite the fact that the solely owned properties accurately reflected the initial financial contributions far more often than the jointly owned ones, they tended to be far more contentious than the joint ownership cases. Only two of the sole ownership cases settled on the question of the beneficial shares without commencing proceedings, in contrast to the joint ownership cases, three quarters of which were settled without the issue of court proceedings (some of the latter in reliance on the presumption that beneficial shares followed the legal title, as now confirmed by *Stack v Dowden*).

Subsequent Financial Contributions

There were at least 11 cases amongst our core sample and seven in the secondary sample in which there were significant later financial contributions, none of which prompted any change to the legal title or were formally recorded between the cohabitants, whether the property was held in joint or sole names. If the initial financial contributions were not accurately reflected in the title, then it was even less likely that the couple would formally record any subsequent contributions.[22] In some cases where earlier contributions had come from one partner, later contributions came from the other. Ben, for example, who owned the family home jointly with his partner, put capital in later, both from the sale of a property which he had owned in his sole name and from an inheritance, whilst his partner had paid the initial deposit from a redundancy payment, and their property was held under a joint tenancy throughout. These later contributions had not been recorded; as Ben himself observed, 'This isn't a business arrangement'.

Baroness Hale acknowledged that the parties' intentions may change over time, producing what Lord Hoffmann referred to as an 'ambulatory' constructive trust, but she went on to say:

> [A]t any one time their interests must be the same for all purposes. They cannot at one and the same time intend, for example, a joint tenancy with survivorship should one of them die while they are still together, a tenancy in common in equal shares should they separate on amicable terms after the children have grown up, and a tenancy in common in unequal shares should they separate on acrimonious terms while the children are still with them.[23]

In fact, we think it highly likely that if we had asked our cohabitants if this was what they had wanted, many would have answered in the affirmative.

Non-financial Contributions

None of this says anything about the parties' non-financial contributions, such as child- and home-care responsibilities, or lack thereof. Currently the law does not recognise such contributions as giving rise to beneficial entitlement, and there were many cases in our study in which the legal title did not reflect such contributions. Amongst these were several examples of the 'Mrs Burns'-type scenario,[24] the most extreme of which was Frances, who had brought up the couple's four children over a 20-year relationship but who was entitled to no share in the family home because she had made no direct financial contribution towards it.

---

[22] *James v Thomas* [2007] EWCA Civ 1212, [2008] 1 FLR 1598 affirms that, as a matter of principle, post-acquisition discussions and conduct can be fully considered, although an inference of agreement as to post-acquisition change of ownership will not readily be drawn from conduct alone in the absence of evidence of express agreement.

[23] *Stack v Dowden* [2007] UKHL 17, [2007] 2 AC 432 at [62].

[24] *Burns v Burns* [1984] Ch 317, CA. Mrs Burns (who had adopted her partner's surname) lived with her partner for 19 years, but failed to establish a beneficial interest in the family home because she could not point to any direct payment towards the acquisition of the home. This was despite the fact that she had given up her job to have the couple's two children and then, when she did begin to earn money, had spent it on household expenses, fixtures and fittings in the house and the family's clothing.

Although they may have a lasting economic impact (see Fisher and Low, chapter eleven, and Price, chapter twelve, in this volume), such non-financial contributions are of course more difficult to quantify and are not directly comparable with capital contributions towards the property (although they may be more easily compared to contributions towards the mortgage and other household outgoings, which we discuss further below). However, there were a few cases in the study where the home had been put into joint names despite the fact that one partner had made a greater financial contribution towards its purchase, and where this may have been seen as a mechanism for recognising the non-financial contributions of the other. Ewan, for example, whose partner, Rosie, was expecting his child, was the sole contributor to the purchase of their home, and rejected the solicitor's advice that he could protect this contribution, commenting at the conclusion of his case:

> The children do need a home—I accept that responsibility. She would still have needed the money, and I think we all make ... mistakes. I'd have done the same thing again.

Alternatively the non-financial contributions may have been reflected in the settlement. Mary, who in some ways regretted not having done anything to record the fact that she had made a far greater financial contribution to the home, took a fairly pragmatic approach to the eventual settlement, commenting: 'I respect the fact that he's been the one to look after the children'.

How the Parties arranged their Finances

A number of studies (Pahl, 2005; Burgoyne and Sonnenberg, chapter five, this volume) have looked at the way that couples in both married and cohabiting relationships arrange their finances, and have found a growing trend towards separate finances. Ashby and Burgoyne (2008), however, found that those using separate financial systems of money management are not always operating as separate financial entities, and they warn that assumptions cannot be made about the meaning of the couple's financial arrangements without exploring the reasons behind them. Our study reflects this caution. Although the majority of the couples in our study operated separate accounts, we found a variety of complex joint and independent systems of money management with no clear pattern emerging.

We looked at the modes by which finances were owned and managed between the partners and at whether the ownership of assets and the mode of banking bore any correspondence to each other, as well as at the actual management of the finances in terms of who took responsibility for ensuring the bills were paid, budgeting and so on. Two thirds of the sample operated their finances from sole accounts, five operated entirely from joint accounts and a few operated additional accounts for specific purposes (for example, holidays and school fees), some of which were held jointly and some in sole names. In the case of joint owners, slightly more than half operated from sole accounts, with the remainder using joint accounts or a combination. Where the home was owned solely by one partner, in the majority of cases the couple also operated sole accounts. For example, Pat and her partner, who were both working full time, always kept separate accounts, he paying her an agreed monthly amount towards the bills, food and holidays. He had moved into her home and this remained in her sole name throughout their six-year relationship. Linda, whose partner was the main breadwinner and owned their home in his sole name, never held a joint account with him, and he just paid her a monthly housekeeping allowance 'in traditional style'. Opening a joint account 'was one of those things we never got round to doing'.

However, the day-to-day management of finances showed an entirely different picture, with little correspondence to the formal modes of ownership. The sample was divided more or less equally between those couples who managed their finances together and those where one partner had taken that responsibility. Men and women were equally likely to take on the responsibility of sole management.

It was difficult to find patterns across the two sets of dimensions. There were cases where one partner—the man—was clearly dominant in terms of economic power, owning the home, operating from a sole account, being the main breadwinner, and managing the finances. However, there were also cases in which the main breadwinner was not the main manager of the finances, even where the account was in the breadwinner's sole name. This was sometimes for pragmatic reasons, for example because one had more time to organise the bills and go to the bank, as in Linda's case referred to above. Another rather extreme example was James, who somehow gave his cohabitant control of the main household account, held in his sole name, to such an extent that he was unable to use it himself. It was clearly not necessarily the case that the economically stronger party always held the reins.

Looking at the couples having the greatest areas of equality—joint ownership, joint accounts, and equal contribution—there appeared to be little correlation with the mode of management. Of the few cases operating from joint accounts, more were in fact managed on a day-to-day basis by one partner alone, usually for pragmatic reasons, and/or because one was more capable of financial management than the other:[25]

> I was always really good on money and set up bankers' standing orders and the managing of the finances. He was rubbish. I knew that when I met him. That's my strength, and he's brilliant at cooking, so he can do that and I'll do the finances.

---

[25] See also Vogler, ch 4, this volume, who suggests that the partner managing the money is not necessarily the one in control.

On the other hand, several such couples organised their finances together, albeit from sole bank accounts. Again, this was sometimes for pragmatic reasons, for example where one partner was employed by a bank and operated the main household account through that bank in his or her sole name because he/she could obtain favourable employee conditions. In two other cases one partner had not previously held an account and so the finances were run from the other partner's already existing sole account.

Using the Smart and Stevens (2000) categorisation referred to above, we also looked at whether the degree of commitment to the relationship had any bearing on the couple's financial arrangements. We could find no obvious relationship between the two, and we found differing degrees of apparent commitment spread across the full range of financial arrangements.

Overall, we found no patterns of financial organisation that would do justice to the myriad of facets which contribute to a full and meaningful picture of how finances were organised. Much financial organisation arose from ad hoc decisions and circumstances requiring specific pragmatic solutions, rather than being based on any systematic principles. Generally speaking, financial arrangements appeared to have little or nothing to do with the couple's intentions with regard to property ownership.

How they Discharged their Outgoings on the Property and their Other Household Expenses

This aspect of the couple's finances is clearly related to those just discussed. Those couples who were contributing more or less equally in terms of income and expenses were more likely to be in the shorter, childless relationships and operated in a slightly more independent business-like way, such as in Pat's relationship described above. Karen and her partner, who were in their twenties and had had a relationship on and off for about four years, also had separate accounts and paid equally towards the outgoings on the property and other household expenses, even though Karen's income was considerably less than her partner's.

Longer relationships, however, were more likely to have created a degree of interdependence between the partners, and the more so when there were children, when there was the added dimension of the division of roles and responsibilities in terms of breadwinning and child care. Not surprisingly, where there were children it was not uncommon for the primary carer to be the lower income-earner and therefore to contribute less to the family expenses. Although there have been changes in the couple division of labour in Britain over the last decade (Scott and Dex, chapter three, this volume), our sample reflected the population at large, with the majority of women taking the child-caring role and a clear bias towards lower-paid employment for women. Brenda, for example, who had one child with her cohabitant and another from a previous relationship, worked part time at various jobs, 'whatever I could fit in, juggling with the kids'. Her partner paid the mortgage and regular bills, whereas:

> For me it was a case of all the in-betweens, clothes, all that sort of thing, but he paid the majority.

As we suggested earlier, however, the fact that one partner was the breadwinner and paying more towards the outgoings did not necessarily mean that he or she was the main manager of the finances or the financial 'boss'. Colin, for example, was the sole breadwinner for most of the relationship, but it was his partner who controlled the finances and had a far better working knowledge of them.

Baroness Hale suggested that in joint ownership/mortgage cases it is:

> easier to draw the inference that they intended that each should contribute as much to the household as they reasonably could and that they would share the eventual benefit or burden equally.[26]

It seems probable that this was the case in our study amongst the majority of those joint owners where there had been no express agreement or understanding about their ownership intentions. However, sometimes there was a difference in approach between the partners, or intentions changed over time, particularly where one was perceived not to be contributing as much as they reasonably could.

The Parties' Individual Characters and Personalities

Our research suggests that the parties' individual characters and personalities were a factor relevant to divining the couple's intentions. However, there were several cases in our sample in which the individuals appeared very different in character from each other, and where it would have been impossible to divine a *common* intention or one which was consistent over time. Colin, for example, who moved into his partner's home and lived with her there as the sole breadwinner for nearly 11 years, accepted that he was not entitled to a share in the house in the earlier years of their relationship, but latterly, having carried out and paid for numerous repairs and improvements, assumed that he would be. His partner, who was clearly the more dominant personality in terms of managing and controlling the finances, had, according to Colin, expressed the same intentions, but she nevertheless sold the property and disappeared abroad with the proceeds before he could get the case to court:

> I guess I'm a bit of a naïve person. I never really—I'm not mercenary minded and I didn't think that far ahead. I just take people as they are and hopefully they'll be as nice as I think I am.

Brenda's was a joint ownership case in which her relatively submissive personality was overwhelmed by her partner's, he being considerably older, more dominant,

---

[26] *Stack v Dowden* [2007] UKHL 17, [2007] 2 AC 432 at [69].

and allegedly abusive. She had a child from a previous relationship, and started living with her partner when she became pregnant with his child. She had been living in a property owned by her parents when they met, and they then purchased it, her partner contributing a sum representing between 50 and 75 per cent of the purchase price (the precise amount never being quite agreed). Neither partner appeared to have thought much about the ownership arrangements, but the property was put into their joint names, more at the request of Brenda's parents for her security than on her own initiative. She showed little understanding or interest in any financial issues, either during the relationship or on its breakdown:

> He was always better with the purse strings than I was. I'm a bit frivolous [laughs]. He basically ran the mortgage, insurances.

Although Brenda was in a relatively strong legal position, in that the property was subject to a joint tenancy, it was her partner's interests which prevailed throughout the relationship, and at the end of it, she moved out of the home with her two children, so that he could remain there with his two teenage sons: 'He saw it that as he had paid the mortgage, he shouldn't move out'. And, without taking any legal advice, she agreed to a settlement which was very much weighted in his favour.

CONCLUSION

As we have sought to demonstrate, the respective contributions—both financial and non-financial—that cohabiting parties make to their relationship and to the acquisition of property that they share during that relationship are not necessarily accurately reflected in the title to that property. This, of course, is why trusts law has been regarded as, at best a blunt, and at worst an unjust, instrument for attempting, after the fact, to determine how the parties' property should be held. In our study, we found that the type of ownership of property—joint or sole, joint tenancy or (rarely) tenancy in common—established at the point of purchase was selected for a variety of reasons or no conscious reason at all. Whilst one would expect that cohabitants might have poor recollections of conversations and advice which had taken place several years before they were interviewed, our discussions with practitioners confirmed that, even at the time, most couples are not interested in such matters. Moreover, as some cohabitant respondents explained, a joint meeting with a conveyancer may not be the right time or setting in which to consider coolly how to protect one's individual interests. At the same time, other, more wily (or more astute) cohabitants may be able to mislead partners so that they fail to assert their own interests or may not have any to protect. The complexity of the law and the opacity of the legal jargon may contribute to the parties' lack of understanding of their positions, and explanations written by lawyers for whom such language is commonplace may not be sufficiently clear to overcome the difficulties.

Couples' relationships vary infinitely, in terms of why they cohabit initially and why they remain cohabiting, their economic and domestic positions, their personalities, the dynamics of their relationship, the changes they undergo as life proceeds, and how far they can or do make financial or other contributions to keeping the relationship going and acquiring property during it. The way they hold property, and the way they organise their finances, as our study and others' demonstrate, may in turn reflect this myriad of circumstances and does not always conform to what one might logically or rationally predict or assume. It is arguable whether, on the breakdown of their relationship, a couple should be held to arrangements which have arisen during their relationship in response to circumstances as if they were by common intention.

Baroness Hale's list of factors was intended to capture and encapsulate this variety and to indicate which elements might be relevant to establishing the parties' 'true intentions', but our study gives little encouragement to the belief that it will provide a clear pointer towards those cases which are 'unusual' enough to warrant a departure from the legal title. On the basis of our findings, we are more inclined to agree with the view of Lord Neuberger:

> To say that factors such as a long relationship, children, a joint bank account, and sharing daily outgoings of themselves are enough, or even of central importance, appears to me not merely wrong in principle, but a recipe for uncertainty, subjectivity, and a long and expensive examination of the facts.[27]

BIBLIOGRAPHY

Ashby, K and Burgoyne, C (2008) 'Separate Financial Entities? Beyond categories of money management' 37 *Journal of Socio-economics* 458.

Barlow, A, Duncan, S, James, G and Park, A (2001) 'Just a Piece of Paper? Marriage and Cohabitation in Great Britain' in A Park, J Curtice, K Thompson, L Jarvis and C Bromley (eds), *British Social Attitudes: The 18th Report* (London, Sage).

Barlow, A, Burgoyne, C and Smithson, J (2007) 'The Living Together Campaign—An investigation of its impact on legally aware cohabitants', Ministry of Justice Research Series 5/07 (London, Ministry of Justice).

Barlow, A, Burgoyne, C, Clery, E and Smithson, J (2008) 'Cohabitation and the Law: Myths, Money and the Media' in A Park, J Curtice, K Thompson, M Phillips and E Clery (eds), *British Social Attitudes: The 24th Report* (London, Sage).

Douglas, G, Pearce, J and Woodward, H (2007) *A Failure of Trust: Resolving Property Disputes on Cohabitation Breakdown* (Cardiff/Bristol, Cardiff University/Bristol University), at www.law.cf.ac.uk/researchpapers/papers/1.pdf and www.bris.ac.uk/law/research/centres-themes/cohabit/cohabit-rep.pdf, funded by the ESRC (Award Reference: RES-000-23-0714).

Hale, B (2004) 'Unmarried Couples in Family Law' *Family Law* 419.

---

[27] ibid at [146].

Haskey, J (2001) 'Cohabiting Couples in Great Britain: accommodation, sharing, tenure and property relationship' 103 *Population Trends* 26.

Kiernan, K and Estaugh, V (1993) *Cohabitation: Extra-marital Child-bearing and Social Policy*, Family Policy Studies Centre Occasional Paper 17 (London, Family Policy Studies Centre).

Land Registry (2008) *Review of the Land Registration Rules 2003: Report on Consultation July 2008* (London, Land Registry).

Law Commission (2006) *Cohabitation: The Financial Consequences of Relationship Breakdown*, Law Com CP No 179 (London, TSO).

—— (2007) *Cohabitation, The Financial Consequences of Relationship Breakdown* Law Com No 307 (London, TSO).

Law Society (2002) *Cohabitation: The case for clear law* (London, Law Society).

ONS (Office for National Statistics) (2008) *Marriage, Divorce and Adoption Statistics*, Series FM2, no 33 (Newport, ONS).

Pahl, J (2005) 'Individualisation in Couple Finances: Who pays for the children?' 4 *Social Policy and Society* 381.

Probert, R (2007) 'Cohabitants and Joint Ownership: The Implications of *Stack v Dowden*' *Family Law* 924.

Smart, C and Stevens, P (2000) *Cohabitation Breakdown*, Family, Parenthood, Policy and Practice Series (London/York, Family Policy Studies Centre in association with Joseph Rowntree Foundation).

8

Financial Arrangements on the Breakdown of Cohabitation

Influences and Disadvantage

JANE LEWIS, ROSALIND TENNANT AND JEAN TAYLOR[*]

INTRODUCTION

ESPITE THE GROWTH in cohabitation, a developing literature on cohabitants' approaches to money management, a growing body of case-law showing what happens when they turn to the courts for help when they separate, and evidence of a disparity between public attitudes and the law when it comes to financial entitlement on separation, we know surprisingly little about how cohabitants actually divide their financial assets when their relationships end. This chapter reports the findings of a study which explored this issue.

As one might expect, the issue is linked to the way in which couples hold their assets during the relationship. Carolyn Vogler's work has been particularly important in shaping our understanding of how cohabiting couples hold money while they are together. Her analysis shows that young childless and older post-marital cohabiting couples generally keep their money partly or completely separate, while cohabiting parents are more like married couples in favouring joint pool arrangements (see Vogler, chapter four, this volume). Analysis of how cohabitants hold money has led to a questioning of the idea of cohabitation as a more egalitarian form of relationship than marriage. Researchers such as Pahl (1999), Elizabeth (2001), and Vogler (2005; see also Vogler, Brockmann and Wiggins, 2006) have shown that holding money separately perpetuates existing financial inequality,

[*] The authors are very grateful to the Ministry of Justice (formerly the Department for Constitutional Affairs) for funding the study on which this chapter draws. The full report of the study was published by the Department for Constitutional Affairs (Tennant, Taylor and Lewis, 2006). This chapter draws extensively on that report. We are also very grateful to the Department for Work and Pensions for allowing access to the Family Resources Survey as a sampling frame. Finally, we are indebted to Jane Craig of Manches and to David Allison of Family Law in Partnership for their advice on legal issues.

creating unequal access to financial resources in the relationship. How couples hold money has also been seen as a factor to take into account when ascertaining their intentions for the purposes of trusts law,[1] although, as both Burgoyne and Sonnenberg (chapter five) and Douglas, Pearce and Woodward (chapter seven) show elsewhere in this volume, couples' money management arrangements are messy and difficult to categorise, do not necessarily arise through explicit nego-tiation, and do not necessarily reflect shared intentions about responsibilities and expectations at the time they are made or subsequently. Even so, as this chapter will show, issues of ownership do influence the arrangements that separating cohabitants actually make.

This then inevitably has an impact on the financial implications of separa-tion. As Fisher and Low in chapter eleven of this volume note, there is very little research on the immediate and longer-term financial implications of cohabitation breakdown. Research in the US (Avellar and Smock, 2005), which involved four-way comparisons in financial outcomes between men and women and between the breakdown of marriage and cohabitation, shows that formerly cohabiting men's financial fortunes decline moderately on separation, whereas those of formerly cohabiting women decline much more precipitously. Married women experience a more dramatic decline in their financial fortunes than cohabiting women (starting from a more affluent position) but they end up with similar levels of poverty, and women fare worse than men irrespective of relationship status.

In this chapter we first describe the study on which we report. We then look at how couples in our study organised their money when they were together, and then look at financial arrangements on separation and the influences on them. We then consider their arrangements from different perspectives on 'fairness' and discuss how disadvantage arises. We finish by considering how far the Law Commission recommendations for legal reform (Law Commission, 2007) address the issues raised by the study.

THE STUDY

The study on which this chapter draws was commissioned by the Department for Constitutional Affairs in England and Wales, now the Ministry of Justice, shortly after the Law Commission was asked to undertake its review of cohabitation law. The objectives were to explore what arrangements couples make for parenting and financial division when cohabitation breaks down, their use of legal and other advice, the influences on their arrangements, and the impact on financial and parenting circumstances, with a particular focus on how disadvantage arises. The study involved qualitative in-depth interviews with 29 people who had separated

---

[1] *Stack v Dowden* [2007] UKHL 17.

from heterosexual cohabiting relationships, as well as qualitative research with solicitors and other advisors.

Since identifying research samples of former cohabitants is always something of a challenge, we provide some details here of our approach. Two national surveys were used to find a sample of former cohabitants. First, a series of questions was placed on the ONS Omnibus, a monthly face-to-face survey with a random general population sample, in April 2005. These questions identified people who had separated from a cohabiting relationship and the recency of this. We then carried out a telephone screen to collect more information about their circumstances.

We suspected that this survey would not yield a large enough sample, as indeed it did not, and so our second approach was to follow up several waves of the Financial Resources Survey, a continuous survey carried out for the Department for Work and Pensions, using face-to-face interviews with a random sample of the general population. We used the survey to identify people who were lone parents, or who paid or received child support, or who were cohabiting either two or four years ago. Since the lone parents and the payers and recipients of child support could have been either formerly married or cohabiting, we then carried out a telephone screen to identify those who were former cohabitants, and then collected more information about their circumstances. The telephone screen also identified, for people who were cohabiting two or four years ago, whether they had since separated.

From the sample frame generated in this way, a purposive sample was selected. We excluded from the study people who had cohabited for less than six months, and those who had separated less than three months or more than four years ago. We also excluded people from same-sex cohabiting relationships. Face-to-face interviews were then carried out with selected former cohabitants who agreed to take part, between late August and early November 2005.

The sample profile is shown in Table 8.1. Within the sample, the overall length of couples' relationships (including the period of cohabitation) ranged from one year to 30 years, with roughly half describing relationships that had lasted four years or less and the other half more than four years. The duration of cohabitation ranged from six months to 23 years. The sample comprised both parents and non-parents and included people with children from former relationships. Their financial circumstances varied greatly. Some were not home owners and had been on low incomes and state benefits even while they were together. At the other end of the spectrum were couples who owned two houses, with cases of substantial savings and high household incomes. Within the sample were couples who lived apart for some of the week but who nevertheless regarded themselves as cohabiting. For them, the fact that they spent most of the week together, or as much of it as possible, meant they considered themselves to be cohabiting. But they also maintained separate households, for example to retain a degree of independence (sometimes reflecting bad experiences of previous relationship breakdown) or to minimise disruption to children's lives.

Table 8.1: Profile of the Cohabitant Sample

	Female Participants	Male Participants	Total
Total	15	14	29
Children:			
Children from relationship	5	6	11
Lived with children from own/partner's previous relationship	5	1	6
Non-resident children from own/partner's previous relationship[1]	2	6	8
Non-resident adult children or no children	5	2	7
The couple's (main) home:			
Jointly owned	3	4	7
Man owned	4	6	10
Woman owned	4	1	5
Joint tenancy	1	1	2
Each had tenancy	0	1	1
Man sole tenancy	1	1	2
Woman sole tenancy	2	0	2
Duration of cohabitation:			
0–2 years	3	5	8
3–4 years	5	3	8
5–10 years	4	3	7
11+ years	3	3	6
Recency of separation			
3 months–2 years	13	8	21
2–4 years	2	6	8
Age of youngest resident child at separation:			
0–5 years	5	1	6
6–10 years	2	3	5
11+ years	3	3	6
Advice used:			
No advice	8	9	17
Solicitor	6	2	8
Citizens' Advice Bureaux	4	0	4
Child Support Agency	3	1	4
Other	2	2	4

[1] Sometimes in addition to children living with the couple.

HOW WAS MONEY ORGANISED DURING THE RELATIONSHIP?

We begin by reporting briefly how money was held in the relationships in our study, since this has important implications for how it was divided, and for the impact on each partner. We used two dimensions of money management in our analysis: joint to individual money management, and equal to unequal financial contributions.

Assessing couples' arrangements against both these dimensions is necessarily approximate. We asked participants to describe their money management and drew on these descriptions in our analysis, rather than using established categories such as those first developed by Pahl (1989; see Vogler, chapter four, this volume). The arrangements couples used were not always deliberately employed: people fell into a pattern of behaviour which was not always discussed, or they discussed some but not all of their arrangements. And there were sometimes internal inconsistencies, for example where some but not all assets were treated as joint, or where an asset was held in one partner's name but treated as joint.

There were four elements to the joint–individual dimension: the title under which assets (such as property or bank accounts) were held; who contributed to them; access, control, and who was seen as entitled to the asset during the relationship; and the perceived divisibility of financial assets. The equal–unequal dimension involved assessing how far the couple's financial assets arose from equal contributions. This is important because it displays economic dependency: the extent to which one partner gained more financially from the relationship than they contributed. There was almost always a degree of financial interdependence among the couples in our study by virtue of the fact that running one household is usually cheaper than running two. But our equal–unequal dimension highlights where one partner was reliant on the contribution of the other partner for their accommodation or living standard beyond what was mutual.

This financial dependency arose in two sets of circumstances from the outset of a relationship, and in two sets of circumstances during the relationship. From the outset of the relationship, it emerged from having fewer financial resources than a partner, either because of being the primary carer of children or for other reasons. During the relationship it arose from earning power being affected by having children, and from becoming ill and having to give up work. This last circumstance was described by only one person in our sample, but among older cohabitants one might expect to see it replicated where one partner retires from work before the other.

Our analysis, shown in Figure 8.1, yields four groups.

Joint equal arrangements involved merged financial assets with broadly equal contributions. This arrangement was typically found among couples who earned roughly equal amounts and who did not have children, or whose children had grown up so that any loss of earning capacity for one partner arising from parenting was largely historical.

Joint unequal arrangements were typically found where couples had had a period of broadly equal earnings when they had built up joint assets, but now had dependent children, which affected the financial contribution made by the mother as the main carer. Despite now making unequal contributions, the assets were still treated as joint.

Individual equal arrangements often reflected the fact that one or both partners had been in previous relationships. In some cases, the partners owned or rented

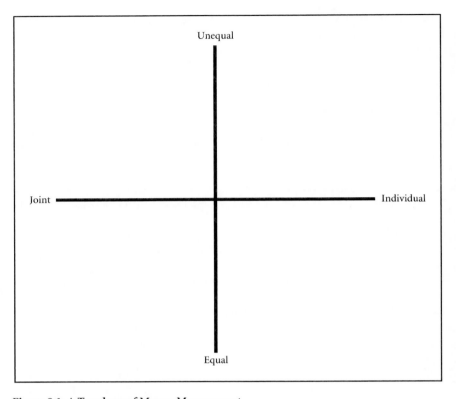

Figure 8.1: A Typology of Money Management

separate properties, living together in either one or both. Their assets were kept separate but they were concerned, and able, to make broadly equal contributions to housing and household expenses.

Individual unequal relationships were characterised by home ownership by one partner, who paid all or most of the housing costs although the other partner might make some contribution to housing or household costs. They had very different earnings levels, and sometimes one partner did not work, particularly if they had children from a previous relationship.

Financial dependency thus arose in the *joint unequal* and in the *individual unequal* arrangements. There was more financial protection in the former since assets were treated or held jointly; in the latter the weaker partner financially was very exposed on separation.

WHAT FINANCIAL ARRANGEMENTS ARE MADE ON SEPARATION?

We turn now to look at how people treated different assets when they separated, and then in the following section consider the factors that influenced this.

Homes

Where homes were held in the sole name of one partner they were almost always retained by that owner, with only one exception. This was true whether or not there were children of the family, and whether or not the other partner had made contributions to the purchase of the house that might have generated a beneficial interest under a trust (see further Miles and Probert, chapter one, this volume). The sole exception was a case where the house had been funded jointly but conveyed into one partner's name because the other was abroad at the time. It had been regarded as jointly owned throughout the long relationship and this was not questioned by either when they separated: the house was sold and the equity shared.

Homes held in joint legal ownership were either retained by one partner or sold. Where they were retained by one partner, this reflected their original ownership and the balance of financial contributions, but not necessarily who would be the main carer for any children. In other words, in some cases the children and their primary carer—always the mother in our study—moved out of a jointly owned home leaving the other parent to occupy it alone. In all but one of the joint ownership cases there was some compensation for the partner who lost the home. The exception here was a couple who remained close after the separation and where the woman had become financially dependent on the man because of ill health. Here the house remained in joint names, occupied by the woman, with no offsetting payment to the man, but on the understanding that he would inherit it from her.

Similarly, in cases involving tenancies, if the tenancy was in the name of one partner, that partner always kept it. This included one case where it was the other partner who had paid the rent throughout the relationship. The implication is that the tenancy was seen as belonging to the person in whose name it was held, but there were no cases where there was a dispute about its retention. Tenancies, including council and housing association tenancies, did not appear to be viewed as a valuable asset. Where the tenancy was in joint names it was either terminated or retained by one partner; again, this was never contested.

Financial Assets

Where couples had joint bank accounts, some divided up the balance and closed the account, but it was more common for the account to be kept, and the balance retained, by the person who stayed in the home. This either reflected the logic that the account was primarily for household bills and so should stay with the home owner for that purpose, or the home owner's generally dominant role in the relationship. Although the person retaining the account was sometimes the person who had made all or most of the contributions to the account this was not always in the case: retaining the home appeared to confer some extra advantage here.

Savings held in one name, even if seen as a joint asset during the relationship, were retained by that person. If they had been in joint names, they were either retained by the person who had generated them or divided between the couple.

Pensions were not taken into account in any of the cases in our sample. They were rarely referred to spontaneously by the people interviewed, and appeared never to have been considered in the arrangements they made. This was the case even where couples had been together for many years, with high levels of commitment to each other, had had children together, and had had a very joint approach to finances. People did not always know whether their partner had a pension, and pensions were not generally talked about as substantial or valuable assets. There were a number of reasons why pensions were not taken into account—couples felt they had not been together long enough to build up either legal or moral entitlement; they were far from retirement age; they thought they had broadly equal provision; they did not want to take what seemed a vengeful or grasping approach; or none of their assets had been shared—but what was more noticeable was that couples did not consider pensions when it came to ordering their finances on separation. This echoes findings from Arthur et al's (2002) study where married couples, as well as cohabitants, rarely considered pension rights on separation (see also Price, chapter twelve, this volume).

Debt

The way in which debts were dealt with on separation reflected whether they were seen as a joint or an individual responsibility during the relationship (see also Finney, chapter six, this volume). Debts which were in the name of one person, or which were seen as their responsibility, remained theirs. This included fairly substantial debts which one woman had accrued covering living expenses in the shared home. Debts which were viewed as joint, arising for example through an overdraft on a joint account or through non-payment of rent, remained a shared responsibility after separation.

Household Assets

Dividing up household goods and equipment could be an important part of the arrangements made by some people. Where people had not owned the home, household goods could be the only things they took away from the relationship, and the cost of setting up and equipping a new household with little or nothing from their previous home could be considerable.

Household goods were generally divided up in ways which reflected who owned or had paid for each item, or whose family or friends had given them, and there seemed generally to be a clear and shared understanding of this between partners. Where things had been purchased jointly they were shared out, or sometimes a financial payment made instead. As with bank accounts, being the partner who stayed in the home conferred some advantage and meant retaining more of the jointly purchased goods. There were also cases where people were particularly shocked and aggrieved to discover that they had no rights in relation to the family home, and took as much as they could of the household goods instead.

> I thought, well, the money I'd put into the house I couldn't take back, I couldn't take the garden with me, I couldn't take carpets, curtains, the lights, the new kitchen units, the new bathroom, I couldn't take any of that with me. So I thought, well it sounds a bit mean, but he had all that and all I did was take anything that wasn't attached to the wall basically. (Former cohabitant, woman, no children)

Child Support

Some form of child support was paid in all the cases involving dependent children of the couple. Some couples agreed to pay at the Child Support Agency (CSA) (now the Child Maintenance and Enforcement Commission) assessment levels, but others paid at a lower level. One couple agreed that the father should pay half the substantial child care costs instead of child support, and others had more ad hoc arrangements, such as paying when funds allowed, or giving money to the child or in one case to the person with whom the mother now lived.

WHAT INFLUENCES FINANCIAL ARRANGEMENTS?

Ownership

By far the most obvious influence on people's arrangements, as will be apparent from the description of arrangements above, was ownership: whose name an asset (especially a house) was held in, or who had bought it or been given it. What was meant here in relation to houses was legal title rather than beneficial ownership—that is, registered ownership rather than any rights that might arise under a trust. Ownership as the dominant motif applied to homes, bank accounts, debts, savings, and assets of all types.

Ownership was very prevalent as an influence where couples had more individual forms of money management—indeed, people sometimes consciously kept assets in their own name to ensure the other partner did not have any entitlement to them. The influences were more varied among couples with more joint arrangements. However, in some cases assets which had been seen as joint during the relationship came to be seen as individually owned on separation. In other words, the 'jointness' of financial arrangements was contingent on the relationship continuing, and it did not confer a sense of ownership or entitlement which survived the end of the relationship.

Establishing individual ownership where assets had been treated as joint involved reference to who had paid for or generated them, or whose family had provided them when the couple first moved in together:

> The fridge freezer was [partner's] mum's, so that was [partner's]. The cooker was from [partner's] mum so that was [partner's]. The telly was [partner's] mum's. It was really an old telly. The sofas were mine because they were off me gran. The CD player was [partner's]. The bed was mine because I bought that with me birthday money. I suppose you could say the carpets were mine because me dad bought me them. (Former cohabitant, woman, children from the relationship)

One woman, for instance, had set up a joint account with her partner when she moved into his house. Both salaries were paid into it until she stopped working upon the birth of their child, both had access to it, and it was used to pay the mortgage and other household bills. When they separated her partner refused to share the contents with her on the grounds that they had been generated from his salary alone since she had given up work.

One man acknowledged the contradiction in describing how the couple's savings, seen as a joint asset during the relationship, were treated as individual when they separated.

> They were in her name but we both talked about them as if they were joint ... There was a sense of both of us that although the mortgage was in my name it was sort of like ours, you know, and everything we did was definitely a sense of us as a couple ... So although they're her investments, it's my mortgage, it was definitely us and ours. [Later in the interview he talks about how his partner's investments were treated when they separated:] This is where, an answer to an early question about whether we saw that money as being ours, this is almost going to go contrary to that 'cos I'm gonna say, no, because it's her money. It's strange isn't it? Because it is her money, but we did talk about it as being our money. And like I would've, you know I would never say, 'well actually, you know, that £70,000 you've got tucked away, £35,000 of that is mine'. (Former cohabitant, man, resident children from previous relationships)

The principle applied very clearly to solely owned houses, including where there had been plans to transfer the house into joint names and where there had been financial contributions to the purchase or to paying mortgages. Such considerations never overrode legal ownership.

Contributions

Contributions often reinforced notions of ownership, for example where the absence of contributions reinforced the sense of individual ownership or where the fact that something had been bought with contributions from both partners meant it was seen as jointly owned. But contributions by one partner to something which on separation was treated as individually owned by the other were generally not recognised.

Where houses were held in one partner's sole name, financial contributions to the purchase—paying part of the deposit or mortgage—were not seen as conferring any sense of joint ownership. Indeed, such contributions were rarely recognised at all in the division of assets. One woman, for instance, had paid half the deposit when the house was bought, but it was conveyed into her partner's name alone because she was on Income Support and thought that owning a property jointly would jeopardise her benefit entitlement. He earned substantially more than her benefit income and paid the mortgage. They subsequently discussed conveying the house into joint names but decided not to because of the legal fees involved. He refused to pay her anything reflecting her contribution until some time after they separated when she threatened legal action, and only then a sum reflecting less than the sum she had contributed. Similarly, one man had paid more than half of the mortgage on his partner's home while they were together for seven years via a joint account from which all bills were paid. But he did not view himself as entitled to a share in the property—he doubted he had a legal right and, since they had a child, thought that he had no moral right.

Indirect financial contributions to the house purchase in the form of paying other household bills, or an arrangement that one partner paid the mortgage and the other the child care costs, were not reflected in any of the couples' financial settlements. Similarly non-financial contributions—paying for or carrying out home improvements, sometimes very substantial ones, or giving up work or reducing earnings to look after children—were never recognised.

However, contributions were seen as relevant in two cases where homes were jointly owned. In the first, the couple held the house as tenants in common with designated shares. When they separated, however, they based the division of the proceeds of sale on what each had contributed rather than on the agreed shares. In the second case, where the house was jointly owned (whether as joint tenants or tenants in common was unclear), despite a very long relationship which included having children, when the couple separated the female partner argued for a larger share of the equity on the grounds that she had contributed more to the purchase. The man rejected this argument but felt she was entitled to more as the children's main carer.

Needs

It was striking that consideration of the needs of children or adults played a relatively small part in the arrangements people made. This is, of course, in stark contrast to the importance that the needs of children in particular play in legal entitlement and the allocation of assets on divorce.

Adults' needs played a part in two cases. In one case the man took a smaller share of the equity in the jointly owned house in recognition of the capital his partner required to meet her housing needs given her lower earning capacity. And in the case where the woman had had to stop working because of ill health, the parties' respective needs influenced the financial arrangements made.

Children's needs also sometimes played a role. Recognition of the needs of the children for a stable home influenced one man's decision to transfer the joint house into his partner's sole name, taking an offsetting payment which reflected less than half the equity.

> I think she did come off well ... but I just accepted it ultimately ... [The children were] a very large factor because it wasn't just the guilt thing, they are my children, I love them dearly. I didn't, I mean the thought again of them having to move to somewhere that wasn't as nice. (Former cohabitant, man, children from relationship)

The fact that it was the children's home, or a home they would sometimes stay in, was an additional reason for some people not to consider whether they had any rights against their partner's solely owned home.

There were also cases where assets were divided with an eye to what adults or children needed, for example where bedroom furniture or a car was given to the main carer despite ownership or contributions, or where furniture or household equipment was given to a former partner to help them set up their new home.

Overall, however, needs did not emerge as a prominent influence on the arrangements people made. Indeed, there were a number of cases where children, and adults, experienced a substantial decline in the quality of their main home because their needs were not taken into account, as we discuss later. This was particularly apparent where there were children from one partner's previous relationship. Similarly, for adults, there was very little recognition of financial dependency in the way in which assets were dealt with, even where this dependency stemmed directly from explicit decisions to have children and for the mother's earning power to be reduced through their parenting arrangements. Thus in the *joint unequal* cases there was some call on assets by the dependent partner if they had been jointly owned as well as treated as joint, but for people in *individual unequal* arrangements there was no recognition of dependency. In other words, financial dependency which was accepted and even explicitly agreed during the relationship, and which arose specifically by virtue of the couple's family arrangements, did not override notions of ownership once the couple had separated.

Equality

Notions of equality rarely informed people's arrangements independently of ownership or contributions. As noted above, homes to which title was held jointly were usually seen as equally owned and this determined how they were treated. Similarly, assets which had been bought jointly were usually divided equally. But this reflected notions of ownership and contribution rather than equality per se. The exception here was a case where the participant stressed equality as the defining motif of the relationship throughout the interview, and the principle by which he and his partner made their financial and parenting arrangements both during and after the relationship. Although equality of impact was relevant in people's assessments of fairness post hoc, it was not clearly an influence on financial division at the time.

> Well, there was no winners ... When nobody comes out winning it's a draw, and if it's a draw it's fair. (Former cohabitant, man, child/ren from the relationship)

Legal Entitlement

Legal entitlement had surprisingly little influence on financial arrangements. For many people, their legal position did not appear to be a significant influence on the arrangements made: it was usually not the rubric by which people approached the settlement. Few people had clear beliefs about their legal position, and where they did, other influences overrode them. For example, one man believed that his partner as a supposed 'common-law spouse' was entitled to a share of the house which he owned, but took the view that there was no way he would give her anything. More generally, there seemed to be the same lack of consciousness of legal issues that people showed when they entered into cohabitation: they seemed simply not to have given any thought when they separated to what their legal position might be.

In the few cases where people did get legal advice this usually had an influence. One woman, for example, gave a payment to her partner reflecting a share in the house which she owned, following legal advice that, although his claim had no merit, it could be expensive to defend it. In other cases people were advised by solicitors or other advisers that they had no rights, and accepted this. In these cases an understanding of their legal entitlement was an influence, although rarely independently strong. And, as we discuss below, there were cases where people appeared not to have exercised their legal entitlement, even where they *had* sought legal advice.

Emotional and Psychological Influences

People's arrangements were also influenced by emotional and psychological influences. First, dominance during the relationship, in terms of financial power, decision-making, and willingness to discuss or negotiate, was reflected in arrangements where people refused to discuss options or simply 'said no'. People were also influenced by wanting to be fair or civil, by continued mutual affection and support, or by not wanting to press for more if they wanted to get away from the relationship as quickly and painlessly as possible. Guilt or pity was relevant where individuals had ended the relationship and recognised they had caused pain to their partner, since this sometimes inhibited them from pressing for what they saw as their full share of the assets. There was also sometimes a desire not to see a partner leave empty handed, or with less than they had brought into the relationship.

> I could have probably got some more money out of her but I would have, you know, I've just broken someone's heart and I don't, I don't really want to be doing that ... I wanted things over and done with. (Former cohabitant, male, no children)

HOW DOES DISADVANTAGE ARISE IN FINANCIAL ARRANGEMENTS FOLLOWING COHABITATION?

Assessing disadvantage in financial arrangements following cohabitation is clearly a complex issue since disadvantage could be conceptualised in a number of ways. It is perhaps unsurprising then that fairness or disadvantage were not clear-cut concepts to the participants in our study. In this section we therefore compare financial arrangements with a number of different concepts of fairness or disadvantage. First, we consider the partners' *material circumstances*: whether they experienced substantial material change in circumstances, whether this was unevenly experienced by the two partners, and whether material needs at the end of the relationship were met. Then, we consider notions of *compensation*: whether people were compensated for what they put into the relationship, for disadvantage or loss accruing during the relationship, or for the loss of protection provided by the relationship. Finally, we consider fairness in relation to *legal entitlement*: looking at whether people secured their legal entitlement under cohabitation law, and whether outcomes would have been different had the couple had the entitlement provided by matrimonial law.

Material Circumstances

Most people experienced some decline in material circumstances. This was most limited where it reflected the loss of small contributions to joint living costs; indeed, where people had supported a partner and paid all or most of the housing and household costs, they sometimes described an increase in affluence on separation (compare the findings of Fisher and Low, chapter eleven, this volume, regarding the situation of men post relationship breakdown). But some people experienced substantial changes in their material circumstances, particularly if they had been living in a house owned by their partner in which they had no share, if they had been dependent on their partner's income, and if they had to bear all or most of the costs of setting up a new household. It was in these circumstances, too, that there appeared to be greatest disparity between the partners' material circumstances on separation.

Similarly, partners' material needs were met in the financial division without any need for external assistance in cases where they had each retained a home or tenancy during the relationship, had independent incomes, and where jointly owned homes yielded enough equity to fund accommodation for both partners. In other cases, however, needs were not met, or at least not without external help. Where a person had lived in their partner's home and had neither the income nor the capital to fund another home, they became reliant on the state, their family, a new partner, or a friend, or simply struggled to manage accumulating debt on insufficient income. This was particularly evident for women with children, although it also emerged for men. The state played an important role in providing external assistance for women and children in these circumstances, while men, and women without children, were more likely to be supported by family and friends. Overall, people in *individual unequal* arrangements were particularly likely to experience material disadvantage.

An important aspect of needs which did not emerge in cohabitants' accounts was longer-term need. From what people were able to tell us, men generally had more pension provision than women, reflecting their higher earnings overall, and the fact that their earnings had not been reduced through having taken time off to care for children. As noted earlier, pensions were not taken into account in any of the arrangements made. It is likely therefore that there is considerable disparity between women and men in our sample in terms of whether longer-term needs were met by financial division (see further Price, chapter twelve, this volume).

Compensation

The dominance of legal ownership in shaping financial arrangements meant that people whose contributions were reflected in legal or agreed ownership were compensated for what they had put into the relationship: they took out what they had brought into the relationship. There were, however, circumstances where what people put in was not reflected in the financial division, because they had made direct or indirect financial or non-financial contributions not reflected in legal title ownership which dominated the outcome on separation regardless of a possible trust claim. For both men and women this arose where they had paid towards mortgages, housing purchase, or other household bills, or where they had funded improvements to property. Non-financial contribution of parenting and household management was sometimes reflected in the division of jointly owned assets in long relationships, but not if assets were owned by the other partner.

In terms of compensation for disadvantage accruing during the relationship, the most obvious forms of disadvantage were loss of the financial support enjoyed during the relationship, and the continued effect of reduced earning capacity mostly arising from parenting roles. There was also one case where a man had moved to part-time employment so that he could do substantial improvements first to his own house and then to his partner's, adding considerably to the value of both, but particularly the latter. He had lived in his partner's house after it was renovated, making some contribution to household expenses (but not to the mortgage), and keeping the rental income from his own house, but otherwise was not compensated for his loss of earnings. And, as noted, there was one case where the woman had to give up work because of ill health.

These forms of disadvantage were reflected in the division of jointly owned assets in longer relationships, but not if assets were owned by the other partner. They were also reflected in payments of child support, although such payments were not always at the level set by the CSA and, even when they were, were not felt to be sufficient to cover the costs of child maintenance, particularly in a separate household.

In terms of loss of protection accruing from the relationship, there was no such loss where the couple had broadly equal financial resources and kept their finances quite separate—the *individual equal* couples in our segmentation. People who had provided financial support to a partner through funding their living expenses also experienced no loss—indeed, were better off—when the relationship ended. But it was more common for there to be a loss for one or both partners. The loss was experienced by both where it reflected the economies of scale involved in a shared household, and where the partners now had to fund two households where they had previously pooled resources to fund one. However, more substantial loss of protection which was not compensated in financial arrangements emerged where one partner owned the house and the other had no share in it, and where one partner had been dependent on the other's income—in the *individual unequal* arrangements in particular.

Legal Entitlement

Assessing arrangements by comparison with the parties' potential entitlement under trusts law is necessarily approximate: we did not collect and assess 'evidence' in the way a lawyer and a court would, and trusts law is full of uncertainty, particularly if there are potential counter-claims. However, we were greatly aided by the advice of two family solicitors who considered 10 of the 29 cases with us and gave us their opinion as to whether the arrangements made were consistent with legal entitlement.

Arrangements were broadly consistent with trusts law in four sets of circumstances: first, where the financial resources of the couple were very limited and they lived in rented accommodation; secondly, if the property was owned jointly and divided broadly equally between the partners; thirdly, if the property was in the sole name of one partner but there were no children from the relationship (so there was no Children Act 1989 Schedule 1 claim[2]) and few or no financial or other contributions had been made by the non-owner (so there was no or only weak potential for a trusts claim); and finally, if child support was paid at CSA assessment levels.

However, in many cases the arrangements made were not consistent with the law. This occurred in various circumstances: first, where there were children from the relationship and thus a potential claim under Children Act 1989, Schedule 1; secondly, where there was potential for a claim against the house under a resulting or constructive trust or proprietary estoppel, whether based on financial contributions, substantial material improvements to the house, dealings suggesting a joint financial enterprise, a stated intention to put the house into joint names, or where one partner had acted to their detriment with the active or passive encouragement of their partner; and thirdly, where child support was paid substantially below CSA assessment levels.

The greatest inconsistency between legal entitlement and arrangements arose where there were both more substantial contributions and a Schedule 1 claim. In one case, for example, the woman moved into the man's solely owned house, they lived together for five years and had a child. She contributed to the mortgage while she was working, via a joint account, and invested £4,000 in capital improvements. They had investigated transferring the home into their joint names and were deterred by the legal costs involved, but were planning to move and to hold their next home jointly. When they separated she moved out into a rented flat and claimed state benefits, getting no financial provision from the relationship except child support. She appeared to have potential claims for constructive trust and proprietary estoppel, and a claim to occupy the house under Schedule 1.

What is striking is that people whose arrangements were not consistent with the law had sometimes received advice, either from a solicitor or from a Citizens' Advice Bureau. But they either said they had been told they had no rights in relation to housing, or had been advised about state support without any apparent consideration of their legal entitlement against their partner. It is possible that people mis-remember or misunderstand what they were told by an adviser, especially given the complexity of trusts law, and so some caution is needed here. However, it seems unlikely that this alone explains apparent shortcomings in the advice they were given.

A fuller use of existing legal rights would therefore have mitigated some of the disadvantage experienced by former cohabitants who had children in the relationship. However, it would not have aided people where no contributions had been made that would have supported a trust claim (for example, purely domestic

---

[2] Schedule 1 of the Children Act 1989 does not apply in cohabitation cases if the child is not the child of both partners.

contributions), where the children were from another relationship so there was no Schedule 1 case, and where income levels were constrained so that occupancy under Schedule 1 could not have been supported by the child's main carer.

The second aspect to be considered is how far cohabitants were disadvantaged by comparison with the likely outcomes had they been married, where again we were helped by the two family lawyers. Under this rubric, the arrangements made by people in the study were broadly in line with outcomes upon divorce where there were no children or low financial resources (see further Hitchings, chapter nine, and Maclean and Eekelaar, chapter two, this volume, on the dominance of practical considerations in this context). But arrangements were very different from likely outcomes upon divorce in the cases where the house was in the sole name of the father, and especially if there was a child from a previous relationship. Had the parties been married, the needs of the children would have been the first consideration for the court, and the primary carer could have expected the house to be transferred to her (sometimes with a charge back to the father), or a substantial share of the equity.

Perhaps the most obvious difference was in a case where the house was bought during the relationship in the man's sole name. The woman had a son from her previous marriage: she received some child support from her ex-husband and had had a small lump sum from the divorce settlement but spent this on her living expenses during the cohabitation. She and her cohabitant lived together for seven years. They had agreed to buy the house in sole names but he signed the deeds in his name alone, saying this was more convenient and he would later transfer it into joint names. She made no direct financial contribution but bought furniture and paid the food bills. She believed that he had very substantial savings and earned around £150,000 per annum; she earned very little and they kept their finances separate. By the end of the relationship, he had bought another house where he was living during the week, and she had acquired debts funding her own and her child's living expenses. She received no support or provision following the separation.

Under trusts law she did not have a particularly strong claim, nor did she have any Schedule 1 rights, so she would have been unlikely to have secured any capital to reflect rights to the house. Had she been married to her partner the settlement would have been based around her needs and those of the child: she could have expected a considerable capital sum and spousal maintenance.

The outcomes might also have been expected to be different, although less significantly so, in other circumstances: first, where the house was jointly owned and divided equally despite there being children; secondly, where the mother owned the house and the father had contributed (he might have expected a deferred capital payment); thirdly, where there were no children and the non-owning partner had made no contributions to the home (upon divorce they might have expected a small capital payment or brief spousal maintenance); fourthly, where there were substantial other assets that would have been taken into account, such as savings, pensions, or another home; fifthly, where the parties' earnings were very different and there might have been spousal maintenance; and finally, in relation to child support, where the child was from a previous relationship: had the parties been married, maintenance for the child might have been awarded if the child's birth father was not providing support.

Overall, and consistently with other assessments of fairness, it is again women whose income and property resources were affected by having children (either prior to or within the cohabiting relationship) who emerge as the most disadvantaged. However, the difference is greatest for women with children from a previous relationship, because of the different interpretation of the mother's partner's responsibilities depending on whether he was married to her or not.

Multiple Forms of Disadvantage

There is a high degree of consistency in who ends up with unfair outcomes, whether this is assessed by reference to material circumstances and needs, to compensation for different forms of economic disadvantage, or to legal entitlement. Multiple forms of disadvantage, where people's arrangements failed to meet several of the criteria by which fairness was assessed, tended to arise where the man was the sole owner, the woman had made unrecognised financial or non-financial contributions, and there were children. These were generally cases where financial arrangements had been *individual unequal.*

The circumstances which contributed to disadvantage are: not being the legal owner of property, especially where this conferred the additional benefit of retaining household goods and bank accounts; not making any financial contributions, or making financial contributions which were not reflected in ownership; and being the main carer, particularly for young children.

Having children from a previous relationship was particularly relevant here. Some previously divorced women had secured the former matrimonial home or a large share of it. But for those who had not done so, having children from that previous relationship underpinned disadvantage on the breakdown of the subsequent cohabitation in three ways. First, it meant they had more limited financial resources to bring into the relationship. Secondly, not having a period of broadly equal earnings limited their ability to make contributions during the relationship and thus, for example, the opportunity to buy a house in joint names or to contribute to a partner's solely owned house. And, thirdly, the fact that the child was from a previous relationship meant there was no legal entitlement under Schedule 1 or to child support.

Some of the multiple forms of disadvantage might have been mitigated by pursuing their full legal entitlement, and for women with children on very low incomes disadvantage was mitigated to some extent by state support. Overall, however, whereas the scheme that operates on divorce is redistributive, financial division on the breakdown from cohabitation sustains the financial power dynamics in the relationship—whether they exist from the start, arise from decisions made during the relationship, or are the result of other factors such as ill health.

WHAT EFFECT WOULD THE LAW COMMISSION
RECOMMENDATIONS HAVE ON DISADVANTAGE?

In this final section we consider how far the Law Commission's recommendations for legal reform would mitigate this disadvantage. Broadly, the Law Commission recommended that eligible cohabitants should have a right to claim financial adjustment for retained benefit or economic disadvantage arising from contributions made during and deriving from the relationship. The proposal is that retained benefits are reversed, that is, the benefit restored to the contributor, so far as possible, and that any residual economic disadvantage is shared equally, subject to the proviso that the applicant should not be put in a stronger financial position than the respondent for the foreseeable future in terms of income and living standards (the 'economic equality ceiling'). Economic disadvantage encompasses loss of future earnings and pension entitlement, loss of the opportunity to build up savings, and the cost of future child care: the applicant is expected to mitigate these losses as far as is reasonable and possible. The welfare of children of both partners should be the first consideration, and that of children living with either partner but not from the relationship a lower-level consideration (Law Commission, 2007).

We consider these recommendations in relation to the four types of economic dependency that we noted earlier: dependency arising from the outset of the relationship, either because of having children from a previous relationship or for other reasons, and dependency arising during the relationship from having children within the couple or from becoming ill.

Dependency arising from having fewer financial resources without there being children would not in itself result in financial entitlement under the Law Commission's recommendations. The typical scenario here was where a man or woman moved into a home owned by their partner, where their partner paid the mortgage and most of the living costs.[3] Under the Law Commission's recommendations there would be entitlement only in circumstances where a person had contributed to the mortgage, or to household costs without which their partner would not have been able to pay the mortgage, or in the form of physical improvements to the property which increased its value. In such cases, there would be entitlement to repayment of the 'retained benefit' which their contribution had yielded. This would have been an improvement on outcomes for some people in our sample, although it would not necessarily provide more than under existing trusts law. Of course, there will be different views about whether a legal remedy is appropriate in these circumstances or whether it is broadly fair that a partner with a lower living standard before the cohabitation should return to that situation when the cohabitation ends. Our purpose here is to highlight that it is a form of material disadvantage, and one that the Law Commission recommendations would address only if a 'retained benefit' arose.

---

[3] This is akin to Example 1 in the Law Commission report (2007: para B.18).

Dependency arising from having children from a previous relationship *may* be better provided for under the Law Commission's recommendations. The typical scenario here was where a woman with a child from a previous relationship moved into her new partner's home, with reduced earnings potential because of her caring role. The Law Commission recommendations say that care for children who are not from the relationship *could* be a qualifying contribution (Law Commission, 2007: para 4.44): it should not normally suffice but there may be cases where it would be appropriate to treat this as a qualifying contribution (Law Commission, 2007: n 36). There is no discussion of the circumstances that might suffice, but the earlier consultation paper (Law Commission, 2006: para 6.209) suggests that the amount of time the child spends in the cohabiting household (rather than in the other parent's household) would be relevant. Our study included cases where such children lived full time in the cohabiting household.

If a claim were eligible, under the Law Commission's recommendations the couple would be expected to share the economic disadvantage, with the women expected to mitigate her loss as far as is reasonable and possible by working where possible, although the fact that children not of the relationship are not the first consideration implies that her entitlement would be less than where the children were from the relationship. If she had contributed to the property purchase or to mortgage payments, or to household costs essential to her partner being able to pay the mortgage, she would also be entitled to provision in the form of a reversal of the retained benefit generated by such contributions. Under these circumstances women with an eligible claim would be better off under the Law Commission's recommendations than under the current legal regime, although possibly not if their contributions could support a substantial claim to a constructive trust within trusts law.

The most generous provision under the Law Commission's recommendations is likely to arise where there are children within the relationship. Assuming a situation where the family lives in a house owned in the man's sole name and where the mother is the main carer during and after the relationship, financial contributions she made to the house purchase would entitle her to share in the retained benefit. The continuing economic disadvantage stemming from reduced earnings capacity and child care costs, including loss of pension and National Insurance entitlement, would also be shared between the parties. The quantum and, in particular, the form of any remedy granted would reflect the fact that the children's welfare is the first consideration for the court when exercising its discretion to grant relief addressing any retained benefit and/or economic disadvantage. Provision to the mother would be capped by the economic equality ceiling so she would not be put in a stronger position than the father 'for the foreseeable future' (Law Commission, 2007: para 4.72), but this could still result in a share of more than half of the assets (para 4.73).

Our final example is where one partner becomes financially dependent during the relationship because of ill health. Our case example here involved a house in the couple's joint names. Under the Law Commission recommendations, there would be no entitlement to financial provision by virtue of the dependency or ill health—because of the requirement for economic disadvantage to be under-pinned by a qualifying contribution. Had the house been in the other partner's sole name but with contributions made to the purchase costs, there would be an entitlement to restoration of the value of the retained benefit.

DISCUSSION

Overall, then, in our study the strongest influence on arrangements following separation from cohabitation was legal ownership. Contributions had some role to play, but particularly where they reinforced notions of legal ownership, or helped to determine respective shares of jointly owned assets. They did not of themselves lead to compensatory payments or an adjustment of ownership. Consideration of needs, notions of equality, and reference to legal entitlement seemed to play little part.

Why the dominance of legal ownership? It is at odds with research on public attitudes to how the law should treat separating cohabitants. Research by Barlow et al (2008) shows that high proportions of the public agree that separating partners should have rights to financial provision in a variety of circumstances, although there remains a stronger endorsement of rights for married couples in the same circumstances. It is also surprising given the fact that joint or sole own-ership can arise in ways that are rather ad hoc and not necessarily clear cut (see Douglas, Pearce and, Woodward, chapter seven, this volume). For example, there were cases in our sample where the house was conveyed in one partner's name as a matter of convenience rather than as a reflection on underlying notions of own-ership or entitlement, or where the couple discussed putting it into joint names but were put off by legal fees, or where a bank account in one partner's name was funded and used by both.

It may be that the objectivity and clarity of title means that it simply has a greater weight in a couple's discussion of financial entitlement, or in their own conception of entitlement, than the complexities of trusts law or more subjective discourses based on fairness. The fact that it is more easily articulated and can be stated as a fact may give it a power much greater than the significance it held to the parties during the relationship. Across our sample the partner who owned assets seemed to be in a stronger position in negotiations defending their ownership, essentially able to say 'no', than the partner petitioning for a share. Legal owner-ship was itself a reflection of power in the relationship—clearly a reflection of financial power, but sometimes also of psychological or emotional power. And at a time when at least one partner's feelings towards the other are likely to be very negative, it is perhaps unsurprising that retentive instincts on the part of a legal owner become dominant.

Ultimately, separating cohabitants appear not to see the cohabitation itself as conferring financial rights or responsibilities—despite public attitudes and stud-ies which highlight that the personal values and assumptions of cohabitants in terms of commitment to the relationship, although varied, are for some people very similar to those of married people (Lewis, 1999, 2001; Arthur et al, 2002; Eekelaar and Maclean, 2004; Barlow et al, 2008). Perhaps cohabitants internalise something of the lower legal and social status of cohabitation despite their exter-nalised views about marriage as 'just a piece of paper'. What is striking is that this lower status seems more relevant at the end of the relationship than during it. Cohabiting couples who do not see the absence of marriage as relevant to their commitment or to the social status of their relationship nevertheless divide assets as if cohabitation itself was of no significance. The lack of formality involved in *ending* cohabitation seems more influential overall than the lack of formal-ity in *beginning* it, raising the suspicion that legal ownership might be the motif to which married couples would default on separation were it not for the legal framework of divorce. Or it may be that the absence of a formal or legal status to the start of cohabitation means there is more scope to reconceptualise the rela-tionship when it ends than there is in marriage—to re-interpret the absence of formality as reflecting limited financial rights and responsibilities even though it did not have this meaning during the relationship.

The current legal framework similarly does not treat cohabitation per se as conferring rights or responsibilities: these arise from what happens within cohabi-tation, such as the nature of financial contributions made and whether there are children in the relationship. The law thus provides particularly poor protection where people have not made contributions, where the children are from a previ-ous relationship (however they are treated and provided for in the cohabitation), and where income levels make Schedule 1 occupancy an unviable option.

The Law Commission recommendations go some way to recognising depen-dency, but again it is not the state of cohabitation (or cohabitation in a form that secures eligibility to apply for relief under the recommended scheme) that cre-ates rights and responsibilities, but the contributions made and losses sustained. Although the conception of these contributions and losses is much wider than under the current legal framework, they still relate specifically to what happens within the cohabiting relationship. Thus, dependency that arises through disabil-ity or ill health is not relevant, and the needs of children not of the relationship are not clearly secured in the recommended scheme. Whereas marriage confers rights and responsibilities irrespective of how money is managed, the current law and the Law Commission recommendations frame rights as contingent on what happened within the relationship. Of course, there is great variation in the intentions and commitments implicit in cohabitations, and for some there is a deliberate decision not to acquire the commitments that marriage would imply. Nevertheless, dependency arises in cohabitation in a number of ways, and it argu-ably needs to be recognised more fully. As one participant in our sample said:

> There's a set of rules and there's reality, and there's injustices happening because of the differences. (Former cohabitant, woman, resident children from previous relationship)

BIBLIOGRAPHY

Arthur, A, Lewis, J, Maclean, M, Finch, S and Fitzgerald, R (2002) *Settling Up: Making Financial Arrangements after Divorce or Separation* (London, National Centre for Social Research).

Avellar, S and Smock, P (2005) 'The Economic Consequences of the Dissolution of Cohabiting Unions' 67 *Journal of Marriage and Family* 315.

Barlow, A, Burgoyne, C, Clery, E and Smithson, J (2008) 'Cohabitation and the law: myths, money and the media' in A Park, J Curtice, K Thompson, M Phillips and E Clery (eds), *British Social Attitudes – The 24th Report* (London, Sage).

Eekelaar, J and Maclean, M (2004) 'Marriage and the Moral Bases of Personal Relationships' 31 *Journal of Law and Society* 510.

Elizabeth, V (2001) 'Managing money, managing coupledom: a critical investigation of cohabitants' money management practices' 49 *Sociological Review* 389.

Law Commission (2006) *Cohabitation: The Financial Consequences of Relationship Breakdown*, Law Com CP No 179 (London, TSO).

—— (2007) *Cohabitation: The Financial Consequences of Relationship Breakdown*, Law Com No 307 (London, TSO).

Lewis, J (1999) 'Relationship Breakdown, Obligations and Contracts' 29 *Family Law* 149.

—— (2001) *The End of Marriage? Individualism and Intimate Relationships* (Cheltenham, Edward Elgar).

Pahl, J (1989) *Money and Marriage* (Basingstoke, Macmillan).

—— (1999) *Invisible Money: Family Finances in the Electronic Economy* (Bristol, The Policy Press).

Tennant, R, Taylor, J and Lewis, J (2006) *Separating from Cohabitation: Making Arrangements for Finances and Parenting* (London, Department for Constitutional Affairs/Ministry of Justice).

Vogler, C (2005) 'Cohabiting couples: rethinking money in the household at the beginning of the twenty-first century' 53 *Sociological Review* 1.

Vogler, C, Brockmann, M and Wiggins, R (2006) 'Intimate relationships and changing patterns of money management at the beginning of the twenty-first century' 57 *The British Journal of Sociology* 454.

9

Chaos or Consistency?

Ancillary Relief in the 'Everyday' Case*

EMMA HITCHINGS

INTRODUCTION: THE RECENT DESCENT INTO
'UNCERTAINTY' AND 'CHAOS'

T HE HOUSE OF Lords decision in *White v White*[1] concerning section 25(2) of the Matrimonial Causes Act 1973 remains the turning point in ancillary relief jurisprudence. The established judicial construct of 'reasonable requirements' as a criterion by which to assess (and limit) ancillary relief in the 'big-money' case was suddenly abandoned. Instead, the House of Lords emphasised the lack of hierarchy in the section 25(2) factors along with the implicit objective of 'fairness' and the yardstick of equality. This had the effect of opening the door to various and varying lines of argument—such as special contributions, conduct, legitimate expectations, and the duration of marriage as the means by which lawyers might seek to obtain a larger proportion of the 'pot' for their client.

Critics have argued that the interpretation of section 25 in recent case-law has led to a lack of clarity and uncertainty within the law. Commenting upon the Court of Appeal's decision in *Miller v Miller*[2] prior to its House of Lords hearing, John Eekelaar described the current uncertainty as 'the descent into chaos' (Eekelaar, 2005); after the House of Lords decision in *Miller v Miller; McFarlane v McFarlane*,[3] he suggested that despite the Law Lords attempting to put into place 'a framework within which property and financial disputes on divorce could be disposed of on a fair and principled basis' the process was 'not yet complete' (Eekelaar, 2006: 754; see also Francis, 2006). Other commentators have also suggested that the House of Lords decision in *Miller; McFarlane* throws up 'very serious practical problems ... in the area of maintenance and periodical payments'

* The research upon which this chapter is based was funded by the Nuffield Foundation through their Small Grants Scheme.
[1] [2000] 2 FLR 981 (hereafter referred to as *White*).
[2] [2005] EWCA Civ 984.
[3] [2006] UKHL 24 (hereafter referred to as *Miller, McFarlane*).

(Moor and LeGrice, 2006: 655; see also Hess, 2006), while Bailey-Harris puts the point more generally:

> For both practitioner and academic, the pattern of the law's development fails to please. It is impossible to predict when an articulated statutory principle will be seized upon in a judgement, or when a new sub-principle will be invented, or when the search for principle will simply be disclaimed (Bailey-Harris, 2005: 240).

The shift away from 'reasonable requirements' and the introduction of the yardstick of equal division has resulted in wives gaining an enhanced share of the assets in the 'big-money' cases. This in turn has enabled lawyers to deploy ingenious arguments in order to reduce the wives' share and thereby depart from the yardstick of equal division. But what of the vast majority of cases in which the higher courts cannot be utilised due to cost? The impact of recent jurisprudential development upon the run-of-the-mill everyday case has been woefully underresearched. As Davis, Cretney and Collins identified in 1994:

> Most of what is written on the subject, whether it be aimed at students, academics or practitioners, is concerned with statute and case law ... These reported cases offer a guide to practitioners who are attempting to settle cases, and to judges when they have to try them. But these case reports offer comparatively little insight into the routine reality of the divorce process, either for practitioners or the parties. (Davis, Cretney and Collins, 1994: 253)

The research upon which this chapter is based was directed at examining solicitors' understanding of the law and, correspondingly, the advice that was given to their clients. Practitioners are currently in a situation where they are faced by the onslaught of new and arguably uncertain case-law which has generated much commentary surrounding the 'chaotic' and 'uncertain' nature of the current law. Nevertheless, this study has found that, overall, there is a pretty consistent approach amongst practitioners in dealing with the everyday ancillary relief case. However, despite this apparent consistency from a practitioner-advice perspective, there appears to be a preference amongst certain practitioners for dealing with particular courts, based on both predictability and insider knowledge of judicial approaches within that court. Furthermore, there are some additional indicators which suggest that there may be some inconsistency of approach between different courts. Likewise, there is an appreciation by certain practitioners of these differences in courts and judicial approaches, with practitioners in one particular area appearing to tailor their approach accordingly.

METHODOLOGY

The research sample contained 24 practitioners, with eight from each of the three chosen areas: one Thames Valley county; one county from the West Country; and one large regional centre in the south of England. The solicitors were chosen at random from the Resolution Directory and the Law Society website. The firms ranged from regional law firms through to specialist family law firms and high street practitioners. Thirteen firms had a legal aid contract for family work, although three of those did not include publicly funded ancillary relief work. Four of the solicitors were trained mediators, and the vast majority considered themselves to be specialists in family work. The experience of the solicitors interviewed ranged from seven who had post-qualifying experience of five years or less, to eight practitioners who had over 20 years' experience. There were 17 women and seven men in the sample.

Clearly the study is limited both numerically and geographically; the sample is small, and there is no northern, midlands, eastern or London representation. Although the study cannot be claimed to be representative, its purpose is to shed light on an area that has been under-researched and to provide a perspective that helps us to evaluate what is happening to the practice of family law in the wake of massive jurisprudential development.

Interviews were digitally recorded and transcribed in full. The main method employed was interviewing. Respondents were given two problem scenarios and asked to comment upon them. That part of the interview was designed to overcome the anticipated problem that family solicitors might not feel able to talk about specific cases and also to assess whether the family solicitors in the sample utilised the established statute and case-law consistently. The scenarios were developed to reflect ordinary ancillary relief cases, the first being a mid-money everyday case, with a working husband, a final salary pension, and a stay-at-home mother with two young children, and the second a low-money everyday case, with a working mother, unemployed father, a small equity, and a large mortgage (proportionately).

The solicitors were then asked to describe in outline (that is, without disclosing confidential details relating to the client) the most recent ancillary relief case in which they had been involved and were asked to comment on whether that case was atypical in any way. The interview concluded with general questions about ancillary relief. The average length of the interviews was approximately one hour.

ADVISING IN THE 'EVERYDAY CASE': CONSISTENCY OF APPROACH

Scenario One

Mr and Mrs Jones were married in 1992 and separated in early 2007. They have two children, aged eight and five. Mr Jones earns £50,000 per annum as a civil servant whilst Mrs Jones is a full-time homemaker and carer for their children. The matrimonial home has been valued at £400,000, with a mortgage of about £160,000. When Mr and Mrs Jones separated, she remained in the matrimonial home with the children, and Mr Jones moved out into rented accommodation. Mr Jones has been paying into a final salary pension scheme whereas Mrs Jones has no pension provision. The parties agree that the children should live with Mrs Jones. Mr Jones comes to you for advice, arguing that he cannot afford to keep up the mortgage repayments on the matrimonial home, in addition to paying rent on his flat and child support. He wants to keep his pension and sell the matrimonial home, retaining at least 50% of the equity, because in his view he was the one who paid the mortgage.

The vast majority of the respondents commented that the husband's desire for 50 per cent of the equity was not realistic, given considerations such as needs, whilst others explained that although they may start off with a 50:50 split in their analysis, thereby utilising the principle of equality (*White* and *Miller; McFarlane*) they will depart from it, especially in a needs case such as this where the first consideration is the housing needs of the parties, and particularly the parent with care.

> One of the first considerations of the court would be that the children are properly housed—she has greater housing needs than he does on a day-to-day basis, so she should be looking at getting the larger amount of things. Plus, on the practical side, she has little to no mortgage capacity if the property is to be sold, whereas he would be able to raise a serviceable mortgage on a lower deposit if there's going to be a purchase of a home ultimately. (Practitioner J)

This manifested itself in a small, but consistent, variation in the type of advice offered in scenario one. Two of the most popular options amongst the practitioners interviewed were advice relating to the wife downsizing in terms of property requirements to either a smaller property or one in a less desirable area (if that was possible) in order to reduce or eliminate the mortgage, and/or the consideration of a *Mesher* order[4]/deferred charge on the property. In addition, a major consideration for the solicitors when giving advice on the division of assets was the practicalities that the parties would face, in particular, where the parties lived and whether they were able to re-house with a more amenable mortgage and also, but not unimportantly, the parties' wishes. The remaining option, which was slightly less popular, was to offset the pension against the wife retaining the bulk of the capital assets.

> Well, traditionally, you'd be thinking about a *Mesher*, but dad's keen to get his money sooner, so perhaps there's an opportunity for raising some money, if she's going to be in a position to generate some income or we could be looking at perhaps an offset against his pension, depending on what his pension is and whether her priority is to have all her eggs in the house basket, or whether she is particularly keen to have a pension as well. (Practitioner R)

As regards the maintenance issue in scenario one, 16 out of the 24 practitioners referred to spousal maintenance in addition to child support. The latter was routinely mentioned during the scenario responses and tied in with the Child Support Agency (CSA) rates. For example:

> Again, child support is going to be the first call on his income and you would adopt, as you know, the Child Support Agency calculation in looking at that, so

---

[4] Based on *Mesher v Mesher and Hall* [1980] 1 All ER 126.

you would start off with 20 per cent, take into account his overnight contact with the children, if any. (Practitioner L)

The majority of respondents in the study suggested that an ongoing maintenance commitment would, on balance, be appropriate at this stage, particularly given the age of the children, the wife's ongoing child care commitments and the husband's salary.

Well, I'd say to him, that he probably is looking at having to pay her maintenance of some form but I'd probably ask him—has she got no qualifications or anything? And when did she give up work? ... I would say to him that the judge will probably take the view that she could work 16 hours a week and therefore she would be able to get tax credit and working tax credit, so she would probably be able to up her income quite considerably, so she may well be able to get £14,000/£15,000 a year. (Practitioner A)

Consequently, the wife's future earning capacity was an important point amongst those practitioners who raised the maintenance issue, particularly in terms of her future capacity to support herself and possibly even have sufficient capacity to borrow for a small mortgage. In all, 13 solicitors referred to the benefits system and the fact that she would be able to work up to 16 hours per week,[5] demonstrating that the practicalities of the situation are an ever-present consideration for the solicitors. The fact that the amount of money in the pot is limited remains a fundamental concern in the everyday case, along with parallel negotiations about the other assets.

It was felt by some solicitors that the amount of maintenance that could be awarded was an area which raised some uncertainty. Some practitioners made reference to the use of the CSA rates as a starting point for negotiation for a higher global sum of maintenance,[6] whereas others drew attention to the problems of advising clients with regard to the amount of maintenance they can expect to pay over and above the CSA rates:

If we can't agree maintenance, obviously the jurisdiction's with the CSA ... Now, just because that's what the CSA say, it may well be that we have a higher

---

[5] A lone parent may claim income support (and other income-related benefits) if they do not have savings of £16,000 or more and are not working, or are working less than 16 hours per week. Tax credits are payments from the government. As a general guideline, if an individual/couple is responsible for at least one child who normally lives with them, then depending on income, they may qualify for Child Tax Credit. If an individual/couple works, but earns low wages, they may qualify for Working Tax Credit, although this also has a child care element.

[6] The current mechanism used to calculate child support (15%, 20%, or 25% of the non-resident parent's net earnings) is relatively straightforward and has been viewed as one of the few successes of the reforms implemented by the Child Support, Pensions and Social Security Act 2000 to the original and complex child support formula. See especially Wikeley (2007). It appears that practitioners do work to the CSA formula, not only in calculating maintenance with the tying-in of CSA rates to the calculation of child maintenance in private cases, but as a starting point for negotiation for a higher global sum. Whether the new and arguably more complex child support calculation (Child Maintenance and Other Payments Act 2008 Sch 4) will be as straightforward as the current mechanism is a matter for experience and discussion. From an ancillary relief perspective, however, it seems a shame that such a simple, workable formula has been altered.

global sum for maintenance overall, because we won't necessarily apportion it between spousal maintenance and children maintenance—what we're looking at are the reasonable needs. (Practitioner R)

Practitioner H, whilst not alone, drew particular attention to the lack of clear case-law in this area and the difficulty practitioners face in arguing a client's case on the maintenance issue, particularly in the lower-end 'needs' cases. He was also not alone in mentioning the one-third rule.[7]

If you're in front of a judge arguing for periodical payments, either on a maintenance pending suit basis, an open-ended periodical payments order, you've got to put your flag somewhere. The judge will say, what order do you think I should make? You will never, you can say categorically, persuade a judge that a husband should pay out more than half of his income, possibly only in a short ... if you've got a total financial crisis, like the mortgage hasn't been paid for six months and there are arrears and effectively it takes the whole of his income just to stop the whole edifice from collapsing, maybe you could persuade a judge to make some sort of periodical payments at that sort of level, otherwise forget it. You've got 20 per cent in hand anyway because you've got the two kids and you've got the CSA, so really you're looking somewhere between 20 per cent and half, that's really the field, so if you say about a third, that's probably the best you're going to get. (Practitioner H)

What is surprising is that, despite the fact that a few interviewees expressed concern about the uncertainty surrounding spousal periodical payments, their concerns do not appear warranted. The advice given in this scenario was pretty consistent and it appears that where ongoing spousal maintenance has been advised (where the wife will either remain in the matrimonial home or downsize to a smaller property with a smaller mortgage), it will be around the one-third level. Two practitioners (A and U) did mention the possibility of a nominal maintenance order if there was to be a clean break, but this was not approached with much fervour:

Also, if she was to have the proceeds of the house, then it's tempting to say, well, she's getting that mortgage-free, maintenance really should be on a clean break. There might be an argument for nominal maintenance which the local court here in [place name] seem to like with children this young—you know, £1 a year, just to keep her foot through the door—although there seems to be a bit of a question-mark about nominal maintenance these days. But that's another possibility. But I think if we were offsetting with that and giving her enough funds to go buy somewhere else which she could do with that sort of sum, I think we'd like to argue from the husband's point of view, clean break, no maintenance. (Practitioner U)

---

[7] The one-third rule is where the income of the husband and wife is added together, divided by three, and the wife receives that third minus her own income. For further discussion, see Hayes and Williams (1999: 602).

The majority of interviewees did not refer to the duration of any periodical payments order in the mid-money scenario specifically, saying that it was an issue for negotiation, but also depended on Mrs Jones' earning capacity/ability to get back to work. Where it was mentioned, five practitioners suggested a fixed period whilst she gets back to work, whereas only one (Practitioner O) suggested joint lives, highlighting once again, a degree of consistency in approach.

Variations to Scenario One

In addition to the main scenario, a couple of variations were added to investigate whether issues that have been raised in the higher-value cases have any impact on the advice given in the everyday case. One of these concerned an inheritance variation, in which the practitioners were asked to consider whether their original advice on the vignette would differ if the matrimonial home had been left to the husband by his parents before he met his wife. Of the 24 practitioners, 22 said that their original advice on scenario one would not vary as a result of this additional inheritance information. The main rationale for this was on the basis of needs.

> I'd tell him that there's no way the court's going to ringfence the asset just because he got it from his parents. Unfortunately, it's a needs-based case and he's agreed the children can stay with his wife. (Practitioner D)

Furthermore, a small number of practitioners actually used *Miller; McFarlane* to bolster their argument that where the inheritance is affecting the matrimonial home, the matrimonial home should be considered separately from the other assets. This is one of the few examples in this research study of where big-money case-law has proved useful to practitioners in the everyday case; rather than the big-money case-law changing current everyday practice in any radical way, *Miller; McFarlane* is used to bolster the pre-existing position that needs predominate in this sort of scenario:

> [I]t would be very difficult in light of speeches of Baroness Hale in *Miller; Macfarlane* for him to successfully argue to ringfence the money from the home. (Practitioner O)

> [T]here's a communal groaning when people bring out *Miller; McFarlane* in your average high street case—but actually the judges that I have seen anyway have been biting on that matrimonial home point … [The matrimonial home point is] one element of those big-money cases which gives you a little bit of extra clout when you're dealing with the matrimonial home … but irrespective of that, there are two children and there's a woman who's got a limited income, so needs mean that the property would have to be utilised anyway. (Practitioner X)

The remaining two solicitors felt that their original advice would differ, although not particularly dramatically:

> Possibly yes, on inherited property. It wouldn't perhaps be looking at a split in the same way. A recent case said it should be a needs basis if there's inherited

property. Having said that, her needs are going to be for a property for the children. He's probably going to feel much more strongly about it. So it may change slightly but I don't think you can get away from the fact that she needs a home for two children. (Practitioner J)

Furthermore, six practitioners, although stating that their original advice still stood, indicated that the inheritance point might encourage them to press for a charge-back or even a slightly higher *Mesher* order:

If it had been his home, it doesn't change the whole strata that the children need a home, they need a roof above their heads and that is a pressing need that has to be addressed at this time. But I think that I would say, depending upon how, if it's money from his side of the family, I think I would be far more pressing about the possibility of him having a charge-back later because I think it does kind of affect the dynamics that this isn't a house that has been created by the two of them during the course of their marriage and they've put everything in together and that's it. But, you know, the needs have got to come first, wherever the money's come from. (Practitioner E)

Scenario Two

Mr and Mrs French have been married for two years, although they cohabited for three years prior to their marriage. The matrimonial home is an average three-bedroom semi-detached worth £170,000 in a rather deprived area and the mortgage amounts to three-quarters of its value. The couple has one daughter (Jennifer), aged four. Three years ago Mrs French used the family home as security for a business loan to start up her florist's business in a rental premises. This was with the full consent of Mr French. Although it was difficult in the beginning, the business is now doing well enough to break even (after her salary of £18,000 has been deducted.) Mr French, however, has recently lost his job as a factory worker. He is unskilled and has been unemployed for approaching nine months, although he has been helping out in the florist's when required. When Mr French was at work, Mrs French's mother looked after Jennifer during the day and has indicated that she is willing to continue with this once Mr French returns to work. As a result of the stress caused by the unemployment and pressure of running the business, Mr and Mrs French have separated and are in the process of obtaining a divorce. Mrs French comes to see you for advice.

In analysing the practitioners' responses to scenario two, it is obvious that this is a scenario that is not only difficult to advise upon, but also contains the type of factual scenario that some of them have witnessed in different guises time and again in either their current or previous practice:

This is more like my [place name] practice. It's much harder isn't it? (Practitioner C)

Again, this is one of those that we spoke about earlier in terms of publicly funded cases where there's just not enough to go round, and they are far more tricky. (Practitioner K)

Unlike scenario one, which contained a number of different issues upon which the practitioners had to advise—house, pension, and maintenance—the practitioners in this vignette were limited in terms of the options available to them. The two most popular options were once again a *Mesher* order over the property, with 14 practitioners suggesting this route, or a complete clean break, with 13 practitioners suggesting this as a possible option:

> [I]f I was acting for her instead of for him, then I would say to her, how much of a bung can you give him to pay him off? And I think it would be a case of her giving him a cash lump sum in return for a complete clean break. (Practitioner B)

Some solicitors advised both options as alternatives. However, unlike the first scenario, the amount to be retained for the charge-back was not as consistent, varying between a 50:50 split (Practitioners H and U), to a middle-range *Mesher* order at 30 per cent charge-back to the non-residential parent (Practitioner S), to a small charge (Practitioners A and I). Perhaps a major reason for this discrepancy in terms of proportion can be found in the limited assets and the fact that the solicitors are trying to do the best that they can with very little in the pot. This is best explained using the reasons given by those solicitors who advocated a clean break, as it highlights how other 'non-legal' factors could lead to a settlement where one may not initially seem possible due to the limited assets. For example, in order to pay Mr French off, a few practitioners suggested using family to help with a lump sum to ensure a clean break, which sounds very pragmatic, rather than legalistic:

> Increasingly you find people's parents being willing to lend money in order to buy out interests of the other spouse—which I find quite surprising—but increasingly you see that, so whether the mum could assist ... (Practitioner I)

Interestingly, one of the legal aid practitioners who dealt with low-money everyday cases on a regular basis initially suggested a *Mesher* order in scenario two, but then, on reflection, turned to the outcome that they tend to experience in practice:

> What I've had clients in this situation do is: fine, in the real world I can't pay this—this is Mrs French talking—we'll sell and if we can agree to pay off my loan as well, that's the best we can do. I shall carry on the business but I don't mind him still working here—we do have this sort of scenario—that will give him some income, but at least I'll get this colossal mortgage off my back and if I got into rented, I can probably pay with that £18,000, and sell it. Husband may be happy with that because he can see that he's not going to come out with much anyway. (Practitioner U).

Although, if a lump sum was to be paid to Mr French, one solicitor sounded a further practical note of caution regarding the implications of that for his future entitlement to state benefits:

> [I]f there is any claim, you're probably looking at a *Mesher* or—as and when mum's in a position to better her circumstances—a very, very small lump

sum payment. But be careful with lump sum payments because if he is on state benefits, if you go over the capital threshold, he's going to be disqualified anyway. (Practitioner R)

It therefore appears that the approach taken by practitioners in the low-value everyday scenario was much more pragmatic compared with the more middle-money everyday case. This is not by any means suggesting that pragmatism was not a factor in scenario one: it was just explicitly on display here. It is therefore suggested that when it comes to the low-value everyday case (scenario two), practicalities are perhaps more important than legal doctrine, the question being simply how the parties (and their advisors) can best manage a bad situation, although, of course, it is legal doctrine that enables the couple to apply for financial provision in the first place. Practitioner U went so far as to describe the process as 'cattle trading':

None of that sounds very scientific but with so little money ... [I]t just gets into good old cattle trading at the end, do the best we can for both of them.

The advice given by solicitors to this particular low-money scenario is particularly illuminating as it corresponds with the recent research by Maclean and Eekelaar, who argue: 'It is hard to see how any more precise rules about property division could have helped in any of [the cases that were observed in their research], all of which were based in the facts of the matter and not in the application of legal doctrine'. (Maclean and Eekelaar, chapter two, this volume).

Distinguishing Between Advice Given in the Different Scenarios

A distinction can be discerned between advice given in the middle-money case (scenario one) and the low-/no-money case (scenario two). Certain practitioners are aware of some impact of the big-money cases (see Hitchings, 2008), in that there appears to be less of a tendency in the higher-money everyday case to go for a clean break, and more likelihood of links between the parties continuing through a *Mesher* order or a periodical payments order:

[P]ost-*McFarlane*—judges much less—there's much less tendency to go for clean breaks as just the assumed automatic default position—unless you've got someone at that sort of level—£50,000. (Practitioner H).

Furthermore, principles such as equality appear to figure slightly more strongly when practitioners were advising in the Jones scenario compared with the French scenario. Both were needs cases, which was reiterated time and again by the interviewees; however, some discussion of additional legal doctrine took place within the Jones analysis, while French was dominated by practicalities rather than legal doctrine. This is highlighted particularly well by Practitioner I:

Well, this one is just needs [French]. That one [Jones], you're much more—there's more money there, isn't there, but you're certainly not going to be looking at 50:50 because he's not going to get as much as that ... Because he [Mr Jones] is in such a stronger position than her that he's going to have to give up some of his strict 50 per cent in order to compensate for the fact that he's in a much stronger position in terms of pension, career and earnings, etc. (Practitioner I)

However, this is not to say that solicitors are unaware of practicalities when advising clients in the mid-money everyday ancillary relief case. Pragmatism and practical issues were not excluded from advice in the Jones scenario: issues such as house prices, the availability of tax credits for the primary carer if working up to 16 hours, and the need for two homes with sufficient bedrooms for each of the children were major considerations for several practitioners. Furthermore, when asked about their priorities when advising in the everyday case, 11 of the 24 interviewees specifically mentioned that practicalities along with needs were the main considerations, the remainder citing needs as the priority. Consequently, although a needs-based approach predominates in the everyday case, whether, and which, other legal issues come to the fore will depend on the assets available and also, importantly, factors other than the law.

PERSPECTIVES FROM THE PRACTITIONERS' 'MOST RECENT CASE'

Although it appears that advice given to clients in the scenarios was pretty consistent across all the practitioners, it has been demonstrated that factors other than the law play a huge part in the everyday case in addition to, or perhaps sometimes as a consideration overriding, the section 25 factors. This finding is not new and is consistent with other studies (Davis, Cretney and Collins, 1994). As Practitioner M explained: 'It's difficult to say where the law leaves off and practicalities take over. So many cases are decided really on practical issues as much as anything else.' This can be seen not only through analysing practitioners' responses to the vignettes, but perhaps to a greater extent in their descriptions of their most recent case. Solicitors were asked to describe their most recent case and compare this with their typical run of cases in terms of factual/legal/procedural complexity. This discussion yet again raised the issue of how it is considerations other than legal doctrine which encourage clients to settle. Perhaps this could be termed as bargaining not only in the shadow of the law (Mnookin and Kornhauser, 1979), but also bargaining under the weight of additional considerations.

Everyday Considerations in the Everyday Case

The array of additional non-legal considerations which influences the parties to come to an agreement is broad. In this study, one of the most common reasons for coming to a settlement was the personalities of the parties. This ranged from clients who agreed to a clean break because they knew that their ex-spouse would be terrible at paying maintenance (Practitioner A) to a client who placed the value of obtaining a clean break higher than obtaining a maintenance order (Practitioner L), because the client did not want ongoing monthly legal battles to enforce the maintenance order. Practitioner L admitted that the case was settled by that route in the end 'largely because of the personalities involved'. Furthermore, some clients ignored the advice of their solicitors just because they were keen to get the whole process resolved, particularly if they were frightened about escalating legal costs. As Practitioner X described:

> Despite advice, she came to an agreement with her husband directly and is receiving a lump sum of £60,000—which is obviously less than 50 per cent of the equity, taking into consideration the pension—which is not what I would want her to do but still, some clients just want it sorted. So that's the settlement they've reached themselves. But there is, certainly in private—I think this is an issue which exists with the current legal aid assessment—there's an issue with clients who are privately paying being frightened of costs and wanting to deal with it as quickly as possible.

These dual issues of a client's personality combined with fear of additional legal costs can also have an impact on encouraging a client to settle, particularly where a client is getting very stressed by the whole situation and just wants it to come to end:

> He was a very, very bullying, manipulative man, and she was struggling with it in the end and she just wanted to settle, get it out of the way, because her legal costs were going up and up and up and she was just seriously stressed out actually. (Practitioner C)

Quotes from these practitioners highlight how the discretionary system can lead to the stubborn or dominant party using the system to get a better deal. This is particularly pertinent given the recent legal aid reforms (see generally Department for Constitutional Affairs, 2005, 2006; Department for Constitutional Affairs and Legal Services Commission, 2006) and the increasing likelihood that parties in the everyday case will not have public funding. The threat of increased costs that would arise from a final hearing is more than sufficient to put parties off striving for their rightful share.

Another non-legal consideration to which two of the practitioners (A and G) referred in relation to their most recent case, and the reasons why it had settled, concerned parental involvement and willingness of one or both of the clients' parents to assist their children in their divorce settlement. For example, when Practitioner A was asked why the case had settled at 85 per cent, the response was: 'I suspect probably that his parents said that they'd help him out'. Furthermore, guilt was another non-legal consideration mentioned by two practitioners (S and T) about why their most recent cases had settled at that particular point—in other words, one party felt guilty, and therefore agreed to a settlement not quite as 'fair' to themselves as it could have been.

The solution was driven solely by two things: one was the children's needs, and the second one was her feeling terribly guilty that she'd walked out on this chap, having decided that he was too boring for her for the rest of her life. (Practitioner S)

In this case, the law would not have taken into account the children's needs as they were not minors. However, in this 'most recent case' the wife ended up giving the husband more than half so that he could stay in the house with the now adult children of the marriage, 'so that they wouldn't be put out into the street—on the basis that the extra that he got he would use to give them a leg up on the housing ladder at the point that they left' (Practitioner S).

Finally, a legally related, although non-doctrinal, consideration that did induce the parties to settle concerned the indication given by a district judge at the Financial Dispute Resolution (FDR) hearing. This was raised by eight of the practitioners:

[T]he wife was a litigant in person when it came to the FDR, but after the FDR she agreed to settle because the judge had expressed an opinion about how he thought settlement would be. And even she then didn't want to keep on going. So you could say that actually the procedure had worked quite well. (Practitioner E)

However, a number of practitioners in the study drew attention to the consequences of an indication at the FDR where the judge's view was unexpected. This could induce a client to settle even though the indication given was contrary to, or right at the boundaries of the acceptable of, the solicitor's advice. In this example, Practitioner O's client received a strange judicial indication:

It was frighteningly easy to sort out at the FDR because of some very strange judicial indications I have to say. Up to FDR, in my view, it wouldn't have been resolved to the extent it was in favour of my client as it turned out without the judicial input ... the judge's indications in my view were completely wrong and were contrary to the advice I had given my client in terms of what realistically he should be expecting, in terms of a settlement, and again I was very surprised that the other side didn't also see that those indications were completely wrong and either try and negotiate with a bit more vigour or take the matter on to a final hearing.

It could be that the other party in Practitioner O's case may have been spooked by the indication given at the FDR, which induced a settlement not in her favour. This also happened to Practitioner P, in whose most recent case a combination of non-legal considerations—such as the potential for increased costs if the client was to go to a final hearing, plus the additional issue of problems with the children of the marriage, encouraged the client to settle:

He ended up with about £66,000. She ended up with £220,000. I actually felt that that was a bit on the low side. This is the difficulty that us lawyers have and I am sure my peer group will endorse this. You'll go before one judge and he'll say, no, 35 per cent—which is quite a lot of money when you're talking about equity of £280,000. Another judge will say 20 per cent is fine. And they're all within the right parameters. Neither of them are wrong. It's just that one might have a higher percentage than the other. So I explained this to the client, 'we could refuse this, go on to a Final Hearing but I cannot guarantee that you'll get a better result. You're not likely to get a worse result but I cannot guarantee that you're going to do better. And you'll end up with £3,000/£4,000 worth of costs between now and the final hearing and also it ups the ante and all the rest of it.' The thing is with FDRs—and I always explain this to the clients—'you do not have to accept anything today. If you're not happy we can go away and think about it some more.' But he was keen to get it resolved. He'd had enough. There'd been problems with the children. She was almost using the children as a bit of a whip to beat him with because of contact arrangements—she wouldn't let him do x, y and z, you know what happens. He was content to settle on that basis even though he had a maintenance liability of £1,100 a month for quite a while.

On a number of occasions, the practitioners in the study described their role not only as about giving legal advice to their clients, but as more diverse. This tallies very well with the way in which these everyday ancillary relief cases are settled. The fact that considerations other than legal doctrine affect the settlement that is ultimately achieved means that practitioners in this area are expected to play a much wider role than that of legal advisor. Practitioner A described it as 'more like being a negotiator with figures' and went on to describe their role as being more like 'a financial, not advisor, but a debt counsellor', whilst Practitioner R explained:

It is the emotive side which I think gives a true flavour of what matrimonial law is all about. It's managing clients as much as dealing with the logistics of the particular case in front of you.

SOME INCONSISTENCY WITHIN THE SYSTEM? THE JUDICIARY AND THE COURTS

By focusing on decisions made by the higher courts in ancillary relief cases, both academics and the judiciary fail to take into account the complex inter-relationship between the law, non-doctrinal factors, and, equally important, the courts and judiciary. This is a major consideration in any discretionary system, and one area of the current process where it appears that local knowledge is of considerable importance in the ancillary relief case:

It's a mixture, isn't it, of the Matrimonial Causes Act—of course, that's there—but that doesn't really help a great deal. It's not really about case law—you won't find any cases about these people to mention. It's more a kind of pragmatism based largely, I suppose, on local practice in the sense that we know who our local judges are. I could pretty much predict what they're going to do in these situations for that sort of reason rather than any case-law—although, you know, the case-law does feed into these things. (Practitioner H)

Two main issues were raised by the interviewees in this study, both of which are very much inter-linked. First, there was a definite preference amongst practitioners to deal with, and thereby issue in, certain courts of which they had knowledge or experience. The second inter-related issue was that certain practitioners, particularly from one of the research areas, perceived a noticeable difference between courts in terms of court approach. This had an impact for those practitioners who identified the divergent approach in terms of where they might issue proceedings.

'Know Thy Judge'

The data demonstrate that there is a definite preference amongst practitioners for dealing with certain courts. In the majority of cases this is their local court. This preference is based on predictability and knowledge/experience of judicial approaches within that court—a classic example of Galanter's 'repeat player' concept (Galanter, 1979). This was expressed particularly well by Practitioner E, who believed that 'undoubtedly there is parochialism in terms of the courts, … judges like people they know and don't like people that they don't know so much, and that's always a factor because we're all human, and I think that's again something that can affect outcomes'. Practitioner E went on to explain this further:

> When I appear in [local place] County Court, I know all of the judges. As it so happens, four of them were solicitors, I've been a solicitor for 30 years in [local place], and they all know me, and if it's then somebody who comes from the outside and is on the other side, I know that in a sense that I'm going to be listened to … and it's the same thing when you go to [different place County Court] where I feel more of an outsider. It's a club. Everyone's greeting each other because they all know each other.

The practical effect of this local knowledge/awareness is demonstrated to the greatest extent in the comments practitioners made about the outcomes they believe that they are able to obtain for their client; from being able to advise within a narrower boundary, for instance, to being able to predict with more certainty which way the judge may go if it gets to court. The problem of not having that local knowledge was described by Practitioner R:

> I don't like going out of my terrain because then I become dependent on counsel telling me, 'we've got so and so district judge and I can tell you what

they're like'. And I don't like that because you're introducing—you clearly can't guarantee an outcome for a client. Litigation by its definition is uncertain and that's introducing a further factor that I can't predict when I'm using somebody that I don't know ... I've got a [district judge] who's an unknown quantity to me, I'm instantly putting myself on the back foot and putting my client on the back foot, so I don't like it.

This solicitor was not alone in always using counsel whom they knew and more importantly, counsel who also knew the court. Practitioner O agreed with this perspective: 'it's often always extremely wise to instruct local agents to do the court hearing or local counsel—that know the idiosyncrasies of the judges that they're dealing with'. Consequently, the nature of judicial decision-making[8] is not necessarily off-putting to some practitioners. They put in place strategies to deal with the additional element of uncertainty, not only through employing local counsel, for instance, but also through structuring a certain argument in a certain way that they know a particular judge is amenable to:

I know that there are some judges in [place name] that I would raise an argument with and others that I wouldn't even waste my breath because I've tried it before and it's just not going to get anywhere. Likewise some of the other judges I know react very well to certain arguments and I will structure my case around that. (Practitioner L)

However, in a few cases, interviewees gave examples of certain judges with whom it was totally impractical to deal:

There are other courts—is this strictly anonymous?—I suppose there are two things. Shortly after I qualified, I worked in [place name 1] for about two years, and I came back to [place name 2] with a huge sigh of relief because the judges down there were much ruder and much more individual, much more whimsical in what they would do, and so you could go into court genuinely not knowing what's going to happen, which isn't an experience you have in [place name 2]. You can be pretty damn sure what's going to be said ... In [place name 3] there are basically two resident district judges, one of whom is excellent, consistent, courteous, thoughtful—all of the things you would want a judge to be. And the other one is absolutely mad. So it's a complete lottery.

---

[8] Through analysing a data set in relation to possession proceedings in the county court, Cowan et al make reference to, and construct three typologies of judicial decision-making which they term 'liberal', 'patrician' and 'formalist'. These three 'ideal types' represent different judicial behaviours and styles and are based on the practices observed in their 'possession proceedings' research (Cowan et al, 2006). Despite a lack of research regarding an analysis of the types of judicial decision-making in ancillary relief proceedings, Cowan et al's research is useful as it demonstrates that varying styles of judging and judicial decision-making are not unusual within a discretionary system. As Cowan et al suggest, their typology operates 'to render more visible and understandable the complex and sometimes contradictory nature of judicial decision-making'. (2006: 549).

When you go down to [place name 3], if you get one judge it could be great. If you get the other one, you're back in that territory of: I don't know what's going to happen. (Practitioner H)

A number of interviewees made similar references to the idiosyncrasies of the judiciary, in particular their local judiciary. However, because those practitioners had an everyday working knowledge of their local court (and judiciary) they were nevertheless comfortable using that court despite the varying styles and typologies of judicial decision-making, as discussed above. As it was a court they knew, the judicial approaches were familiar and within an expected range. According to Practitioner D:

[Y]ou get some judges who are pro-wife and some who are pro-husband. I used to work in [place name] and you'd get that up there and you could more or less predict the outcome of the case once you knew who the district judge was going to be who was hearing it.

This was described succinctly by two interviewees (Practitioners O and P) as 'know thy judge'.

At the other end of the spectrum were 11 practitioners who felt that their local county court and judiciary were pretty consistent in their approach: '[B]y and large it's very consistent and also very intelligent' (Practitioner O). The reasons given for the consistent approach was put down to the background work the judiciary do to ensure consistency amongst themselves: practitioners in two of the three areas referred to good practice such as 'model scenarios' used by the judiciary in their local county court. Practitioner H, for example, suggested that the judiciary in his local court 'confer a lot', whilst Practitioner L, who used the same local court, raised an identical point: 'I know they do speak to each other, not necessarily about individual cases but certainly they will have theoretical discussions about things'. However, although it appears that a number of practitioners in this study have reported a good level of consistency between district judges *within* the same court, consistency *between* courts appears to be rather a different matter.

Scrutinising Different Courts

In assessing whether there was any inconsistency between courts, some practitioners in the study were convinced that a typical judicial approach could be discerned from certain courts. This was particularly interesting in one region, where five of the eight interviewees drew the researcher's attention to the difference in approach between their local county court compared with another county court that they would use in certain situations. In this area, a significant number of the interviewees suggested that the court that they would issue proceedings in would vary, depending on the perceived judicial approaches at those courts and the consequent impact that would have on their client.[9]

First, the practitioners from this particular area explained not only that their local county court expects a wife to go out to work, but that the usual order in a case where there is a full-time stay-at-home mother, for example, is a limited term maintenance order. This was compared with a different county court from a region not in one of the study areas which favours lifelong maintenance:

> It's more subtle than this but I can state it quite baldly. I mean there's a general perception that wives do well in [other] county court and [local] county court certainly in the past was rather more robust with the idea that wives need to go out to work, so that effectively in particular circumstances you might feel, well, you'd do better for the wife in [the other county court], but if you were for the husband you might think you'd do better in [local] county court. There are reasons when you practise why you know which court you might want to be in and which court you might not want to be in. There's another discretion inbuilt in the process. (Practitioner E)

> I think in [local county court] they are keen to limit joint lives maintenance whereas in [the other county court] they're not. That actually became clear when we had a Resolution seminar and the people who were presenting it were from [area which contains other county court] and everyone in the room from [local area]—we were doing scenarios similar to your ones—and everyone in the room said, five years of maintenance with a bar, and the presenter said: are you serious? No way! It became clear that there was a huge difference of approach. (Practitioner B)

It appears that in one of the regions in this study there is a glaring difference in approach when one compares practitioners' perspectives of two different county courts. Five of the eight interviewees were quite adamant about the impact that this can have for a client in two respects. First, it can have a massive impact on the outcome for the client as by issuing in one court they may be saddled with a joint lives maintenance order for example, but by issuing in a different court, a limited term periodical payments order may be much more likely. Secondly, it is important that that the solicitor 'gets it right' in terms of issuing in the place appropriate to the outcome desired for their client. This is highlighted by the response of Practitioner A: 'so generally what we do, if there isn't very much money, then generally, we will issue in [local court], and if there's a husband, we will always issue in [local court]; but if there is a lot of money and it's the

---

[9] Under r 2.6(1)(a) of the Family Proceedings Rules 1991 (FPR 1991), a petition can be filed at any divorce county court in England and Wales. This is regardless of where the petitioner lives and is subject only to the normal domicile and residence requirements. If the court chosen is nowhere near where the parties live, then either party can apply to have the matter transferred to a local court (FPR 1991 r 2.32(4)). There is case-law to suggest that where the matter is complex or involves a trust (*Re C* [2007] EWHC 1911 (Fam) at [17]), the application should be heard in the High Court.

wife, because the wife will get a better deal [we will issue in the county court further afield].'

This approach was not unique to the five practitioners from this particular region. Four other interviewees from the other two areas of the study admitted that they also tailor the court that they issue in to the facts of the case and who they are acting for. They explained that there were a number of reasons why they might do this:

> If you're acting for a wife on a big-money case, notwithstanding the horrendous delays, you would normally look at issuing in [another county court further away]. If you're acting for a wife on a low- to middle-money case, then you would issue locally [at local county court]. If you're looking at achieving a settlement that is not going to, if you want an early resolution with a sensible indication, then you will issue in [regional, bigger city, county court], for example, if it was a big-money case. (Practitioner O)

Of course, this is not to say that all practitioners tailor their court so precisely. Some solicitors specifically mentioned that they do not adopt a different approach. Practitioner P's comment is interesting as it highlights how she is aware of other solicitors' methods, despite the fact that she does not adopt a different approach:

> Well, I don't get to know the judges at other courts. I've been all over the country, not necessarily for ancillary relief. I definitely don't adopt a different approach. I never phone up to find out who the judge is on the day. I know a lot of people do but I don't. I have the same approach to things. Providing you stick to the rules and you don't make any wild submissions, I don't think you can do anything else. I don't have any views on any other judges elsewhere.

It therefore appears that there is an awareness of varying judicial approaches in the courts that solicitors practise in on a regular basis; the mantra 'know thy judge' proves to be an essential non-doctrinal influence on the ancillary relief process if the case has failed to settle outside the doors of the court. The repeat players' insider knowledge of court culture and approaches ensures a certain amount of consistency when it comes to judicial approaches in a certain area surrounding a county court.

It would be all too easy to generalise and suggest that there is geographical inconsistency in decision-making across the county courts of England and Wales in the everyday ancillary relief case. However, it would be inappropriate to do so because not only is this research study based on the perceptions of solicitors, rather than an objective study of the county courts themselves, but the sample is limited to three regions in southern England. Consequently it is impossible to make any sweeping generalisations that this research has found evidence of geographical inconsistencies in approach. However, from the limited perspective of this study, the findings demonstrate inconsistencies between various county courts and a noticeable difference in approach between two county courts in particular. In order to assess whether there is any geographical inconsistency across a wider spread of courts, or even differences in application of the rules by district judges within the same court, it would be necessary to undertake specific court-focused research, including analysing judicial responses to the type of scenarios utilised in this research.[10]

CONCLUSION

In *Cowan v Cowan*,[11] Thorpe LJ suggested that the removal of reasonable requirements as an aid to quantification 'leaves specialist practitioners and judges facing a period of considerable uncertainty'.[12] He continued by suggesting that the decision in *White* has made the case for statutory reform more compelling as a result of the considerable uncertainties emanating from the decision.[13] Furthermore, a number of highly respected commentators have suggested that, post *White*, the law lacks 'predictability in practice or policy coherence' (Bailey-Harris, 2005: 231), and Joanna Miles (2005, 2008), for example, has highlighted the difficulties of juggling the principles of sharing, compensation and need that arise in the wake of *Miller; McFarlane*.

Nevertheless, I would suggest that the findings in this study do not support the argument that the law of ancillary relief is uncertain and chaotic. At the everyday level at least, there does not appear to be a pressing need for additional principle to increase certainty of outcome. In the everyday case where needs dominate, the findings demonstrate that the advice given to clients is pretty consistent, subject to local court culture and the practicalities of the individual case. However, the identification by practitioners of the diversity of approaches between different courts demonstrates some inconsistency which may need further research. This appears to have had the effect of inducing some practitioners to tailor the approach of their cases accordingly. However, this finding is not new. Given the wide-ranging research over the years which has looked at judicial discretion within and between courts on a range of different legal matters (see especially Barrington Baker et al, 1977; Ingleby, 1989 and Cowan et al, 2006), the finding in this study of some inconsistency between county courts in a discretionary system of law is not particularly surprising. For example, in 1989, when examining the regulation of out-of-court activity in matrimonial proceedings, Richard Ingleby stated: '[s]olicitors commented on the different levels of behaviour required by various county courts with which they dealt, some of which were regarded as "softer" than others' (Ingleby, 1989: 240). In a similar vein, Cowan et al have analysed the differing styles and types of judicial decision-making in their possession proceedings research (Cowan et al, 2006).

---

[10] It has been noted in a previous study that district judges are a notoriously 'hard-to-reach' group to research with 'a range of gatekeepers determining access arrangements, including the Department of Constitutional Affairs (now the Ministry of Justice) and the individual courts' (Cowan et al, 2006: 548).

[11] [2001] 2 FLR 192.

[12] At [41].

[13] At [38]–[41].

It therefore appears that only a further in-depth study which focuses on the approaches between different courts across a much larger area than the one in this research will determine whether different courts do have different (and inconsistent) approaches in the everyday ancillary relief case.

Whilst a finding of potential inconsistency between courts in a discretionary system is not new, what is surprising is that this inconsistency has not necessarily led to practitioners giving widely differing advice to clients in the everyday case. On the contrary, the responses to the scenarios in this study suggest a large amount of consistency, if only in the areas studied here. This runs counter to the long-standing position of Resolution. Even before the rapid jurisprudential developments witnessed in the post-*White* case-law, Resolution has been calling for clearer guidelines for practitioners. In 1993, Mark Harper suggested that 'the widely differing approaches of district judges makes it impossible to predict the outcomes of cases. Clearer guidelines would enable solicitors to advise their clients more confidently' (Gilvarry, 1993: 8). Likewise, in 2007, the National Chair of Resolution likened ancillary relief to a 'gambling game' where the 'stakes are high' and uncertainty reigns (Greensmith, 2007: 203). However, these opinions are not consistent with the findings in this study. As the law currently stands, the research project upon which this chapter is based found that it is consistency, rather than inconsistency of approach that is perhaps the most adequate way of describing the everyday ancillary relief case in England and Wales. Indeed, rather than practitioners' advice to clients being widely variable on a scale of A–Z, it is perhaps more appropriate to label it on a scale of A–E in terms of options available to the client. It is the practicalities of the case and the needs of the parties which dominate the settlement in the everyday case.

BIBLIOGRAPHY

Bailey-Harris, R (2005) 'The Paradoxes of Principle and Pragmatism: Ancillary Relief in England and Wales' 19 *International Journal of Law, Policy and the Family* 229.
Barrington Baker, W, Eekelaar, J, Gibson, C and Raikes, S (1977) *The Matrimonial Jurisdiction of Registrars: The Exercise of the Matrimonial Jurisdiction by Registrars in England and Wales* (Oxford, Centre for Socio-legal Studies).
Cowan, D, Blandy, S, Hitchings, E, Hunter, C and Nixon, J (2006) 'District Judges and Possession Proceedings' 33 *Journal of Law and Society* 547.
Davis, G, Cretney, S and Collins, J (1994) *Simple Quarrels: Negotiations and Adjudications in Divorce* (Oxford, Oxford University Press).
Department for Constitutional Affairs (2005) *A Fairer Deal for Legal Aid*, Cm 6591 (London, TSO).
—— (2006) *Legal Aid Reform: the Way Ahead*, Cm 6993 (London, TSO).
Department for Constitutional Affairs and Legal Services Commission (2006) *Legal Aid: a Sustainable Future*, CP 13/06 (London, TSO).
Eekelaar, J (2005) '*Miller v Miller*: The Descent into Chaos' 35 *Family Law* 870.
—— (2006) 'Property and Financial Settlement on Divorce—Sharing and Compensating' 36 *Family Law* 754.

Francis, N (2006) 'If It's Broken—Fix It' 36 *Family Law* 104.

Galanter, M (1974) 'Why the "Have's" Come Out Ahead: Speculations on the Limits of Legal Change' 9 *Law and Society Review* 95.

Gilvarry, E (1993) 'News—Savings by reform say family lawyers' 90 *Law Society Gazette* 8.

Greensmith, A (2007) 'Let's play Ancillary Relief' 37 *Family Law* 203.

Hayes, M and Williams, C (1999) *Family Law: Principles, Policy and Practice* (London, Butterworths).

Hess, E (2006) 'Assessing the Quantum of Periodical Payments after *McFarlane*' 36 *Family Law* 780.

Hitchings, E (2008) 'Everyday Cases in the Post-*White* Era' 38 *Family Law* 873.

Ingleby, R (1989) 'Rhetoric and Reality: Regulation of Out-of-Court Activity in Matrimonial Proceedings' 9 *Oxford Journal of Legal Studies* 231.

Mnookin, R and Kornhauser, L (1979) 'Bargaining in the Shadow of the Law: The Case of Divorce' 88 *Yale Law Journal* 950.

Miles, J (2005) 'Principle or Pragmatism in Ancillary Relief: The Virtues of Flirting with Academic Theories and Other Jurisdictions' 19 *International Journal of Law, Policy and the Family* 242.

—— (2008) '*Charman v Charman (No 4)*—Making sense of need, compensation and equal sharing after *Miller; McFarlane*' 20 *Child and Family Law Quarterly* 378.

Moor, P and Le Grice, V (2006) 'Periodical Payments Orders following *Miller* and *McFarlane*: A Series of Unfortunate Events' 36 *Family Law* 655.

Wikeley, N (2007) 'Child support reform—throwing the baby out with the bathwater' 19 *Child and Family Law Quarterly* 434.

10

Self-determination or Judicial Imposition?

Translating the Theory into Practice

SALLY DOWDING

INTRODUCTION

THERE ARE MANY urban myths and hypotheses surrounding the financial implications of relationship breakdown. These vary from the erroneous assumption that the departing spouse or partner forfeits all entitlement to a share of any assets to the equally misguided but opposite belief that the briefest of marriages or civil partnerships leads inexorably to an equal share of all assets. Misconceptions of whatever variety militate against amicable resolution of family disputes: realistic expectation is essential if parties are to have the confidence to negotiate and compromise. The purpose of this chapter is to examine, from the perspective of practice rather than academic theory, the various forms of assistance available to facilitate settlement—and the powers of the courts when agreement proves elusive.

The rights of the parties on dissolution of a marriage are governed by the statutory regime enshrined in the Matrimonial Causes Act 1973—as amended at various stages in the course of its 35-year existence and as interpreted and explained in a multitude of significant judicial decisions. The law is intended to be gender-neutral, favouring neither husband nor wife, but specifically requiring that first consideration be afforded to the needs of any relevant children throughout the period of their dependency. Parallel legislation applies to separating registered civil partners.

However, court-imposed divorce settlements in England and Wales are not formulaic but rather are decided within the broad spectrum of what a judge perceives to be a fair solution in the light of the statutory principles and in the particular circumstances of that couple. This element of uncertainty provides a powerful incentive to resolve issues with minimal or no resort to litigation with its attendant expense in both human and financial terms, which in turn leads many family lawyers to place increasing and welcome emphasis upon the virtue of a negotiated settlement. Moreover, family lawyers know—and, it is to be hoped, explain to their clients—that even the most reluctant litigant can be obliged by the court to confront reality, as will be shown later in this chapter.

As recently as the 1970s, family law was considered to be part of general, contentious litigation rather than a discrete legal specialism. One of the greatest forces for change, in that context, was the creation in December 1982 of the Solicitors Family Law Association (SFLA) (now known as Resolution)—an organisation whose core value is the sensible and non-confrontational resolution of domestic disputes. Members of the Association subscribe to a Code of Practice which has evolved over the years and which has been endorsed by the Law Society's Protocol as a model of good and effective family law practice.[1] An early information sheet published by SFLA explains its rationale thus:

> The SFLA was formed in December 1982 in response to demands from the public and the legal profession for a different approach to 'matrimonial litigation'. Traditionally matrimonial litigation was treated in the same adversarial manner as commercial disputes. This approach saw both parties confronting each other in a determined effort to secure the 'best' settlement often regardless of the emotional and psychological stress experienced by clients. By contrast, members of the SFLA seek to replace time consuming and costly conflict with skilful negotiation and conciliation. This approach has proven highly successful and has received enormous support and backing from the public and legal professions alike.

By 1998, the Association was launching the fourth revision of the Code. In an article published to mark the revised Code, David Hodson commented:

> In the late 1970s/early 1980s, there were very few specialist family law solicitors. Most also undertook general civil and criminal litigation. They applied the tactics and approach of those areas of work in the sensitive and relationship-orientated area of family breakdown. It was little wonder, therefore, that the founding members of the Association were concerned that solicitors and the Court process were unnecessarily adding to the distress, emotion and anger that can arise on the breakdown of a relationship.

The Code of Practice has been revisited during the 25 years of the Association's existence and now appears on the Resolution website as a short statement of principle which binds its members to a number of Guides to Good Practice dealing with numerous aspects of family litigation.[2] The first point of principle enshrined in the original Code of Practice and replicated in substance, if not in form, in all subsequent editions is as follows:

> 1.1 The Solicitor should endeavour to advise, negotiate and conduct proceedings in a manner calculated to encourage and assist the parties to achieve a constructive settlement of their differences as quickly as may be reasonable whilst recognising that the parties may need time to come to terms with their new situation.

---

[1] Law Society Family Law Protocol, 1st edn, 2002, Appendix 2; 2nd edn, 2006.
[2] Resolution, *Code of Practice and Practice Guides*, www.resolution.org.uk

It is perhaps that last point—the time required for people to come to terms with their situation—which is most often overlooked by professionals, and the neglect of which can constitute the greatest obstacle to constructive, negotiated resolution of family disputes. It is, after all, common sense that a partner who has been planning departure from the family home for several weeks or months will be ready far sooner to address the financial consequences of that decision than the unsuspecting, abandoned partner.

ALTERNATIVES TO COURT PROCEEDINGS

The alternatives to litigation may be summarised as follows:

(a) adhering to a prior agreement between the parties—whether entered into before marriage (ante nuptial—commonly referred as a 'pre-nup') or during the marriage (post nuptial, or 'post-nup');
(b) walking away from everything—although this will not guarantee the other party taking an equally laissez-faire approach;
(c) mutual agreement without the benefit of advice;
(d) a mediated settlement;
(e) a settlement achieved through the use of collaborative lawyers;
(f) settlement by conventional negotiation between solicitors.

Pre- and Post-nuptial Agreements

It is increasingly common, if perhaps unromantic, for those embarking upon marriage later in life—perhaps with children of earlier relationships and/or with significant wealth—to enter into agreements as to the financial arrangements in the unhappy event of separation. Some parties will simply honour such agreements and thus pre-empt any dispute upon separation. Others will wish to depart from their terms, and seek to enlist the support of the legal process in the furtherance of that desire. The issue of pre-marital agreements was thrust into the forefront of public consciousness by the activities of Mrs Crossley.[3] In that particular case, both spouses had a history of previous marital ties and each had substantial financial resources independently of the other. Their 14-month marriage had been preceded by a pre-nuptial agreement, the nub of which was that, in the event of breakdown, each party would walk away with their pre-marital assets and neither would make any claim against the other. Despite that agreement, Mrs Crossley initiated a claim against her husband, citing his failure to provide full and frank disclosure of the extent of his assets prior to the conclusion of the agreement. In the event,

---

[3] *Crossley v Crossley* [2008] 1 FLR 1491.

Mrs Crossley, having unsuccessfully appealed a preliminary ruling by a High Court judge, thought better of her application and withdrew it. However, the case retains significance, not only in terms of the operation of the procedure for resolving financial cases through the courts, but also on account of the comments of Lord Justice Thorpe in the course of his judgment—including reference to 'a developing view that prenuptial contracts are gaining in importance in a particularly fraught area that confronts so many parties separating and divorcing'.[4]

As the law stands at present, pre-nuptial agreements are simply one of the factors to be taken into account when the judge arrives at a decision on the division of the matrimonial assets. The weight to be attached to the agreement will depend upon a number of matters, including the length of the relationship; whether the interests of minor children need to be protected; whether each party gave full and frank disclosure of assets before the agreement was concluded and whether there has been any change in circumstances since the agreement was entered into, for example the birth of a child or the onset of unexpected disability. Cases such as *Crossley* demonstrate the inexorable development of the law towards the goal of recognition of voluntary agreements—a development foreshadowed by the Home Office Consultation Paper *Supporting Families* (Home Office, 1998) which contained the specific proposal to make pre-nuptial written agreements about property legally binding on those who wish to make them. It is pertinent to observe that in the summary of responses to the consultation paper, the Home Office reported that of the 157 responses to that proposal, 80 agreed that it would be helpful to allow nuptial agreements to be legally binding whilst, on the other hand, 77 felt that making such agreements binding would foster negative expectations on the part of those contemplating marriage. The response from the Women's National Commission highlighted one obvious conundrum: if according binding status to nuptial agreements reduced post-separation conflict, then this was a development particularly to be welcomed in families with children; however, the birth of a child or children post agreement would be likely to render the agreement non-binding (Home Office, 1999: 23–24). Unless and until Parliament summons the legislative will to change the status of pre- or post-nuptial agreements, all that can safely be said is that they are most likely to be upheld where a court is satisfied that they were entered into in an informed fashion and without duress, and where there has been no significant change of circumstances since the agreement was concluded. In all cases they form part of the factual matrix upon which the court reaches its decision.

Walking Away

The partner who walks away may be, at one extreme, a partner fleeing domestic violence; at the other extreme, he or she may have formed a new relationship and feel too guilty to address the financial implications of the relationship breakdown.

---

[4] ibid at [17].

If there are few assets to consider then this may not be such a high-risk strategy. However, if the couple own a house—whether in the sole name of one partner or jointly—or if there is any risk of personal maintenance being payable, then they are sitting on a litigation time-bomb which might explode unexpectedly at any time in the future.

By way of example, a wife may be left in the family home to bring up three young children. She may be too distraught to contemplate taking legal advice let alone commencing legal proceedings, or she may feel that she simply cannot afford to do so. The husband may feel it inappropriate to add to her distress by pressing for a sale of the home or other form of settlement. Time goes by. She feels grateful not to have to contemplate moving house and does nothing. Eventually the children leave home. At that point the husband wishes to realise his share of the property.

Had the wife taken advice at an earlier stage, and assuming the property was reasonably modest and suitable for the family's needs, she might well have been granted either an outright transfer or a transfer with a charge-back in her spouse's favour—very possibly for less than 50 per cent, and quite probably not to be exercised while she required it as a home, absent her remarriage or cohabitation with another party. As it is, by waiting until the children cease to be dependent she forfeits the protection inevitably extended to the parent with care by virtue of the statutory obligation requiring courts to give first consideration to the children's welfare. All she has by way of comfort is the duty of the court to consider the issue of delay when exercising its statutory discretion. This may or may not result in the court determining that she should continue to have the benefit of occupation of the family home. In any event, it is highly unlikely that it would have been in her interests to defer resolution of the matter.

Another example might be the husband who leaves a wife in her mid-forties for a new partner. The children may be approaching independence and no longer preventing her from seeking employment but the husband feels reluctant to press the issue and prefers instead to pay regular maintenance. After more than 10 years of separation the husband considers seeking a divorce. By this time the wife is in her mid-fifties and may not have been in the workplace for 30 years or more. In all probability the husband is facing lifelong payments to the wife unless he is sufficiently affluent to provide a capital sum to buy out her right to maintenance. Had he acted more promptly, the court may have been more disposed to attribute to the wife an earning capacity and at least thereby reduce her dependency upon the husband.

Essentially, in any case where either or both parties are likely to be seeking some form of financial settlement, there is rarely anything to be gained from allowing the metaphorical sword of Damocles to remain suspended over the parties' heads.

DIY Settlements

Some separating couples reach agreement between themselves and are sufficiently confident in the outcome to find it unnecessary to trouble solicitors to advise them, or courts to endorse the fruits of their negotiations. Sometimes such agreements will be perfectly sound and sensible, particularly after short marriages with few assets. Some, however, will be the product of an inequality of bargaining power, whether or not coupled with scant disclosure of assets.

Any agreement reached without comprehensive disclosure and independent legal advice is vulnerable to costly challenge in the event that either partner subsequently becomes dissatisfied with the arrangement. As with ante- and post-nuptial agreements, the existence of a separation agreement is simply a factor which the court will take into account if invited by either party to determine the allocation of financial resources. It does not—as the law stands at present—bind the court in the exercise of its discretion, although case-law strongly favours the upholding of agreements made with proper advice and frank disclosure of assets.[5]

It follows that separating couples with any assets at all are well advised to take proper professional advice before embarking upon the formulation of any separation agreement.

Mediation

Increasingly, couples are turning to family mediation to assist in resolving disputes relating, in some cases, to the arrangements post-separation for any children, in some to financial arrangements, and in others to both children and financial issues. Family mediation has grown exponentially over the last quarter-century, and is now a well-regulated profession with a number of organisations dedicated to training and regulation. One such organisation—National Family Mediation—defines mediation in its promotional material[6] thus:

> Mediation is a confidential, voluntary, 'without prejudice' process in which a neutral third party, the mediator helps you to discuss and negotiate all issues surrounding your divorce or separation.

Successful financial mediation presupposes a willingness on both sides to be honest about the extent of their resources and further presupposes that there is no insuperable power imbalance. For the latter reason, mediators may feel constrained to decline to assist couples where historical domestic violence militates against a level playing-field. It is fair to say in the context of the climate eventually resulting in the proposals for divorce reform enacted as Family Law Act 1996 Part II—but later abandoned—that the government was actively considering compulsory mediation, even in the shadow of domestic violence. This climate prompted a flurry of activity in the academic press designed to highlight the difficulties of this approach. Notably, Kaganas and Piper (1994) reviewed the

---

[5] *Edgar v Edgar* [1980] 1 WLR 1410.
[6] National Family Mediation website: www.nfm.org.uk/index.php?page=Home (last visited 29 August 2008).

research on domestic violence and mediation with the object of highlighting the theoretical and practical difficulties which must be addressed if mediation is to be pursued in the context of domestic violence, and Greatbatch and Dingwall (1999) spoke of the marginalisation of domestic violence in divorce mediation.

In those cases where mediation is an option, many couples choose to enter mediation with the benefit of concurrent legal advice, particularly when the mediation concerns the parties' financial affairs. The process requires both parties to complete a comprehensive statement of financial means: whilst mediators ought to be able to recognise any gaps in disclosure, lawyers for the parties are uniquely well qualified to spot any attempt at concealment. Lawyers will also advise as to proposed terms of settlement and will, if settlement is achieved, reduce the agreement to an application for a consent order for the court's approval. It is not until the court approves the negotiated terms that the agreement is placed on the firm footing which in the majority of cases is beyond challenge.

It has been suggested in some sceptical circles that family lawyers may have difficulty with supporting mediation by the same analogy which disinclines turkeys to vote for Christmas. On the contrary: many family lawyers train as mediators and the vast majority of constructive family lawyers recognise the value to their clients of achieving a solution which is tailored to their specific needs and aspirations rather than imposed by a judge in the exercise of statutory discretion. This view should of course be considered in tandem with the views reported by Emma Hitchings in chapter nine of this volume suggesting that many solicitors have concerns about mediation as a tool for resolving financial disputes. Clearly, successful mediation presupposes the skills and willingness to address those very valid concerns. If that can be achieved, lawyers have no reason to fear that mediation will be contrary to their clients' best interests.

Collaborative Law

An emerging form of dispute resolution is the employment of collaborative lawyers. The movement for collaborative law started in the US but has in more recent years migrated to the UK. UK practitioners have formed the Collaborative Family Law Group, which describes collaborative family law as:

> The alternative to 'divorce as usual'. It is designed to minimise the hurt, the loss of self-esteem and the anger and alienation that occurs all too frequently with divorce or separation.[7]

Collaborative family law is intended to manage the divorce process in a dignified way, in which both lawyers and clients agree in writing to reach settlement on the children and financial issues arising from the clients' separation without

---

[7] Collaborative Family Lawyers' website: www.collaborativefamilylawyers.co.uk/WhatisCollabLaw. asp (last visited 29 August 2008).

involving the court. Collaborative family lawyers then help their clients to shape a fair agreement, using their various skills of client representation, negotiation and problem-solving. Their mantra is control of the process: agreement without involving court proceedings and a saving of costs. Underpinning the collaborative process is an understanding that the participants—lay and lawyer—will act in good faith in all of their dealings one with another. It is therefore by definition unlikely to be suitable for those cases where there is a substantial level of mistrust between the separating partners.

For those cases deemed to be suitable, the collaborative process begins with a meeting with each partner's lawyer to discuss the preparations for the first stage in the collaborative process: a four-way meeting consisting of each of the separating partners and their respective solicitors. At that meeting the participants are expected to commit to seeking to work out an agreement without recourse to the courts; the parties will be invited to consider priorities for the next meeting and to embark upon the process of exchange of financial information. The course of subsequent meetings will be dictated by the particular needs of the couple concerned: for example, arrangements for the children may loom large or the parties may need to agree to commission expert advice on specific matters such as the tax efficiency of particular proposals or the best way to maximise pension provision for the parties.

If all goes according to plan, the process will result in a negotiated agreement to which both parties are happy to subscribe. If collaborative law fails to produce a solution, rendering proceedings inevitable, then the parties must instruct different lawyers. It follows from this that whilst collaborative law is a valuable service for couples who are motivated to strive to achieve settlement, it is less successful where either or both parties are not fully committed to the process—and indeed in those circumstances could prove a more costly alternative to standard divorce litigation by requiring the fresh instruction of different lawyers upon the breakdown of the collaborative process.

Settlement by Solicitor Negotiation

It is well recognised that legal professionals are the first port of call for the majority of people faced with relationship breakdown. Some are then willing to be guided by their solicitors towards some form of alternative dispute resolution but others simply wish the solicitor to 'sort it out'.

The first step in the process of 'sorting it out' is to exchange details of income, assets and liabilities. If comprehensive disclosure is volunteered, experienced solicitors should have little difficulty in determining what would be a fair solution and in reaching agreement either by exchange of correspondence or by meeting, with or without the presence of the clients. Clearly agreement is unlikely to be achieved if either client is unreasonable in their expectations or is not motivated to reach a sensible settlement. It must also be recognised that solicitors have differing levels of experience and of the confidence necessary to advise a client as to the merits of any particular solution. It is also right to say that the discretionary system which operates in England and Wales may trigger debate as to what is 'fair' in any given case. However, experienced solicitors will be well aware of the parameters of any settlement which a court might be minded to impose and will take into account in advising their clients the costs which will be saved by a negotiated settlement. They will also be vigilant to ensure that their client's needs are met as fully as circumstances allow.

Many solicitors deal with financial matters from start to finish without recourse to counsel. However, and particularly in a complex or high-value case, it is not unusual for solicitors to instruct a barrister to advise the client either on paper or by means of a conference. If counsel is retained then round-table meetings to discuss settlement are likely to involve both barristers and solicitors—adding to the cost of the process but thus increasing the incentive for the parties to reach an agreement before yet further costs are incurred.

It is fair to say that a great many cases resolve with or without legal assistance without troubling the courts in any contentious sense. It is also right to point out that the increasing restrictions upon the availability of legal aid (and the reduction in the numbers of experienced legal aid lawyers) is perhaps one of the greatest threats to the resolution of matters without recourse to the courts: without proper advice, many may simply lack the confidence to conclude an agreement which, with advice, might be easy to achieve.

Converting an Agreement to an Order of the Court

If agreement is reached as between divorcing clients or separating civil partners—by whatever method—the terms can be reduced to a form of order to be approved by the court on or after pronouncement of decree nisi or conditional order. This ensures that the agreement has binding force. Whilst, as noted above, it is possible for the parties to enter into a formal separation agreement without court endorsement, such an agreement is not beyond challenge, whereas a court order—absent an appeal based upon potentially vitiating factors which might in appropriate circumstances cast doubt upon the validity of an agreement, for example non-disclosure or an unforeseeable change in circumstances,[8] and possibly, in an appropriate case, duress—binds the parties and thus renders the arrangements secure. Before approving a proposed order, the court will require to be made aware of not only the terms proposed but also, in summary form, each partner's financial positions, details of where they and any children will live, and whether either or both has any intention to remarry, enter a further civil partnership or cohabit. If the judge then approves the order it becomes final and binding upon the parties.

---

[8] *Livesey v Jenkins* [1985] AC 424; *Barder v Calouri* [1988] AC 20.

However, approval is a judicial act, not a mere rubber stamp, and the court will reject any settlement proposals which appear manifestly unfair. Alternatively, if there is doubt about the appropriateness of the terms proposed, the court may insist upon both parties attending a short hearing at which the judge will further consider the proposals in the light of any representations made.

Increasingly, parties are unrepresented, and it is the practice of many courts to insist on seeing the parties before approving terms of settlement where one or both do not have the benefit of a solicitor. This practice is designed to guard against parties submitting to terms under duress or with limited appreciation of their implications. This can be particularly important where the financially weaker partner—typically but not exclusively the wife—is submitting to a termination of any maintenance rights on terms which the judge may consider to be ill advised. It must, however, be recognised that the absence of judicial blessing does not prevent the parties from implementing whatever agreement they may have reached: however, the parties would not in those circumstances have the security of a court order and they would therefore run the risk of renewed litigation in the future if one party became disenchanted with the agreement reached.

RESOLUTION IN DEFAULT OF AGREEMENT

However conciliatory an approach may be adopted by one party and/or solicitor, there will always be a hard core of cases where consensual resolution cannot be achieved. There will also be a body of cases where settlement is elusive, rather than unattainable, and can be achieved only in the shadow of the court, when the reluctant party's mind is concentrated by the reality of being required to address the situation.

The starting point for such cases is the Pre-action Protocol annexed to a Practice Direction of the President of the Family Division.[9] This begins by citing the words of Lord Woolf in the final *Access to Justice* report (Woolf, 1996) commending the rationale of pre-action protocols 'to build on and increase the benefits of early but well informed settlement which genuinely satisfy both parties to the dispute'. The Protocol specific to ancillary relief proceedings extols the necessity of full and frank disclosure, exhorts solicitors to be mindful of the appropriateness of mediation, reminds the parties of the need to consider costs implications, cautions against unnecessary use of experts and warns of the danger of infelicitous correspondence:

> The impact of any correspondence upon the reader and in particular the parties must always be considered. Any correspondence which raises irrelevant issues or which might cause the other party to adopt an entrenched, polarised or hostile position is to be discouraged. (para 3.7)

---

[9] *Practice Direction (Ancillary Relief Procedure)* [2000] 1 FLR 997.

The final paragraph of the Protocol (paragraph 3.15) summarises its purpose thus:

> The aim of all pre-application proceedings steps must be to assist the parties to resolve their differences speedily and fairly or at least to narrow the issues and, should that not be possible, to assist the court to do so.

The Protocol was introduced to support a radical change in procedure piloted in a number of centres and then introduced universally in modified form as from 5 June 2000. Prior to that date, and subject to local court practices, it was possible for financial cases to languish in the court system for a considerable period of time without any obvious structure or timetable. The new procedure was designed to bring to bear a rigorously enforced procedure to guard against delay with all its attendant cost and uncertainty. For this reason, and perhaps optimistically, the Protocol attempts to provide reassurance that:

> Making an application to the court should not be regarded as a hostile step or a last resort, rather as a way of starting the court timetable, controlling disclosure and endeavouring to avoid the costly final hearing and the preparation for it. (para 2.4)

It is, unfortunately, a rare litigant who does not perceive the issue of proceedings against him or her as a hostile step, and the extent to which this perception impedes amicable resolution depends very much upon the quality of advice given by solicitors and upon whether the litigation is being conducted in a constructive or confrontational manner. Certainly the ethos underpinning the whole structure of litigated financial settlement demands continuous attempts to resolve matters without recourse to a final hearing, and that aspiration is much more likely to be fulfilled in the absence of intemperate behaviour and acrimonious correspondence.

Court Procedure

Proceedings may begin at any time after filing a petition for divorce, judicial separation or dissolution of civil partnership, although no final order may be made before pronouncement of a decree of divorce, judicial separation or separation order.

The process of commencing proceedings is straightforward, requiring the filing of one single-sided form (Form A) accompanied by a cheque in respect of the prescribed court fee (currently £210). This sets in train a timetable, as required by the Family Proceedings Rules 1991(as amended), to deal successively with the following:

(1) The filing and exchanging of standard-form affidavits (Form E) setting out each party's financial position and a summary of matters such as the standard of living enjoyed during the relationship, arguments relating to claims that either party made a special contribution to the welfare of the family, and so on; and the order sought. Each Form E must be supported by a number of prescribed documents, including evidence of income and 12 months' worth of bank and building society statements.

(2) The filing and exchange of chronologies; a concise statement of the issues in the case, and any questionnaire seeking further information or documents.

(3) The first directions appointment at court (FDA): this must be fixed no less than 12 weeks and no more than 16 weeks after the filing of Form A.

(4) At the FDA the court will in the vast majority of cases fix a Financial Dispute Resolution hearing (FDR).

(5) If matters are not resolved at FDR stage, the court will fix a final hearing.

First Directions Appointment

The rules envisage that the FDA will in most cases be utilised as an opportunity to give directions to progress matters to the next stage. Directions may include:

(a) valuation (usually by a jointly instructed expert) of any properties if the parties cannot agree as to their value;

(b) the date by which parties must respond to any questionnaire raised by the other party (the court having first satisfied itself that the questions are appropriate and proportionate);

(c) where absolutely necessary, provision for the filing of statements dealing with particular issues—for example where one party is suggesting that their share of the assets should be enhanced by virtue of an alleged special contribution, such as the bringing into the marriage of significant entrepreneurial skills or a substantial inheritance;

(d) fixing the next stage of the process—the FDR. In very rare cases the judge may decide to dispense with the FDR if there is a compelling reason to do so.

It is fair to say that there is less than universal full compliance with the rules as to filing of the documents necessary for a fully effective FDA. However, most people make some attempt to produce a Form E within a reasonable approximation of the prescribed timetable; generally at least one party will be armed with a schedule of issues and other supporting documentation. The court will then give directions designed to remedy any deficiencies, in addition to the more typical directions mentioned above.

Very occasionally, all the necessary information is marshalled by the parties before the FDA, which can then be utilised as the FDR, thus saving the expense of an additional hearing. Such model litigants are, sadly, few and far between.

Financial Dispute Resolution Hearing

The purpose of the FDR is to provide an opportunity for the litigants to resolve matters without the stress, delay, and expense of a final hearing. The judge conducting the FDR is required to assist the parties by explaining to them the sort of order which a court is likely to make at a final hearing.

The parties are required to prepare for the FDR by complying with all previous directions and by filing copies of all offers to settle, such offers to be seen only by the judge conducting the FDR. Most advocates file and serve on the other party a useful position statement summarising the parties' financial positions and explaining what resolution is proposed. The parties will usually have been directed to attend at least an hour before the court appointment in order to discuss a possible settlement or at least to refine those issues which present an obstacle to settlement.

The FDR was, when introduced, an innovative process: it requires the judge to be proactive in encouraging the parties towards resolution and to give indications on particular issues which might otherwise present an obstacle to settlement. The difficulty for the judge is that indications are given solely on the basis of the documentary evidence filed: there is no opportunity for the purposes of the FDR to test any of that evidence by hearing cross-examination of the parties. Nevertheless, except in the most unusual case, few judges would encounter great difficulty in taking a view of the case and giving a clear indication as to the likely outcome on the basis of the information then available.

The facility for judicial intervention is particularly valuable where litigants are intent upon conducting their cases with scant regard to what is reasonable and are perhaps paying limited attention to their solicitors' advice. It is also particularly useful in cases involving litigants in person—an increasingly common phenomenon in a climate of severe restriction, as noted above, upon the availability of publicly funded legal advice.

Two practical examples illustrate the type of reality check which a district judge can bring to bear upon a case. The incidence of urban myths has already been mentioned: a common scenario might involve a separation after very many years of marriage, where the husband may have formed a new relationship, leaving a wife close to retiring age, or thereabouts, with no job history and little prospect of financial independence. A settlement in such circumstances is far more likely to be achieved if the husband accepts the reality that, having given up her career to look after the family, the court is not likely to expect the wife to be left devoid of his support simply because the husband aspires to a clean break. Such a wife is likely to be provided for either by an additional lump sum to capitalise her maintenance claims, by personal maintenance, by pension sharing, or, indeed, by some permutation of those three possibilities. Conversely, a wife left behind in a property too large and expensive for her needs may struggle with the idea that her much-loved home must be added to the catalogue of losses which she associates with the breakdown of the marriage. Once the realities of the situation are firmly (and, it is hoped, sympathetically) explained, cases which appeared to be destined for a contentious hearing become capable of settlement.

It is fair to say that couples requiring the intervention of the court to resolve their financial disputes are in the minority, and of that minority, a very substantial proportion of cases settle at the FDR stage, eliminating the need for a final hearing. Many judges extol the virtues of agreeing something which the couple can at least live with, rather than risking the imposition of a judicial decision potentially unpalatable to both—together, of course, with the attendant escalation in costs of a final hearing.

If the FDR does not resolve matters, the FDR judge has no further contentious involvement in the case, and all documentation relating to proposals for settlement is removed from the file. The trial judge thus approaches the matter knowing only the parties' open positions—not the positions that they would have been prepared to adopt for the purpose of seeking to agree terms of settlement.

Final Hearing

The final hearing may occupy as little as two hours or may extend to several days or even weeks. A substantial majority require between one and two days. Most final hearings are conducted by district judges, although some circuit judges may hear such cases, and the most complex—especially if likely to involve some innovative point of law—will be heard by a High Court judge. If the matter is suitable for hearing in the High Court then it is highly likely that the FDR will also have been conducted by a High Court judge.

At the final hearing the judge should be in possession of a trial bundle containing all the documents relevant to the determination of the proceedings. Inevitably, the size and weight of the bundle varies according to the type and value of case, but may be very substantial. The judge will hear oral evidence from the parties and submissions from the parties' lawyers—or from the parties themselves if unrepresented. Sometimes it is necessary to hear oral evidence from an expert involved in the case—perhaps a forensic accountant, a pensions expert, or a property valuer. It is fair to say that oral expert evidence is rarely required in the small- and middle-money cases which make up the majority of the divorcing community.

After the conclusion of evidence and submissions, the judge will make a decision based upon the factors set out in section 25 of the Matrimonial Causes Act 1973.[10] The court is obliged to give first consideration to the welfare of any minor children; thereafter the judge must consider a range of issues including needs, resources, contributions, length of marriage, health, and, occasionally, conduct.

CONSISTENCY OF DECISION-MAKING: IS IT ALL A LOTTERY?

It is common sense that people are more likely to settle their differences without recourse to litigation if they have a clear understanding of the likely outcome of such litigation. Some jurisdictions—notably Scotland—provide greater certainty on issues such as spousal maintenance by virtue of the clear principles embodied

---

[10] As amended by, inter alia, the Matrimonial and Family Proceedings Act 1984, the Pensions Act 1995, and the Welfare Reform and Pensions Act 1999.

in the Family Law (Scotland) Act 1985. The Child Support Agency in its original incarnations provided a formula for the calculation of child maintenance, although its complexity meant that it did not always clarify individuals' understanding of the law.

In England and Wales principles rather than formulae govern applications for ancillary relief, and 12 judges applying the same principles to the same case may produce 12 slightly different answers. Should we therefore heed the call for 'limited discretion being exercised against the background of reasonable certainty'? (Greensmith, 2007). In May 2003 the Law Society's Ancillary Relief Working Group published *Financial Provision on Divorce Clarity and Fairness—Proposals for Reform*. One of the key proposals was a recommendation that the Matrimonial Causes Act 1973 be amended to provide guidelines for the sharing of assets, to be read in conjunction with the factors set out in the Act. The hope was expressed that this would provide greater certainty and clarity and thus fewer cases would reach trial. That particular recommendation has yet to be put into practice. However,the reality is that for most middle-income families, resolution is driven by need—for example, the need for the parent with primary care to retain the family home. Any judicial variations are likely to encompass secondary considerations such as the exact percentage of the value of the property which the dispossessed spouse might be entitled to realise when the children attain their majority.

The situation is arguably less clear for those of greater wealth. Most litigants can only dream of the income and capital enjoyed by the majority of those who feature in the cases which come before the higher courts and thus form part of the body of binding legal precedent which dictates how judges throughout the land exercise the discretion conferred upon them by statute. However, greater wealth makes it much easier to satisfy the reasonable needs of the parties and then to achieve fairness in relation to the division of other assets by reference to the jurisprudential wisdom contained in the various authorities—notably, for example, *White v White*,[11] in which the House of Lords promulgated the 'yardstick of equal division' whilst reminding all concerned that the factors set out in Matrimonial Causes Act 1973 section 25(2) have no particular order of importance, and *Miller v Miller; McFarlane v McFarlane*,[12] in which their Lordships articulated the three principles of need, sharing, and compensation. Competent lawyers should be able to assess within a reasonable band the likely award for the client even within the bounds of a discretionary system—and the very positive advantage of such a system is the ability to tailor the arrangements to the very specific circumstances of the individual family. Some might consider this to be less a lottery and more a reflection of the system's capacity to deliver very personalised and tailored justice for any given family. It is also worthy of note that the lack of absolute certainty as to the outcome of any final hearing provides a powerful incentive to the parties to reach an agreement rather than risk a result which may be to the liking of neither.

---

[11] [2001] AC 596.
[12] [2006] UKHL 24, [2006] 2 AC 618.

RELUCTANT OR OBSTRUCTIVE LITIGANTS

In an ideal world, parties exchange properly prepared Forms E within the pre-scribed period of 35 days before the FDA: the Forms E will be supported by all the right documents; the parties will co-operate to agree a chronology and statement of issues, and any questionnaires will be concise, relevant, and timely of delivery. The matter will then proceed to FDR in an orderly fashion and it is to be hoped they will resolve there. Sadly, those immersed in the unhappiness of relationship breakdown rarely inhabit that utopian world, and even at an early stage in the proceedings it may be necessary to consider a number of strategies to extract co-operation and thus to make the steady and inexorable progress envisaged by the architects of the ancillary relief scheme.

Reluctance to participate in the litigation process can, on one level, be wholly understandable. Some, as mentioned above, are simply not be ready to accept the reality of relationship breakdown and its practical consequences; some may be intent upon making life as difficult as possible for the former partner; some may feel that it is not in their interests to address the issues in a timely fashion (for example, if they suspect that the other party is about to inherit a substantial estate); some may be suffering from physical or mental ill health which prevents their engagement in the process; some may be terrified by their inability to afford legal advice; and yet others may simply be indulging in ostrich-like behaviour, in the hope that it will all go away. The approach of the courts in those circumstances depends upon the judge's view of the underlying reason or reasons for non co-operation. Inevitably, the deserted spouse who struggles to come to terms with the peremptory termina-tion of 30 years' marriage is likely to excite more judicial sympathy than the party who is suspected of playing for time in the hope of disposing of part of the assets.

The first indication to the court of any problems with compliance is likely to be a delay in filing Forms E. Sometimes one party might write in to alert the court to the absence of compliance, thus providing the court with an opportunity to give directions requiring the errant party to remedy the matter within a particular time scale, in the hope of preserving the FDA as an effective hearing.

If the Form E is not filed sufficiently in advance of the first appointment to enable all necessary documentation to be prepared, there will be little choice but to adjourn the FDA to a later date to accommodate the revision to the timetable. If that is the consequence of delay on both sides then it is unlikely that the court will make any adverse costs orders. However, if only one party is in default, an order requiring the miscreant to pay the costs of the abortive FDA might well be all that is necessary to emphasise the importance of compliance.

If the default continues, then the court may well be persuaded to attach a penal notice to a further order requiring the provision of Form E by a particular date. That order must then be personally served upon the defaulting party, and further failure to comply would place that party in contempt of court, with the attendant prospect of a prison sentence. Such a prospect does tend wonderfully to concen-trate the mind of the defaulting party in the vast majority of cases.

Not all parties invite the court to go down the route of threatening contempt proceedings, and not all cases are in any event suitable for such measures. It may be that a party lacks capacity to deal with the proceedings: this may be a permanent or transient state, possibly associated with the stress of the relationship breakdown and its consequences for that person's mental health. In such circumstances, consideration would be given to appointing a litigation friend to stand in the incapacitated party's shoes. It may also be the case that the means of the parties are limited and the defaulting party's absent Form E is unlikely to contain any significant surprises. In that event, the complying party (or the court) may take the pragmatic view that the court has sufficient information to arrive at a fair decision in the matter and that committal proceedings would be expensive and unnecessary. In other cases, the applicant may be concerned simply to meet their primary needs—for example for a transfer of ownership or tenancy of the former matrimonial home in order to ensure accommodation for the applicant and any children.

Where the applicant is clear what order is likely to be sought as a final disposal of the matter, even though the other side has not given proper disclosure, an effective strategy may be to adjourn the FDA with a clear endorsement on the face of the order that if the defaulting party continues to neglect to file Form E then on the next occasion the court may be minded to make an order in accordance with the applicant's request. It is helpful if the applicant drafts the proposed order to be annexed to the court's directions: seeing the possible outcome of the proceedings in black and white can prove to be the catalyst which spurs even the most ostrich-like litigant into action. The court's duty is to be fair to both parties, subject to the overriding imperative to give first consideration to the interests of the children, and obviously it is very much easier for the court properly to discharge that duty if it has full information at its disposal. However, it is not inconsistent with that duty to make an order depriving the defaulting party of the home—on whatever terms appear appropriate—if the court is satisfied that this is a proper disposal of the matter and provided that the court is satisfied that both parties have had every opportunity to participate in the litigation process—even if one party has declined to take that opportunity.

In some cases, there are concerns that the reluctant litigant is devoting the time and energy which should be spent on preparing the case to seeking to frustrate the process by dissipating assets. The court has a number of weapons in its armoury for dealing with such activities. Orders can be sought to freeze bank accounts and restraining the disposal of assets. The court also has power to unscramble dealings intended to put property beyond the reach of the court proceedings and thus to frustrate the other party's claims.[13] With the increasing incidence of marriages with an international element, ever more complex remedies are required and it is possible, for example, to apply to the court to restrain anticipated dealings in

---

[13] See, eg, Matrimonial Causes Act 1973 s 37.

property pending an application in this country for financial order after a divorce conducted overseas.[14]

Finally, it should be noted that although there is a clear framework prescribed by the Family Proceedings Rules 1991 for dealing with ancillary relief claims, there is now judicial authority for adopting a creative approach to those rules to meet the needs of each particular case. In *Crossley*, Lord Justice Thorpe provided the following reassurance: 'I am quite unpersuaded … that these individual rules were intended to be some sort of straitjacket precluding sensible case management'.[15] Thus the converse of the uncertainty perceived as a possible evil of our discretionary system is that each fractured family has the luxury of an individual, tailored approach to its particular circumstances.

AND THE CHILDREN?

Child support has been a major political issue for many years. Whilst many parents are happy to accept their responsibility to support their children post separation, there is a divergence of view as to how best to deal with the reluctant parental contributor. The advent of the Child Support Agency substantially reduced the ability of the courts to ensure proper support for children, even, perhaps curiously, when all other aspects of the fractured family's financial arrangements were the subject of scrutiny. The new Child Maintenance and Enforcement Commission, created pursuant to the Child Maintenance and Other Payments Act 2008 is charged with maximising agreement between separating parents but provides—potentially—a new array of enforcement possibilities for those who prevaricate. That Act is yet to be exposed to the test of time and it is impossible to say therefore to what extent children will derive greater—or lesser—protection from the acknowledged mischief of parental reluctance to support them. In the meantime, Children Act 1989 Schedule 1 remains at the disposal of all parents, married and unmarried alike, to provide for capital sums and transfers in the relatively limited circumstances when this is deemed to be appropriate. The same principles of disclosure and encouragement to settle apply to such applications as they do to an application for financial relief after divorce, and in many courts a financial dispute resolution hearing is offered in substance if not in name to assist the parties in resolving matters without recourse to a final hearing.

CONCLUSION

As suggested above, the majority of separating spouses and partners are able to resolve their financial issues without recourse to the courts, save perhaps for the purpose of inviting the court to endorse their agreed terms of settlement. It is beyond peradventure that it is far less costly, both in human and

---

[14] Matrimonial and Family Proceedings Act 1984 s 24(1).
[15] [2008] 1 FLR 1476 at [15].

in financial terms, if litigation can be avoided, even though all methods of achieving settlement—except perhaps the exclusively DIY variety—will incur some costs. However, those who achieve settlement after engaging in mediation, solicitor-led negotiation, or the collaborative law process are likely to regard the money as being well spent and an investment designed to provide a fair outcome.

Those who are compelled—for whatever reason—to embark upon the litigation process will be obliged at both FDA and FDR stage to confirm to the court and to the other party the costs incurred to date. This helps to concentrate minds on what may be very substantial expenditure which the parties can ill afford, and is one of the factors which may assist in reaching agreement at FDR. It is highly probable that at that stage the judge will not only give a clear steer to the parties as to the likely outcome of a contested final hearing, but will also remind the parties of the money already lost in terms of legal costs, and the substantial further costs which a final hearing will entail. For the most part, legal costs are regarded as liabilities which must be taken into account in determining the distribution of the family assets, but which are not generally payable by one party on behalf of the other. However, the small minority who constitute the body of reluctant, evasive, and downright dishonest litigants will be left in no doubt not only of the court's powers to arrive at the truth of the parties' financial situation—or to draw inferences as to the position—but also that they face the prospect of adverse costs orders in the event that they seek to sabotage a fair and expeditious resolution of the proceedings.

Whilst no arrangements for resolving domestic disputes can ever claim to be perfect, those litigants who have the misfortune not to settle their differences do have the benefit of a system which concentrates on the detail of each individual case and strives to find the fairest solution tailored to the particular circumstances of that case. It must, however, be acknowledged that those who embark upon family litigation are rarely happy to be in court, are likely to have incurred considerable legal costs and to have found the process highly stressful, however sympathetic the judge may seek to be. The parties may therefore require some persuading that the outcome of their case was fair, balanced, and just. It is a truth universally acknowledged amongst family law professionals that if both parties feel slightly aggrieved after a court-imposed settlement, the judge probably reached the correct decision.

BIBLIOGRAPHY

Greatbatch, D and Dingwall, R (1999) 'The Marginalization of Domestic Violence in Divorce Mediation' 13 *International Journal of Law, Policy and the Family* 174.
Greensmith, A (2007) 'Let's Play Ancillary Relief' 37 *Family Law* 203.
Hodson, D (1998) 'The new fourth edition of the SFLA Code of Practice', *Solicitors' Family Law Association Review,* issue 71.
Home Office (1998) *Supporting Families: A Consultation Document* (London, Home Office).

Home Office (1999) *Supporting Families: Summary of Responses to the Consultation Document* (London, Home Office).

Kaganas, F and Piper, C (1994) 'Domestic Violence and Divorce Mediation' 16 *Journal of Social Welfare and Family Law* 265.

Law Society (2006) *Family Law Protocol*, 2nd edn (London, The Law Society).

Law Society Ancillary Relief Working Group (2003) *Financial Provision on Divorce Clarity and Fairness—Proposals for Reform* (London, The Law Society).

Woolf, H (1996) *Access to Justice: Final Report to the Lord Chancellor on the Civil Justice System in England and Wales* (London, HMSO).

11

Who Wins, Who Loses and Who Recovers from Divorce?

HAYLEY FISHER AND HAMISH LOW

INTRODUCTION

T HIS CHAPTER ANALYSES the economic consequences of divorce, focusing on two issues: first, how large and persistent is the fall in income on divorce for each party; and secondly, how might alternative arrangements for divorce settlements affect this income fall and affect behaviour both within the marriage and following divorce. Our main finding is that there is a striking difference between the experience of men and women on divorce, alongside substantial variation within the sexes. If divorce settlements were to be based on compensation for decisions made within marriage, some of these differences would be offset.

Part of the drive for reform of the basis for divorce settlements comes from the unequal experience of men and women following divorce. Much of the evidence for this comes from the US. For the UK, Eekelaar and Maclean (1986) provide evidence using a retrospective cross-section survey, while Jenkins (2008) follows individuals in the UK over time through divorce, finding that the financial impact on women exceeds that for men, but with a weakening impact of divorce over time.[1] However, these conclusions are problematic for exploring the implications of divorce because they are based on a sample in which separation following cohabitation is not distinguished from separation from marriage and because data from England and Wales are pooled with data from Scotland where divorce law differs. The evidence we show in this chapter provides a detailed analysis of what happens after divorce in the short and long term, distinguishing marriage from cohabitation, and focusing on England and Wales.

---

[1] There is some evidence from the US that documents the differences in the experience of men and women after divorce, with large short-term falls in household income for women and smaller absolute falls for men. For example, Duncan and Hoffman (1985) report that women's household income is on average 70% of its pre-divorce level in the period after separation, whereas men's is 93%.

We examine the short- and longer-term impact of divorce on the income and financial resources of both men and women in the UK. We do this using data from 15 years of the British Household Panel Survey (BHPS). We consider the size of the fall in income after divorce and how long that fall persists. Following divorce, the income of men increases by about 23 per cent, while that of women falls substantially by 31 per cent, after controlling for household size. Underlying these numbers are two offsetting effects: first, each spouse is living in a household with less household income; secondly, household size is smaller (in the absence of repartnering) meaning increasing per capita income for a given income level. For men, this second effect dominates, leading to the increase in 'equivalised' income. For women, the loss of partner income dominates the smaller household size, and equivalised income falls. Over time, the income loss faced by women is mitigated and average post-divorce income returns to average pre-divorce rates nine years later. We examine whether this recovery is due to repartnering, labour supply changes or government-provided benefits, finding that the main driving force behind recovery is repartnering. Benefits matter substantially for a small group of women, mostly among the low educated, but labour supply changes post divorce are insignificant. Our data work compares these conclusions to the results for cohabiting couples: income falls on divorce are more substantial and more persistent than those on separation from a cohabiting relationship. Of course, part of this difference arises because of differences in the type of people and circumstances of those who are married compared with those cohabiting.

These figures on the recovery of household income post divorce suggest that changing divorce settlement mechanisms will not alter long-term outcomes, instead merely replacing alternative forms of insurance. However, it is important to stress that the short-term consequences for household income on divorce are substantial, and this reduces welfare. This effect is particularly severe for those without savings or access to borrowing (see Finney, chapter six, this volume). Further, repartnering may be viewed as an unsatisfactory way for many to recover their standard of living. Most importantly, we show that this option is least likely for certain groups, such as older divorcees and those with children, and as a result these people are hardest hit by divorce.

Drawing conclusions about appropriate settlements on the basis of standard of living after divorce is akin to basing settlements on need, which ignores the investments (and their costs) made during the relationship by both partners, and so fails to consider the honouring of implicit contracts within marriage. To clarify this argument, we draw a conceptual distinction as to whether the divorce settlement should be calculated on the basis of each party's income or on the basis of their consumption (that is, spending power). A consumption-based measure could be needs determined or could be determined by expectations within marriage. A calculation based on income allows allocations to be made dependent on the investments each spouse has made to the marriage and to each other's career, or dependent on current earnings potential. A key part of such a calculation concerns the role of accumulated human capital in determining earnings. There is extensive evidence that earnings are dependent on past labour force participation (Eckstein and Wolpin, 1989), and so differences in earnings potential between spouses are affected by labour supply decisions within marriage (as to which see further Scott and Dex, chapter three, this volume). This suggests a requirement to compensate parties for losses incurred in good faith. This issue lies at the heart of the *McFarlane v McFarlane* ruling.[2] We therefore discuss some of the incentive effects of these alternative mechanisms.

This chapter proceeds as follows. The second section presents empirical results on income loss and recovery after divorce, and the third compares these trends with those after the end of cohabitation. The fourth section presents a simple model to show the implications for income and consumption of alternative resource allocation mechanisms on divorce, and the final section presents our conclusions.

ESTIMATES OF FINANCIAL LOSS ON DIVORCE

The aim of this section is to use data from the UK to show the consequences of divorce for men and for women. We begin by discussing some of the existing literature on the economic impact of divorce and then by describing the data source that we use. The bulk of the section uses that data in two ways. First, we present descriptive statistics on the economic effects of divorce in the UK. We focus on income changes for those who divorce at some point in our 15-year time frame, without comparison to those who do not, and our focus is therefore on how the timing of divorce affects behaviour. Implicitly, we are assuming that the timing of divorce is independent of changes in income. Secondly, we use regression analysis to identify more carefully the magnitude of effects.

Background

There is a literature, predominantly from the US, which attempts to measure the economic effects of divorce on both men and women. Duncan and Hoffman (1985) use US panel data from 1967 to 1981 and find substantial falls in household income and increases in the poverty rate for women at the time of divorce. Income falls are mitigated by a strong labour supply response and by remarriage. However, there is selection into remarriage, which means that not all of those who divorce would be able to achieve this improvement. Smock, Manning and Gupta (1999) find that women who remain married would experience similar losses to those who divorce if they were to divorce. McKeever and Wolfinger (2001) study more recent US data from the late 1980s and early 1990s (using the National

2 [2006] UKHL 24.

Survey of Families and Households), and find that falls in women's household income on divorce are smaller in magnitude than in previous studies. This moderation is attributed to better labour market attachment and human capital.

The study of the UK most related to this one is Jenkins (2008), which builds on Jarvis and Jenkins (1999), using the BHPS to assess the income changes associated with partnership dissolution. Both these papers pool separations from cohabitation and marriage, and so we cannot draw conclusions about the effects of divorce or changes in divorce patterns. In addition, the analysis in these two papers is focused on descriptive statistics. The key findings are of substantial declines for the household incomes of women and children, after controlling for household size, but little change for men. The declines in household incomes for women and children are mitigated by increases in those receiving income support and housing benefit. There is a moderation in these effects over time, which Jenkins (2008) notes is contemporaneous with changes in in-work benefits that increased the rewards from paid work relative to not working.

For the European Union, Uunk (2004) and Aassve et al (2006) use the European Community Household Panel (ECHP) to assess short-term income losses on divorce. They find that social welfare and public child-care provision matters in explaining women's economic circumstances: women in countries with a social-democratic regime experience smaller income declines than those in Southern European countries, where public policy assumes that family will ensure an individual's welfare. Further, the losses from divorce are shared more equally between the man and woman in a more egalitarian society such as Sweden (with high female labour market participation rates) than they are in Italy.

There is less evidence on the experience of men. McManus and DiPrete (2001) consider the economic impact of divorce on men in the US using data from the Panel Study of Income Dynamics from 1980–93, and point out that there is substantial heterogeneity across men. Those men who contributed over 80 per cent of household income in the married state tend to gain (in terms of equivalised household income), whereas those who contributed less suffer losses.

Overall, the literature supports the view that there is a severe, negative impact of divorce on the economic well-being of women, and either no effect or a small gain for men. There is less evidence on how fast recovery occurs and the mechanisms of recovery.

Data

We use panel data from the first 15 waves of the BHPS, from 1991 to 2005. The first wave of this survey covered a nationally representative sample of all adults in each of around 5,000 households. This gave an initial sample of approximately 10,000 individuals. All individuals in this initial sample have been followed since, where possible. Where an original sample member (OSM) forms a new household, all adults in the new household are interviewed whilst they remain part of that household, but they are not followed if the household is disbanded unless children have been born to the couple. For this reason, the BHPS does not necessarily track both partners after a separation. All sample members provide wide-ranging information including incomes, demographic information, and social attitudes. For more information about the BHPS see Taylor et al (2007).

We restrict attention to working-age individuals residing in England and Wales. Various additional socio-economic variables are used to control for changes in income, including age, race, education level and whether there are young children in the household.

We restrict our sample to individuals who we observe undergoing a separation from their partner. For couples who divorce, we define the point of divorce as the point at which the couple no longer live together, rather than the granting of an official divorce (in the spirit of Duncan and Hoffman, 1985), and similarly for cohabiting couples we define separation as the point at which the couple stop living together.[3] Where an individual has undergone more than one separation, each is treated as a separate record. This leaves us with a sample of 339 male and 475 female separations from marriage, and 342 male and 457 female separations from cohabitation, where survey information is available for both the year preceding and the year succeeding separation.[4]

Since the BHPS was intended to be a nationally representative sample, we would expect roughly equal numbers of male and female separations in our data. The disparity is due to differences in attrition rates between women and men: men are more likely to leave the sample than women. There are two reasons why individuals leave the sample: first, the individual may not be an original sample member, and so is not followed after separation; secondly, the attrition may be as a result of choices by the individual. Whether an individual is an original sample member or the partner of an original sample member is random, and so the first type of exit from the sample is not problematic. The second type of exit is potentially problematic if attrition is related to variables which drive income paths because this could bias our results. To shed light on the extent of this problem, we consider the sample of individuals who respond at time $t = -1$ and are eligible to respond at time $t = 0$ (note that this excludes temporary sample members who are not followed when they split from the original sample member). Amongst those who split from a marriage, we have potential responses from 446 males and 509 females. Of these, 107 males and 34 females leave the sample, giving no data at $t = 0$. Amongst those who split from a cohabitation, we have potential responses from 401 men and 473 women, with 59 men and 16 women leaving the sample.[5]

---

[3] We disregard partnerships that have ended through the death of a partner.

[4] Note that, in contrast with Jarvis and Jenkins (1999), we do not require the separating partnership to have children.

[5] The indicated lower attrition rate for cohabitation is misleading since a larger proportion of those splitting from cohabitation are temporary sample members (29% of the partners in question vs just 7% of those splitting from marriage) and so are not followed. However, this is not the natural attrition we are concerned with here.

For women divorcing, we analyse the extent that the probability of exiting the sample is correlated with characteristics of the household.[6] We find that there are a number of characteristics predicting attrition: attrition is more likely when a woman has fewer children and is non-white. On the one hand, this leads us to be slightly cautious about the conclusions drawn about the experience of women on divorce because our effects underweight women with no children who might suffer less from divorce, meaning our results may overstate the effects. On the other hand, the natural attrition rate is low at seven per cent. For men, where the attrition rate is much higher at 24 per cent, there are no key variables that predict attrition. This lack of correlation between observable characteristics at time $t = -1$ and future attrition gives us some confidence that the results presented below for men are not significantly affected by attrition.[7] For men who separate from cohabitation, attrition is more likely among those with children. The low level of natural attrition for women splitting from cohabitations makes it difficult to draw conclusions about the existence of selective attrition.

Since these sample sizes are large relative to previous studies, we are able to examine the experience of separations from marriage separately from those separations from cohabitation. Moreover, in 45.5 per cent of separations from marriage and 54.7 per cent of separations from cohabitation, we have data for at least five years following the separation, so we are able to consider the longer-term economic impact of divorce and the mechanisms which drive any recovery. The year immediately following separation is denoted as $t = 0$, and all observations of separation are pooled over the 15 years of the sample.

It is important to note that, since we are restricting our attention to those who separate, our results need to be interpreted as the average effect of separation *for those who separate*. Since separating or becoming divorced is not a random event, we cannot draw inferences about the potential experiences of separation on those who remain in a couple.

We measure economic well-being using traditional income measures. The BHPS allows us to split household income into individual labour, benefit and other income. Our variables of interest are household income, and the labour and benefit income of the individual undergoing the separation (all deflated to 1991 prices using the retail price index). We attribute the full household income at time $t = -1$ to the individual who separates. Implicitly, we are assuming that expenditure within the household is determined by a joint decision irrespective of the source of income, rather than reflecting an allocation of income between the parties, followed by individual expenditure decisions. This is not an

---

[6] We perform this analysis through regression with 'exiting the sample' as the dependent variable. We use 'probit estimation' because the dependent variable is either a 0 (remains in sample) or a 1 (exits the sample). The probit therefore calculates the effect of different explanatory variables on the probability of exiting the sample or not. The coefficient on a particular characteristic is the difference in this probability associated with a change in the characteristic.

[7] However, attrition may be related to unobservable characteristics and we cannot test for this.

uncontroversial assumption. For example, in chapter five of this volume, Burgoyne and Sonnenberg present evidence on differing financial arrangements made by cohabiting couples, which may reflect differences in attitudes towards sharing income and making joint expenditure decisions. Further, the degree to which income is shared underpinned the *Stack v Dowden* ruling.[8] However, to identify the actual allocation of resources within a relationship requires data on expenditure that can be attributed specifically to a particular individual (a possible example is spending on clothing), and also a way of accounting for expenditure on goods which are jointly valued by both individuals (such as heating). If the only data are details of income in each bank account, we cannot infer the actual allocation of resources within a partnership or the mechanism for determining expenditure decisions (Chiappori, Fortin and Lacroix, 2002).

A household with more individuals will require more resources to maintain each individual's standard of living. To control for this extra cost of having a larger household, household income is adjusted using the McClements (before housing costs) equivalence scale. Rather than just converting household income to income per head, this adjustment acknowledges the economies of scale inherent in maintaining a household. For example, adding a spouse to a household of one adult requires only the addition of 67 per cent of the existing resources to maintain the previous individual standard of living. The weights for children vary with their age. Clearly, as the economies of scale from sharing a household increase, the implied cost of divorce (and the removal of the economies of scale) will increase. Our results will therefore be sensitive to the equivalence scale used. As pointed out by Jarvis and Jenkins (1999), income changes for men following separation are likely to be more sensitive to this since their change in household size on divorce is generally greater.

Results: Separation from Marriage

We restrict our attention here to those who separate from a marriage. We present our results in three stages. First, we discuss the characteristics of those who become divorced compared with those who do not divorce within a given time frame. Secondly, we present summary results on financial loss on divorce; and, finally, we present the results of regression analysis which explore the raw trends in more detail. Throughout this analysis we are assuming that the timing of divorce is unrelated to the timing of income changes.[9]

---

[8] [2007] UKHL 17.

[9] This is not an innocuous assumption. If income changes influence the timing of divorce then we would be measuring this influence as well as the impact of divorce on income. For example, if unexpected declines in income precipitate divorce, then we would over-estimate the decline in income brought about by divorce because causality flows from income to divorce, not vice versa.

Characteristics of Divorcees

Since we focus on the subsection of the population who get divorced, it is instructive to consider how this group may differ from the rest of the population. We consider all those who are married in 1995 (wave 5 of the BHPS). We then split this group into those who remain married for the subsequent five years, and those who get divorced within that time period (ignoring those who drop out of the sample or experience separation due to the death of one partner). The influence of key characteristics on the probability of divorce is shown in the probit regressions presented in Table 11.1. The coefficients on each variable show the change in the probability of divorce for a one unit change in that variable, relative to the probability of divorce of an individual with average characteristics For example, home owners are 1.3 per cent less likely to be in the sample of those who divorce, once we take account of other characteristics; cohabiting before marriage is associated with an increase in the probability of divorce of 4.6 per cent.

In terms of individual characteristics, the table shows that divorce is more likely for younger people. A higher score on the General Health Questionnaire

Table 11.1: Characteristics of Divorcees

	Women	Men
Age	**−0.0013**	**−0.0023**
Number of children	0.0013	−0.0010
Race (not white)	0.0108	0.0021
In poor health	**−0.0173**	−0.0073
Score in GHQ	**0.0865**	**0.0750**
Household size	0.0012	−0.0013
Home owner	**−0.0132**	−0.0059
Asset income > £100 pa	−0.0042	−0.0028
Highly educated	−0.0057	0.0003
Working	−0.0005	−0.0046
Hours worked per week	0.0001	**−0.0003**
Has second job	0.0109	0.0140
Personal labour income (£000s)	−0.0007	**0.0007**
Equivalised household income (£000s)	0.0000	−0.0003
Household benefit income (£000s)	−0.0007	−0.0002
Reports financial difficulties	0.0078	0.0182
Previously married	−0.0108	0.0206
Marriage tenure (years)	−0.0004	0.0005
Cohabited before marriage	**0.0456**	**0.0362**
Mean divorce probability	0.0289	0.0267
Observations	3,097	2,347

Note: Variables in bold are significant at 10% confidence level.
Variables which are not in bold are statistically insignificantly different from zero. Standard errors and details available on request.

(GHQ)[10] is also associated with a higher divorce probability, indicating that those who divorce subsequently are (unsurprisingly) less happy within marriage than those who remain married. Women in poor health are less likely to divorce. Men who work more hours have a lower probability of divorce, but those who earn more labour income have a higher probability of divorce.

Having cohabited before marriage increases significantly the probability of being in the sample of those who divorce, which is consistent with previous studies (see, for example, Axinn and Thornton, 1992).[11] These differences in key characteristics suggest that there are important differences between households that divorce and those that do not, and this is why we do not use those who remain married as a counterfactual for those who divorce.

Extent of Financial Loss on Divorce

We turn now to considering how the household incomes of those who do divorce change in response to the shock. Figures 11.1 and 11.2 show the evolution of

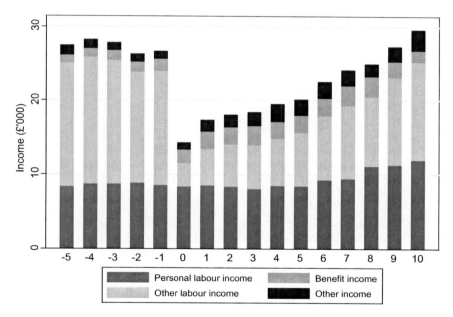

Figure 11.1: Breakdown of Household Income for Women with High Education

---

[10] The GHQ is a questionnaire originally designed to assess psychiatric illnesses, but now commonly used as a measure of subjective well-being, with a lower score indicating higher levels of well-being (see Taylor et al, 2007 for more information).

[11] This should not be interpreted as arguing that cohabitation *causes* divorce, rather that the type of person who cohabits before marriage is more likely to be the type of person who gets divorced (Lillard, Brien and Waite, 1995).

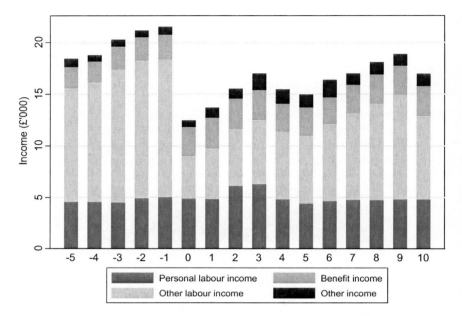

Figure 11.2: Breakdown of Household Income for Women with Low Education

the composition of household income for highly and low-educated women, respectively.[12,13] Both figures show a large drop in household income at the time of divorce of 42 per cent for low-educated women and 46.5 per cent for highly educated women. Despite this, personal labour income does not appear to change at time zero in response to divorce. Recovery does occur, with average household incomes reaching their pre-divorce level nine years after separation for highly educated women. This appears to be driven by the growth of other labour income, namely the addition of income of any new partner.

The literature discussed earlier emphasises the role of state benefits in cushioning the short-term consequences of divorce for women. The bar graphs above are suggestive of a similar role in our sample. However, this effect is likely to be important only for a small fraction of families, and so a bar chart reporting average incomes may be understating the importance of this benefit income for a subgroup of low-income women.

Discussion so far has neglected the potential economies of scale deriving from sharing a household. Figure 11.3 shows how income changes over time since

---

[12]   Highly educated is defined as having qualifications above A-level or their equivalent.
[13]   Note that Figures 11.1 and 11.2 report as 'other income' sources of income that include periodical payments received. 17% of divorced women receive such payments, while 2% make payments. The cost to those making payments is not subtracted from the income figures shown.

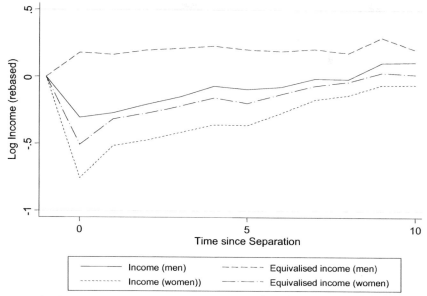

Note: The four lines show the average of (log) income by number of years since separation for men and for women, both controlling for changes in household size (equivalised income) and not controlling for changes in household size. Income in each series is rescaled to begin at 0 at time t = −1. The scale on the y-axis should be read as the proportional change in income relative to time t = −1. For example, for women, the proportional fall in equivalised income at divorce is 0.5 (ie a 50% decline).

Figure 11.3: Evolution of Actual and Equivalised Household Income after Divorce

divorce for men and women both in terms of absolute household income and household income equivalised using the McClements scale.[14] All series show the change in log income[15] relative to time $t = -1$, and so the scale on the y-axis shows the *proportional* change in income compared with the pre-divorce level. For women, absolute income falls more dramatically than equivalised household income. This is because household size has decreased: the husband's income has been lost but one fewer person needs supporting. This means that the fall in absolute income overstates the fall in the standard of living, and the increase in absolute income from adding an extra person to the household overstates the rise in the standard of living on repartnering. In order to increase her equivalised

---

[14] We repeat our analysis using the McClements after housing costs equivalence scale, which does not significantly alter our conclusions.
[15] We report the natural logarithm (log) of income rather than the actual monetary value of income because the comparison between two values of the log of income can be interpreted as a proportional difference rather than a monetary difference.

income, the woman must repartner with a man who brings in at least 67 per cent of her current income.

Men's household income and equivalised household income show a different pattern. Absolute income falls, although not to the same extent as women's. However, since women are usually the primary carers for children following separation, men's household size falls, on average, by more than women's, and this leads to average equivalised household income actually rising on divorce, giving men a higher standard of living following divorce. This result is sensitive to the equivalence scale used and also to the measure of welfare. The greater the economies of scale, the less likely men are to increase their standard of living on divorce.

There are three key sources of recovery for women in the data: repartnering, benefit income, and labour income. Figure 11.4 shows the role of benefit income and labour income more clearly. These figures plot the log of equivalised household income, personal labour income, and benefit income around the time of divorce (for low-educated women). As shown in the earlier figures, there is a clear drop in household income, and little response in labour income. It is also clear that there is an increase in benefit income received by separating women at the time of divorce. The highly educated women experience a similar (though

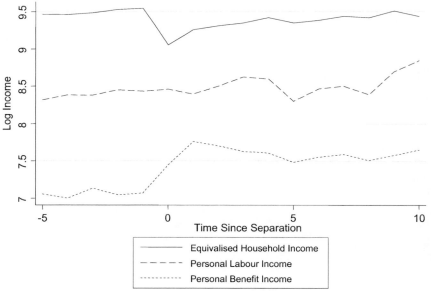

Note: The three lines show the average of (log) income by number of years since separation.

Figure 11.4: Income Levels Before and After Divorce for Women with Low Education

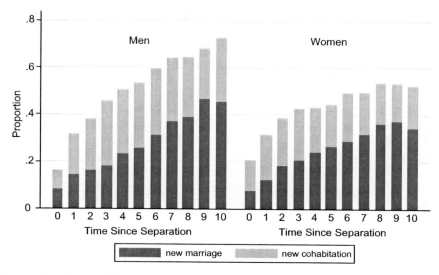

Figure 11.5: Rates of Repartnering after Divorce

smaller) increase in benefit income. This suggests that welfare benefits are important in providing an initial income boost. However, as seen in Figures 11.1 and 11.2, this is only a small proportion of total household income.

The importance of 'other labour income' in driving the recovery in women's household income after divorce is indicative of repartnering. Figure 11.5 illustrates the proportion of our sample who have repartnered (either into cohabitation or marriage) in the 10 years following separation. First, it is clear that men are more likely to repartner and to remarry. Secondly, the rate of repartnering is striking: within four years 51 per cent of men and 43 per cent of women are either remarried (24 per cent and 24 per cent respectively) or cohabiting (27 per cent and 19 per cent respectively).

Regression Analysis

In this section, we use regression analysis to establish whether the raw numbers presented so far are robust to controlling for individual and household characteristics.[16] We carry out four regressions, separately for men and women. The four dependent variables in these regressions are equivalised household income, total household income, benefit income, and equivalised household income when the wife was not working prior to divorce ('male single earner').

---

[16] It is important to stress that the results we report show correlations between variables, and do not necessarily imply causation.

Income Changes

The graphs discussed above provide a strong indication of the divergence in experience of men and women on divorce, and the reasons for the recovery of household income after divorce. However, changes in household income may be driven by changes in other characteristics, such as changes in the number of children in the household. In order to ascertain if the trends discussed above are robust to observable characteristics, we regress the change in log income on a set of demographic and other characteristics as well as time dummies (related to the time before and since divorce).[17]

The results for women are presented in Table 11.2. The first column shows the results with the rate of change in equivalised household income as the dependent variable (that is, the proportion by which equivalised household income changes year on year). The coefficients report the correlation between each variable and that rate of change. For example, the coefficient on the variable $t = 0$ indicates how income grows over the time of separation. We see a significant fall (57 per cent) at time $t = 0$, accompanied by a smaller rebound (13 per cent) at time $t = 1$. The act of repartnering has a significant, positive impact on income (44 per cent).

The change in absolute household income shows a larger immediate drop (83 per cent), a larger rebound (20 per cent), and a larger response to repartnering (56 per cent). Benefit income increases significantly in the year of separation and the subsequent year, but falls on repartnering. The fourth column shows the equivalised household income equation just for women who were not active in the labour market in the year before separation (that is, time $t = -1$). The income fall is more severe (72 per cent) for this group, but the recovery greater (38 per cent), perhaps suggesting a greater ability for this group of women to increase their household income on divorce (for example, enter the labour market). Unreported regressions with the change in personal labour income as the dependent variable show no trend over time.

Similar unreported regressions for men's data confirm the trends described in Figure 11.3 above: equivalised household income increases by 13 per cent on divorce, whereas absolute household income falls by 27 per cent. Repartnering has a significant effect in increasing absolute income, but no significant effect on equivalised income. This suggests that men repartner with women whose personal income is cancelled out by the extra costs to the household. There is no clear trend in benefit income, and there are no clear trends for these men who split from a more traditional partnership. Indeed, we see no significant improvement in equivalised household income on divorce for these men. This is in contrast to the findings of McManus and DiPrete (2001) who, using US data, find that a traditional family structure is associated with greater gains for men on divorce.

---

[17] The explanatory variables in the regressions take values of either 0 or 1, and so the use of log income as the dependent variable means the coefficients on each variable should be interpreted as the proportional change in income associated with a change in the variable from 0 to 1.

Table 11.2: Explaining Income Growth for Women

Variable	Equivalised Household Income	Household Income	Benefit Income	Equivalised Household Income (single male earner)
t = –1	–0.003	0.014	0.072	0.018
	(0.039)	(0.039)	(0.051)	(0.081)
t = 0	**–0.572**	**–0.826**	**0.266**	**–0.721**
	(0.044)	(0.045)	(0.061)	(0.090)
t = 1	**0.129**	**0.199**	**0.376**	**0.377**
	(0.047)	(0.047)	(0.065)	(0.095)
t = 2	–0.035	–0.014	0.003	0.037
	(0.048)	(0.048)	(0.066)	(0.096)
t = 3	0.004	0.034	0.013	0.067
	(0.048)	(0.049)	(0.066)	(0.096)
t > 3	–0.026	0.022	0.027	0.065
	(0.037)	(0.037)	(0.050)	(0.075)
Repartnered	**0.440**	**0.557**	**–0.330**	**0.294**
	(0.054)	(0.054)	(0.071)	(0.099)
Partner	0.008	0.045	0.006	0.057
	(0.027)	(0.028)	(0.039)	(0.057)
Child present	**–0.082**	**–0.047**	**0.111**	**–0.089**
	(0.022)	(0.022)	(0.034)	(0.050)
Home owner	–0.017	–0.002	–0.013	–0.002
	(0.023)	(0.023)	(0.030)	(0.045)
Asset income > £100 pa	**–0.075**	**–0.077**	0.027	–0.107
	(0.029)	(0.030)	(0.043)	(0.071)
Working	**0.064**	**0.055**	**–0.105**	0.075
	(0.022)	(0.022)	(0.028)	(0.047)
Receives transfer	0.033	0.046	**0.085**	0.081
	(0.030)	(0.030)	(0.037)	(0.065)
Makes transfer	0.044	–0.007	**–0.208**	**–0.297**
	(0.055)	(0.056)	(0.082)	(0.127)
Observations	3,766	3,766	2,738	1,253
People	417	417	297	138

Note: The coefficients on each variable show the effect on the rate of growth of income of that variable. For example, the coefficient on the variable t = 0 in the first column indicates that the rate of income growth is 0.57 lower over the time of separation (ie income falls by 57% over this period compared with other periods).

Variables in bold are significant at a 10% confidence level. Variables which are not in bold are statistically insignificantly different from zero. Standard errors are given in parentheses. Other controls: age at separation and age at marriage, current age, marriage tenure, previous marriage, education, race, prior cohabitation, poor health and holding a second job. Further details available on request.

Overall, these results reinforce the conclusions drawn earlier: some men do benefit from divorce in terms of their equivalised income, and women recover over time from the initial income falls, mainly due to repartnering. Benefit income provides some support for a subset of women in the short term.

Recovery after Divorce

We have so far emphasised that a majority of women benefit from a recovery over time in household income. At $t = 5$, the median fall in household income relative to income prior to separation for women is 4.1 per cent, which is a substantial improvement on the initial fall of 57 per cent. However, there is a large minority of women who suffer a more persistent loss in household income: even five years after divorce, the fall in income at the 25th percentile is 40.1 per cent. We now look more closely at the characteristics associated with the recovery in household equivalised income from time $t = -1$ to time $t = 5$. This uses a sub-sample of 204 women who separated from marriage and who have valid income data for both time periods in question.

The first two columns of Table 11.3 show how the rate of recovery of household income depends on characteristics of women. We separate out characteristics known at the time of divorce from characteristics revealed since divorce. These characteristics revealed since divorce are likely to be affected by what happens to income and so it is harder to interpret the coefficients in a causal way. The first column considers only the role of characteristics observable before divorce. Greater recovery is associated with women who held a second job whilst married. This effect may be picking up lower-income households, or may indicate greater flexibility in responding to divorce. A more limited recovery is associated with older woman and women in poor health. Cohabiting before marriage is associated with a greater recovery. The second column shows that these characteristics have their impact through their effect on repartnering: the coefficients on age, cohabitation and poor health are no longer significant when repartnering is controlled for. In addition to repartnering, an increase in hours worked since divorce is associated with recovery. Finally, the table shows the effect of retraining. In our sample, 41 women (20 per cent) retrain following divorce. Some of those retraining have children and some do not. This distinction turns out to be important for the impact of retraining on income recovery: for those without children, training has no statistically significant impact on recovery; while for those with children, training is associated with income growth being 53 per cent lower. This latter surprising effect may indicate that retraining is undertaken to accommodate child-care responsibilities.

As mentioned above, the key trend underlining recovery in household income for women is repartnering. The third and fourth columns of Table 11.3 examine the characteristics of women who repartner by looking at how the probability of repartnering in the five years after divorce is affected by various characteristics. Younger women and those who previously cohabited are significantly more likely to repartner, which supports the results in the first two columns.

Table 11.3: Explaining Recovery after Divorce for Women

Variable	Growth in Household Income		Probability of Repartnering	
Characteristics before divorce				
Age	**−0.030**	−0.019	**−0.028**	**−0.026**
Child present	−0.154	0.126	**−0.219**	0.002
Race (non-white)	0.449	0.581		
In poor health	**−0.398**	−0.221	−0.088	−0.189
Household size	0.079	0.088	−0.019	−0.015
Home owner	−0.090	−0.153	0.037	0.160
Asset income>£100 pa	0.064	0.081	0.188	0.101
High education	0.102	−0.027	−0.026	−0.027
Working	−0.212	−0.299	0.040	−0.075
Hours worked	0.008	**0.021**	−0.005	−0.008
Holds second job	**0.446**	**0.583**	0.159	0.128
Marriage tenure	**0.026**	0.022	**0.022**	0.016
Previously married	−0.226	−0.252	0.027	−0.080
Cohabited before marriage	**0.273**	0.163	**0.451**	**0.431**
Characteristics at t = 5				
Partner		**0.409**		
New child		−0.094		**−0.399**
Started work		−0.068		−0.195
Stopped work		−0.017		−0.012
Retraining (if no children)		0.138		0.021
Retraining (if child present at t = −1)		**−0.534**		−0.171
Change in hours		**0.021**		−0.004
Mean probability of repartnering			0.430	0.424
Observations	204		200	

Notes: For columns 1 and 2, the coefficients on each variable show the effect on the growth of income from the year prior to separation to five years after separation. For example, the coefficient on the variable 'Cohabited before marriage' indicates that the rate of income recovery is 0.27 higher (ie 27% higher) five years after divorce for those who cohabited prior to marriage compared with those that did not, after controlling for other characteristics. Column 1 includes as explanatory variables only those variables which were known at the time of divorce, column 2 adds as explanatory variables characteristics of the individual five years after divorce (these characteristics will be affected by what happens to income and so their interpretation is less clear cut).

For columns 3 and 4, the coefficients on each variable show the change in the probability of repartnering for a one unit change in that variable, relative to the probability of repartnering for an individual with average characteristics (and the average probability of repartnering). The coefficient 'Cohabited before marriage', for example, shows that those who cohabited before marriage have a probability of repartnering after divorce which is 0.451 (ie 45%) higher than those who did not cohabit before marriage.

Variables in bold are significant at a 10% confidence level. Variables which are not in bold are statistically insignificantly different from zero. Other controls: changes in home ownership and health status. Further details and standard errors available on request.

This analysis suggests that those groups of women who suffer most from divorce are those who are older and those who have children. Part of the reason for their inability to recover financially compared with others is the lower chance of repartnering. The persistence of the fall in equivalised household income for these women highlights the importance of divorce in driving outcomes for women and their children.

Changes in Effects Over Time

Our data covers separations occurring over a 15-year period. However, our analysis so far has assumed that the effects of divorce are constant over time and that the average income fall on separation is the same in the early 1990s as in 2004. Over this period there have been various social changes including increasing divorce rates (albeit at a slower rate than previously), falling marriage rates, and increased female labour force participation, as well as some key House of Lords rulings regarding the division of assets at the time of divorce,[18] and we might therefore expect that the extent of the income fall on divorce has changed over time. Due to the limited sample size we are unable to run the regressions using a full set of time-to-divorce and year dummy interactions. Instead, we run the regression with equivalised household income as the dependent variable on two sub-samples: an earlier period covering separations from 1992 to 1997, and a later period covering separations from 1998 onwards.

The results for women are presented in Table 11.4. We see clearly that the impact of divorce is reduced in the later period, with women suffering a 42 per cent fall in income relative to a 65 per cent fall in the earlier period. Recovery is, however, less pronounced in the later period. This suggests improved insurance against divorce in the period after 1997 as compared to the 1990s, which might be attributed to higher labour force attachment. This is consistent with McKeever and Wolfinger's (2001) findings for the US, and also with Jenkins' (2008) findings for the UK, which stress the increased role of in-work benefits as a means of providing insurance. For women, the positive effect of repartnering remains, as does the negative effect of having a child. Unreported results for men, however, show that their experience on divorce does not change over the two periods.

This analysis is suggestive of a reduction in the divergence between the experience of men and of women after divorce: women have become better insured against the income loss, and men do not make the gain in equivalised income they did previously.

FINANCIAL LOSS FOLLOWING COHABITATION

Due to sample size restrictions, a number of previous studies have estimated income changes for a sample combining individuals who separated from marriage

---

[18] *White v White* [2001] AC 596, and *Miller v Miller; McFarlane v McFarlane* [2006] UKHL 24, [2006] 2 AC 618.

Table 11.4: Explaining Income Growth for Women in Different Time Periods

	To 1997	From 1998
$t = -1$	−0.026	0.016
$t = 0$	**−0.648**	**−0.417**
$t = 1$	**0.146**	0.069
$t = 2$	−0.048	−0.036
$t = 3$	−0.004	−0.005
$t > 3$	−0.048	0.040
Repartnered	**0.430**	**0.456**
Partner	0.001	0.023
Child present	**−0.090**	**−0.075**
Home owner	−0.005	−0.042
Asset income > £100 pa	**−0.090**	−0.051
Working	**0.071**	0.047
Receives transfer	0.031	0.035
Makes transfer	−0.009	0.125
Observations	2,368	1,398
People	213	204

Note: The coefficients on each variable show the effect on the rate of growth of income of that variable. For example, the coefficient on the variable $t = 0$ in the first column indicates that the rate of income growth is 0.65 lower over the time of separation (ie income falls by 65% on separation) in the period before 1997, but the coefficient in the second column indicates only a 42% fall for those who divorce after 1997.

Bold denotes variables which are significant at 10% confidence level. Variables which are not in bold are statistically insignificantly different from zero. Other controls: age at separation and age at marriage, current age, marriage tenure, previous marriage, education, race, prior cohabitation, poor health and holding a second job. Further details and standard errors are available on request.

and those who separated from cohabitations (see, for example, Jenkins, 2008). Our larger sample size allows us to make comparisons between income changes resulting from splits from marriage and cohabitation. Figure 11.6 shows the evolution of log equivalised household income for men and women, split into those separating from cohabitations and those from marriage. The graph shows the change in log income since time $t = -1$.

On average, the income fall is smaller for those splitting from cohabitations. This might be explained by the fact that only 36 per cent of women separating from cohabitations have children, compared with 69 per cent of those from marriage. Further, those splitting from cohabitation tend to be younger than those divorcing. Recovery from cohabitation also occurs more quickly. We do not see the same instant jump upwards in equivalised household income for men splitting from cohabitations as described above for men divorcing their wives. This is consistent with the lower prevalence of children, meaning that

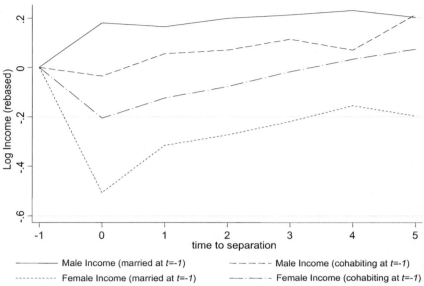

Note: The four lines show the average of (log) income by number of years since separation for men and for women, separately for splits from marriage and for splits from cohabitation, controlling for changes in household size (equivalised income). Income in each series is rescaled to begin at 0 at time t = −1. The scale on the y-axis should be read as the proportional change in income relative to time t = −1. For example, for women, the proportional fall in equivalised income at the end of cohabitation is 0.2 (ie a 20% decline) compared with a 50% decline at the end of marriage.

Figure 11.6: Evolution of Income after Split from Marriage vs Cohabitation

the equivalence scale changes less. However, the differences between cohabitation and marriage persist even when we control for age, duration and children as in Table 11.2: comparing the income losses for cohabitants with those for divorcees as in Table 11.2 shows an average loss on separation of 32 per cent in equivalised income for cohabitants compared with 57 per cent for divorcees, and a 45 per cent loss in household income for cohabitants compared with 83 per cent for divorcees.

These figures indicate that a split from cohabitation is associated with a smaller economic impact than a split from marriage. This is especially pronounced for women, who experience much smaller falls in income, and recover more quickly than from divorce. It is difficult to draw stronger conclusions about the evolution of income over time after the separation because the data become more noisy as time since separation increases. However, our data suggests that a split from cohabitation is a less traumatic experience in terms of household income than a divorce.

This is consistent with the analysis of Manting and Bouman (2006), who studied data from the Netherlands from 1989 to 2000, finding that cohabiting women experience a smaller income decline on cohabitation, and also that gender differences after the split disappear over time when considering cohabitation. Avellar and Smock (2005) find a similar pattern in the US.

Even though our conclusion about the difference between divorce and the end of cohabitation persists when we control for observable characteristics, it is important to stress that there may be differences between the types of person who marry and those who cohabit which may underlie this conclusion: a woman divorcing from marriage may in fact be better off than she would have been had she been splitting from cohabitation. This would arise if the population of those splitting from cohabitations are less vulnerable (in terms of income) to separation than the population of those divorcing. This would imply that had those divorcing instead separated from a cohabitation, they would have seen an even larger income fall owing to the lack of financial remedy from the male partner.

THE EFFECTS OF DIVORCE ON INCOME AND CONSUMPTION

The conclusion from our analysis of the BHPS is that recovery from separation occurs, but that it can be slow, and is less likely for older women or when children are present. This motivates the discussion of possible bases for settlement. There are therefore three aims of this section: first, to show the implications for earnings of alternative decisions within marriage; secondly, to show the implications for income post-divorce of alternative mechanisms for allocating resources; and, finally, to discuss the implications of the alternative allocation mechanisms for consumption.

In discussing alternative methods for calculating divorce settlements, the focus is on methods for allocating earned income and assets combined. There is discussion in the divorce literature of the desirability of 'clean breaks'. There are two separate issues: one is the desirability of calculating the amount of the settlement at the time of the divorce; the second is the desirability of making all payments associated with a settlement at the time of divorce. Whilst full payment clean breaks would have the advantage of allowing the individuals to go their separate ways and prevent any dependency on the ex-spouse, such an arrangement is not feasible when human capital is an important component of wealth.

Wages and the Return to Work

To make the analysis more transparent, we make the following assumptions, although the conceptual framework does not require these assumptions:

A1 The potential income process faced by husband and wife is identical at the time of marriage, that is, they have the same career prospects and so it may be supposed that the wife could have had the same future income as the husband;

A2 No individual assets prior to marriage and no inheritances;

A3 No retirement.

Figure 11.7 shows potential earnings at each age following different decisions about participation in the labour force. We consider what happens to potential wages after exit from the labour force. Individuals who remain single and continue working full time are estimated to increase their wages each year by about 2.4 per cent in real terms (Eckstein and Wolpin, 1989). After 10 years of work, at D, their wages will have increased by 27 per cent. For married individuals, there is potentially an extra return, leading them to E. Antonovics and Town (2004) estimate the benefit to marriage as a 20 per cent wage premium, after controlling for selection, and show that this premium persists after divorce. Other evidence from the US (Korenman and Neumark, 1991) suggests that only a small portion of this benefit derives from support from a wife who is not working, with the rest accruing from marriage whether or not the spouse works. This is therefore a benefit of being married independent of the decision to work or not. However, this finding is not uncontroversial. For example, Bardasi and Taylor (2005) analyse the male marriage premium for the UK using BHPS data, using a fixed effects approach, and find a much smaller marriage premium (around four per cent), which declines with the hours of market work undertaken by the wife. The source of the marriage premium is important to determine whether there is double counting of the effects of decisions within marriage: double counting would arise if both the loss to the wife from not working and the ongoing gain to the husband following divorce arising from the support provided by the wife during the marriage are

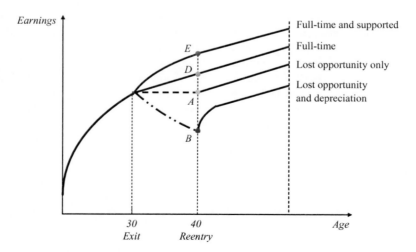

Figure 11.7: Earnings over the Life-cycle

compensated (in the latter case, by sharing that gain). Double counting would not arise if the gain from the wife's support was simply a marriage premium which was independent of whether the woman was working.

Those who exit from the labour force are not able to obtain the wage increases from extra experience, and, in addition, their skills are likely to depreciate. Without depreciation, they would be at A after 10 years, with potential earnings 66 per cent of those of their partner. With a depreciation rate of two per cent a year (as estimated in Mincer and Ofek, 1982), potential earnings on returning to work after 10 years are 54 per cent of their partner's earnings.[19] These numbers are, of course, only indicative and are based on average returns to experience and depreciation and ignore any gender wage gap. In reality, returns to experience are likely to be age dependent and higher for younger workers. This would make the earnings deficit harder to recover from for individuals who are older when re-entering the labour market. The numbers also differ substantially across occupation and education groups: better-educated workers tend to receive greater returns to experience and are subject to faster wage depreciation.

Divorce Payments

This discussion of the cost of non-participation is in terms of lost realised earnings and lost earnings potential. Clearly, however, there are benefits of not participating in the labour market, both from the support this may offer to a partner, and from not having to pay for child care. To the extent that costs and benefits are both realised within the marriage, divorce payments should be independent of such costs and benefits. The difficulty is that decisions within marriage have costs and benefits after divorce. Figure 11.8 puts Figure 11.7 into the context of divorce. In this example, divorce happens before re-entry into the labour force.

At the time of divorce, the earnings of the partner who has kept working are at E, whereas the wife, who exited 10 years previously, is at 54 per cent of this level, at B. This difference can be broken down into the higher wage that arises if married (z_1) and the opportunity cost of not working (z_2). The amount z_1 is referred to as the 'restitution damages' and the amount z_2 as 'reliance damages' (Dnes, 1999). However, using z_1 and z_2 as calculations of the benefit and cost of not working underestimate both the cost and the benefit. The boost to wages from being supported within marriage persists after divorce, generating the benefit x_1 and y_1. Similarly, the cost to wages from not working persists beyond divorce, with the additional cost to potential earnings of $x_2 + y_2$. However, *actual* earnings after divorce depend on when the non-working partner re-enters work, with each year of non-participation lowering potential wages further. In the figure,

---

[19] If we ignore the 'marriage premium' benefit accrued by the working husband where the estimates are less reliable, potential earnings would be 65% of the husband's.

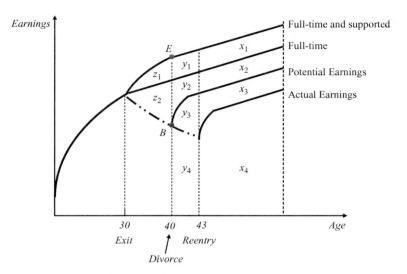

Figure 11.8: Divorce and Earnings over the Life-cycle

this occurs three years after divorce, when the potential wage has fallen a further 6 per cent.[20]

These decisions mean that total resources post-divorce are given by:

$$\text{Total} = \underbrace{x_4}_{\text{Wife's actual income}} + \underbrace{x_4 + x_3 + x_2 + x_1 + y_4 + y_3 + y_2 + y_1}_{\text{Husband's actual income}}$$

The realised monetary loss post-divorce as a result of non-participation (that is, the difference between actual earnings after divorce and potential earnings if there had been no period of exit) is given by:

$$\text{Loss} = x_3 + x_2 + y_4 + y_3 + y_2$$

However, this is misleading as an estimate of the cost of decisions within marriage, because part of this loss is due to decisions after divorce. The monetary loss we should be considering is the impact on potential earnings of decisions within marriage. This is given by:

$$\text{Potential Loss} = x_2 + y_2$$

---

[20] We can relax the assumption of equal income processes, so that, eg, the spouse with the greater earning potential works while the other takes time out of the labour market. The simplest way to model this is to assume that Figure 11.8 shows the earnings process for the spouse who is not working, whereas the spouse who is working has a greater income. This implies that the total resources post-divorce will be greater than if earnings are equal. However, the potential earnings post-divorce of the non-working spouse will not vary with the income of the working spouse.

This potential loss is the 'compensable loss' to the woman. An allocation mechanism based on compensation would split this loss 50:50 between the husband and wife. In the example where: (i) the marriage lasted 10 years; (ii) the wife was not working for any of that period; and (iii) potential earnings before marriage were identical, then the husband would be paying approximately 17 per cent of his earnings.[21]

This, however, ignores the ongoing benefit to the husband of marriage. Allowing for these benefits generates the difference in potential earnings that arises from the marriage:

$$\text{Difference in potential} = \underbrace{x_2 + y_2}_{\text{Loss to wife's potential earnings}} + \underbrace{x_1 + y_1}_{\text{Increase in husband's potential earnings}}$$

This would imply the husband making a payment of 23 per cent of earnings in the example above. If there are benefits that accrue to the husband only if his wife is not working, then either the costs or the benefits should be used in determining the amount, but not both.

To focus on the incentive effects of this allocation, we start by assuming that the decisions to marry and to divorce are unrelated to current earnings and earnings potential, and that decisions about labour market participation do not affect the bargaining position within marriage. The allocation mechanism then has a potential incentive effect on labour market participation and on spousal support within marriage. A mechanism which under-rewards the benefit of marriage to the husband's career that persists after divorce (underestimating $x_1 + y_1$) or underestimates the loss after divorce to potential earnings of not working within marriage (underestimating $x_2 + y_2$) will impose financial losses disproportionately on the woman. This is the context in which the *McFarlane* ruling should be assessed. The *McFarlane*[22] ruling can be interpreted as arguing in favour of using estimates of this 'difference in potential': the marriage had been long and Mrs McFarlane had stopped work to bring up the children, thereby incurring the loss of earnings potential, in addition to the support provided to her husband. If this difference in potential earnings were not accounted for in divorce settlements, then the lost earnings potential could be mitigated by increasing labour market participation within marriage. If this were the case, then the choice within marriage would be distorted towards excess labour market participation as a form of protection or insurance against the possibility of divorce. By contrast, if the compensable loss were correctly calculated, there would be no distortion to the labour market participation decision. In

---

[21] This assumes that if the wife had worked, her wage would have grown by 3% per year, instead of declining by 2% per year. After 10 years, the obtainable wage is 60% of the wage that would have been earned and this difference is then split 50:50.

[22] [2006] UKHL 24.

this sense, the *McFarlane* ruling reflects the removal of a distortion to decisions within marriage.[23]

Two other points about the *McFarlane* ruling are important in this context: first, there is a focus on the retraining possibilities after divorce and a suggestion that the payments should be time limited. This would be appropriate from an economic perspective if retraining could offset the lost opportunities within marriage and if the higher wage for men associated with being married did not persist beyond divorce. However, the evidence is that retraining is only partially effective and that the higher wages associated with marriage are highly persistent after divorce. Secondly, there was concern in the ruling about payments being used for savings, but since savings are a mechanism for deferring consumption, the use of a payment would not be relevant if earnings were the basis for the calculation.

It is, however, worth distinguishing between basing compensable loss on potential earnings after divorce compared with actual earnings after divorce. If the basis for calculating loss were actual earnings, then the choice by the woman not to work would impose a cost on her ex-husband for a decision which was not a joint-decision. By contrast, potential earnings after divorce include the implications of decisions to work within marriage, but leave the choice and consequences of whether or not to work after divorce solely with the woman.

Dnes (1999) argues that one of the principal difficulties with using allocation mechanisms based on the costs and benefits of decisions within marriage is that it may make divorce too cheap for one party relative to expectations of the cost of continuing with the marriage. This arises in particular when the underlying earnings potential of the husband and wife differ. This would give rise to opportunistic behaviour and the incentive for the higher-earning partner to divorce and thereby renege on the implicit agreement within the marriage. Discussion of such implicit agreements and expectations raises the issue of allocation on the basis of consumption rather than earnings loss.

Allocations on the Basis of Consumption

An alternative to making divorce payments dependent on earnings or earnings loss is to use a measure of consumption (or spending power). The rationale for this lies in a desire to use allocation mechanisms to ensure needs are met, or insurance is provided against divorce, or that allocations should be set to compensate for lost expectations. However, this is the issue of whether divorce allocations are about maintaining a standard of living and honouring a commitment within marriage, as compared to ensuring an appropriate allocation of the benefits and costs arising from the marriage. The former leads to a consumption-based rule, the latter to an income-related rule.

---

[23] One criticism of the equal split of the costs and benefits of decisions within marriage is that the incentive to divorce lies with the party who in practice bears more than 50% of the net costs.

Irrespective of the mechanism, it is important to understand the effects of divorce on consumption because this is more closely related to welfare than income. The main point about divorce in this context is that even if resources are split equally, the standard of living of each individual will fall because it is cheaper for two people to live together than separately: divorce means that these economies of scale from sharing a house are lost. This was highlighted on pp 235–238 above, where allowing for household size and composition was shown to be crucial to conclusions about the consequences of divorce. This is reiterated in Figure 11.9, which superimposes consumption choices pre- and post-divorce. To make this simple, we assume that consumption (or spending power) does not vary over time before divorce and does not vary over time after divorce (although consumption after divorce may be at a different level). On divorce, if we ignore saving, the total consumption of the former couple will fall because of the lost economies of scale, and this is reflected in the fall to $c_{Div,Equal}$ in the figure. This is the heart of the problem for divorce: there is insufficient income for both parties to maintain their pre-divorce standard of living. It is, of course, possible for one party to maintain their standard of living if the other party receives less, with the lowest level of spending power being the consumption level from complete independence (or autarky), labelled on the figure as $c_{Div,None}$. Indeed, as shown earlier, men do better on these measures after divorce than they did within marriage.

A further issue is that these graphs showing potential earnings and actual earnings ignore the possible presence of fixed costs of work associated with child care. This suggests that the graphs overstate the potential earnings (and consumption) of the spouse, and the earnings net of child-care costs are likely to be substantially lower. An alternative way of allowing for child-care costs associated with work would be to calculate the utility value of alternative income paths. This would

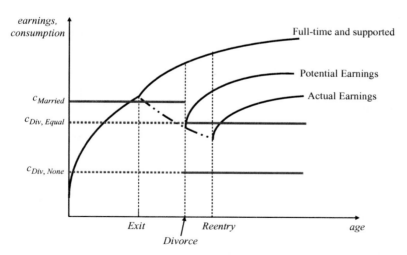

Figure 11.9: Consumption and Earnings over the Life-cycle

recognise explicitly that the value of different income streams may differ between spouses depending on their obligations. In principle, this notion could be made more precise by considering consumption paths over the life-cycle and the impact of divorce on those consumption paths. Implicitly this recognises that the costs of decisions taken within marriage (for example, having children) should be split between the parties—exactly analogously to the argument for splitting the compensable loss to earnings.

Where there are substantial differences in the underlying earnings potential or asset holdings of the two parties, the compensation basis for settlement makes divorce 'cheap' for the wealthier party, as discussed above. Therefore, this discussion of allocation on the basis of spending power is most appropriate when there are substantial differences in the underlying earnings potential or asset holdings of the two parties, as with the *Miller*[24] ruling.

The *Miller* case arose from a childless marriage of short duration. The consequences of decisions within the marriage for earnings would appear to be minimal in this case, arising only from the increase in Mr Miller's earnings during the marriage. It is hard not to draw the conclusion that the basis for settlement was maintaining the consumption level for Mrs Miller that had implicitly been promised by Mr Miller. This would imply that the judgment was based on an assessment of what the implicit contract of marriage is, rather than being based on the economic consequences of decisions within marriage. However, the notion of legitimate expectation is explicitly excluded and so the basis of the ruling is less clear. Further, although the settlement was substantial, Mrs Miller would not have been able to maintain her level of consumption over the longer term. The incentive problem with a legitimate expectation ruling is that marriage becomes potentially very costly when there are differences in earnings potential—the basis for divorce settlement will act to discourage marriage in these cases.

CONCLUSIONS

The aim of this chapter was to analyse the economic consequences of divorce. The stark conclusion is that men's household income increases by about 23 per cent on divorce once we control for household size, whereas women's household income falls by about 31 per cent. There is partial recovery for women, but this recovery is driven by repartnering: the average effect of repartnering is to restore income to pre-divorce levels after nine years. Those who do not repartner tend to be older and have children. For these individuals, and for those in poor health at the time of divorce, the long-term economic consequences of divorce are serious. For some, these long-term consequences are offset by increased labour supply, but the effects are small, and this ignores any extra costs such as child care which

---

[24] [2006] UKHL 24.

may arise from working. For others, government-provided benefits provide some cushion to the cost of divorce. On the positive side, we present evidence that these costs of divorce for women have been mitigated over time and more recent divorces have not led to the same falls in household income as earlier divorces.

These conclusions on the financial consequences of divorce highlight the importance of the basis on which post-divorce settlements are calculated. The *McFarlane* case is an example of the scenario when the economic consequences of divorce are most severe for the woman. The key change highlighted by the *McFarlane* ruling was an attempt to consider the impact on post-divorce income arising from decisions within the marriage. In particular, this involved considering the lost return to work experience that would have occurred if Mrs McFarlane had kept working and considering the increase in her husband's post-divorce earnings due to the marriage. Correctly calculating the difference to post-divorce earnings arising from decisions within marriage removes some of the distortions to decisions about labour supply within marriage. However, given the difficulty of these calculations and given the difficulty of accurately modelling behaviour within relationships, these are problems that are not going to go away.

BIBLIOGRAPHY

Aassve, A, Betti, G, Mazzuco, S and Mencarini, L (2006) 'Marital Disruption and Economic Well-being: a comparative analysis', ISER Working Paper 2006–07 (Colchester, University of Essex).

Antonovics, K and Town, R (2004) 'Are All the Good Men Married? Uncovering the Sources of the Marital Wage Premium' 94 *American Economic Review* 317.

Avellar, S and Smock, PM (2005) 'The Economic Consequences of the Dissolution of Cohabiting Unions' 67 *Journal of Marriage and the Family* 315.

Axinn, WG and Thornton, A (1992) 'The Relationship between Cohabitation and Divorce: Selectivity or Causal Influence?' 29 *Demography* 357.

Bardasi, E and Taylor, MP (2005) 'Marriage and Wages: A Test of the Specialisation Hypothesis', ISER Working Paper 2005-01 (Colchester, University of Essex).

Chiappori, P-A, Fortin, B and Lacroix, G (2002) 'Marriage Market, Divorce Legislation, and Household Labor Supply' 110 *Journal of Political Economy* 37.

Dnes, AW (1999) 'Applications of economic analysis to marital law: concerning a proposal to reform the discretionary approach to the division of marital assets in England and Wales' 19 *International Review of Law and Economics* 533.

Duncan, GJ and Hoffman, SD (1985) 'Economic Consequences of Marital Instability' in M David and T Smeeding (eds), *Horizontal Equity, Uncertainty, and Economic Well-Being*, Studies in Income and Wealth vol 50 (Chicago,IL, National Bureau of Economic Research).

Eckstein, Z and Wolpin, K (1989) 'Dynamic Labour Force Participation of Married Women and Endogenous Work Experience' 56 *Review of Economic Studies* 375.

Eekelaar, J and Maclean, M (1986) *Maintenance after Divorce* (Oxford, Clarendon Press).

Jarvis, S and Jenkins, SP (1999) 'Marital splits and income changes: Evidence from the British Household Panel Survey' 53 *Population Studies* 237.

Jenkins, SP (2008) 'Marital splits and income changes over the longer term', ISER Working Paper 2008-07 (Colchester, University of Essex).

Korenman, S and Neumark, D (1991) 'Does Marriage Really Make Men More Productive?' 26 *The Journal of Human Resources* 282.

Lillard, LA, Brien, MJ and Waite, LJ (1995) 'Premarital Cohabitation and Subsequent Marital Dissolution: A Matter of Self-Selection?' 32 *Demography* 437.

Manting, D and Bouman, AM (2006) 'Short- and Long-term Economic Consequences of the Dissolution of Marital and Consensual Unions. The Example of the Netherlands' 22 *European Sociological Review* 413.

McKeever, M and Wolfinger, NH (2001) 'Reexamining the Economic Costs of Marital Disruption for Women' 82 *Social Science Quarterly* 202.

McManus, PA and DiPrete, TA (2001) 'Losers and Winners: The Financial Consequences of Separation and Divorce for Men' 66 *American Sociological Review* 246.

Mincer, J and Ofek, H (1982) 'Interrupted Work Careers: Depreciation and Restoration of Human Capital' 17 *The Journal of Human Resources* 3.

Smock, PJ, Manning, WD and Gupta, S (1999) 'The Effect of Marriage and Divorce on Women's Economic Well-Being' 64 *American Sociological Review* 794.

Taylor, M, Brice, J, Buck, N and Prentice-Lane, E (2007) *British Household Panel Survey User Manual Volume A: Introduction* (Colchester, University of Essex).

Uunk, W (2004) 'The Economic Consequences of Divorce for Women in the European Union: The Impact of Welfare State Arrangements' 20 *European Journal of Population* 251.

12

Pension Accumulation and Gendered Household Structures

What are the Implications of Changes in Family Formation for Future Financial Inequality?

DEBORA PRICE

INTRODUCTION

A S THE UK population has rapidly aged over the last decades, marked gender disparities in income and poverty in later life have been exposed. Older women have much less income and far higher rates of poverty than men (Arber and Ginn, 2004; DWP, 2005). These inequalities are the result both of gendered differences in the life-course and a pension system designed to reward full-time employees with full working histories working for large employers. Women have historically been much more likely than men to undertake care work and housework within the household, to work part time, for low pay, for small employers, and to have interrupted histories of paid work. They have been correspondingly less likely to participate in state, occupational and private pensions, or to remain in the paid workforce as they approach state pension age.

Particularly noticeable, however, is the low income of *married* older women (Ginn, 2003). It is this low income within marriage that accounts ultimately for the relatively high rates of poverty among older female divorcees and widows, both disproportionately poor groups in later life, as they cannot compensate for the loss of their financial dependency on their former husbands (Price, 2006). This is so even though widows usually inherit some pension rights from their deceased husbands, unlike divorcees, who are the poorest group of older women (Arber and Ginn, 2004).

The question arises whether this will remain so for future cohorts. Many aspects of social life have changed dramatically, particularly the increasing education, labour force participation, earnings and independence of women. As rates of cohabitation and divorce have also risen over the decades, this too poses questions for understanding the cultures and structures that might affect older women's income in later life. Legal marriage provided some protection in terms of derived social security, pension, and widow's benefits, but partnering outside legal marriage has grown, those living alone have increased in number, and the incidence of separation and divorce has risen. If women are potentially acquiring independent incomes in later life through their own pension accumulation regardless of their marital status, then we need not perhaps be too concerned about changes in family formation and dissolution for the later life income of women. If, however, women in couples continue to exhibit high levels of financial dependency on their male partners within marriage or cohabitation, then the consequences for later life income of all women bear further examination.

Behaviour within couples affects not only the individuals concerned, but (in circular feedback loops to policy and from policy back to behaviour) will also have an impact on the policy environment, the labour market and gendered hours of working, child-care provision, and patterns of partnering and dissolution (Lewis, 1992, 1997; O'Connor, Orloff and Shaver, 1999; Pfau-Effinger, 1999; Orloff, 2002). These wider social and policy impacts will also affect the ability of women who are not in couples to earn and to accumulate pensions.

Moreover, cultures of gendered financial dependency within couples will probably themselves impact on long-term financial decision-making. Qualitative research has shown that women who are dependent on men for income are generally also dependent on them for pensions, despite generally high risks of the partnership breaking down (DWP, 2005). In a study of women's pension choices in the mid 1990s, Peggs (2000: 356) found that many women saw their employment as temporary and 'second to caring'. Without taking on a breadwinning role, which involved planning ahead financially, these women did not—and with low earnings had few options to—participate in private pension schemes. In a comprehensive study of women's pensions in Northern Ireland, Evason and Spence (2002: 35–41) found that older cohorts of women depend heavily on their husbands for pension provision; similarly, while younger cohorts would have liked to have been independent of their partners in providing pensions for themselves in retirement, or even felt that they ought to be independent, where they had children this was simply not the case, and they thus continue to rely on their husbands or partners to accumulate pensions for both of them.

Understanding cultural patterns of earnings and pension accumulation within working-age couples is therefore important for understanding potential gender disparities in later life income. Yet despite its importance, very little research has examined these issues. In this chapter, I use data from the General Household Surveys (GHS) 2001 and 2002 to address five questions:

(1) To what extent do couples in the UK still organise themselves around breadwinner models of coupledom?
(2) What is driving these modes of organisation? In particular, does the degree of financial inequality between partners vary according to the woman's level of educational attainment?

(3) Is the extent of financial inequality within couple relationships related to the extent to which women participate in pension accumulation? If so, what are the drivers for this?

(4) How, if at all, is financial inequality within relationships related to legal marital status and history?

(5) What are the implications of these modes of organisation for the pension accumulation of working-age women, whether single or in a couple?

These questions are all asked within the context of a social structure in the UK where women are particularly likely to work part time for low pay, in a system for pension accumulation which privileges those in full-time work on high pay.

COUPLES, EARNINGS, AND NORMS OF PARTNERING

In a low-waged economy for women coupled with a lack of state support for care and caring roles in the UK, household decisions are often made for women to prioritise within-household family care over paid work (see further Scott and Dex, chapter three, this volume). While between 60 and 70 per cent of 'working-age' women in the UK are in the paid labour force, 45 per cent of these work part time (Women and Equality Unit, 2005). This pattern has been remarkably resilient to change over time (Woods et al, 2003). Research also confirms that part-time work for women in the UK is often not directly associated with child care (Johnson and Stears, 1996; Walby and Olsen, 2002; Manning and Petrongolo, 2004: table 1 and figure 3.2); almost 30 per cent of women with no child under 16 in the household work part time, compared with 8 per cent of men (Women and Equality Unit, 2005). Women may well be making the best of what is available to them, given the competing demands on their lives and on their time (Warren, 2004). These patterns nevertheless point to a model of gender relations within families that is socially, normatively, and structurally embedded. Policies supporting part-time work often reinforce the identity of women as carers (McKie, Bowlby and Gregory, 2001), and serve to reinforce gender differences in pay, prospects, and conditions (Smithson et al, 2004).

The extent of part-time working for women in the UK suggests that women probably remain financially dependent on men within couples to some extent (see further Vogler, chapter four, Burgoyne and Sonnenberg, chapter five, and Lewis, Tennant and Taylor, chapter eight, this volume). Women's dependency arises from the extent to which they are unequal contributors to the household (Ward, Dale and Joshi, 1996b). They are not necessarily 'dependent' in the sense of being unable to form an autonomous household (although these two forms of dependency will often coincide), but they have much to lose from the ending of the relationship (Millar, 2003). The lifestyle of many women is closely tied to the financial resources provided or sustained by their partners, including housing, furniture, household goods, cars, holidays, entertainment, and other material things.

Warren (2001: 555) describes women in this position as having a 'distinctly contingent role'. Full-time work is recognised as the route by which women generally achieve greater financial independence from their partners (Ward, Dale and Joshi, 1996a), although even among full-time workers, disparities in working hours and in pay may leave couples with wide disparities in earnings.

Using data from the late 1980s, Arber and Ginn (1995) showed that gender inequality in earnings was more pronounced within households than in society generally. They found that among wives aged 20 to 59, about a third were not in paid work, with just over a third working part time, and the remainder working full time. Among dual-earning couples, a quarter were approximately equal earners, and only 11 per cent of wives earned more than their husbands. Similar findings were obtained in an analysis of couples in the 1958 cohort at age 33 in 1991 (Ward, Dale and Joshi, 1996b), and then again by Warren (2003) using 1995 data from the British Household Panel Study. Warren showed that among working-age dual-earning couples a third of men earned more than 75 per cent of household wages, just over half earned more than 65 per cent, and three quarters more than 55 per cent. Only 9 per cent of women in dual-earning couples earned more than 55 per cent of combined wages. These three studies paint a picture of substantial and surprisingly static continuing inequalities of earnings within couples.

Given these patterns, what are the implications of this inequality for women's participation in private and occupational pension schemes?

FINANCIAL DEPENDENCE IN LATER LIFE: A GENDERED PENSION REGIME

The UK pension system is a mixture of insurance-based state provision (through the system of National Insurance, and National Insurance credits), other state benefits (including means-tested benefits), and occupational or private pensions. The Pensions Commission has described the system as one of 'bewildering complexity', indeed, as the most complex pension system in the world (Pensions Commission, 2004: xiii, 238). The system has been designed over many decades to encourage and incentivise private and occupational pension provision over state provision, so that citizens are largely dependent on private and occupational pensions for adequate income in later life (Glennerster, 2006). The state pensions (basic state pension and state second pension) together provide an income well below the poverty line for most people, but particularly for women (Arber and Ginn, 2004; Price, 2006).

This means that citizens in the UK are particularly reliant on employer or personal private provision for adequate income in old age. Men over 65 have far higher occupational and private pension incomes than women (Arber and Ginn, 2004; Ginn, 2007) exacerbating gender differences in income in later life. Women are therefore generally reliant on a partner's pension, or, if they live alone, on means-tested state benefits, for an adequate income in retirement. Means-testing is, however, a flawed system for reaching those most in need. Somewhere between 30 per cent and 40 per cent of pensioners who are entitled to Pension Credit (the principal means-tested benefit for pensioners) do not claim their entitlements (DWP, 2007).

The government has spent the last five years shaping reform of the pension system. The reformed system will have an improved basic state pension, but this will still provide income well below the poverty line, and participation in paid work throughout the life-course, and in private or occupational pensions, will remain central to building adequate income in later life (Price, 2007, 2008).

Analysis in this chapter is therefore of participation in 'third-tier' pension provision, meaning occupational and private pensions over and above the current (low) levels of mandatory provision in the state pension schemes or their compulsory equivalent. It is participation in this tier of pension scheme provision that will determine the extent to which people have an adequate income for a comfortable later life.

DATA AND METHODS

The analysis combines cross-sectional data from two years of the General Household Surveys (2001 and 2002). The General Household Survey is a multi-purpose continuous cross-sectional survey carried out by the Office for National Statistics, collecting information on a range of topics from people living in private households in Great Britain, including current pension scheme participation, marital and cohabitation histories, and maternal histories. A stratified, clustered probability sample of about 13,000 households is selected, and each adult individual in the household is interviewed. The survey achieves response rates of approximately 70 per cent. The combined data set yields 10,314 men and 11,087 women aged between 20 and 59. Included in the data is information about the earnings of 5,772 partnered men and 6,141 partnered women aged 20 to 59.[1]

Where contributions to private pensions are shown in this chapter, these are either occupational pension schemes provided by an employer, or personal pensions provided by an insurer, but if the personal pension is *only* a contracted-out replacement for the state scheme, then it has been excluded. Those included are described here as 'third-tier pensions'. Women have been grouped into those who have never had children, those whose youngest child is under six, those whose youngest is between 6 and 16, and those whose youngest is over 16. For individual earnings analysis, all those in paid work have been divided into quintiles according to gross weekly earnings. Partnerships have been classified according to the combined earnings of partners. Those partnerships in receipt of any income from earnings have again been divided into joint earnings quintiles.[2]

---

[1] Same-sex partnerships are excluded from the analysis.
[2] The cut points are available from the author.

EARNINGS INEQUALITIES WITHIN COUPLES:
THE MODERN BREADWINNER

In order to assess earnings inequalities within couples, for each person the amount that they contribute to joint earnings has been expressed as a proportion or ratio of joint earnings. A ratio of 0.5 means that the person contributes one half of joint earnings, ie both partners are equal earners. In Figure 12.1, the mean ratio of own earnings to joint earnings has been calculated for each five-year age group. Figure 12.1 shows that men still earn about two thirds of couples' joint earnings across all age groups, varying from 64 per cent in their late twenties and late fifties to more than 72 per cent in their early forties. The late twenties represents the most equal period in the lives of men and women—before gender pay gaps are much in evidence and before many women have begun having children—although even at this stage women are not equal earners, providing on average only a third of joint earnings. The late fifties is likely to represent a time of early or semi-retirement for men while their (often younger) partners are still working, possibly full time, as children are likely to have grown up or left home; at this stage women make their highest mean contribution, of just over 40 per cent. Between these ages, however, women's contributions dip, to less than 30 per cent in their late thirties.

While the increased equality of couples in their twenties may reflect a cohort change in attitudes to earnings equality, it is difficult to discern any evidence here of cohort changes in the balance of earnings among couples over different age groups. There is little difference between partnered women in their twenties and in their forties. The U-shaped pattern implies strongly that the dip from age 30 to age 44 is related to child-rearing and not cohort changes. Women aged between 30 and 35, for example, are probably not materially different in education, training, attitude, and partnering patterns to women aged between 20 and 29.

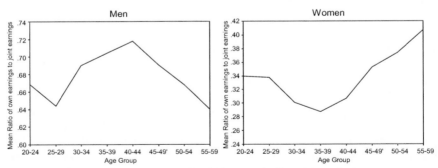

Note: Y axis for men from 0.6 to 0.74; Y axis for women from 0.24 to 0.42

Source: GHS 2000/1 and 2001/2; author's analysis; Couples with no earnings between them have been excluded.

Figure 12.1: Mean ratio of own to joint earnings across age groups. Partnered men and women aged 20 to 59

MOTHERHOOD AND INEQUALITY WITHIN COUPLES

As the interaction with age just shown suggests, and as Figure 12.2 makes explicit, these persistent-looking patterns of earnings inequality between partners are to a large extent the result of child-care and allied household responsibilities that women still take on to such a substantial degree in the UK. Here, the extent of women's contributions to joint household earnings is shown by joint earnings

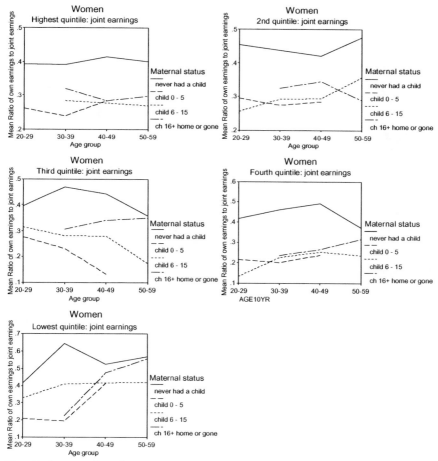

Note: Scale on y axis varies

Source: GHS 2001 & 2002, author's analysis; Couples with no earnings between them have been excluded.

Figure 12.2: The impact of motherhood on earnings' equality within couples. Women aged 20 to 59 living with a spouse or cohabiting

quintile and by maternal status in 10-year age groups. Joint quintiles are shown to establish whether different patterns of dual earnings emerge across the joint income distribution—that is, does it make a difference if the woman is in a high-earning or low-earning couple? In general, it makes surprisingly little difference. The solid line in each graph denotes women who have never had a child. The next two lines represent the age group of the youngest child in the family unit: either 0–5 or 6–15. The final line shows that the youngest child is either still at home but over 16 or has left home—that is, these are women who have had children, but none of their children, save in exceptional circumstances, could be considered as in need of daytime care.

The impact of motherhood on gender inequality among couples across all levels of joint earnings is clearly shown. In each graph the solid line floats well above the others. Women who have never had children (which will, of course, be a diminishing group with age) are contributing between 40 and 50 per cent of joint earnings on average within each age group, and an even higher percentage in the lowest quintile. Whilst clearly not representing complete equality between the sexes, it is, in historical context, a reasonably close approximation. Interestingly, there is no substantive dip among childless couples with age, which would suggest that changes in society in the sense of expectations of dual earning within couples are impacting as much on the financial relationships between mid-life couples as on younger couples.

The effect of having children depends to some extent on which earnings bracket a couple falls into, but the broad picture is similar across all five quintiles. Women whose youngest child is under six contribute on average between 24 per cent and 29 per cent to joint earnings in all age groups in the highest two quintiles, while women in mid-earning couples (3rd quintile) in their forties with young children are contributing just 13 per cent to joint earnings. In the lowest two quintiles for women, the contributions of women in their twenties and thirties with a very young child are reasonably constant, at around 20 per cent, but for the lowest-earning couples women's contribution rises sharply if they are in their forties, reaching 41 per cent. Despite being relatively 'equal' compared with women in better-off households, this reflects the low earnings of their partners, rather than their own higher earnings. Women in their forties with their youngest child aged 0–5 in the lowest joint earnings quintile were contributing on average just £90 a week, or £4,680 per year, from earnings to household finances in 2002.

Thus, women with very young children in the two highest joint earnings categories are contributing a slightly higher proportion on average than women in other categories, which is likely to be a factor in the classification of the couple into those higher earnings brackets in the first place. But they are not anywhere near equal contributors, and the differences in proportions among the various women shown here are surprisingly slight. The low average percentage of joint earnings of women with a child under six years old is, of course, in part a reflection of the higher likelihood that mothers of such young children will be out of the paid labour market ($p = 0.345$), but neither are those who are in the labour market, on the whole, high

relative contributors (data not shown). Although overall there is some improvement towards equality where the youngest child in a family is at school (aged
6–15), this change is barely discernible in some earnings brackets.

The impact of ever having had a child is more difficult to interpret. The lowest
quintile apart, women who have ever had a child do not in any age group contribute more than 35 per cent to joint earnings, and there is no evidence here to suggest change for younger cohorts. This could be because of the effects on human
capital of years out of the labour market and/or in part-time work, or a gendered
accommodation in the household of work, housework, and care in a balance that
couples are reluctant to disturb if finances do not require it.

The highest quintile stands out for its persistent inequality for mothers of all
ages and with children of all ages; the lowest quintile for the degree of earnings
equality among couples where a woman is over 40, regardless of the ages of her
children. This is most likely a 'needs must' situation—with relatively low-earning
women partnered with men who are not earning or are themselves low earners.

The result of this analysis is that while couples without children are on average
reasonably close to each other in earnings, substantial inequalities persist among
couples of working age across the economic distribution where they have children, or have ever had children. Women who have ever had a child do not, in any
age group or any part of the earnings distribution on average contribute more
than about third to joint earnings, unless they and their partners are among the
lowest earners.

The most equal-earning couples with children are therefore those in the lowest
earnings quintiles, rather than the high-powered dual-earning couples prevalent in
media discourses. This raises the question of whether higher educational qualifications lead to greater egalitarianism among couples, or whether this too is a myth.

EDUCATION

Policy on equality, driven by the liberal agenda of equality of opportunity, has
largely focused on reducing discrimination in education and at work. The theory
is that if women are as well qualified as men and workplace discrimination is
reduced, then equality between the sexes will follow. But, as just shown, inequality
between the sexes within partnerships remains manifest, especially if the parties
have children. Lack of available affordable child care and ungenerous maternal/
paternal leave policies could in theory lead to an earnings sacrifice by either parent, but in practice, it seems to be women's earnings that are sacrificed. The question arises whether this inequality is evident for the most educated women too.

Research has shown that new opportunities, particularly for reduced economic
dependence, are largely available to highly educated, middle-class, partnered
women, and that there is increasing divergence between childless women and
mothers (Dex, Joshi and Macran, 1996; Crompton and Harris, 1998; Warren,
2000; Elliott, Dale and Egerton, 2001; Ginn, 2003). Davies, Joshi and Peronaci

(2000) and Rake et al (2000) have suggested that while the loss of gross earnings from motherhood over a lifetime remains substantial, these losses are mostly borne by less-educated women. Ginn and Arber (2002), however, have challenged these assumptions in so far as they relate to highly qualified mothers, showing that in the mid 1990s fewer than half of graduates who have children were in full-time employment, regardless of age, cohort, and the ages of their children, with sizeable commensurate financial losses.

Indeed, in an institutional and cultural setting that encourages it, patterns of educational homogamy in marriage and partnership can theoretically lead to highly educated women being *more* likely than other women to sacrifice a career for child-rearing, since they are more likely to have high-status, high-earning partners who can afford to maintain the family.

Figure 12.3 shows the relationships between women's education level, their age group, and the degree of earnings inequality in their relationships. The clusters of lines representing different age groups are situated fairly closely together in each case. This means that a woman's own age is a less important determinant of inequality than the age of her youngest child. The impact of educational attainment is shown by the way the lines in each cluster tend to slope upwards from left to right, with the left-most data points representing those with no qualifications, and the right-most data points women with the highest qualifications, such as degrees.

The extent of equality of earnings in relationships varies little according to educational attainment for women who have never had a child, with such women generally contributing about 40 to 50 per cent of family earnings, whatever their age and educational attainment, indicating a relatively high degree of earnings homogamy among partners without children. Looking at those with a young child under the age of six in the family, in each age range higher education means women are more equal than those with lower education. However, here even women with degree-level education are contributing only around 30 per cent of joint earnings—while their children are young they earn on average less than half of the earnings of their partners. With children this young, educational attainment has a notably stepped impact on equality within the household—higher education implies greater equality but not even near-equal earnings.

Women with degree-level education are also the most equal in terms of earnings within their partnerships when they have children at school, but the mean ratio of their own to joint earnings is still only about a third. They are also the most equal controlling for age group when their children have grown up, but it is only among degree-educated mothers in their fifties that virtual equality of earnings is reached. Moreover, it is only degree-level education that has this effect once children are of school age. While women with no qualifications at all are always, on average, lower relative contributors to household earnings, among other women with school-age or older children, qualifications make little difference to equality, whatever the age group.

In summary, women's degree-level education brings greater earnings equality to relationships, but not as much as one might think. Degree-educated women with

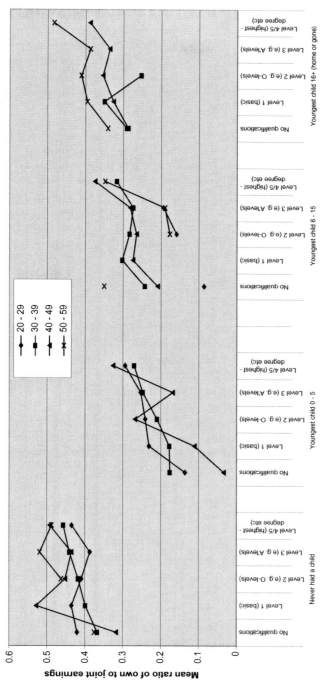

Source: GHS 2001 & 2002, author's analysis; those in partnerships where neither party earns are excluded; also excluded are cells where n <15, and those with unclassifiable or unknown qualifications.

Figure 12.3: Mean ratio of own earnings to joint earnings by maternal status, educational qualifications and age group. Partnered women aged 20 to 59

young children and children at school experience marked inequality in earnings at home, whatever their age, and it is only if they do not have children, or their children have grown up, that this changes. Educational attainment and age are also not the most important drivers of earnings inequality for women with educational attainment short of a degree. The most important influencing factor is once again the presence of dependent children in the household, or having ever had a child.

PARTNERSHIP, DEPENDENCY AND PENSION PROVISION

Mothers, therefore, remain particularly dependent on their partners for household income. The question then arises whether this economic dependency matters for participation in pension schemes. Figure 12.4 shows the percentage of partnered women aged 20 to 59 who are participating in third-tier pensions according to the degree of earnings inequality in their relationship. This shows that women who earn less than a fifth of joint earnings (a third of partnered women) are the least likely to contribute to pensions, with barely 10 per cent making such contributions. Equal and better earners are more likely to contribute, but only just over half of the few women who are the primary earners in their relationships (earning more than 80 per cent) do so.

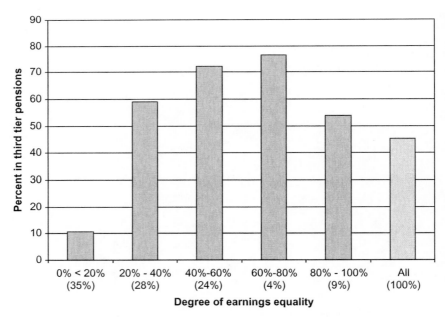

Figure 12.4: **Percentage of partnered women aged 20 to 59 participating in third-tier pension schemes according to degree of earnings equality. Brackets show distribution of partnered women**

It is not necessarily the case, however, that these patterns are related to the degree of economic dependency in the relationship. They might be a result of the amount that the individual women are earning, or how much income comes into the household, since we have shown that it is in the lower quintiles of earnings that women are most equal. It may also be related to the lower educational qualifications of these relatively low-earning women, or to the fact that low-earning women might on average have younger children. To elucidate the mechanisms by which the inequality within partnerships is related to making provision for additional private pension during the working life, multivariate analysis is needed, controlling for a number of possibly influencing factors simultaneously.

Table 12.1 presents the results of a multivariate logistic regression analysis for partnered women aged 20 to 59. The analysis in this table shows how earnings inequality is related to third-tier pension coverage, while taking into account all of these other variable factors in each model. The results show the odds ratios for being in this privileged category of those with pension coverage relative to a reference category for which the odds have been defined as 1. The number in the table tells you, relative to the reference category, how much greater the odds are that a person with that characteristic has a third-tier pension compared with the reference category, while the other attributes in the model are controlled. In Model 1, the odds ratios are shown according to the extent and direction of earnings inequality within a relationship, with reference to the category '40%–60%', who for these purposes are considered 'equal' earners, while age group is controlled. So we see that the odds of a woman who earns 20 to 40 per cent of joint earnings contributing to a third-tier pension are only approximately half (0.49) the odds of an equal earner, controlling for age group; and for someone contributing 0 to 20 per cent of joint earnings, the odds of contributing to a third-tier pension are only four per cent of the odds for an equal earner—the odds for an equal earner are 25 times higher.

Moving from left to right across this table shows how the impact of inequality of earnings on third-tier pension contributions is affected by other variables. Model 2 also controls for individual earnings, and Model 3 for joint earnings. In Model 4, maternal status is controlled, together with educational qualifications. This is to test whether, apart from their influence on individual earnings, joint earnings, and degree of inequality within partnerships, these variables have any independent impact on participation in pension provision, and whether they affect the association between inequality and pension scheme participation.

The primary question of interest here is the effect of gender inequality of earnings within couples on participation in third-tier pension schemes. Although these models contain much other information, this analysis will comment only on the coefficients across models for the first category, that is the percentage of joint earnings (or the degree of earnings inequality). As indicated in these tables, almost two thirds of women contribute less than 40 per cent to joint earnings, and fewer than one in ten more than 80 per cent. The odds ratios in this category after all these controls (that is, for Model 4) are presented graphically in Figure 12.5.

Table 12.1: Odds ratios for contributing to additional pensions. Partnered women aged 20 to 59

	Model 1	Model 2	Model 3	Model 4
Percentage of joint earnings	***	**	***	***
0 < 20% [35% of women]	0.04***	0.76*	0.35***	0.34***
20% < 40% [28% of women]	0.49***	1.13	0.81*	0.80*
40% < 60% [24% of women]	1.00	1.00	1.00	1.00
60% < 80% [4% of women]	1.15	0.85	1.17	1.14
80% < 100% [9% of women]	0.40***	0.76*	1.63**	1.51**
Age group	***	***	***	***
20–29	0.43***	0.41***	0.42***	0.40***
30–39	1.00	1.00	1.00	1.00
40–49	1.13	1.05	1.04	1.10
50–59	0.82*	1.06	1.14	1.20
Earnings quintile: own earnings		***	***	***
Highest		1.00	1.00	1.00
2nd		0.53***	0.67*	0.70
3rd		0.31***	0.57**	0.64**
4th		0.14***	0.36***	0.43***
Lowest		0.02***	0.10***	0.12***
No earnings		0.00~	0.00~	0.00~
Earnings quintile: joint earnings			***	***
Highest			1.13	1.06
2nd			1.00	1.00
3rd			0.60***	0.63***
4th			0.46***	0.49***
Lowest			0.18***	0.20***
Maternal Status				*
Never had a child				1.00
Youngest 0–5				1.22
Youngest 6–15				0.91
Youngest over 16 (home or gone)				1.20
Educational qualifications				***
Level 4/5- highest (degree etc)				0.94
Level 3 (e.g. A-levels)				0.80
Level 2 (e.g. O-levels)				1.00
Level 1 (basic)				0.61***
No qualifications				1.43***
Other or unknown				0.69*
-2LL	5540	4407	4333	4275
Change in chi square	1741	1133	74	58
DF	3	5	4	8

***$p < 0.001$; **$p < 0.01$; *$p < 0.05$ (no asterisk = not statistically significant at 5%)
~odds of contributing to a pension defined as 0
Source: GHS 2000/1 and 2001/2, author's analysis, Excludes couples where neither earns.

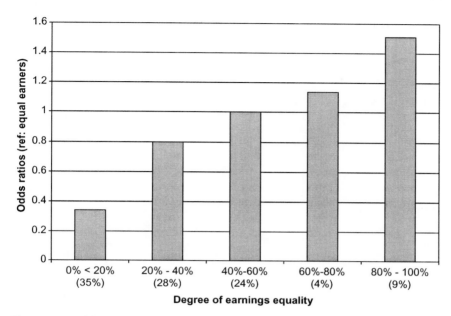

Figure 12.5: Odds ratios for participation in third-tier pension schemes according to degree of earnings inequality in relationship, partnered women aged 20 to 59, after controlling for age group, own earnings, partner's earnings, maternal status and educational qualifications

Female breadwinners are more likely to be low earners. This is shown by the dramatic increase in the odds ratios for women providing over 80 per cent of joint earnings from 0.4 in Model 1 to 0.76 in Model 2, when the strong association between low earnings and low third-tier pension scheme participation is taken into account. Women providing 80 per cent plus of earnings as well as being low earners themselves are also much more likely to be in the low end of the joint earnings distribution. Thus it is only when both personal earnings and joint earnings are controlled that we see the odds ratio for the pension contributions of 'breadwinning' women jump from 0.76 to 1.63 ($p < 0.01$), relative to an equal earner.

Model 3 shows that the degree of earnings inequality in a relationship has a significant impact on whether women contribute to pensions. Women who are more financially dependent are less likely to contribute to additional private pensions. For women earning 0–20% of joint earnings, the odds are only a third of those for equal earners, and for those earning between 20% and 40% of joint earnings, the odds ratio is 0.81. All other things being equal, women who have assumed the role of major breadwinner *are* more likely than equal earners to make additional pension provision, conforming to a breadwinning norm. But all other things are not equal—the starting odds ratio for women in couples where they are the major breadwinners is only 0.4 because these effects are counterbalanced by their higher probability of low earnings and low joint earnings where third-tier pension provision is very unlikely. The additional statistical controls of maternal history and educational qualifications do not affect these relationships.

These results suggest that financial dependency within a partnership is normatively associated with lack of third-tier pension accumulation. Being a 'second earner' has implications beyond immediate access to financial resources—it is also related to relying on a partner or the state for pension provision. This is important given the high risk of partnership dissolution or widowhood over the life-course.

PENSIONS AND PARTNERSHIP STATUS

Within partnerships, where there are children, women are likely to be financially dependent and to have low rates of contribution to third-tier pensions. Yet they risk separation and divorce, and living alone in later life. It is important to establish how likely women are to contribute to third-tier pensions once partnerships have ended, and this is the final question addressed in this chapter.

Unravelling whether it is partnership status or children that influence pension scheme participation is complex. Women in different partnership statuses are not equally likely to have children at home, and children are an important factor in women's earnings and pension accumulation. Also, women in different partnership statuses are likely to be of different ages, and age is also strongly associated with pension accumulation. This is because pensions become more salient to people as they age. Table 12.2 shows the percentage with children in each marital status, and the mean age of that subgroup, among women aged 20 to 59.

The age profiles of divorced lone women and divorced women who are cohabiting are very similar, but divorced lone women are more likely to have a child under 16 (48 per cent as opposed to 42 per cent) and also more likely to have a child who is over 16 (13 per cent as opposed to 8 per cent). Divorcees with children have lower prospects of repartnering (Haskey, 1999; Lampard and Peggs, 1999). There are substantial age difference between those in second marriages, cohabiting divorced women, and cohabiting women who have never been married—in particular, never-married cohabitants are much younger on average. Never-married cohabitants are more likely to be childless ($p = 0.63$), but, notably, more than a quarter have a child under six at home. A quarter of never-married lone women have a child under 16 to look after—a smaller proportion than in any other subgroup, but substantial nevertheless. More never-married lone mothers have a child under six to care for than do divorced lone mothers.

The percentage of men and women in third-tier pension schemes in each partnership status is shown in Table 12.3. Although the variation among women is not that great, lone women are much less likely to have current pensions than partnered women (27–35 per cent, compared with 38–45 per cent), and among partnered women, divorced cohabitants are the most likely to be contributing (45 per cent).

Table 12.2: Percentage of population with dependent children and mean age by selected marital statuses

Women	Never married, lone		Never married, cohabiting		In first marriage		Sep from first marriage, lone		Div from first marriage, lone		Div from first marriage, cohabiting		In second marriage	
	%	*Mean age*	%	*Mean age*	%	*Mean age*	%	*Mean age*	%	*Mean age*	%	*Mean age*	%	*Mean age*
Never had a child	71	30	63	29	35	39	31	36	40	44	49	41	43	56
Youngest 0–5	14	27	27	29	24	32	28	31	13	33	20	33	16	37
Youngest 6–15	12	34	10	34	25	40	28	38	35	38	22	39	25	42
All children 16+ (home or gone)	3	45	1	42	17	52	13	50	13	51	8	48	16	51
All	100%	30	100%	29	100%	42	100%	39	100%	44	100%	42	100%	46
n=	1,746		849		5,131		341		650		281		813	

Source: GHS 2001 & 2002, author's analysis.
Notes: Mothers whose dependent children live elsewhere and those looking after others' children have been excluded.

Table 12.3: Percentage in third-tier pension schemes according to partnership status, men and women aged 20 to 59

	Percentage in third-tier pensions	
	Women	Men
Never married, lone	35	36
Never married, couple	40	52
First marriage	40	65
Separated (1st mar), lone	29	58
Divorced (1st mar), lone	33	40
Divorced (1st mar), couple	45	58
Widowed (1st mar), lone	27	47
Second marriage	38	56
Complex history (2+ mar ended)	35	39

Source: GHS 2001 & 2002, author's analysis.

Note: Separated men and women who are cohabiting, and cohabiting widows and widowers are excluded for small numbers; those with complex histories include both lone men and women, and couples, who have lived through the breakdown of at least two marriages.

To establish the extent to which this is related to the legal marital status and marital history of any women, as opposed to age or the presence of children, once again, multivariate analysis is needed. Table 12.4 presents odds ratios resulting from a logistic regression analysis, again predicting whether the respondent participates in a third-tier pension. The odds ratios presented compare the odds of participation for women in other marital statuses to those in a first marriage, where the odds have been set to 1. Age group, fertility history, gross earnings quartile, social class, and highest educational level have been controlled with dummy variables, and again odds ratios are presented compared with the reference group (age 40–49, having a child age 0–5 in the family, lowest quartile, social class IIIM, and Level 3 (one or more A-levels or equivalent) in education). Nested models are presented, with the predictor variables added one by one to see the effect at each level on the association between partnership status and pension scheme participation.

The first model shown, Model 1, controls for age group and fertility history. This shows the importance of fertility history, with the odds of contributing to a third-tier pension 3.3 times higher for a woman who has never had a child than a woman who has a pre-school child at home, and twice as high as for a woman whose youngest child is now 16 or over (3.3 compared with 1.6), once age and partnership status are controlled. Similarly, the low participation of women at the extremes of the age range is highlighted, with the odds of contributing to a third-tier scheme for women in their twenties and fifties about half the odds for those in the middle age-ranges (30–49), controlling for children.

Table 12.4: Odds ratios for participation in third-tier pension schemes. Women aged 20 to 59

	n=	Model 1	Model 2	Model 3	Model 4
Partnership status		***	***	***	***
Never married, lone	1,514	0.67***	0.63***	0.64***	0.64***
Never married, couple	771	0.92	0.65***	0.66***	0.66***
First marriage	4,534	1.00	1.00	1.00	1.00
Separated (1st mar), lone	284	0.65**	0.57**	0.57**	0.58***
Divorced (1st mar), lone	581	0.73***	0.64***	0.66***	0.67***
Divorced (1st mar), couple	260	1.02	0.79	0.81	0.83
Widowed (1st mar), lone	139	0.56**	0.80	0.85	0.87
Second marriage	735	0.86	0.80	0.81*	0.82
Age group		***	***	***	***
20–29	1,835	0.49***	0.47***	0.46***	0.45***
30–39	2,725	1.00	1.00	1.00	1.00
40–49	2,372	1.13	1.17*	1.17	1.17*
50–59	2,237	0.62***	1.15	1.12	1.18
Fertility history		***	***	**	***
Never had a child	2,818	3.33***	0.86	0.91	0.93
Dependent child 0–5	1,574	1.00	1.00	1.00	1.00
Dependent child 6–15	2,113	1.13	0.66*	0.71**	0.72*
Child 16+, home or gone	2,664	1.65***	0.72	0.80	0.86
Gross earnings, £ per week			***	***	***
Highest quartile	934		26.36***	17.98***	16.63***
Second quartile	1,395		12.50***	9.45***	8.99***
Third quartile	2,065		5.34***	4.71***	4.67***
Lowest quartile	2,268		1.00	1.00	1.00
No earnings	2,507		†	†	†
Social Class				***	***
I	281			2.65***	2.15***
II	2,664			2.40***	2.06***
IIINM	3,282			2.01***	1.92***
IIIM	786			1.00	1.00
IV	1,654			1.18	1.21
V	502			0.79	0.89
Highest Educational Level					***
Level 4/5 (highest)	2,499				1.26*
Level 3	1,355				1.00
Level 2	2,233				1.04
Level 1	687				0.86
No qualifications	1,819				0.69***
Unknown	576				0.84

(continued)

Table 12.4 (Continued)

	n=	Model 1	Model 2	Model 3	Model 4
-2LL		11,793	7,262	7,142	7,109
change in -2LL		535	4,531	120	33
df		14	4	5	5
Significance		***	***	***	***

Source: GHS 2001 & 2002, author's analysis.

Notes: *$p < 0.05$; **$p < 0.01$; ***$p < 0.001$ (no asterisk = not statistically significant at 5%);
† – probability of third-tier pension provision defined as zero; Same sex cohabitees, separated women cohabiting, and widows cohabiting have been excluded due to small numbers; those with complex marital histories whereby more than two marriages have ended are not shown due to conceptual difficulties in analysis.

Model 1 shows an apparently clear distinction between women who live alone, and those who live with a partner. Like for like in maternal status and age group, lone women (never-married, separated, divorced and widowed) are much less likely than married women to have third-tier pensions (odds ratios of 0.67, 0.65, 0.73 and 0.56 respectively), whereas there are no statistically significant differences[3] between women who are living with a partner, whether never married, in a first marriage, divorced, or in a second marriage. The apparently higher rate of contribution to third-tier pensions of divorced cohabiting women in Figure 12.5 is shown to be a function of their lower likelihood of having children, and their higher likelihood of being in their forties (peak age for pension accumulation for women); once these variables are controlled they are shown in fact to be *less* likely than married women to be making contributions to third-tier pensions.

When earnings are controlled (Model 2), the very great difference that earnings make to third-tier pension scheme participation is obvious, with the odds for a woman in the highest quartile of earnings 26 times higher than for a woman in the lowest quartile. Controlling for earnings explains the differences in odds ratios for women in their fifties, for women who have never had a child and those with grown-up children. It does not explain the lower odds for women in their twenties, confirming that this is an age-related factor. After controlling for earnings, it is shown that women with a school-age child are the least likely to make current contributions to third-tier pension provision.

Controlling for earnings (Model 2) serves to accentuate the distinctions between women of different partnership statuses. Despite their low pension contributions, never-married women, divorced women and women in second marriages are all on average higher earners than women in first marriages, after controlling for age and children. Thus when earnings are controlled, the odds ratios for all these groups of women contributing to pensions compared with married women fall

---

[3] At 5%.

even lower than in Model 1. For lone separated women, the odds ratio is 0.57, for lone divorced women 0.64 and for lone never-married women, 0.63. Controlling for earnings also shows that, like for like on other controlled factors, cohabiting women who have never been married are also much less likely than married women to have third-tier pensions, with an odds ratio of only 0.65. The differences between odds for married women, cohabiting divorced women, and women in a second marriage remain statistically non-significant.

It might be thought that the lower contribution rates of lone mothers could be explained by the known correlation between lone motherhood and lower social class and educational attainment (Rowlingson and McKay, 2005). However, class differences and educational differences between women in different marital statuses do not account for these findings. As Models 3 and 4 show, controlling for social class and for highest educational qualifications does not alter the coefficients for the partnership status variables, which are in fact fairly robust from Model 2 through to Model 4.

This analysis shows that the impact that children have on women's earnings—both while the children are dependent and afterwards, and whatever the mother's marital status—is extremely important in pension accumulation. It also suggests that it is important to think of the ways in which having children might affect women's pension accumulation apart from a simple effect on earnings—if mothers return to paid work when their children are at school, social norms about how mothers spend money on child care and children while they are dependent (or beyond) may be diverting women's earned income towards children at the expense of their pensions, thus explaining the robust lower odds of pension contribution for women with children of school age. Women's exit from paid labour and lower earnings in their fifties—likely to be for social reasons as well as labour market reasons—has a further deleterious effect on their pensions.

Partnership status and partnership history are also important. Cohabiting women who have never married are higher earners than other women, but once earnings are controlled, married and divorced cohabiting women are more likely to have third-tier pension provision. This may mean that there is something about having been in or through a marriage that focuses women's minds on pension accumulation, or may indicate a selection effect—those women who are more likely to make pension provision are also more likely to marry.

However, significantly, compared with women in couples, lone women are the least likely to be contributing to third-tier pension provision despite the importance of doing so for their financial well-being in later life. Once age, motherhood, earnings, social class, and educational level are controlled, lone women are much less likely than those in couples to make pension provision. The reasons are unrelated to their earnings, social class, or educational attainment. Despite the already low rates of pension accumulation among married women, among lone women rates are even lower.

Very little is known about what happens to the financial well-being of divorced men and women in the UK after divorce (see Fisher and Low, chapter eleven, this volume), but what is known suggests that women emerge from the process with considerable financial burdens. Few fathers pay child support. Estimates vary for the percentage of lone mothers in receipt of any maintenance from the fathers of their children from 23 per cent (Rowlingson and McKay, 2005) to 31 per cent (Marsh and Perry, 2003). Rowlingson and McKay (2005) report that among manual workers the figure is only 16 per cent. These data support the notion that the financial constraints of single living are such as to prevent lone women securing a financial future for themselves through the acquisition of third-tier pensions. The association holds even for those without children, however, suggesting that being part of a couple seems to act as an enabling or normative mechanism for third-tier pensions for women, or that personality factors or economic incentives are associated both with contributing to pensions and being in a couple.

This is especially worrying given that on average married women start from a low base. The wide disparity in pension rights as between husband and wives (Field, 2000) led ultimately to government adding to the courts' discretionary powers on divorce a further power to allocate or 'share' pensions between spouses.[4] The government declared that pension-sharing was 'an important step towards security in retirement for women' (DSS, 1998: Foreword by the Secretary of State). Despite several years of operation, it is little used (Price, 2003). In 2006 there were 13,630 pension-sharing orders made (Ministry of Justice, 2007: 91, table 5.6), approximately one per cent of divorces.

If women cannot expect the divorce courts to provide them with a share of accumulated 'family' pension provision, then they are likely to emerge from their marriages with no or little pension. These data suggest that if they have not repartnered, they are far less likely than married women to be accumulating third-tier pensions, particularly if they have children.

CONCLUSIONS

The pension structure in the UK demands that for adequate later-life individual income, individuals must accumulate private pensions. Despite forthcoming reforms to the state system, and better financial incentives for many to participate in private pensions, histories of involvement with paid work, earnings, and private pension accumulation will remain crucial in determining pension outcomes for women (Ginn, 2003; Price, 2007, 2008). To the extent that work biographies remain highly gendered, private pension systems will continue to disadvantage women.

---

[4] In England and Wales, by Parts III and IV of the Welfare Reform and Pensions Act 1999. The Act also applies in Scotland, but the legal system for the division of matrimonial property in Scotland is quite different.

However, this chapter has shown that it is not only work biographies but also gendered cultural norms which influence women's participation in third-tier pension schemes. The UK has a prevalent culture of women becoming 'second earners' in relationships once children are born. Large disparities in earning as between mothers and their partners persist in all income and educational strata. Mothers are likely to be dependent on their spouses or partners to provide the bulk of household income. This financial dependency appears to continue once children have grown up, with little evidence so far of cohort changes.

The culture has implications for pension provision, since women on low incomes, and in low income households are much less likely to be making third-tier provision. Financial dependency itself also affects pension provision, even after controlling for income and various other demographic variables. This analysis suggests that women who rely on their partners for income during their working life continue to anticipate that their partners will also provide for them in old age.

When partnerships break down, lone separated and divorced women are disadvantaged in pension accumulation. Lone mothers especially do not generally participate in a third-tier pension. Whether single, separated or divorced, lone mothers have lower rates of third-tier pension accumulation than married women, even taking into account likely selection effects such as education and social class. Separated mothers, bearing the financial strains of the immediate aftermath of family breakdown, have the lowest rates of all. After family breakdown, mothers are likely to spend many years as a lone mother, with re-formed partnerships themselves fragile. Multivariate analysis confirmed that divorced women who are cohabiting do not accumulate pensions at any greater rate than other partnered women, thus conforming to the same social and financial patterns of behaviour as married women, and as are prevalent around them in society. Neither lone divorced women nor cohabiting divorced women show the higher rates of pension accumulation after divorce that we might expect to see if they were 'catching up' in pension building. If anything, the data suggest strongly that lone divorced mothers are falling further behind.

Advocates of gender equality and a reduction in income poverty experienced by older women have argued for a reformed system where pensions are accrued universally regardless of participation in paid labour (often called a 'citizen's pension'), paid at a rate that provides at least a poverty-line income, and that will be increased once in payment in line with national average earnings (PPI, 2006). This would reduce the associations between paid work history, earnings history, and pension income and therefore benefit women who have tended to fare poorly in the UK's employment-based system. Such a reform has now been rejected by government, which, with cross-party support, has committed to a pension system where work-based contributions and private pensions remain important elements for income adequacy in later life. Without substantial changes in gender relations within households and in the policy and labour market structures that support them, mothers who may live alone in later life continue to face a high risk of financial insecurity.

BIBLIOGRAPHY

Arber, S and Ginn, J (1995) 'The mirage of gender equality: occupational success in the labour market and within marriage' 46 *British Journal of Sociology* 21.

—— (2004) 'Ageing and Gender: Diversity and Change' in Summerfield, C and Babb, P *Social Trends 34* (London, The Stationery Office).

Crompton, R and Harris, F (1998) 'Gender relations and employment: the impact of occupation' 12 *Work, Employment and Society* 297.

Davies, H, Joshi, H and Peronaci, R (2000) 'Forgone income and motherhood: what do recent British data tell us?' 54 *Population Studies* 293.

Dex, S, Joshi, H and Macran, S (1996) 'A widening gulf among Britain's mothers' 12 *Oxford Review of Economic Policy* 65.

DSS (Department of Social Security) (1998) *Pension Sharing on Divorce: Reforming Pensions for a Fairer Future. Part I: Consultation* (London, DSS).

DWP (Department for Work and Pensions) (2005) *Women and Pensions: The Evidence* (London, DWP).

—— (2007) *Pension Credit Estimates of Take-up in 2005/6* (London, DWP).

Elliott, J, Dale, A and Egerton, M (2001) 'The influence of qualifications on women's work histories, employment status and earnings at age 33' 17 *European Sociological Review* 145.

Evason, E and Spence, L (2002) *Women and Pensions* (Belfast, Equality Commission for Northern Ireland).

Field, J (2000) *Pensions and Divorce: the 1998 Survey* Department of Social Security Research Report No. 117 (Leeds, Corporate Document Services).

Ginn, J (2003) *Gender, Pensions and the Lifecourse: How Pensions need to Adapt to Changing Family Forms* (Bristol, The Policy Press).

Ginn, J (2007) 'Poverty and Financial Inequality in Later Life' in T Ridge and S Wright (eds), *Understanding Inequality, Poverty and Wealth: Policies and Prospects* (Bristol, The Policy Press).

Ginn, J and Arber, S (2002) 'Degrees of freedom: do graduate women escape the motherhood gap in pensions?' 7 *Sociological Research Online.*

Glennerster, H (2006) 'Why so different? Why so bad a future?' in H Pemberton, P Thane and N Whiteside (eds), *Britain's Pensions Crisis: History and Policy* (London, The British Academy).

Haskey, J (1999) 'Divorce and remarriage in England and Wales' 95 *Population Trends* 18.

Johnson, P and Stears, G (1996) 'Should the Basic State Pension be a contributory benefit?' 17 *Fiscal Studies* 105.

Lampard, R and Peggs, K (1999) 'Repartnering: the relevance of parenthood and gender to cohabitation and remarriage among the formerly married' 50 *The British Journal of Sociology* 443.

Lewis, J (1992) 'Gender and the development of welfare regimes' 2 *Journal of European Social Policy* 159.

—— (1997) 'Gender and welfare regimes: further thoughts' 4 *Social Politics* 160.

Manning, A and Petrongolo, B (2004) *The Part-time Pay Penalty* (London, Women and Equality Unit, Department of Trade and Industry).

Marsh, A and Perry, J (2003) *Family Change 1999 to 2001*, Department for Work and Pensions Research Report No 180 (Leeds, Corporate Document Services).

McKie, L, Bowlby, S and Gregory, S (2001) 'Gender, caring and employment in Britain' 30 *Journal of Social Policy* 233.

Millar, J (2003) 'Gender, poverty and social exclusion' 2 *Social Policy & Society* 181.

Ministry of Justice (2007) *Judicial and Court Statistics 2006*, Cm 7273 (London, Ministry of Justice).

O'Connor, J, Orloff, A and Shaver, S (1999) *States, Markets, Families: Gender, Liberalism and Social Policy in Australia, Canada, Great Britain and the United States* (Cambridge, Cambridge University Press).

Orloff, A (2002) *Women's Employment and Welfare Regimes: Globalization, Export Orientation and Social Policy in Europe and North America* (Geneva, United Nations Research Institute for Social Development).

Peggs, K (2000) 'Which pension? Women, risk and pension choice' 48 *The Sociological Review* 344.

Pensions Commission (2004) *Pensions: Challenges and Choices. The first report of the Pensions Commission* (London, The Stationery Office).

Pfau-Effinger, B (1999) 'The modernisation of family and motherhood in Western Europe' in R Crompton (ed), *Restructuring Gender Relations and Employment: The Decline of the Male Breadwinner* (Oxford, Oxford University Press).

PPI (Pensions Policy Institute) (2006) *Shaping a Stable Pensions Solution: How Pension Experts would Reform UK Pensions* (London, PPI).

Price, D (2003) 'Pension sharing on divorce: the future for women' in C Bochel, N Ellison and M Powell (eds), *Social Policy Review 15: UK and International Perspectives* (Bristol, The Policy Press).

—— (2006) 'Why are older women in the UK poor?' 7 *Quality in Ageing* 23.

—— (2007) 'Closing the gender gap in retirement income: what difference will recent UK pension reforms make?' 36 *Journal of Social Policy* 1.

—— (2008) 'Towards a new pension settlement? Recent pension reform in the UK' in T Maltby, P Kennett and K Rummery (eds), *Social Policy Review 20: Analysis and Debate in Social Policy* (Bristol, The Policy Press).

Rake, K, Davies, H, Joshi, H and Alami, R (2000) *Women's Income over the Lifetime* (London, Women's Unit, Cabinet Office).

Rowlingson, K and McKay, S (2005) 'Lone motherhood and socio-economic disadvantage: insights from quantitative and qualitative evidence' 53 *The Sociological Review* 30.

Smithson, J, Lewis, S, Cooper, G and Dyer, J (2004) 'Flexible working and the gender pay gap in the accountancy profession' 18 *Work, Employment and Society* 115.

Walby, S and Olsen, W (2002) *The Impact of Women's Position in the Labour Market on Pay and Implications for UK Productivity* (London, Women and Equality Unit/Department for Trade and Industry).

Ward, C, Dale, A and Joshi, H (1996a) 'Combining employment with childcare: an escape from dependence?' 25 *Journal of Social Policy* 223.

—— (1996b) 'Income dependency within couples' in L Morris and E Lyon (eds), *Gender Relations in Public and Private: New Research Perspectives* (Basingstoke, Macmillan).

Warren, T (2000) 'Women in low status part-time jobs: a class and gender analysis' 4 *Sociological Research Online* 113.

—— (2001) 'Divergent female part-time employment in Britain and Denmark and the implications for gender equity' 49 *The Sociological Review* 548.

—— (2003) 'Class- and gender-based working time? Time poverty and the division of domestic labour' 37 *Sociology* 733.

—— (2004) 'Working part-time: achieving a successful "work–life"' balance?' 55 *The British Journal of Sociology* 99.

Women and Equality Unit (2005) *Women and Men in the Workplace* (London, Women and Equality Unit/Department for Trade and Industry).

Woods, L, Makepeace, G, Joshi, H and Dolton, P (2003) 'The world of paid work' in E Ferri, J Bynner and M Wadsworth (eds), *Changing Britain, Changing Lives. Three Generations at the Turn of the Century* (London, Institute of Education).

Part IV

A Rational Approach?

13

Rational Decision-making and Intimate Cohabitation

ANTONY W DNES

INTRODUCTION

IN THIS CHAPTER, I discuss the approach taken in 'law and economics' studies of the family to questions concerned with intimate unmarried cohabitation. I refer henceforth simply to 'cohabitation', in line with the practice in standard legal writing, accepting that most readers will realise that the discussion relates to lovers, not grandmothers. Work in law and economics is simplistically associated, in many minds, with models and applied work in which humans are expected to behave purposively and may display rational intent; in fact, much of the work actually recognises strategic interaction, which is not conventional rational decision-making. I propose to analyse several strands of work focused on marriage, making some comparisons with cohabitation along the way, and thereby illustrating particularly useful contributions made by the law and economics approach. Broadly, these strands include the search for a satisfactory theory of marriage, compared with cohabitation, the significance of empirical studies of trends in marriage and cohabitation, and policy design—approached as a special case of the economic analysis of regulation. My hope is to show that such rationality-based studies yield fruitful results that could not be generated by alternative approaches to family law.

I begin, however, by distinguishing between normative and positivistic (often referred to as 'positive') studies in economics, keeping in mind the family area of application.[1]

NORMATIVE AND POSITIVISTIC ANALYSIS

Many questions concerning intimate cohabitation can be beneficially analysed using approaches based on the enlightened thought[2] characteristic of modern

---

[1] My practical focus on the adult-relationship side of family law reflects the balance of my own interests. Economists have also contributed to debates on surrogacy, adoption, domestic violence, child abuse, inheritance and the treatment of elders (Dnes, 2005: ch 9).

[2] I mean enlightened in the sense of its being a product of the Enlightenment and the development of scientific method emphasising measurement and testing of hypotheses.

studies in law and economics. It is essential in carrying out such exercises to distinguish between normative analysis that considers intelligently designed social policy and positivistic[3] analysis that predicts how people might respond when faced with changes in socio-economic or legal variables. We should bear in mind that economic benefits come in many shapes and sizes, are defined as elements that contribute to a person's sense of well-being, and are not limited to pecuniary effects.[4] To some extent, what follows gives an insight into the economist's view of rationality, which really requires little more than people preferring more over less of some beneficial quantum. The qualification is important because, beyond this extent, there are many studies, particularly of human happiness (Layard, 2005), that recognise the influence of apparently irrational behaviour on well-being. From my own observations, mixing with people across different academic camps, there is often a striking need to distinguish between (i) the explanation of what is happening to the family and (ii) an acceptable basis for analysing the desirability of particular policy approaches toward the family: distinguishing positivistic studies from normative analysis helps enormously in this regard.

Normative Analysis

Generally, normative analysis formulates objectives and recognises constraints. Economists draw on the principles of welfare economics, in the sense of figuring out how people are made better or worse off by policy changes, which, in relation to jurisprudence, reflects an underlying utilitarianism (Dnes, 2005). Welfare economics could use alternative perspectives from jurisprudence, such as Rawls' (2005) egalitarian focus, or Nozick's (1974) individualist focus, although often this would make no difference to the result. Utilitarianism, in its modern guise of welfare economics, and even possibly simplified to wealth maximisation (Posner, 1984: ch 1), provides an analytical system for the analysis of the settling-up aspects of relationship breakdown: it broadly tells us the rule on which the parties would have agreed had they thought about dissolution ahead of time. From this perspective, the parties should choose a settlement rule maximising their joint welfare and leaving each *at least as* well off as they would be if they had never married. In relation to settling up, utilitarianism does not generate the problems with which it is associated in other contexts.[5]

The use of 'what the parties might have chosen' as a guide to settlements has surfaced in the House of Lords' continuing discussion of 'imputation' and

---

[3] Richard Lipsey popularised the term 'positive economics' back in the 1960s: see Lipsey (2008). I prefer the term 'positivistic', which is historically more accurate. Modern economics comes straight to us from the Scottish Enlightenment, via Adam Smith, David Ricardo, Jeremy Bentham, and John Stuart Mill.

[4] A focus on pecuniary effects would give a kind of 'law and accountancy.'

[5] English jurisprudence emphasises the context-dependency of the reasonable application of systems of moral philosophy, of which utilitarianism is one example.

'inference' of parties' intentions regarding the ownership of the shared home by spouses and cohabitants (and in other 'domestic' contexts), most recently in *Stack v Dowden*.[6] The distinction between imputation and inference is blurred by the majority in *Stack*, who acknowledge that there is a distinction but then go on to use the two terms interchangeably. Lord Neuberger's dissent in *Stack* does distinguish between inference and imputation[7] Inference entails discerning the parties' actual (albeit unexpressed) intentions, which is a positivistic exercise in keeping with the idea of ascertaining the true nature of the parties' property rights. In contrast, imputation entails ascribing to the parties the intentions that we think they would have had, had they thought about the issue of settling up, when in fact they did not think about it: there is no agreement or trust to find or infer. Imputation corresponds to an exercise in normative analysis. An example of an imputation is deciding that the separating couple would very likely have agreed on a settlement based on joint wealth maximisation, with division of the ownership of the wealth set to support that maximisation and keep each party at least as well off as they might be under any other plan. Although it is easy to see how imputation in practice may be thought difficult to distinguish from the court's deciding what it thinks would be 'fair' (the approach that the majority reject in *Stack*), it is different because of the possibility of adopting a coherent welfare standard as a guide.

The House of Lords has been extremely wary of lower courts imputing common intentions to the parties, preferring to look for actual (express or implied) bargains typically creating beneficial interests under a trust. In *Stack v Dowden*, Lord Walker's examination of Lord Diplock's argument in *Pettitt v Pettitt*[8] in favour of the court's task being to impute the 'common intention' of the parties, using the whole course of the relationship as evidence, rather than relying more narrowly on evidence of an actual bargain, emphasises evidential difficulties rather than the disentanglement of inference from imputation. Lord Diplock acknowledged in *Gissing v Gissing*[9] that his argument in *Pettitt* over imputation was not in the majority, but then uses the term 'infer' in a remarkably similar way to 'impute' in considering the same issues of beneficial interests, in fact joining in with the current muddle. Subsequent cases up to *Stack v Dowden* show the judges to be uncomfortable with the process of inference owing to a perception of unreality about the process and a recognition that it is often difficult in practice to maintain a distinction between inference and imputation.[10] One could regard this reluctance as embodying a libertarian welfare principle, respecting the integrity

---

[6] [2007] UKHL 17 (property division between an unmarried couple).

[7] ibid at [125]ff, which carefully discusses the distinction between inference and imputation that I make use of here. I am grateful to Jo Miles for discussions on the significance of the legal debate over the distinction between inference and imputation in relation to positivistic and normative economics.

[8] [1970] AC 777 at 822E.

[9] [1971] AC 886.

[10] According to Griffiths LJ in *Bernard v Josephs* [1982] Ch 391 at 404, cited by Lord Walker in *Stack v Dowden* at [21].

of the individual in choosing not to consider the issue of relationship breakdown rather than constructing the fix that the parties would have recognised if only they had been like some other, hypothetical, people.

Having clarified the distinction between imputation (normative) and inference (positivistic), can we say anything about the current direction of the law on settling up between former cohabitants? I think so: one can in fact *infer* that the modern move toward equal division of joint property implies true imputation by the courts. Baroness Hale's opinion in *Stack*,[11] used by her to suggest a rebuttable presumption of equal shares, could be seen as a form of imputation:

> At first blush, the answer appears obvious. It should only be expected that joint transferees would have spelt out their beneficial interests when they intended them to be different from their legal interests. Otherwise, it should be assumed that equity follows the law and that the beneficial interests reflect the legal interests in the property.

Does this answer use the joint transferees' failure to do anything else as inferred evidence, or move beyond factual matters to consider what rational people would have done had they thought about it? I interpret the resulting assumption as imputing rational assessment by the parties of their best interests, even where this may not have actually occurred: after all, doing nothing is in fact consistent with more than one outcome, such as its being too costly to spell out the beneficial interests, or the parties not having considered the matter. Silence is not generally acceptance, so acceptance is imputed here. To some considerable extent, the issue of imputation could be eased by providing a more solid foundation within which to work: an agreed welfare focus, in the terms favoured by economists. The normative approach coming out of mainstream law and economics would focus on situations where there is no evidence of a 'bargain', even allowing that the bargain could be inferred by citing an entire history of things said and done. The norm ('arrangements likely to have led to joint-wealth maximisation') would be deduced *separately* on the basis of what would have been in the joint interest of the couple, given that they had not agreed anything, in any terms, at the commencement of the relationship. The norm could then be widely debated and eventually emerge from legislation as a clarification of public policy.

The major contribution of normative economics is in clarifying the steps taken in moving from setting policy objectives, that is, a clear target or set of compatible and weighted targets known as a 'welfare function' in the terms of economics, to checking how policies affect the target/s. Much debate in social policy areas such as those connected with cohabitation looks unfocused to an economist, in not clarifying objectives. Once objectives are set, and assuming recognition of the need for compatibility for multiple aims, the debate needs to move on to methods of achieving the objectives. Incompatibility between multiple objectives is not a particular objection to rational decision-making, but is a *general* objection to *any* solution to the underlying problem.

---

[11] [2007] UKHL 17 at [54].

A good example of normative analysis, illustrating the need for greater clarity of reasoning, arises in comparisons of different standards that might guide settling up following divorce, and which might be extended to other forms of relationship break-up. Trebilcock (1994: 156) examines several arguments that all make a case for compensating the economically weaker party, typically, although not necessarily, the female, for the costs incurred as a result of the relationship.[12] These costs often reflect the giving up of a career to stay home and raise children, which would be regarded, *ex post*, as 'sunk costs', or, equivalently, as 'detrimental reliance'. Regardless of terminology, the key point is that the woman was initially committed to the relationship and gave up opportunities in anticipation that it would last and provide a range of benefits to her of both a pecuniary and non-pecuniary, and of both an individually and a jointly enjoyed, kind.

Arguments over compensating the sunk costs associated with relationship-specific investment by the female have generally settled into modern family law, but as just one factor to be recognised, actually in competition with others. The point is well recognised in recent English cases. In *Miller; McFarlane*,[13] the House of Lords recognised three rationales standing behind judicial discretion exercised by virtue of the Matrimonial Causes Act 1973: (i) need; (ii) equal sharing of matrimonial property; and (iii) compensation. Much discussion in the literature is about possible conflicts between the compensatory principle and rationales (i) and (ii), as considered by Bridge (2006) in relation to the Law Commission's (2006) consultation paper on the reform of cohabitation law. One can see that the notion of a rationale corresponds with an objective and that the three rationales taken together give a more complicated welfare function crying out pitifully for the application of a clear system of weighting. Every time the court applies the rationales it will be assigning weights, at least implicitly, to need versus sharing versus compensation. The exercise amounts to welfare economics writ small, more properly recognised as the court's following what in the legal literature has for some time been referred to as a 'liability rule', that is, a rule whereby an objectively determined value is ascribed to the parties' entitlements (Calabresi and Melamed, 1972).

There are alternative normative approaches to settling up in the literature. Leaving aside the 'I think it should be *x* per cent shares, and that's that' kind of argument, we can easily identify two serious alternatives. One is associated with Parkman (2002) who has argued for the use of a 'property rule', in the terms popularised by Calabresi and Melamed (1972), in which divorce is permitted by mutual consent only, and the court abandons its liability-rule, interventionist approach. A spouse seeking a divorce would compensate the other, who could insist on being at least as well off as before the divorce, as far as money can do

---

[12] Trebilcock is critical of the reliance standard, arguing instead for a share in accumulated benefits that is likely to be kinder to women with low opportunity costs in entering the marriage.

[13] [2006] UKHL 24 (assessing claims of equal shares in property and income in a longer and shorter marriage).

it, before consenting. The implied welfare standard of this approach is a variant on the requirement that gainers must be able to compensate losers and still gain from a change, before the change is permitted (Dnes, 2005: ch 1), often referred to as a Kaldor-Hicks test for a welfare improvement.[14] Parkman's approach at least preserves the expected benefits of the old marriage for both parties, because the divorce-seeker would back off if personal benefits from the change were not high enough to leave a surplus after compensating the other spouse's losses. There is a strong sense here of finding the rule likely to be agreed on before the marriage, had the parties thought about a later possible divorce. Most folk do not want to consider such issues when getting married, so perhaps it behoves the court to come up with an approach reflecting the veto-entitlement rule that can be inferred or imputed in Parkman's sense.

Secondly, we could require the court to use a liability rule to award damages comparable to those emerging from Parkman's bargaining approach. This variant would lead to the award of expectations damages to an unwilling divorcing party, since preserving at least the status quo benefits for him or her would be the minimum award that could be extracted by bargaining under the shadow of a veto entitlement. Compensation using expectation damages should normally exceed the reliance damages contemplated in *Miller; McFarlane*[15] (Dnes, 1998). Preserving expectancy should stop 'inefficient' divorces, in which, as at present, the spouse seeking a divorce may be able to make off with personally enhanced benefits, regardless of the costs imposed on the other party.

There are many more normative approaches that could be explored: for example, consider what settlement rule might be adopted under a Rawlsian veil of ignorance, which, in the context of family law, would involve not knowing whether one is male or female. Indeed, there is a significant struggle with the basics of a welfare comparison of compensatory approaches in the recent Law Commission (2007) recommendations concerning post-dissolution obligations between unmarried intimate cohabitants, and possible double-counting as a result of not quite getting to the bottom of the link between opportunities forgone and the generation of advantages flowing from cohabitation.[16] The main point made here is simply a plea for clarity, in particular in distinguishing normative from the positivistic analysis to which we now turn.

---

[14] The welfare standard is named after Lord Nicholas Kaldor and Sir John Hicks, who both popularised it in the 1940s, albeit in a form that accepted a hypothetical ability to compensate but did not require actual payment to be made.

[15] [2006] UKHL 24. The House of Lords rejected expectations damages in *Miller; McFarlane* mainly in terms of avoiding a return to the earlier and abandoned 'tailpiece' to s 25 of the Matrimonial Causes Act that required the court to put the parties into the position they would have been in had the marriage continued: in actual fact an impossible thing to do and not strictly comparable to the expectations damages approach of contract law, which requires mitigation of costs by all and maintained expectancy for the breached-against party only (see Lord Nicholls' dicta at [58]). The breaching party may be assumed to be better off if continuing to move on to greener pastures, notwithstanding a requirement to compensate his/her spouse.

[16] This is the subject of a separate paper available from the author.

Positivistic Analysis

Positivistic analysis typically uses insights from social theory, including information theory, economics and psychology, qualitative inquiry, and applied statistical analysis, in order to understand social changes concerning cohabitation. Examples would include the analysis of the response of marriage and divorce rates (Binner and Dnes, 2001), the age of first marriage (Mechoulan, 2006), and the age of first child-bearing (Brinig and Crafton, 1994) to legal changes such as the introduction of no-fault divorce, or no-fault settlements, and socio-economic changes such as increased female participation in the economy. Fisher and Low's chapter 11 in this volume is a good example of statistical enquiry aimed at assessing the impact on spouses of the current divorce settling-up regime in the UK. The level of sophistication of these studies is high, increasingly eschewing data analysis at a point in time, which cannot capture secular change (that is, changes in attitudes and underlying institutions), in favour of pooling data over lengthy periods of time.

Mechoulan's (2006) paper is an excellent example of state-of-the-art approaches, based on panel data techniques, covering the statistical analysis of longitudinal data for substantial cohorts of people, and permitting variations over time and between the groups under study to be explored. Mechoulan links convergence of first-marriage rates across US states to increased marital selectivity by females in response to an increase in the risk and cost of divorce associated with the introduction of no-fault property settlements.[17] It is fair to say that some clear results, for example the link between increased female labour market participation and marriage rates, have by now emerged in these studies, and would be very difficult to discern and explain in any other framework. The test that is generally applied to positivistic studies is to ask whether they predict some variable well: whether the theory and applied work give a compelling version of events.

Judging whether theory and applied work give a compelling version of events is not a matter related to the unschooled judgement of the observer, although the choice to adopt a scientific methodology should still be regarded as a value judgement of sorts. Over the centuries, certain criteria have been recognised as encouraging fruitful research, such as preferring simple over complex theory if the explanatory power of the two is identical. More recently, attention to the lag structure of explanatory variables in statistics, for example checking whether an earlier shift in the explanatory variable is a significant influence on the dependent variable in the longer term, does give a basis for deducing causality between variables in certain well-defined cases (see the analysis of the growth of the US Army after the Civil War in relation to increasing Indian settler battles in Anderson and McChesney, 1994 for an interesting demonstration). In a positivistic study, in order to provide a satisfactory explanation of events, capable of predicting

---

[17] The introduction of the no-fault divorce procedure, which has no significant impact in the study, should be distinguished.

the future course of those events, it is, strictly speaking, enough to show that the world is behaving as if a particular theory is correct.

Quantification is usually important in that *modelling*, and it is likely to matter less what people think they are up to compared with independent indicators of their behaviour. A good example arises in family law in studies of marriage and cohabitation. In qualitative studies (see the discussion in chapter fourteen of this volume by Anne Barlow), interviewees often insist that money matters, or changes in family law affecting money, have nothing to do with their decisions to marry or cohabit. In a very narrow sense this may well be true, even leaving aside the issue of a natural tendency to answer such questions in a perceived tasteful manner. However, statistical studies, based more on hypothesis testing and relying on survey or census data, tend to show that such variables as the levels of divorce and marriage *do* respond to legal changes, and in particular to variables reflecting rules affecting financial settlements (Mechoulan, 2006) and to those reflecting welfare benefits and the workplace-based growing independence of women (Binner and Dnes, 2001). It is likely that many people would not have these financial influences in mind when answering a question framed in terms of simple legal or financial impetuses toward relationship structures. Another useful point of reflection is the introduction of legal aid for divorce cases in post-war Britain: this has been identified as a statistically significant influence on the level of divorce in our time-series study (Binner and Dnes, 2001), but whilst legal aid clearly did make it easier for wives to initiate proceedings, it is unlikely that a questionnaire study would pick this up by asking about financial influences on the subject.

The main purpose in separating normative and positivistic strands of analysis is to be clear as to the distinction between ought and is, but real world studies are often aimed at a mixture of complex questions. In practice, many studies will examine a variety of questions, some normative and some positivistic in nature, and one sometimes even encounters 'normative analysis as positive theory' (Viscusi, 2007) indicating that one predictor of behaviour could be the parties deciding to follow some aim on which they agree. In general, however, it clarifies debate if one understands when a prediction is being made about the effect of a legal change on the parties' behaviour (positivistic), and the effect relative to a desired effect on their welfare (normative).

I now consider some largely positivistic studies that focus on the feedback from legal rules on to human behaviour. Incentive structures, as noted by Fisher and Low (chapter eleven, this volume) are somewhat neglected in discussions of cohabitation legal reforms.

STUDIES OF THE NATURE OF MARRIAGE: LIFE PROFILES, OR 'SHE GAVE HIM HER BEST YEARS'

The life profile theory of marriage is positivistic, and hence testable. It is associated with Cohen (1987, 2002), who then went on to make an influential normative argument that, to avoid encouraging opportunistic divorce, the equivalent of contract (expectations) damages ought to be awarded to the fault-free party in a divorce. Actually, there is no reason to attach the liability to fault, as traditionally interpreted in family law, since for one spouse to indicate a wish for no-fault divorce is itself a breach of contract. The purpose of marriage, as a form of heavily-obligated cohabitation governed by a standard contract, could be seen as being to protect the economically weaker party from a form of exploitation taking the form of opportunistic behaviour emanating from an asymmetry in the life-cycle of men compared with women. This theory regards the defining aspects of marriage as being the rules governing divorce and post-dissolution obligations.[18]

According to Cohen, getting the rules of divorce settlement wrong, in his terms, risks creating an extremely worrying incentive structure characterised by opportunistic exploitation of the traditional wife. This concern is supported empirically by many papers, including Allen (1998), showing how the introduction of no-fault divorce, far from simply releasing a one-time bottleneck of unhappy spouses, encouraged divorce, thereby adversely affecting the interests of traditional wives. Studies not supporting a permanent impact on divorce rates appear to be statistically faulty, or show adjustments occurring in marriage rates that are consistent with law having a permanent impact.[19] Cohen's argument is firmly based on a life-profile theory of traditional marriage, characterised by an asymmetry over the timing of investments made by the man and the woman as he specialises in the labour market and she specialises in homemaking.

According to the life-profile theory, in a traditional marriage, the woman invests in children and home-making early on in marriage, incurring detrimental reliance by giving up alternative labour market opportunities, or, possibly, alternative marriage possibilities, and expects to remain with her husband enjoying the family income and home over the long term. He is freed of domestic responsibilities, enabling him to build up a career that will yield high earnings later on in the life-cycle, as is frequently observed (Bardasi and Taylor, 2008). Cohen

---

[18] Note that in modern family law, the enforcement of obligations *within* marriage, eg for support, is becoming increasingly less important. Suits for spousal support are a rarity. Earlier work by Becker (1981) on the family was based on gains from specialisation in forming the family unit, which do not give a reason for marriage compared with simple cohabitation possibly with one's granny. Modern work (Bardasi and Taylor, 2008) sees the gains from being married as at least ranging over those from specialisation, male human-capital formation (the enhancement of earning capacity discussed in *Miller, McFarlane* and in *Charman v Charman (No 4)* [2007] EWCA Civ 503), and signalling (of male sobriety, according to Akerlof, 1998).

[19] Binner and Dnes (2001) used 50 years' worth of UK data in a time-series model and showed that no-fault divorce laws had a permanent effect on divorce rates, and did not simply release a bottleneck. We noted that one of the frequently cited contrary (time-series) papers, Ellman and Lohr (1998), misinterpreted a spike in changes in divorce rates as release of a bottleneck, when a spike in *changes* is a long-term shift in *levels*. As noted earlier, the debate has moved on: Mechoulan (2006) finds a temporary effect from changing to no-fault *settlement rules*, in this case in a panel data study working on age of first marriage across US states and through time, but examines the response to the law, which includes increased search activity given unreliable marital promises.

observed that males more readily remarry in middle age than women,[20] and might be tempted to abandon older spouses and move off without sharing the long-term returns of the marriage: the life profiles show an asymmetry between the sexes. In fact, her early investments have seriously reduced her ability to form a new relationship: while her child-bearing years may be over, she may still be encumbered by child-care responsibilities.

Cohen's analysis is economic in the broadest sense: the returns to marrying include companionship and related matters—the abandoning male may be looking for different company as well as retaining material assets, and the abandoned woman loses companionship as well as material claims. Its traditional focus needs updating to recognise a more egalitarian but still sexually unequal world, but is a starting point for analysis and is not a significant problem unless we think there are no asymmetries in life-cycles (on these persisting inequalities see further Scott and Dex, chapter three, this volume).

The life-profile theory broadly implies that marriage may be a mechanism for protecting the female's early marriage-specific investments over time in the face of possible later mistreatment by the male. Given uncertainties over the precise impact of domestic responsibilities, or growth in market-led family earnings and wealth, both male and female may wish to defer ultimately to court governance of their relationship by adopting a standardised marriage contract. He should wish to signal commitment to maintain a valuable level of support for her, and she would be encouraged to make the early marriage-specific investments. Marriages based on asymmetric relationship-specific investment patterns are particularly subject to possible opportunism after the introduction of no-fault rules that do not tie financial provision and property division to the equivalent of breach of contract, which is not necessarily fault as understood in family law. In terms of traditional marriage, it is now possible for the man to tire of an older wife and move on to a new relationship without maintaining the promised lifestyle, providing courts do not require the payment of expectations-based settlements. Divorce settlements based on meeting the *needs* or 'reasonable requirements' of an ex-wife, as in applications of the Matrimonial Causes Act 1973, especially before *White v White*,[21] may effectively make divorce rather cheap, at least for wealthier men, and encourage such male opportunism (Dnes, 1998). The same is true of jurisdictions, such as Scotland or California, which require equal division of community property, since a half-share of the marital acquest may not yield the promised lifestyle. There is some empirical support for the worry that legal changes of this sort have increased divorce rates.[22]

---

[20] Higher remarriage rates for divorced males appear as a statistical regularity in most international family law studies. And see Fisher and Low, ch 11, this volume on different repartnering rates by men and women post-divorce.

[21] [2001] AC 596.

[22] The modern trend to introduce reliance (opportunity cost) or restitution (returning the value of domestic contributions) will also under-compensate (certainly if taken as the sole measure of relief), as I explain in an earlier paper (Dnes, 1998). Think of the low opportunity cost of a waitress who marries a millionaire, or the low market value of hosting and domestic management compared with a promised wealthy lifestyle.

Lest we think it only the men who are capable of opportunistic exploitation, modern settlements could also make divorce too cheap from a female perspective: for example, the wife might tire of marriage and may know that, in a moderate-asset setting, 'needs' could dominate contributions and lead to her keeping a significant proportion of the assets, particularly as a parent with care of minor children (see, for example, Hitchings, chapter nine, this volume).

In terms of the debate over unmarried cohabitation, creating post-dissolution obligations could be a mechanism for protecting relationship-specific obligations, if there is some reason for thinking that there is an obstacle to marriage and the asymmetry over investment timing exists: this use of the life-profile theory and associated observations implies that we look for functional equivalence in designing marriage and cohabitation law.[23] However, the failure of divorce law to enforce implied support promises, or to recognise fault, might well imply that unmarried couples of whatever kind could protect themselves better using private cohabitation agreements, although the complexity attached to these is potentially problematic.[24] Ideally, we would not want a disaffected cohabitant to be able to move to a new relationship without having first to compensate the losses of the abandoned cohabitant, and it is doubtful that current marital law requires this of divorcing spouses.

THE COASE THEOREM AND FAMILY LAW

There is a theoretical argument, following Coase (1960), associated with Peters (1986) and tested in many papers including Mechoulan (2006), that the legal regime affecting divorce settlement may not influence the level of divorce, or of marriage. A modern variant on the approach would suggest that requiring unmarried cohabitants to opt into, or opt out of, a standardised set of obligations would not affect the level of cohabitation, marriage, or single living. Such an argument depends upon bargaining to offset the effect of a legal change, and requires bargaining costs to be insignificant and the mechanism for offset to have no visible effect. A visible effect would occur, for example, if divorce rates settled down after an initial response but we discovered that fewer people were marrying.

The analogy is with Coase's argument that nuisance cases[25] could, at least in a textbook sense, be settled by bargaining once the tortfeasor and victim knew their legal entitlements to carry out or stop the offending activity, resulting in

---

[23] In *Burns v Burns* [1984] Ch 317 and in *Marvin v Marvin* 122 Cal Rptr 815 [App 1981] the unmarried ladies would be treated as if married.

[24] There are good reasons for considering simplicity in legal doctrines as likely to enhance the quality of legal enforcement. See Dnes and Lueck (2009) for further details.

[25] This note may help non-lawyers. Nuisance is the area of civil law settling conflict over resources (land-based activities). The court must decide whether conflicting uses of neighbouring land represent 'reasonable' uses of land, or not. The traditional remedy for nuisance is to stop ('enjoin') it whenever it is judged to be unreasonable, although financial compensation for continuing nuisance is developing in some jurisdictions. A nuisance roughly corresponds to an 'externality', or unpriced spillover effect, in economic analysis. Analysis of cases suggests that courts tend to see as unreasonable those uses of land that impose high costs on neighbours.

the best use of the underlying resources. In a case discussed by Coase, *Sturges v Bridgman*,[26] a confectioner who could make more profitable, but noisy, use of property than a physician would carry on to the detriment of the physician's medical practice, if the court refused to enjoin him. The value of the medical practice would be too low to enable the physician to buy out the noise. Conversely, if the physician received an injunction against the confectioner the physician could still be induced to allow the noise if the confectioner compensated him for lost medical fees. Either way, the *same* (joint profit-maximising) level of noise should result, as explained in more detail in Dnes (2005: ch 3). By analogy, if we were suddenly to move English family law from the current system of equitable distribution towards a community property system, or, say, move a community-property system from equal shares to 25 per cent or 75 per cent sharing, according to this theory it is possible that there would be no response in divorce, or marriage rates, since bargaining between the parties would reflect such changes.

For there to be no response to the settlement rule, however, a number of heroic assumptions would need to be borne out in reality, or at least the world would need to behave as if they were true.[27] These assumptions, apart from the obvious requirement for insignificant bargaining costs, include a requirement that all elements of value in the marriage could be rearranged, so that it would be broadly possible to redistribute early benefits from marrying to offset the change in post-divorce entitlements. Yet it may not be possible to divide all benefits from the marriage to facilitate bargaining: some assets/benefits may be inherently 'indivisible'. Zelder (1993) examines such possibilities in detail and, importantly, notes that 'indivisibilities' really do exist that make bargaining difficult—children of the marriage whose future is to be determined by the court's assessment of their best interests rather than efficient bargaining between the parties.

The legal regime affecting settlement can allow marriages to end even when they could be reorganised to show a clear benefit to both parties, in which case, following the Coase (1960) theorem, one might have expected bargaining to take care of any problems. This inefficiency follows if one party can hold enough of the benefits of the marriage under the legal rules to put that amount beyond bargaining, which would otherwise focus on factors such as transferring beneficial use assets, consumption patterns, or altering the domestic division of labour. Such indivisibilities explain why there may be a failure to bargain in the shadow of the divorce court to rearrange individual benefits and prevent divorce occurring when there is a positive overall benefit from the marriage (Zelder, 1993; Brinig and Allen, 2000).

In any case, the world does not behave as Coase's theorem might suggest. The disruption of marriages by changes in divorce law is implied by empirical studies showing either a significant and permanent shift in divorce rates following

---

[26] [1879] 11 Ch D 852 (injunction awarded to Sturges stopping a noise nuisance next to a Wimpole Street consulting room). Incidentally, the neighbouring properties are now occupied by law firms.

[27] Note the positivism.

the introduction of no-fault divorce laws (Binner and Dnes, 2001), or increased search activity during marriage formation (Mechoulan, 2006)[28] that affects marriage rates. Even if bargaining around legal change is a possibility, the world currently behaves as if bargaining is impeded.

STUDIES OF COHABITATION

The move away from marriage and towards cohabitation represents one of the most significant shifts in society during the post-war period. The trends over 1960–2000 are similar across North America and many European countries, although detailed patterns may vary across countries.[29] On average, first marriages fell from approximately 70 per 1,000 to 30 per 1,000 of the male population. The age at which first marriages occur has typically risen, with both men and women waiting an extra three years. Births outside marriage have increased from 5 per cent to over 40 per cent of all births. In addition, the proportion of cohabiting women between the ages of 20 and 50 has trebled.[30]

First, this change is clearly a major change in behaviour and is unlikely to be a random, inexplicable phenomenon. A puzzling aspect of the substitution is that cohabitation is against the interests of many women. Marriage is potentially a rather good mechanism for supporting long-term family investments, even taking a very approximate view of the fit of Cohen's (2002) life-profile model, and without marriage women might predict their vulnerability to opportunistic behaviour (there might also be some men in such a position). It seems unlikely that changes in women's economic activity and in techniques of child-rearing have reached a point where the sexes no longer show *any* asymmetric interdependence over life profiles.[31] Therefore, one would expect a man's willingness to offer marriage to remain a very important signal for young women, giving a 'separating equilibrium' distinguishing committed from uncommitted life partners. Inquiries have been made, but interviewed cohabitants give a variety of reasons for not marrying, or they believe erroneously that cohabitation is legally like marriage (Barlow, 2009), and, in general, one has an impression of tremendous confusion in the face of massive social change.

Secondly, cohabitation has not generally been subjected to the same kind of settling-up regime as marriage in the event of dissolution. Up to now, there has been no intervention by a family court with powers to reallocate assets between partners or to create maintenance obligations.[32] Cohabiting parties must rely

---

[28] The argument that divorce rates may not change following legal reform because of bargaining adjustments is associated with Peters (1986).

[29] See Kiernan (2002).

[30] For a summary of recent demographic data, see Law Commission (2006: Part 2).

[31] See Scott and Dex (ch 3), Price (ch 12) and Fisher and Low (ch 11), this volume.

[32] But note the opinions in *Stack v Dowden* [2007] UKHL 17, followed in *Fowler v Barron* [2008] EWCA Civ 377, that support a rebuttable presumptive equal beneficial division of assets held jointly at law.

largely on natural 'hostages' that emerge in the relationship to limit opportunism. Such hostages may be provided by the presence of children, with whom parents may wish to maintain easy contact. Also, the search costs of finding a new partner may act to hold people together over a long period of time. In the case of marriage, such hostages will typically be bolstered by legal obligations between the ex-spouses to divide marital property and share earnings.

Cohabiting parents have for some time been subject to child support obligations affecting all non-resident parents, regardless of marital status, to pay child support. Nonetheless, it is clear that it would be rational to choose to cohabit, if the parties actually wished to avoid, or perhaps in some jurisdictions just to lessen, the legal obligations towards each other in the event of dissolution. One can conclude from research findings that, to the extent that people think they are trying out partners (Lewis, Datta and Sarre, 1999) they are indeed *avoiding* marriage at that stage in their lives. 'Trying out' is consistent with the findings in Mechoulan (2006).

From a life-profile perspective, if there were evidence that women were making early investments in family life that created benefits to be shared later, and that men were taking advantage of them by *imposing* cohabitation rather than marriage and then abandoning them later on, there would be the basis for a claim of exploitation. Even a tremendous libertarian might then reasonably seek to outlaw cohabitation by effectively turning it into marriage, or at least removing the basis for doing harm, just as we might wish to prohibit other frauds. Such reasoning might cause marriage-like obligations to be enforced when cohabitation came to approximate marriage (for example after children had been born within the union, or after a period of time during which one party had been economically dependent). However, the presence of exploitative cohabitation is not supported by the evidence (Lewis, Datta and Sarre, 1999) which suggests some form of shared expectations rather than one party creating an erroneous perception of common law marriage.[33] At best one could claim that some people are misinformed about the likely outcome of cohabitation and the life-profile problem. There might then be a case for providing information and education, which the Ministry of Justice currently tries to do for England and Wales, but hardly one for the suggestion emerging around the world that would render consensual non-obligated cohabitation impossible without a specific agreement.[34]

A key issue, from a rational decision-making perspective, is that parties are free to avoid cohabitation as they could choose marriage. What if the meaningful sense of that freedom disappears? Choices are typically constrained. It may well be that

---

[33] Common law marriage (ie an informal claim by a couple to be married) is recognised in some US states such as Montana.

[34] The argument to change cohabitation obligations because people overestimate the obligations is perilously close to an argument that 'the people could be different': one of the fallacies of nirvana economics identified by Demsetz (1969), who argues that we need to fashion policy to reflect the welfare of people we actually have in society, not those whose preferences would be different if only they were wiser, fitter, younger, or whatever you wish.

the terms of cohabitation have changed in favour of males, following a reduction of pregnancy risk for unmarried females (Akerlof, Yellen and Katz, 1996), so that more women are willing to engage in unmarried sexual activity and fewer men seek marriage. Akerlof, Yellen and Katz (1996) demonstrate theoretically that there can be a tipping point in a population such that it moves from all single women benefiting from a male-provided marriage guarantee in case of pregnancy, whether they feel a need for the guarantee or not, to a position in which so many women no longer seek the guarantee that few couples end up married.[35] There is no implication here that males are exploiting females, it is just that 'terms of trade' have moved adversely for women. Everyone is exercising free choice, under new constraints, but what to make of it? Indeed, the story told here is consistent with late twentieth-century developments, and with the reports on survey respondents' views in qualitative inquiries (Barlow, chapter fourteen, this volume). Women are unsure why no one is marrying these days, whereas their mothers mostly did, and reassure themselves with the thought that it is all the same really. And, the men cannot believe they are getting away with so little commitment and also reassure themselves that cohabitation is really marriage, so as not to appear opportunistic. The alternative is to conclude that we are living among people who are systematically stupid or misinformed, which seems unlikely. Something really changed: after all, their parents probably[36] had the same beliefs but *did* get married, as do people in jurisdictions with common law marriage.

It is meddlesome, but entirely consistent with regulation in several areas, to intervene in an unregulated outcome such as the one just described if the outcome has wider implications in some way worrying for the rest of society. There are worries over the impact of relationship break-up on children, especially in relation to an absence of fathers (Popenhoe, 1996). There are also concerns that, once into unmarried cohabitation, the parties will begin to make joint pecuniary investments, for example in housing, and that hard-to-value non-pecuniary inputs may be involved (Bridge, 2006). So, in just the same way that certain free choices, such as those involving child labour or selling organs, are limited in broadly free and pluralistic societies (Novak, 1982: 55), so we might alter the legal constraints on cohabitation.

It is important to realise that cohabitants are likely to respond to legal changes, and that there may be additional effects on the married and on the single. Rowthorn (2002) has argued that marriage has declined precisely because the courts have failed to keep the commitment signal clear: one can promise to love and support for life, and back out a few years later. Introducing a further form of

---

[35] In some sectors of society the impact of the welfare system favouring single-person claims could also encourage such a result, as could greater female labour market participation. Akerlof, Yellen and Katz (1996) concentrate on the legalisation of abortion in a US context as the initiating change.

[36] Although it is possible that previous generations did *not* have the same belief in common law marriage: see Probert (2008) for the argument that the common law marriage myth is of recent origin in England and Wales, and that common law marriage was not a part of the pre-eighteenth-century legal landscape in that jurisdiction.

marriage, which is what obligated intimate cohabitation would amount to, could further confuse the signals over commitment for couples. If people now think that unregulated cohabitation is marriage, what will they make of something like marriage but different? This reflection might also suggest caution over allowing enforceable pre-nuptial, or private cohabitation contracts: ultimately the clarity of signals of obligation and the quality of legal enforcement may depend on simplicity of doctrine. I have made similar observations in other areas of law, such as land-use servitudes (Dnes and Lueck, 2009).

Also, there may be unintended consequences. The real importance of positivistic studies in family law and policy is in warning of what might happen if laws are changed. Is it possible that marriages might be displaced into less-obligated cohabitation? It is not good enough to say we do not think that will happen.

IN CONCLUSION: INFREQUENTLY ASKED QUESTIONS (IFAQS)

The practical results of my discussion of normative and positivistic studies of family law can be summarised in a number of answers to questions that should be more frequently asked than is typically the case.

— Does economic rationality imply a financial motive for entering marriage or unmarried cohabitation? *A.* Not in general, as there could be a variety of reasons, or combinations of reasons, for marrying, all of which contribute to the welfare of the individuals concerned and affect their incentives.
— Does this imply that legal and financial changes affecting dissolution obligations will have no effect on behaviour? *A.* No, not least because empirical work by economists, sociologists, and economist/lawyers picks up statistically significant impacts on marriage and divorce rates following on from legal change.
— Should we just make marriage and cohabitation legally the same, given that so many people are receptive to the idea or believe in a common law marriage myth? *A.* The effect of this would either be to prohibit unobligated unmarried cohabitation in the absence of an agreement between the parties opting out of the scheme of financial remedies, or to create a new category of marriage—interpreted as a standardised set of obligations—and it is likely that this would have an effect on behaviour, possibly leading to undesirable repercussions. Normative questions would remain: in general, we have not allowed our legal approach to emerge from majority decision-making (consider capital punishment).
— Are marriage and cohabitation really functionally equivalent? *A.* Apparently not, since empirical work of many kinds picks up differences between the two populations within a country and across countries. Social change has propelled a move towards cohabitation that differs in different places where social conditions differ, and that has increased across time where beliefs over

the legal status of cohabitants are unlikely to have varied, and has increased in places where common law marriage does exist, such as Montana.

— Do studies of incentive effects from legal change suggest no need for legal support for cohabitants? *A.* No, there are issues concerning the current law's encouragement of opportunistic behaviour. Most studies of incentive impacts suggest considerable caution over inadvertently making the cure worse than the disease by formulating policy that does not examine what amounts to regulatory impact. Most people seem to wish to avoid further destabilisation of relationships that include marriage and cohabitation.

Before we consider whether a new rule should be adopted for either married or cohabiting couples, perhaps we should consider whether we are asking the right questions.

BIBLIOGRAPHY

Akerlof, GA (1998) 'Men without children' 108 *The Economic Journal* 287.

Akerlof, GA, Yellen, JL and Katz, ML (1996) 'An analysis of out of wedlock childbearing in the United States' 111 *Quarterly Journal of Economics* 277.

Allen, DW (1998) 'No-fault divorce in Canada: its cause and effect' 37 *Journal of Economic Behavior and Organisation* 129.

Anderson, T and McChesney, F (1994) 'Raid or trade? An economic model of Indian-White relations' 37 *Journal of Law and Economics* 39.

Bardasi, E and Taylor, M (2008) 'Marriage and Wages: A Test of the Specialization Hypothesis' 75 *Economica* 569.

Becker, G (1981) *A Treatise on the Family* (Chicago, IL, University of Chicago Press).

Binner, J and Dnes, A (2001) 'Marriage, Divorce and Legal Change: New Evidence from England and Wales' 39 *Economic Inquiry* 298.

Bridge, S (2006) 'Money, Marriage and Cohabitation' 36 *Family Law* 641.

Brinig, M and Allen, DW (2000) 'These boots are made for walking: why most divorce filers are women' 2 *American Law and Economics Review* 126.

Brinig, M and Crafton, S (1994) 'Marriage and opportunism' 23 *Journal of Legal Studies* 869.

Calebresi, G and Melamed, AD (1972) 'Property rules, liability rules, and inalienability: one view of the cathedral' 85 *Harvard Law Review* 1089.

Coase, RH (1960) 'The problem of social cost' 3 *Journal of Law and Economics* 1.

Cohen, L (1987) Marriage, divorce and quasi rents: or, 'I gave him the best years of my life', 16 *Journal of Legal Studies* 267.

—— (2002) 'Marriage: the long-term contract', in A Dnes and R Rowthorn (eds), *The Law and Economics of Marriage and Divorce* (Cambridge, Cambridge University Press).

Demsetz, H (1969) 'Information and efficiency: Another viewpoint' 12 *Journal of Law and Economics* 1.

Dnes, A (1998) 'The Division of Marital Assets' 25 *Journal of Law and Society* 336.

—— (2005) The Economics of Law: Property, Contracts and Obligations (Boston MA, Cengage).

Dnes, A and Lueck, D (2009) 'Asymmetric Information and the Structure of Servitude Law' 38 *Journal of Legal Studies* 89–120.

Ellman, IM and Lohr, SL (1998) 'Dissolving the relationship between divorce laws and divorce rates' 18 *International Review of Law and Economics* 341.

Kiernan, K (2002) 'Cohabitation in Western Europe: Trends, Issues and Implications' in A Booth and A Crouter (eds), *Just Living Together: Implications of Cohabitation on Families, Children and Social Policy* (Mahwah, NJ, Lawrence Erlbaum Associates).

Law Commission (2006) *Cohabitation: The Financial Consequences of Relationship Breakdown*, Law Com CP 179 (London, TSO).

—— (2007) *Cohabitation: The Financial Consequences of Relationship Breakdown*, Law Com No 307 (London, TSO).

Layard, R (2005) *Happiness* (London, Allen Lane).

Lewis, J, Datta, J and Sarre, S (1999) *Individualism and Commitment in Marriage and Cohabitation*, Research Paper 8/99 (London, Lord Chancellor's Department).

Lipsey, RG (2008) 'Positive Economics' *The New Palgrave Dictionary of Economics*, 2nd edn.

Mechoulan, S (2006) 'Divorce Laws and the Structure of the American Family' 35 *Journal of Legal Studies* 143.

Novak, M (1982) *The Spirit of Democratic Capitalism* (New York, Simon and Schuster).

Nozick, R (1974) *Anarchy, State, and Utopia* (New York, Basic Books).

Parkman, A (2002) 'Mutual consent divorce' in A Dnes and R Rowthorn (eds), *The Law and Economics of Marriage and Divorce* (Cambridge, Cambridge University Press).

Peters, HE (1986) 'Marriage and divorce: informational constraints and private contracting' 76 *American Economic Review* 437.

Popenhoe, D (1996) *Life Without Father* (Cambridge, MA, Harvard University Press).

Posner, R (1984) *The Economics of Justice* (Cambridge, MA, Harvard University Press).

Probert, R (2008) 'Common-law marriage: myths and misunderstandings' 20 *Child and Family Law Quarterly* 1.

Rawls, J (2005) *A Theory of Justice* (Cambridge, MA, Harvard University Press).

Rowthorn, R (2002) 'Marriage as signal' in A Dnes and R Rowthorn (eds), *The Law and Economics of Marriage and Divorce* (Cambridge, Cambridge University Press).

Trebilcock, M (1994) *The Limits of Freedom of Contract* (Cambridge, MA, Harvard University Press).

Viscusi, WK, Vernon, JM and Harrington, JE (2007) *The Economics of Regulation and Antitrust*, 4th edn (Cambridge, MA, MIT Press).

Zelder, M (1993) 'Inefficient dissolutions as a consequence of public goods: the case of no-fault divorce' 22 *Journal of Legal Studies* 503.

14

Legal Rationality and Family Property

What has Love got to do with it?

ANNE BARLOW

INTRODUCTION

F AMILY LAW, IN so far as it is trying to regulate disputes relating to money and property on relationship breakdown, has its work cut out. For it is trying to deal in a rational way with issues between people who are in an emotionally charged relationship situation and where most might predict that rationality is unlikely to prevail (Beck and Beck-Gernsheim, 1995). Whilst some, such as John Dewar, see the answer as conceding to what he terms 'the normal chaos of family law' which nonetheless works on a practical level due to the pragmatic solutions of professionals operating within a discretionary legal framework (Dewar, 1998), others have argued that this is not the optimal way forward for family law in general (Henaghan, 2008) and the regulation of new family forms in particular (Barlow et al, 2005).

This chapter will therefore consider whether family law can avoid the trap of a 'rationality mistake'—whereby legislators overestimate the law's ability to steer behaviour in a particular direction (Barlow and Duncan, 2000; Barlow et al, 2005)—yet still develop a coherent theory of family law to apply in this field (Eekelaar, 2006; Henaghan, 2008). It has been argued convincingly by critical theorists that family law 'needs to be socially located' (see eg Freeman, 1985: 153–54). Given shifting attitudes and more complex married and unmarried families resulting from changed parenting, partnering and repartnering patterns and behaviours, this presents a real challenge. In rising to this, it will be argued that it is now time to take stock of both the emotional and economic foundations and commitment on which modern couple relationships are built in order to consider how family law should weigh the competing values of promoting personal financial autonomy yet providing legal protection for the economically weaker partner on relationship breakdown. Arguably this has already been done in the cohabitation context by the Law Commission in its consideration of proposals for the reform of cohabitation law (Law Commission, 2007). But has the right balance been struck here? Is the current legal hierarchy still fit for purpose or are we drawing the regulatory lines in the wrong places? These are the questions this chapter aims to pursue. In so doing, it will draw on empirical research to examine whether family law in this area can find a way to cope with its chaotic raw material, avoid the legal rationality mistake yet become sufficiently coherent to provide satisfactory outcomes for those it serves.

LEGAL RATIONALITY AND THE NORMAL CHAOS OF LOVE

At its foundation, law is a system predicated on its power to bring about what might be termed 'legally rational' behaviour. It is a closed system which assumes that its deterrents and rewards are known (or should be known) and will shape behaviour. Whilst this classical positivist formulation of the working of the legal system has been much critiqued (see, eg, Dworkin, 1977), an assumption of 'legal rationality' still underlies the way law is expected to work. This approach remains visible in the family law field, where different styles of family receive different legal treatment in different contexts but according to a preferential hierarchy which has developed in an ad hoc manner, with only sporadic legislative review.

The assumption of a legally rational reaction to family law is certainly a matter which has influenced legislators and which dominates discussions surrounding any family legislation which might potentially detract from more traditional moral standards. Whilst the same-sex civil partnership legislation (the Civil Partnership Act 2004) was able neatly to side-step allegations of undermining heterosexual marriage (with which, after all, it was not a direct competitor), by focusing debate on the government's equality and non-discrimination agenda (Department of Trade and Industry, Women and Equality Unit, 2003), attempts to introduce greater legal rights for informal cohabitants—often dubbed 'marriage-lite' (Morgan, 2000)—are seen to pose a greater threat. This has been observed most recently in the government's cautious reaction to the Law Commission's recommendations for reform of cohabitation law (Law Commission, 2007). Rather than acknowledging the case for reform made out very strongly in the Law Commission's report, more research into Scotland's experience of similar but very recent legislation was deemed necessary prior to legislative action.[1] Despite the already overwhelming statistics showing the decline in marriage and increase in heterosexual cohabitation (National Statistics Online, 2008), the belief in law's power to influence the future direction of these social phenomena remains undiminished and is deeply influential within party politics. As Baroness

---

[1] Ministerial Statement to Parliament by Bridget Prentice, Parliamentary Under-Secretary of State for Justice, *Hansard* HC vol 472 col 22WS (6 March 2008).

Young asserted in the parliamentary debates surrounding the Family Law Bill 1996 proposing divorce reform, 'law influences behaviour and it sends out a very clear message. There would be no point in legislating at all if law did not influence behaviour.'[2] It is this concept of legal rationality which is used in this chapter where its role as a useful tool or inhibitor of progress in the family law field will be explored.

Love, on the other hand is the very antithesis of rational thought and behaviour, legal or otherwise. Indeed, sociologists such as Beck and Beck-Gernsheim (1995) talk convincingly of 'the normal chaos of love', a phrase which encapsulates the way in which rationality is overpowered by love, which is something far stronger and beyond control, leaving the 'victim's' reason in a distant parallel universe and at least temporarily beyond recall. When the first flush of love fades, a semblance of rationality may return, but its roots are not deep. It can easily be dislodged by the all-too-powerful emotions which accompany love's rejection or a fear that love might be lost. Thus when relationships based on love break down, rationality is not restored. On the contrary, often more chaos is fuelled, which poses the question of law's suitability for resolving disputes born out of such emotionally charged situations.

This leads us to ask whether family property disputes are social problems for which law, at least in its present form, is altogether unsuited or whether it is indeed possible to use law to help find more imaginative solutions. Dewar (1998) identified the normal chaos of family law, endorsing Bourdieu's suggestion that the logic of following a rule ceases at the point at which logic ceases to be practical. How practical are legal rules in a sphere dominated by emotions where diverse social (and behavioural) norms are no longer reined in by a set of moral and religious values shared across society that can be reflected in law? Should we instead be asking ourselves how long can we go on pretending that society is well served by such a mismatching of social problems and legal solutions?

Or is this to overstate the case? Can people, even those in love-based relationships, be persuaded to take legally rational steps to protect their interests? According to Barlow et al (2005), to assume this is generally possible is to fall prey to the legal rationality mistake, whereby law assumes people act according to the logic of the law whereas in reality they act in accordance with the social imperatives within their own lives:

> [P]olicymakers risk falling into what we have called a 'rationality mistake' ... They may create policy assuming a particular sort of public behaviour and rationality, whereas in fact most people make their decisions according to different criteria ... according to moral, relational and emotional judgements of what is the proper thing to do in their situation. To preserve this rationality mistake by not reforming cohabitation law, may be to risk a permanent rupture between social and legal norms. This could completely undermine the credibility of the law in relation to families.' (Barlow et al, 2005: 97–98)

---

[2] *Hansard* HL vol 569 col 1638 (29 February 1996).

Avoiding the Legal Rationality Mistake

How then might law avoid the rationality mistake? Barlow et al's view was formed following a two-year study focused on the social and legal attitudes of a nationally representative sample of people in England and Wales. One key finding was that in the British Social Attitudes Survey conducted in 2000, the majority of people (56 per cent) and a bigger majority of cohabitants (59 per cent) believed in a 'common law marriage myth' whereby people falsely believed cohabiting couples have a 'common law marriage' in which they gain the same rights as married couples after a period of time (Barlow et al, 2001, 2005). Another important finding, however, was that the vast majority of those cohabitants who did *not* believe this myth and *were* aware of the legal position they were in did not respond by taking available legal steps such as making wills or declarations of ownership regarding the family home, often despite a desire and intention to do so. Reasons for this included the cost of legal advice, the perceived need for advice only when things go wrong, the complexity of the various legal steps needed, and a general inertia surrounding putting one's affairs in order (Barlow et al, 2005: 78–79).

One possible solution if one does not want to reform the law is to make people more legally aware and to better facilitate the taking of appropriate legal steps; and this was indeed the government response. A web-based public information campaign, The Living Together Campaign (www.advicenow.org.uk/living-together/), which aimed to inform cohabitants of their legal situation and help dispel the common law marriage myth, as well as provide downloadable forms to enable people to take the requisite legal steps more easily and cheaply, was funded by the Department for Constitutional Affairs (now the Ministry of Justice) over a three-year period from summer 2004.

However, this campaign was launched against the background of a legal culture which, it could be argued, has actually discouraged those in love from being legally rational about family property. Its unwillingness to enforce pre-marital agreements on divorce[3] in a sense endorses the view that legal rationality and love do not and should not go hand in hand. Similarly, the Law Commission's strong recommendation that, regardless of whether other reform was enacted, cohabitation agreements should be made unequivocally enforceable and explicit confirmation that they are not regarded as contrary to public policy be provided (Law Commission, 2007: [5.8]–[5.9]) has so far gone unheeded by Parliament. Add to this the inconsistencies within our law as to whether to treat cohabitants as married—as in the case of social security, tax credits, and private tenancy succession law; two single individuals—as in the case of capital taxes and pensions; or somewhere in between—as for compensation under the Fatal Accidents Act 1976 or a claim from a deceased partner's estate under the Inheritance (Provision for Family and Dependants) Act 1975), and one begins to understand why the falsely

---

[3] *F v F (Ancillary Relief: Substantial Assets)* [1995] 2 FLR 45; *NG v KR* [2008] EWHC 1532; cf *K v K (Ancillary Relief: Pre-nuptial Agreement)* [2003] 1 FLR 120.

supposed existence of common law marriage (Barlow et al, 2005, 2008a) seems far more credible than the actual state of the law and the legally rational yet disparate and complex steps which it consequently requires.

If public information might not then be the whole answer, what else might be considered? Could family law mould itself differently so as to better fit the needs of the community it serves? Is there any public consensus on how law should tackle these problems which can be used to better socially locate the role of family law as the arbiter in the (gendered) power struggle which often erupts on heterosexual relationship breakdown? Is there, perhaps, an optimum moment at which to focus a couple's minds on a marital or cohabitation agreement perhaps, if private ordering is part of the solution? What about views of those who have experienced marriage or cohabitation on what the law *should* do for people when relationships break down and there are disputes about property and post-relationship support? Is there any room for a bottom-up approach to legislating in this sphere, where the very nature of family law's impact on a person's exercise of their right to private and family life (guaranteed by Article 8 of the European Convention on Human Rights) might justify the legislature taking into account public attitudes in this sphere more than in any other? In other words, how best can we deliver family law solutions in this field which are socially located? In order to address these issues, let us now consider the messages from recent research as it relates to relationships, separation, property, and attitudes to legal reform in this field.

MARRIAGE, COHABITATION AND FAMILY PROPERTY—TIME FOR RESPONSIVE MODE?

Research confirms that the decision whether to marry or cohabit is now considered a lifestyle choice by the vast majority of people in Britain, and the legal consequences of these different family forms have little or no bearing on the choice of family structure, at least on entering a first relationship (Barlow et al, 2005; Hibbs, Barton and Beswisk, 2001; cf Dnes, chapter thirteen, this volume). Love clearly triumphs over legal rationality in this situation. Similarly, the need for 'a proper wedding'—a powerful social symbol—trumps any desire to have the security of a legal contract in the eyes of many.

A lawyer's response to this might well be '*caveat emptor*'—let the buyer beware—and if you know you are not married, then you know you are getting something other than the legal contract of marriage, however marriage-like you might think your relationship is. However, if despite the government-funded information campaign people still wrongly believe that cohabiting for a period of time gives couples the same legal rights as if they were formally married, as the most recent British Social Attitudes Survey suggests (51 per cent of people in general and 53 per cent of cohabitants so believe (Barlow et al, 2008a)), then this gives pause for thought. Furthermore, the proportion of people who correctly do not believe in the myth has remained constant (37 per cent) since 2000 (although among cohabitants this had increased from 35 to 39 per cent), but there has been a growth in the percentage of those who are unsure of the legal position which has risen from six to 10 per cent. Whilst there was a significant increase in the numbers who agreed that marriage provided greater financial security than cohabitation, this still left less than half of all cohabitants agreeing with this view, which is a matter of concern given the financial consequences of the legal disparities between the two styles of relationship.

The Living Together Campaign, whilst moving things in the right direction, has not, according to these results from the latest British Social Attitudes Survey, significantly dismantled the common law marriage myth. Neither has it persuaded large numbers of people to put their cohabitation affairs in order, either by marrying or by taking appropriate legal action, such as making wills (only 12 per cent of cohabitants in the recent national study had done so), taking legal advice (19 per cent had done this), or entering into cohabitation agreements. There is some evidence of an increase in the number of declarations of trust relating the family home made when property is jointly purchased (15 per cent, compared with eight per cent in 2000), probably in large part due to the change in Land Registry Rules requiring declarations to be lodged prior to registration of a purchase.

The study of the campaign's effectiveness on legally aware cohabitants (Barlow, Burgoyne and Smithson, 2007) showed how difficult it is to have any great impact even with a well-publicised media and website campaign that provided free legal information and documentation and was relatively easy to use. Although there were some positive outcomes, particularly on how useful the site was perceived to be, most people found it too difficult to take action for a variety of reasons. Even when people wanted to behave in a legally rational way, there were many obstacles. Reasons given included: there was no appropriate action that could be taken to achieve what the couple wanted; a fear that action might cause problems in their relationship; that a partner would not agree to the proposed action; or, for the largest category, they had not yet got around to it. Others mentioned the cost, either financially or emotionally, of legal action against the likelihood of needing the benefits of that action at a later stage. There was also a recurring view that filling out a living together or cohabitation agreement was 'too negative'. Optimism also made it difficult in a relationship which was going well to think of things turning sour:

> You've got to weigh up the cost of these sort of legal transactions and think, well, …, is it really worth going into it for, you know, something that's probably not going to happen. (Laura, cohabitant)

Overall, it was concluded that policies directed at encouraging legally rational behaviour over relationship choice were useful but not transformative in changing behaviour, impacting only at the margins (Barlow et al, 2007, 2008).

Thus both the continued existence of the common law marriage myth and the lack of behaviour transformation through awareness campaigns pose problems for the continuation of family law's current hierarchy of relationships where law privileges marriage and now civil partnerships, yet deals with the increasing numbers of informal relationships differently in different contexts.

Another more radical response might be for law to give people the rights they think they already have. For if people are making decisions on a false premise but which they sincerely believe is imbued with a 'common law' legal truth drawn from the lived 'social truth' that married and cohabiting couples are functionally similar and deserving of equal treatment, particularly where there are children, should the law then not consider aligning itself with that social truth? This is the approach that has been taken in other common law jurisdictions such as Australia and New Zealand (Atkin, 2001, 2003; Graycar and Millbank, 2007) but is met here with the criticism that to go down this road is oppressive to those who are deliberately avoiding marriage and its legal obligations and encourages women's dependency on men (Deech, 1980; Freeman, 1984). Certainly research has characterised different types of cohabitant. Smart and Stevens (2000) identified a continuum of cohabiting and married relationships which range from the contingently committed to the mutually committed, with more marriages falling at the mutually committed end and cohabiting relationships being far more mixed. Lewis's study revealed most cohabitants in her sample as mutually committed rather than individualistic (Lewis, 2001), and Maclean and Eekelaar's study (2004) did not find that the moral obligations felt towards family members in unmarried as opposed to married families differed significantly. Barlow et al (2007) found diversity among their sample of legally aware cohabiting couples who had used the Living Together Campaign website. This included a typology of four main styles of couple—ideological, pragmatic, romantic, and uneven—and concluded that different legal solutions were needed to meet the different needs of each group. Protection of uneven cohabitants, where one of a couple wanted to marry or take legal action whilst the other did not, was seen as particularly necessary, for these couples could never agree to resolve the situation for themselves, leaving one partner very vulnerable and in need of legal protection, particularly on relationship breakdown. Enforceable cohabitation agreements which were accompanied by an acknowledged legal status similar to but other than (as they viewed it) patriarchal marriage would, on the other hand, be very welcome to ideological couples. Pragmatic couples would all be prepared to take legal steps or even marry for legal reasons if necessary, even though they may delay taking such action and would prefer not to have to do so. Romantic couples, on the other hand, many of whom were in a trial marriage and were building towards a big wedding that might still be years away, felt it would be wrong to marry for purely legal or financial reasons. However, very few (10 per cent) even in this study of legally aware cohabitants, many of whom were ideologically opposed to marriage, were opposed to the extension of legal rights currently enjoyed only by married couples to cohabitants with children. Nor were views expressed that this type of legislation would be oppressive, providing a couple could jointly agree to opt out from the presumptive scheme.

At the time when the Law Commission was looking at reform of cohabitation law on separation and death, social attitudes nationally were again tested in the British Social Attitudes Survey 2006 and follow-up study (Barlow et al, 2008a, 2008b). This looked, inter alia, at which behaviours within different styles of (heterosexual) cohabiting relationships warranted claims for financial support on relationship breakdown or death. As with the Living Together Campaign Study discussed above, there were few signs that an extension of legal rights would be viewed as oppressive and this was particularly the case where there were children of the relationship. Public attitudes were tested by putting forward 10 scenarios which explored how meritorious a partner's claim for financial provision was viewed where the law currently metes out different treatment to married and cohabiting couples on relationship breakdown on death and which was under review by the Law Commission. The aim was to see how views changed according to variables such as: the presence or absence of children; whether the parties were married; the length of the relationship; financial and domestic contributions to the relationship; and the circumstances leading to the claim for financial provision.

Table 14.1 below summarises the findings of what was viewed as appropriate on relationship breakdown.

Table 14.1: Beliefs regarding Rights to Financial Provision on Separation for Married and Unmarried Couples

% agree partner should have right to financial provision on separation if ...	If couple not married	If couple married
... couple living together for 20 years, 3 children, woman reduced work to part-time and then gave up work to look after family and home, man supported family financially and owns home, woman has no income and poor job prospects.	89	N/A
... couple for ten years, no children, one partner worked unpaid to build up other partner's business, partner who runs business also owns family home, other partner has no property or income of own.	87	93
... couple for ten years, one partner has well-paid job requiring frequent moves, other partner has worked where possible but has not had a settled career.	69	81
... couple for two years, one has a much higher income than the other and owns the family home.	38	62
... couple living together for two years with young child and now separating. She will be child's main carer and he will pay child support.	74	N/A
Base	*3197*	*3197*

This confirmed a different hierarchy of relationship status after short couple relationships to that embodied in law.

Similarly, when asked about the situation where a cohabitant died, even after a two-year short childless relationship, there was clear support for a functional approach to regulating couple relationships. Two-thirds felt the same remedies should be available to cohabitants as married couples, with 98 per cent believing this after a 10-year childless relationship.

This research found little support nationally for the law to distinguish between financial remedies for separating married and cohabiting couples where the relationship was long term; where there are children of relationship or where there is evidence of joint enterprise contributions, for example to a business.

There was evidence that views change across the generations and this supports the idea put forward by Eekelaar (2006) that it might be important to bear this in mind when attempting to legislate for future generations in this field. Whilst it is difficult to know for certain if this variance in views is a periodic or generational effect which may change as people get older, younger people without children tended more readily to endorse the promotion of financial autonomy on relationship breakdown. However, this was more so in scenarios which did not involve children. Most people were found to be very child-centred in their thinking, which does reflect one of the main tenets of family law. Those who were older or who had more than one child tended to favour more equal recognition of financial and non-financial contributions, and where there was a child in the scenario this approach broadened across all categories of research participants, endorsing the functional approach favoured by participants in earlier research (Barlow et al, 2005; Cooke, Barlow and Callus, 2006; Barlow, Burgoyne and Smithson, 2007).

Why does this Differ from what Law Currently Does?

If law could justify its different treatment of approaches to family property in the married and cohabitation contexts in a convincing manner, then perhaps the legally rational approach could be endorsed. As things stand, whereas cohabitants' assets are divided according to property law on relationship breakdown with little or no attention being given to the nature of the relationship (*Burns v Burns;*[4] *Stack v Dowden*[5]), a completely different approach is taken on marriage breakdown where the aim is to achieve fairness as between the parties. For financial and non-financial contributions to the marriage are viewed as equal and justify an equal division of assets on divorce, unless other factors such as the needs of the parties, a truly exceptional contribution by one party alone, or inherited wealth or other non-matrimonial assets justify a different approach

---

[4] [1984] Ch 317.
[5] [2007] UKHL 17.

(*White v White*;[6] *Miller v Miller; McFarlane v McFarlane*[7]). However, much of the logic as to why we do as we do in the married context, has been lost. Why is an economically weaker spouse rewarded for the public commitment given on marriage at the point of divorce when that commitment has been broken? We have no-fault divorce and so assets are in the vast majority of cases redistributed regardless of who is to blame—we are not compensating an innocent party for a breach of contract, as was reiterated forcefully by the House of Lords recently in *Miller; McFarlane*.[8] Often, quite the reverse is true. On divorce, pre-marital cohabitation may in effect lengthen the duration of the marriage for the purpose of deciding how assets should be redistributed, accepting that the private commitment of cohabitation is valuable if it translates into marriage.[9] Yet we do not redistribute assets on the basis of a long-lasting private commitment if a long cohabitation relationship breaks down.

If the rationale behind the messages being sent by the current state of the law is itself confused and at odds with what is socially acceptable, clear messages are not likely to get through to the public, let alone encourage 'legally rational' behaviour. Either we need to accept this as Dewar's normal chaos of family law or questions need to be posed about what law is doing and whether it can justify the different treatment of cohabitants from that of functionally similar married couples. What are we rewarding on divorce exactly? If it is the fact that one party has sacrificed their own financial position for the greater good of the family, perhaps by giving up work to care for children, why is this rewarded only in the married context when exactly the same benefits are being gained by the partner, children and, indeed, society when cohabitants order their lives in this way? The empirical evidence clearly shows that it is not public attitudes nor, indeed, those of cohabitants that are standing in the way of such a development.

Furthermore, the strength of public support for maintenance on separation following a short childless relationship is also questioned by the results from the most recent British Social Attitudes Survey (see Table 14.1 above). Whilst there was little support for cohabitants without children who separate after two years to receive financial provision (just 38 per cent were in agreement), more surprisingly there was less support for maintenance following a two-year childless marriage, where 62 per cent agreed this was appropriate, than for maintenance for the primary caring cohabitant following a two-year cohabitation relationship with one child, for which 74 per cent were in favour.

This begs the question of whether the regulatory lines have been drawn correctly in providing financial provision on separation. Clearly to use marriage

---

[6] [2001] 1 AC 596.
[7] [2006] UKHL 24.
[8] ibid.
[9] See, eg *W v W (Judicial Separation: Ancillary Relief)* [1995] 2 FLR 259; *GW v RW* [2003] EWHC 611.

and now civil partnership as the sole determining factor for providing financial provision is convenient from the point of view of the legal system. Whether or not you hold the required status is easy to prove by production of the marriage certificate or civil partnership document. There may be more arguments about whether or not a couple fall within the definition of cohabitants, yet this is something that the courts already deal with quite competently in those areas where rights have been extended to such couples. Ease of regulation cannot really stand up as a very good reason not to endorse a change of approach, particularly where this has been achieved in other common law jurisdictions with seemingly minimal difficulty.

The feminist argument that the law should, at the beginning of the twenty-first century, be discouraging rather than promoting further financial dependence of women on men might hold more sway. Yet where there is relationship-generated need or disadvantage which falls principally on women, who are most often the primary carers of children in all styles of relationship, should the law continue to discriminate against those who have done this outside marriage yet not require financial autonomy from divorcing childless women in the name of fairness?

The last and most cited justification for the continuance of the status quo is so as not to undermine marriage. Marriage is more stable than cohabitation and is seen as special. Indeed, only nine per cent of the public in the most recent British Social Attitudes Survey agreed that marriage is only a piece of paper (Barlow et al, 2008). Yet, retaining the status quo has not in this jurisdiction stemmed the tide of those cohabiting nor, indeed, the decline of the numbers marrying each year. Policy documents from both the major political parties talk of supporting marriage in the name of creating more stable families for children (Home Office, 1998; Social Justice Policy Group, 2007). However, there is an argument that it is those families that are likely to break up that need most to be regulated. Certainly, research shows that the current law can produce great economic disadvantage for cohabitant parents on relationship breakdown (Tennant, Taylor and Lewis, 2006; Lewis, Tennant and Taylor, chapter eight, this volume). Furthermore, where is the logic in encouraging marriage whilst providing a perverse incentive not to marry by denying legal remedies for other styles of families with children who are in need of them when relationships break down? Generally, it is not clear how extending rights and obligations which appertain to marriage to functionally similar cohabiting couples will in any way undermine marriage further than is already happening.

What is it that we are concerned about in extending remedies to the cohabitation context, given the seemingly uncomplicated experiences of other jurisdictions that have awarded legal status and family property rights to cohabitants (see eg Atkin, 2001; Graycar and Millbank, 2007) and the fact that countries that have gone down this route have not suffered any observable decline in marriage rates above and beyond existing rates of decline (Kiernan, Barlow and Merlo, 2007)?

RECONSIDERATION OF HIERARCHY TO REFLECT
CHANGING CIRCUMSTANCES?

The Law Commission for England and Wales has recently reviewed the law governing the financial consequences of cohabitation breakdown and, after a two-year project in which it consulted widely, it made recommendations for reform of cohabitation law in its report in 2007 (Law Commission, 2006, 2007). However, the idea that cohabitation law should be put on a par with marriage was rejected. In its consultation paper, the Law Commission explained the view as put to it by one consultee:

> Some account should be taken of the decision of the parties not to marry: it is one thing to relieve the unequal impact of the relationship, but quite another to treat the parties as if they had actually married. (Law Commission, 2006: [6.239])

The report confirmed this view:

> Applying the MCA would impose an equivalence with marriage which many people would find inappropriate, and some consultees suggested that it is unlikely that a scheme which equated cohabitation with marriage in this way would be politically attainable. (Law Commission, 2007: [4.8])

Rather it put forward a radical new presumptive scheme which does not mirror marriage but which proposed acceptance of cohabitation contracts and redress for relationship-generated economic disadvantage or retained benefit.

The Law Commission recommended that its scheme should apply to all cohabitants with children and other childless cohabitants (whether of same or different sex) who have lived together for a qualifying period, which they suggested should be between two and five years. Couples should be able to opt out of the scheme in order to protect individual autonomy providing certain conditions were satisfied, notably that the agreement was in writing, signed by both parties and made clear the parties' intention to disapply the scheme (Law Commission, 2007: [5.56]). In the case of manifest unfairness, a court would have power to set aside an opt-out agreement ([5.61]).

The idea of the scheme was to base a former cohabitant's claim upon the 'economic impact' of cohabitation. On separation, an eligible applicant in making a claim against their partner would have to prove that either the respondent had a retained benefit, or the applicant had an economic disadvantage as a result of qualifying contributions the applicant had made. It recommended that the same style of orders would be available for financial provision as is currently the case on divorce or civil partnership dissolution with the exception of periodical maintenance payments, although the grounds for making the orders were to be quite different.

A qualifying contribution was defined as any contribution to the shared lives or welfare of members of the family, and could be non-financial ([4.34]). An economic disadvantage was stated to be a present or future loss. It could include a diminution in current savings as a result of expenditure or of earnings lost during the relationship, lost future earnings, or the future cost of paid child care ([4.36]).

A retained benefit, on the other hand, could take the form of capital income or earning capacity that had been acquired, retained or enhanced ([4.35]).

The remedy in respect of retained benefit was straightforward. The court would be able to order the reversal of any retained benefit 'in so far as it is reasonable and practical and having regard to the discretionary factors', which were:

— the welfare of any minor child of both parties (which was to be the court's first consideration);
— the financial needs and obligations of both parties;
— the extent and nature of any financial resources of each party now and in the foreseeable future;
— the welfare of any child living with, or who might reasonably be expected to live with, either party;
— the conduct of each party, defined restrictively but including a qualifying contribution made despite the express disagreement of the other party.

With regard to a finding of economic disadvantage, however, how exactly this would be calculated in practice was cause for concern among commentators, with a crystal ball being seen as a useful piece of equipment in the calculation of lost future earnings (Probert, 2006). In any event, only one half of any economic disadvantage would be paid over according to the principle that any loss should be shared equally, and in making any order, the court should not place the applicant for the foreseeable future in a stronger economic position than the respondent. Whilst this sharing of risk and loss sounds very egalitarian, it might well have meant that where there was an unequal distribution of assets between cohabitants, an economically weaker primary carer partner would not on separation have been able to recover their full loss from a very wealthy former partner. Equal sharing of loss would not always have been fair.

The attractiveness of the scheme is its promotion of financial autonomy between the partners. Indeed, some respondents to Barlow et al's most recent BSA (see Table 14.1) and follow-up study recognised the Law Commission's approach to be appropriate for married and unmarried childless couples. As Noreen, a cohabitant in her thirties with one child, explaining her view on the position in the scenario where a childless couple breaks up after a two-year marriage or cohabitation, confirmed:

... there's no children involved, why should one person be responsible for supporting you financially?

However, the fact that the Law Commission scheme deliberately did not directly address the financial needs of those facing separation, and so would have been likely to have operated harshly on those who were post-separation primary carers of children of the relationship in some cases was not universally welcomed. The Law Commission took the view that relationship-generated economic disadvantage was a fairer and more specific way of defining and thereby addressing (albeit indirectly) the sort of post-cohabitation relationship need worthy of legal redress where, unlike in marriage, the parties had not publicly declared their commitment to the relationship (Law Commission, 2007: Appendix C, [C9]–[C12]). Indeed the BSA Survey did reveal some support for this approach (see Table 14.1 above) as did the follow-up study. As Ruth, in her thirties and a cohabitant with three children, saw it:

> [I]n a partnership people make compromises and quite often it's the woman that makes compromises and that's part of the deal. If it then turns sour ... they shouldn't be penalised because they've made sacrifices.

Where there were children, though, the appetite for a difference in approach between married and cohabiting families was greatly reduced, and evidence of thinking that there should be a functional approach to families with children based on their needs is found across the recent studies:

> I don't think it [legal protection] should be automatically tied into marriage or cohabiting or just living separately. It should be to do with the rights everybody has to have a minimum safety net. It should be to do with the rights that children have to have their parents have an income with which to bring up the children, regardless of, you know, whether the parents are still in a relationship or not. (Daniel, cohabitant of nine years, two children, respondent in Barlow et al's 2007 study)

Similarly, in Cooke, Barlow and Callus's 2006 study, when asked for reasons why a cohabiting mother with children should have the same rights to the family home owned by her partner as a married mother on relationship breakdown, a married respondent explained:

> I think she should be allowed to stay in the house and then the property sold.... [*Why?*] ... Because they've still got the same responsibilities to each other and their children. (Cooke, Barlow and Callus, 2006: 32)

However, probably the biggest problems with the Law Commission's scheme were its apparent complexity and its unfamiliar approach which resulted in being received less enthusiastically than it in fact deserved.

Despite the Law Commission's misgivings about equal treatment of functionally similar married and cohabiting couples, research does now clearly show that there is public (if not political) support for reconsideration of the hierarchy of those whom the law provides may obtain financial provision on relationship breakdown. As has been seen, there is greater support for financial provision after a two-year relationship for a cohabitant who has a child than there is for a spouse after a two-year childless marriage. It is not clear to people why Mrs Miller should have got £5 million after a two-year childless marriage to a very rich man (*Miller; McFarlane*[10]), whereas Mrs Burns, a cohabitant of 19 years' standing with another rich man, who brought up two children and worked part time, received nothing (*Burns v Burns*[11]).

---

[10] [2006] UKHL 24.
[11] [1984] Ch 317.

If we can agree that it is couples with children who are the most deserving of the law's remedies, as public opinion seems to confirm, then we need to reformulate the hierarchy to reflect society's consensus on this point, which is one with which, outside the sphere of family property, family law agrees. At the very least, it should be possible to extend to cohabitants the provision of reasonable requirements—a needs-based approach to financial provision on separation—as existed for married couples before the cases of *White v White*[12] and *Miller; McFarlane* introduced the principle of equal sharing of matrimonial assets on divorce in higher asset cases under the Matrimonial Causes Act 1973. The Law Commission rejected its consultees' call for a needs-based redistribution of assets on relationship breakdown as it felt there was not

> a clear, principled justification for needs-based relief that would help to determine how 'need' should be measured, which 'needs', if any, should be met by a partner, in what circumstances and for how long' (Law Commission, 2007: Appendix C, [C9]).

However, these are all matters which the courts have had to address in the divorce context. In the majority of cases where assets do not exceed needs, it is the housing needs of the children and then those of the primary carer which are addressed first, followed by the housing needs of the other parent. The future income needs of all would then be considered and addressed. Before *White* and *Miller; McFarlane*, the other assets were left undisturbed (see Bird, 2000) but would now be subject to the equal sharing principle if they were classified as matrimonial assets in the divorce context. The courts are familiar with exercising their discretion in this context and could, as they used to on divorce, generously interpret needs in higher asset cases. Thus implementation of such a scheme would, from a practical point of view, be relatively easy and address the concerns of the public without wading into the difficulties which the equal sharing principle poses in the non-contractual cohabitation context (see Law Commission, 2007, Appendix C, [C5]–[C8]).

Where there are no children, on the other hand, then financial autonomy may be a better goal for both the married and unmarried cohabitants and would encompass the call for enforceable pre-marital and cohabitation agreements, alongside a safety net of legal redress based on relationship-generated economic disadvantage and retained benefit.

CONCLUSION

Love then has everything to do with it, as it makes law's subjects far less susceptible to legally rational behaviour, within the current legal framework, in the context of their private lives. This means that we follow our hearts, often with the best of motives, and social norms endorse this approach. People do what is right for them in the context of their own lives and to act legally rationally, given the demands

---

[12] [2001] 1 AC 596.

of the current law, is often seen as inappropriate or too difficult. To ignore the social trends away from marriage leaves law looking rather inadequate in the face of social change. It is failing to protect the most vulnerable 'uneven' partners and it is failing to recognise that there are many ways to 'do family' (Morgan, 2000) which serve society well and which are worthy of support when things go wrong. Certainly, in the public mind, there is an equality discourse between functionally similar couples—where there are children and where there is 'marriage-like' behaviour which is borne out of a freedom to choose which partnering and parenting structure to adopt according to the context of your own life, perhaps best understood as a social interpretation of the meaning of one's right to private and family life free from state interference.

Indeed, this idea fits with some legal dicta—Hale LJ (as she then was) in *SRJ v DWJ (Financial Provision)*[13] observed:

> It is not only in [the child's] interests but in the community's interests that parents, whether mothers or fathers and spouses, whether husbands or wives, should have a real choice between concentrating on breadwinning and concentrating on home-making and child-rearing, and do not feel forced, for fear of what might happen should their marriage break down much later in life, to abandon looking after the home and the family to other people for the sake of maintaining a career.

To find a way forward, we need to consider regulation of family property disputes across both married and cohabitation contexts in the light of twenty-first century values. The only clear alternative is to allow chaos to continue to reign, rather than socially locate family law within the real-life situations found in society. The best way forward, in my view, involves coming back to Teubner's solution of reflexive law (Teubner, 1993), which, as King and Piper (1995) explain:

> is offered as an answer to the crisis caused by the failure of legal rationality under modern conditions to provide law with the necessary tools to restore consensual, moral and political values.

This approach offers a 'bottom-up' solution, which departs from the normal uniform standard-setting role that law has traditionally played and would permit a pluralistic approach to family regulation. That is not to say it would abandon standard-setting altogether. Rather that it would attempt to meet the needs of a society where partnerships founded on love take diverse forms, by being better attuned to shifting public attitudes and respecting the need for greater flexibility for couples to make their own arrangements whilst acknowledging minimum standards.

Family property is surely a good starting point to examine how this could be done and protection for weaker economic partners where there are children, and regardless of whether or not they happen to have married, is clearly publicly acceptable, if not politically so. There is also a taste for private ordering where

---

[13] [1999] 2 FLR 179 at 182.

there are no children or where a couple have carefully thought through the implications of their separation for themselves and their whole family. Pre-marital and cohabitation agreements must surely have their day and allow couples to separate their financial and emotional layers of commitment where they are both fully cogniscent of their choices. By combining these features of autonomy and protection, we should at lest be en route to achieving a new normal order of family law as advocated by Henaghan (2008) and Eekelaar (2006) which is firmly socially located in current family practices and public expectations and yet is flexible enough to empower rather than enslave future generations.

BIBLIOGRAPHY

Atkin, B (2001) 'Reforming property division in New Zealand: from marriage to relationships' 3 *European Journal of Law Reform* 349.
—— (2003) 'The challenge of unmarried cohabitation—the New Zealand response' 37 *Family Law Quarterly* 303.
Barlow, A, Burgoyne, C, Clery, E and Smithson, J (2008a) 'Cohabitation and the law: myths, money and the media' in A Park, J Curtice, K Thompson, M Phillips and E Clery (eds) *British Social Attitudes: The 24th Report* (London, Sage).
—— (2008b) *Cohabitation and the Law: Myths, Money and the Media: Key Findings* (London, Nuffield Foundation).
Barlow, A, Burgoyne, C and Smithson, J (2007) *The Living Together Campaign—An investigation of its impact on legally aware cohabitants* (London, Ministry of Justice), available at http://www.justice.gov.uk/publications/research250707.htm.
Barlow, A, Duncan, S, James, G and Park, A (2001) 'Just a piece of paper? Marriage and cohabitation in Britain' in A Park, J Curtice, K Thomson, L Jarvis and C Bromley (eds) *British Social Attitudes: The 18th Report* (London, Sage).
—— (2005) *Cohabitation, Marriage and the Law: Social Change and Legal Reform in the 21st Century* (Oxford, Hart Publishing).
Barlow, A and Duncan, S (2000) 'Family law, moral rationalities and New Labour's communitarianism: Part II' 22 *Journal of Social Welfare and Family Law* 129.
Beck, U and Beck-Gernsheim, E (1995) *The Normal Chaos of Love* (Cambridge, Polity Press).
Bird, R (2000) 'Ancillary relief outcomes' 30 *Family Law* 831.
Cooke, E, Barlow, A and Callus, T (2006) *Community of Property: A Regime for England and Wales?* (Bristol, The Policy Press).
Dewar, J (1998) 'The normal chaos of family law' 61 *Modern Law Review* 467.
Department of Trade and Industry, Women and Equality Unit (2003) *Civil Partnership: A Framework for the Legal Recognition of Same-sex Couples* (London, Department of Trade and Industry).
Deech, R (1980) 'The case against the legal recognition of cohabitation' 29 *International and Comparative Law Quarterly* 480.
Dworkin, R (1978) *Taking Rights Seriously* (Cambridge, MA, Harvard University Press).
Eekelaar, J (2006) *Family Law and Personal Life* (Oxford, Oxford University Press).
Freeman, M (1984) 'Legal ideologies, patriarchal precedents and domestic violence' in M Freeman (ed), *State Law and Family: Critical Perspectives* (London, Tavistock).
—— (1985) 'Towards a critical theory of family law' 38 *Current Legal Problems* 153.

Graycar, R and Millbank, J (2007) 'From functional family to spinster sisters: Australia's distinctive path to relationship recognition' 24 *Journal of Law and Policy* 121.

Henaghan, M (2008) 'The Normal Order of Family Law' 28 *Oxford Journal of Legal Studies* 165.

Hibbs, M, Barton, C and Beswisk, J (2001) 'Why marry? Perceptions of the affianced' (2001) 31 *Family Law* 197.

Home Office (1998) *Supporting Families: A Consultative Document* (London, TSO).

Kiernan, K, Barlow, A and Merlo, R (2007) 'Cohabitation Law Reform and its Impact on Marriage: Evidence from Australia and Europe' 63 *International Family Law* 71.

King, M and Piper, C (1995) *How the Law Thinks about Children* (Aldershot, Arena).

Law Commission (2006) *Cohabitation: The Financial Consequences of Relationship Breakdown—A Consultation Paper*, Law Com CP No 179 (London, TSO).

—— (2007) *Cohabitation: The Financial Consequences of Relationship Breakdown*, Law Com No 307 (London, TSO).

Lewis, J (2001) *The End of Marriage? Individualism and Intimate Relationships.* (Cheltenham, Edward Elgar).

Maclean, M and Eekelaar, J (2004) 'Marriage and the moral bases of personal relationships' 31 *Journal of Law and Society* 510.

Morgan, D (1999) 'Risk and family practices: accounting for change and fluidity in family life' in S Smart and E Silva (eds), *The New Family* (London, Sage).

Morgan, P (2000) *Marriage-lite: The Rise of Cohabitation and its Consequences* (London, Institute for the Study of Civil Society).

National Statistics Online (2008) *Focus on gender: living arrangements* London, available at www.statistics.gov.uk/CCI/nugget.asp?ID=1652, accessed 31 October 2008.

Probert, R (2006) 'Cohabitation: contributions and sacrifices' 36 *Family Law* 1060.

Smart, C and Stevens, P (2000) *Cohabitation Breakdown* (London: FPSC).

Social Justice Policy Group (2007) *Breakthrough Britain, Volume 1: Family Breakdown*, available at http://povertydebate.typepad.com/home/files/family_breakdown.pdf.

Tennant, R, Taylor, J and Lewis, J (2006) *Separating from Cohabitation: Making Arrangements for Finances and Parenting* (London, Department for Constitutional Affairs), available at http://www.dca.gov.uk/research/2006/07_2006.pdf.

Teubner, G (1993) 'Substantive and reflexive elements in modern law' *Law and Society Review* 239.

Index